THE FLAME AND THE CANDLE
War in Mayo 1919–1924

DOMINIC PRICE grew up in Rathfarnham in Dublin close to Padraig Pearse's Scoil Éanna, and often visited his grandparents near Kilmainham Jail. This sparked an interest in Irish history. He also served in the 20th Infantry Battalion, FCA. A teacher of history, religious education and music, he has a keen interest in traditional Irish music and plays the uilleann pipes, traditional flute and guitar.

This book is dedicated to John & Mary Goggins
and Rachel Price

Ar dheis Dé go raibh a n-anamacha dílse

THE FLAME AND THE CANDLE

War in Mayo 1919–1924

DOMINIC PRICE

The Collins Press

First published in 2012 by
The Collins Press
West Link Park
Doughcloyne
Wilton
Cork

Reprinted 2012

British Library Cataloguing in Publication Data
    Price, Dominic.
    The flame & the candle: Mayo's war.
    1. Mayo (Ireland: County)—History—20th century.
    2. Mayo (Ireland: County)—Social conditions—20th century.
    3. Ireland—History—War of Independence, 1919–1921.
    4. Ireland—History—Civil War, 1922–1923. I. Title
    941.7'30821-dc23

ISBN–13: 9781848891364
EPUB ISBN: 9781848899513/mobi ISBN: 9781848899520

Typesetting by Carrigboy Typesetting Services
Typeset in Garamond Premier Pro
Printed in Denmark by Nørhaven A/S

Cover photographs

Front (from top): Jack Leonard with Lewis gun (courtesy Anthony Leonard);
ammunition (courtesy Brendan Hughes); armoured car (courtesy Michael Ring TD).
Back: (top, l–r): Irish Volunteer Mayo Brigade cap badge (courtesy Abie and Annie
Allen); RIC Insignia (courtesy Raymond and Jean Shearer and Neil Harrison
Photography); (*bottom*): West Mayo Brigade Flying Column (courtesy Anthony Leonard)

Contents

Acknowledgements

Love to my wife, Catherine, and children, Heather, Emma and Shane, for walking with me through Mayo 1919–24.

My gratitude to The Collins Press for their confidence, support and belief in this project from its beginning.

Sincere thanks to my friends Peter Molloy and Michael Hastings for their kindness, endless patience, advice and support.

To my teachers, Colm Brady of Coláiste Éanna and John Corcoran of Ballyroan Boys National School, for their inspirational teaching of history.

My thanks to my colleagues at Drimnagh Castle CBS, particularly Dr Ray Walsh, John Hayes, John Flood, Clodagh O'Byrne and Tom Lenihan, for their energy and enthusiasm in supporting this book.

My sincere thanks for the expertise and professionalism of the archivists and others who were most generous with their time and assistance: Rod Mackenzie, Argyll and Sutherland Highlander Museum; Fr Pádraig Ó Cuill, Capuchin Archives; Ivor Hamrock, Castlebar County Library Local History; Lynsey Robertson, Churchill Archives Centre; Patria McWalter, Galway County Council; Tom Kilgarriff, Galway Diocesan Archive; Gerry Kilgallon, Garda Museum; Kelley Proctor and Martin Fagan, Irish College Archives, Rome; Linda Memery, Judicial Support Unit of the Courts Service; Anne-Marie Ryan, Kilmainham Gaol Museum; Stuart Eastwood, King's Own Royal Border Regiment Museum; Anthony Leonard, J. J. Leonard Historical Photographic Archive; Clement McGann and Pat Sweeney, Maritime Institute of Ireland; County Manager Des Mahon, Secretary John Condon and Clare Kenny, Mayo County Council; Commandant Victor Laing, Captain Stephen MacEoin, Lisa Dolan, Noelle Grothier and Hugh Beckett, Military Archives; Christy Allen, Elizabeth McEvoy, David O'Neill, National Archives of Ireland; Sandra McDermott, Glen Dunne and Berni Metcalf, National Library of Ireland; Finbarr Connolly, National

Museum of Ireland; Eileen O'Donoghue, Matthew Day and Seamus Haughey, Oíreachtas Library; Clare Elsey, Parliamentary Archives, London; Hugh Forrester, Police Museum, Belfast; Neil Cobbett, Public Record Office, London; Peter Devitt, RAF Museum; Mary Furlong, Representative Church Body Library Dublin; Harriet Wheelock, Royal College of Physicians of Ireland Heritage Centre; Claire Skinner, Swindon and Wiltshire Archives; Claire McGuirk, Trinity College Library; Canon Kieran Waldron and Fr Fintan Monahan, Tuam Diocese Archive; Seamus Helferty, UCD Archives; and Aiden Clarke, Westport Heritage Centre.

Throughout the course of my research for this book I was over-whelmed at the openness, sincerity, generosity and warmth of so many with an interest in Mayo and who did all they could to assist. In particular I would like to thank: Richard Abbott, Paddy Allen, Trevor Ardill, Joan Boyd-Ó Cléirigh, Christine Bradly, Eoin Brennan, Captain Dónal Buckley, Celio Burke (née O'Keefe), Anne Butterly (née Moylett), Tom Campbell, Kevin Carr, Michael Coleman, Thomas Collins, Fintan and Reggie Darling, Peter and Mary Delaney, Barry Donnelly, Dominick and Mary Dunleavy, Martin Dwyer, Micheline Egan, Paddy Furlong, Toby Gibbons, Neil Harrison, Dan Hoban, Brendan Hughes, Eamonn Hughes, Dr Clare Kilgarriff, Peadar Kilroy, Brian McCarthy, Jim Maguire, Johnny Mee, Dr Roderick Maguire, Dr Seán Maguire, Eileen Molloy, Martin Mortimer, Susan Moylett, Tom Murtagh, William O'Keefe, Michael O'Malley, Tomás P. Ó Móráin, Bernadette and Margaret Quinsey, Michael Ring TD, Tommy Ruane, Tommy Ryder, Raymond and Jane Shearer, Thomas Smith, Brendan Smyth, Averil Staunton, Tom Waldron and Paraig Walsh.

A special thank-you to Cormac K. H. O'Malley for the privilege of working alongside him in transcribing Ernie O'Malley's military notebooks detailing interviews with IRA veterans from County Mayo.

A heartfelt thanks to all who ensured the men, women and children who lived the history of Mayo during the War of Independence and Civil War could be heard once more.

Míle buíochas díobh
DOMINIC PRICE

Abbreviations

CI	County Inspector
DC	Divisional Commissioner
DI	District Inspector
GAA	Gaelic Athletic Association
GHQ	IRA General Headquarters
IRA	Irish Republican Army
IRB	Irish Republican Brotherhood
ITGWU	Irish Transport and General Workers Union
O/C	Officer Commanding
QMG	Quartermaster General
RAF	Royal Air Force
RIC	Royal Irish Constabulary
UDC	Urban District Council
UVF	Ulster Volunteer Force

Author's Note

In 2008 I attended the launch of a book by Captain Dónal Buckley in Mayo County Library on *The Battle of Tourmakeady*. It told a story of courageous men and women from Mayo during Ireland's War of Independence. Captain Buckley's book was inspiring, and I set out to discover more about Mayo during this period. This proved more difficult than I imagined. I was convinced there had to be more and so I set out on the road that led to this book. Throughout this account every attempt has been made to allow the people who lived through Mayo's turbulent history between 1919 and 1924 to speak for themselves, through the use of their letters, diaries and speeches. This is Mayo's story.

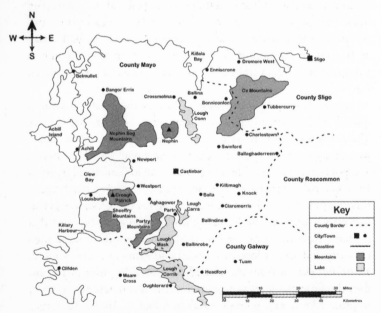

Map of County Mayo 1919–24. (Courtesy Eoin Brennan)

Introduction

The years 1919–24 were the defining era in Ireland's centuries-long struggle to win independence from Britain. The beginning of the twentieth century had seen the growth of a new nationalism that appealed to a younger generation of Irish men and women. This nationalism appeared in the form of organisations like the Gaelic Athletic Association (GAA), founded in 1884, the Gaelic League, founded in 1893, and Sinn Féin, founded in 1905. Nevertheless, there appeared at first to be little threat to the established order. The Irish Parliamentary Party under the leadership of John Redmond had recovered from the split caused by Charles Stewart Parnell's involvement in a divorce scandal in 1890. Under Redmond, the Irish Parliamentary Party allied with the governing Liberal Party in Britain in an attempt to achieve Home Rule for Ireland. Although control of finance and defence would have remained with the parliament at Westminster, Home Rule would give a significant amount of autonomy to Ireland within the United Kingdom and greater British Empire.

Not all Irish people saw Home Rule as the great panacea. A quarter of the population viewed themselves as loyal to the Crown. These unionists, as they were known, lived mostly in Ulster. Being part of a great world power brought tremendous social, economic and political advantage. The Home Rule crusade embarked upon by Irish nationalist parliamentarians was seen by unionists as a threat to their very existence. Unionists were in the main Protestant whereas nationalists were mostly Roman Catholic. Unionists believed that if Home Rule was implemented they would become a persecuted minority and would lose their social and economic well-being in an Ireland cut off from the United Kingdom. In order to prevent this, the Orange Order was revived in the late nineteenth century to protect Protestant-unionist ideals and society. The Order forged strong political links with the British Conservative Party.

A Third Home Rule Bill was introduced to Parliament in 1912; John Redmond looked set to become the first Irish Prime Minister. Unionists realised they would have to depend on more than the political alliance with the Conservatives in Westminster to prevent Ireland breaking away from the United Kingdom. They established the Ulster Volunteer Force (UVF) in 1913 with the clear intention of resisting Home Rule by force of arms. Led by General Sir George Richardson, it became an army of 90,000 trained soldiers. Irish nationalists responded with the formation of their own military force – the Irish Volunteers. In 1914 the position of the British Army in Ireland was thrown into doubt when officers at the Curragh military camp mutinied and threatened to resign rather than fight the Ulster Volunteers. Conflict between the Ulster Volunteers and the Irish Volunteers seemed increasingly likely, with both sides importing arms. An anxious King George V called Liberals, Conservatives, unionists and nationalists to a conference at Buckingham Palace at the end of July 1914. Although Redmond conceded that some areas of Ulster might opt out of an Ireland under Home Rule, the conference failed to agree on the specific areas. Then, on 4 August 1914, the First World War began. The introduction of Home Rule, although placed on the Statute Book, was shelved until the end of hostilities.

As Britain became more deeply involved in the First World War, a secret revolutionary group called the Irish Republican Brotherhood (IRB) planned an overthrow of British power in Ireland. The IRB were the inheritors of a long tradition of opposition to British rule in Ireland, including the United Irishmen of 1798, the Young Irelanders of 1848 and the Fenians of 1867. These organisations were committed not just to the overthrow of British rule but also the establishment of an independent Irish Republic. By 1914, the IRB had infiltrated most nationalist organisations like the GAA, the Gaelic League, Sinn Féin and the Irish Volunteers. The Irish Volunteers had in fact split over Redmond's decision to support Britain in the First World War. The majority, some 150,000, went with Redmond, who argued that support for Britain would guarantee Home Rule at the war's end. These soldiers, who became known as the National Volunteers, joined Irish regiments of the British Army. A minority of 12,000 remained in Ireland refusing to support Britain's war. They retained the title of

Irish Volunteers and became the nucleus of a new attempt to achieve Irish independence. The UVF also joined the British Army, forming the Ulster Division. Their aim was to prevent the introduction of Home Rule by supporting Britain in her hour of need.

On Easter Monday 1916, the IRB, having secretly organised the Irish Volunteers and co-opted the Irish Citizen Army into their plans, seized key buildings around Dublin. A proclamation declaring an Irish Republic was read outside the General Post Office in Sackville Street (now O'Connell Street) by Patrick Pearse, the commander of the revolutionary forces. The Rising continued throughout the week, leaving the centre of Dublin destroyed. However, it failed to ignite nationally, in part due to orders to stand down being issued by Éoin MacNeill, the commander of the Volunteers, who had discovered the IRB's real intentions. The capture of the *Aud*, a German ship carrying additional arms and ammunition, off the coast of Kerry was a further blow.

In the aftermath of the Rising, the British commander in Ireland, General Sir John Maxwell, ordered the court martial of 183 people. Of these, fourteen were executed at Kilmainham Jail in Dublin and another in Cork. Sir Roger Casement was hanged in London in August 1916. The Irish public was deeply shocked at the executions, especially that of the socialist James Connolly. Connolly, the leader of the Irish Citizen Army, militant trade unionists in the main, had to be tied to a chair to face a firing squad as he could not stand up due to a gangrenous ankle wound. The executions were the catalyst in transforming Irish public opinion from being content with a measure of Home Rule to demanding complete independence in the form of an Irish Republic.

Sinn Féin was wrongly blamed for the Rising and over 3,000 people were arrested and imprisoned. This imprisonment gave the younger members of the IRB and the Irish Volunteers time to analyse the military failure of the Rising. Among them were men like Michael Collins and Richard Mulcahy, who now planned for a resumption of the fight against the British but on very different terms. In this planning lay the origins of the guerrilla tactics and intelligence operations that were to characterise the War of Independence. As the prisoners were released in late 1916 and early 1917, they set about reorganising the Irish Republican movement. The conscription crisis of 1918 saw Irish men and women from many backgrounds unite in opposition to the demand for more recruits to be used as cannon fodder for the British Army in closing stages of the First World War. Sinn Féin's handling of this crisis ensured its place as the leading political voice of the Irish people. Through the leadership of Éamon de Valera, Sinn Féin emerged triumphant in the General Election of December 1918, consigning the Irish Parliamentary Party to the annals of history. John Redmond did not live to see his life's work in ruins, having passed away the previous year.

Sinn Féin had campaigned on a policy of withdrawing from Westminster and establishing an independent Irish Constituent Assembly. This assembly, which became known as Dáil Éireann, met for the first time on 21 January 1919 despite being banned by British authorities. A number of those elected were still being held in prison. Therefore, of the seventy-three Sinn Féin elected representatives, only twenty-seven were in attendance at the first Dáil. The unionist party ignored the Dáil Assembly. On the same day the first Dáil met in the Mansion House in Dublin, the first shots of the Irish War of Independence were fired at Soloheadbeg in County Tipperary. Two Royal Irish Constabulary (RIC) constables were killed in an ambush organised by the 3rd Tipperary Brigade of the Irish Volunteers.

The rest of the war followed a similar pattern. Ambushes and assassinations became the main tactics of the Irish Volunteers, or Irish Republican Army (IRA) as they were known from 1920. The RIC, as the linchpin of British control over Ireland, bore the brunt of the attacks. The British responded with the introduction of a new terror of their own – the Black and Tans and Auxiliaries. These specialist forces, supplementing the falling numbers in the RIC, brought in their wake a wave of looting, arson and murder. Another side to the War of Independence was the intelligence war that was played out by the IRA and British forces, with spies and informers seeking to give each side the edge in the conflict.

As the war progressed, both sides sought the establishment of contacts that would facilitate an end to the violence. The Truce of July 1921 was the result of many months of secret negotiations. This was followed by the signing of the Anglo-Irish Treaty on 6 December 1921.

The Treaty gave enhanced formal recognition to the Government of Ireland Act 1920, which had established six Ulster counties as the new State of Northern Ireland alongside the southern Irish Free State. De Valera and his supporters opposed the Treaty but were defeated in a Dáil vote by sixty-four votes to fifty-seven. This vote split the Dáil, the Sinn Féin movement and the IRA. The anti-Treaty bloc led by de Valera could accept neither the required oath of allegiance to the British Crown nor the partition of Ireland. The pro-Treaty bloc led by Michael Collins and Arthur Griffith, both of whom had signed the Treaty, argued that acceptance of the agreement would lead to greater independence for the island of Ireland.

The anti-Treaty IRA led by Rory O'Connor seized control of the Four Courts in Dublin. De Valera continued to lead their political wing, Sinn Féin. The pro-Treaty IRA established a standing army equipped with arms and ammunition from Britain. A bitter Civil War ensued, with terrible violence, death and destruction. It began in June 1922 with General Michael Collins' orders to shell the Republican forces in the Four Courts. The victorious Provisional Government then launched a conventional military campaign in the south and west of Ireland, quickly retaking the Republican strongholds of Munster and Connaught. The Republicans resorted to the old IRA tactics of guerrilla warfare, employing ambushes and blowing up railway lines and bridges as part of their campaign. The torture and murder of captured prisoners became a hallmark of the newly established National (or Free State) Army. The Republicans, too, engaged in intimidation, beatings and the execution of suspected spies. Finally, the Free State government, led by W. T. Cosgrave, Kevin O'Higgins and Richard Mulcahy, embarked on a policy of executing Republican prisoners in order to end the Civil War. Many of those who fought to give Ireland independence did not live to see it realised. Michael Collins, Cathal Brugha and Harry Boland, to name but a few, were killed in the war that divided Ireland. Arthur Griffith died exhausted from his efforts to bring about Irish freedom. The Civil War has defined the Irish political landscape into the modern age.

The history of this period in counties such as Cork, Dublin and Tipperary is well documented. Events in many other counties are less well known. This book sets out to tell the story of County Mayo during the War of Independence and the Civil War that followed. Chapter 1 begins with an in-depth look at the policing duties of the RIC in Mayo and how it evolved into an increasingly militarised force. Part of this chapter looks at the command structure and the personalities involved and the impact their decisions had on the lives of Mayo communities. The chapter concludes with an examination of the unsolved murder of Resident Magistrate John Charles Milling in Westport.

Chapter 2 explores the nationalist organisation in County Mayo, and in particular the manner in which the old Irish Volunteers gave way to the Mayo brigades of the IRA in preparation for a guerrilla war. The chapter concludes with a detailed account of the Mayo brigades' difficulties in acquiring weapons and ammunition. Chapter 3 recalls the sudden outbreak of agrarian unrest in Mayo in 1920, and how it threatened to undermine the Sinn Féin movement for national independence. In order to prevent this, Arthur Griffith agreed to the establishment of the Republican courts, the first of which was held in Mayo. These Republican courts proved so successful that the British court system all but collapsed across Ireland. The move was to come too late, however, for two Mayo men who were savagely murdered by their own neighbours.

Chapter 4 carefully examines the decisions made in 10 Downing Street that led to the introduction of the Black and Tans and the Auxiliaries, and how such decisions had terrible consequences for men, women and children throughout Mayo. Pivotal in retelling these events are contemporary eyewitness accounts of Black and Tan atrocities, collected on the orders of Dr Gilmartin, the Archbishop of Tuam. Chapter 5 sees the IRA's military campaign begin in earnest. The IRA ambushes are examined in considerable detail as they offer a great insight into the minds of the combatants, their tactics and attitudes towards their enemies in time of war. Also included is perhaps one of the RIC's greatest victories in the War of Independence, the ambush at Kilmeena. This chapter also demonstrates the considerable difficulty the IRA had in maintaining security. Spies and informers were prevalent and some of their letters and statements are reproduced here.

Chapter 6 describes the role of Patrick Moylett, a Mayo man, as an intermediary for Arthur Griffith in establishing preconditions for peace with the British government. His correspondence offers startling revelations about the terms some in Sinn Féin had already conceded as early as 1920. This chapter also shows how the British Prime Minister David Lloyd George anticipated an Irish Civil War as early as 1920, and had explored solutions to deal with that eventuality. There is a detailed analysis of the role played by the Mayo TDs in the Treaty debates that led to acceptance of the Anglo-Irish Treaty of 1921, and how the split in Sinn Féin was mirrored in Mayo County Council. As the county descended into chaos, an IRA hit squad attempted to settle old scores by murdering retired RIC personnel and civilians. The final act before the outbreak of Civil War was a controversial visit by Michael Collins to Castlebar, after which there was no turning back from a war between former friends.

Chapter 7 investigates the Civil War in Mayo through the actions of the National Army's Claremorris Command and the IRA's flying columns. There are distinctive campaigns and commanders whose different personalities determined the course of events. Perhaps the most heartbreaking event of the Civil War in the Claremorris Command was the execution of six young men in Tuam in April 1923, just days before the formal end of hostilities. Despite the official end of the Civil War, Mayo's strife continued, with hundreds of her men and women in government prisons or camps. As they endured the last desperate act of hunger strike to achieve freedom, a new police force was introduced to Mayo, the Civic Guards or Garda Síochána. The last section of this book looks at how the Civic Guards established themselves in the county and were slowly accepted.

How Mayo as a society reacted to the various victories and defeats, challenges and traumas tells us much about the human spirit. The events in Mayo between 1919 and 1924 were both surprising and shocking. Mayo's war witnessed the very best of human attributes in loyalty, sacrifice, belief, compassion and bravery. But it also saw the very worst human beings are capable of through ruthlessness and betrayal. This history shows how an Irish county steered its way through very difficult times with an inner belief and certainty that kept it together in spite of occasional dissension and discord. Much of the information uncovered will make a serious contribution to the historical knowledge of Mayo and the period under study. This book is intended to stimulate further debate among historians and provide a signpost for those who wish to explore a little further the events in Mayo from 1919 to 1924. This history dispels forever the myth that little or nothing happened in Mayo during Ireland's War of Independence and Civil War.

1

'I Beg to Report': The Mayo RIC

Owen Spellman walked into his office and sat down. At 6 foot 2 inches and dressed in the dark green of a RIC District Inspector, the Roscommon man cut an imposing figure. He removed his peaked cap and gazed upon the black harp and crown. It looked very distinguished on the red background. Head Constable Maunsell brought him a cup of tea. As Spellman sipped his brew he felt very satisfied with himself. Claremorris was his first command as a District Inspector (DI). The town was a good posting for a man who had worked his way up through the ranks. Having joined the force in 1892, Spellman was promoted to Acting Sergeant in 1898 while stationed in Kilkenny. In 1917 he married Mary McDonnell from Stoneyford, County Kilkenny. Transferred upon marriage in accordance with the usual RIC practice, Spellman found himself appointed to Galway West Riding as a Head Constable. Just two years later the couple were in Claremorris, a growing town in south Mayo served by two rail links, one to Dublin and the other to Galway. The town was also the hub through which British forces and the RIC were distributed throughout the county of Mayo to the larger towns and villages.

The RIC county headquarters were further north in Castlebar, the administrative centre of Mayo. The RIC divided the county into districts based on the major towns of Ballina, Claremorris, Newport and Westport. A district barracks had a garrison of between ten and

RIC Insignia. (Reproduced with kind permission of Raymond and Jane Shearer.
Photograph courtesy Neil Harrison Photography)

twenty constables. Garrisons like Westport were to rise to thirty or
more constables during the War of Independence. Each district was
in turn divided into sub-districts with minor barracks in towns and
villages and additional RIC huts situated in rural townlands. The
sub-district barracks had a complement of five to ten men. They were
able to draw down reinforcements from the main district and county
headquarters during times of crisis. The huts, manned by around four
constables, were placed in areas noted for agrarian unrest. Mayo, with
an area of 2,159 square miles and a population (according to the 1911
Census) of 192,177, was one of Ireland's largest counties.[1] It was thus
a considerable challenge for the RIC to police effectively, requiring
one of the highest numbers of sergeants and constables – over 400 –
in the country.[2]

DI Spellman was a dedicated police officer who had trained at the
RIC Depot in the Phoenix Park, Dublin. The instruction provided

Constable James Hopkins from Mayo pictured here on joining the RIC in April 1907. Hopkins joined the RIC from Ballina where he was recommended by District Inspector Shier. Hopkins was stationed in Galway West Riding and then in Limerick during the War of Independence. He was promoted to Sergeant in June 1921. His nephew, Constable Thomas Hopkins, was murdered by the IRA while home on leave at Leface, Ballindine in May 1921. (Reproduced with kind permission of Bridie Hopkins and family)

was exemplary, and a benchmark for police forces throughout the British Empire. One of Spellman's first ceremonies as a young recruit had been to take the following oath:

> I do swear that I will well and truly serve Our Sovereign, the Queen, in the office of Constable without favour or affection, malice or ill-will; that I will see and cause Her Majesty's peace to be kept and preserved and that I will prevent to the best of my power, all offences against the same; and that while I shall continue to hold the said office, I will, to the best of my skill and knowledge, discharge all the duties thereof, in the execution of

Claremorris RIC Barracks. (Author's photograph)

warrants and otherwise, faithfully according to the law; and
that I do not now belong, and that I will not, while I shall
hold the said office, join, subscribe, or belong to any political
society whatsoever, except the Society of Freemasons. So help
me God.[3]

Spellman looked at the large stack of files in front of him. The
first assignment he had given himself was to review the actions of
the Mayo RIC over the past few years. It would be the best way of
familiarising himself with the major issues of his new command. He
thought the Crown and Peace Papers[4] would be a good starting point
as he finished off his tea and settled down to work.

At first glance, the Crown and Peace Papers revealed that the
Mayo RIC's work was similar to that of other districts throughout
Ireland. Some of the crimes included theft of bicycles, dealing with
cattle, sheep and pigs on the loose, hurley fights, trespass of geese

on crops, fist fights, assaults, disputes over bog rights, no lights on carts or bicycles, use of abusive language and no number plates on motors. But there were also more menacing crimes. Land agitation had been a focus of law and order concerns in Mayo since the RIC was established in 1822. In April 1916, Edward Walsh, a landlord at Castlehill, had discovered a coffin placed outside his home with a note attached stating he would lie in it within the month.[5] Spellman was glad to see the dispute had been settled peacefully. He read on through the files. Some stories told of the more human and tragic stories that Mayo constables faced. One report ran as follows:

> On 17th May 1916, John Reilly, a tramp, observed a bundle under a dry gullet in the village of Belderrigmore, Glencalry Sub Dist [north Mayo]. It was found to contain the dead body of a newly born male child wrapped up in two old womens' coats. The whole tied in a piece of canvass. Inquest held on 18:5:16 and following verdict returned viz that death was caused by exposure and want of attention at birth. No person made amenable as yet but police inquiries are still being pursued.[6]

There were also a number of cases relating to members of the Irish Volunteers and Sinn Féin. The most serious concerned the arrest of Colum O'Geary, a teacher, on 30 April 1916. The incident began with a raid by the RIC:

> Sergeant D. Fitzgerald 55670 who with an armed party of police went to Ryan's Hotel, Cong, for the purpose of questioning Colum O'Geary a Gaelic Teacher, a reputed Sinn Feiner. O'Geary answered unsatisfactorily whereupon the Sergeant asked him had he any arms and immediately O'Geary threw himself on a bed put his hand in his hip pocket and drew a colt revolver (magazine charged with nine cartridges) and presented it at the Sergeant. Const O'Donnell who was with the Sergeant threw himself upon O'Geary and wrenched the revolver from him. When searched O'Geary was found to have in his possession 159 other cartridges for revolver and £81 6[s] 6[d] in money.

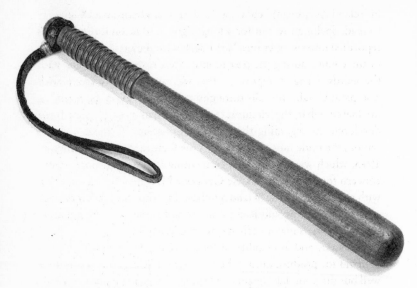

RIC Baton of District Inspector J. C. Milling. (Reproduced with kind permission of Raymond and Jane Shearer. Photograph courtesy Neil Harrison Photography)

A postscript in red ink followed the initial statement: 'Dealt with by court martial and sentenced to 15 years penal servitude – 5 years remitted.'[7]

Spellman was intent on burning the midnight oil. Putting away the Crown and Peace Papers he called for more tea and turned his attention to the County Inspector's monthly reports. The County Inspector was the senior ranking RIC officer in each Irish county. David Adie Steadman, a 54-year-old Presbyterian from Fifeshire, Scotland, had served as a District Inspector in Moate, County Westmeath, before his promotion to County Inspector of Mayo in 1911. The County Inspector was rather harsh in his attitude towards local people, as this statement reveals: 'The Out of Work donation scheme has not helped matters following as it does the idea of getting something substantial for doing nothing and there are no lack of claimants in these parts whose wily cunning and mendicancy are more predominant attributes than self-respect and independence.'[8]

On the last day of each month, the County Inspector submitted a report to Dublin Castle, the headquarters of the British administration in Ireland. Steadman's reports were always handwritten and not easy to read. Spellman was in for a long night. Each County Inspector's report fell into two sections. Part I dealt with the prevailing situation in the county during the past month. Steadman always began with the words 'I beg to report ...' This was usually followed up with 'comparative calm prevails throughout this County at the moment', no matter what the circumstances. Steadman usually related any developments regarding the Irish Transport and General Workers Union, the trade union that had led the General Strike in Dublin in 1913, which was always 'busy fermenting unrest'.[9] Of more serious concern for Steadman was the Congested Districts Board's inaction with regard to the issue of land purchase. He was worried that the lack of available land would lead to unrest and violence. Land agitation was to become a major challenge for the Mayo RIC.

The price and availability of food was another problem. Due to demand for produce during the First World War, farmers had done well but the poor 'felt the pinch of things'.[10] Steadman often reported on the prospective turf yield and potato crop during the summer months. Shortages of turf and potatoes meant hardship for many Mayo people. It also raised the possibility of increased unrest due to high prices. Mayo had relatively few local industries but Steadman always referred to developments that offered hope of employment. Some examples were a small knitting industry in Keel on Achill Island, a woollen factory at Foxford and a bacon factory at Castlebar. Steadman also listed indictable offences reported during the month. This was a good indicator of the level of crime the RIC was facing. The crime of 'inflicting malicious injury while driving cattle' was to become very frequent. Steadman usually concluded Part I of his reports with a reference to the general level of drunkenness in the county. In July 1919 drunkenness was reported to be on the decrease due to high prices and scarcity of poitín.

Part II of the County Inspector's monthly reports dealt with political activity on the part of Sinn Féin, the Gaelic League and the Irish Volunteers. The RIC kept Sinn Féin activists under constant surveillance. After Sinn Féin's stunning election victory in December 1918, Steadman reported political activity to be decreasing or inactive. This was a cause for concern among committed Sinn Féin members

RIC officer's belt buckle of J. C. Milling. (Reproduced with kind permission of Raymond and Jane Shearer. Photograph courtesy Neil Harrison Photography.

in the county. They feared an opportunity was being lost. Mayo had elected four Sinn Féin TDs (Teachtaí Dála/Members of Parliament) in 1918. However, Dr John Crowley for Mayo North was the only Mayo representative present when the Ceann Comhairle (Speaker) Cathal Brugha called the roll of TDs for the first time. Éamon de Valera, Mayo East, Joseph MacBride, Mayo West, and William Sears, Mayo South, were all recorded as '*fé ghlas ag Gallaibh*' (under lock and key of the British).

On the day the first Dáil met in Dublin, eight Irish Volunteers of the South Tipperary Brigade under the command of Seán Treacy and Dan Breen ambushed a cartload of gelignite escorted by two RIC constables at Soloheadbeg. Both men were shot dead. One of them was Mayo man James McDonnell, a 54-year-old widower with seven children. McDonnell, originally from Belmullet, was the first of twenty-three Mayo men in the RIC to be killed over the next four years.[11] Events at Soloheadbeg marked the beginning of the Irish Volunteers' military campaign against the RIC and the British military that was to be called the War of Independence or the Anglo-Irish War.

The RIC witnessed little Irish Volunteer activity in Mayo beyond training and collecting arms. The County Inspector's reports detailed that in the first half of 1919 there were Sinn Féin meetings at Ballyhaunis, Crossmolina, Westport, Foxford and Keelogues to demand the release of interned prisoners. The *Ballina Herald* was allowed to reopen on 6 January following the seizure of its plant for printing 'seditious election literature'. There were also court appearances for eight men in connection with rioting in Louisburgh and Ballycastle at the end of December. Among Sinn Féin activists in the county who received special mention were William Sears, TD for Mayo South, Conor Maguire, a solicitor from Claremorris, J. J. Collins, editor of the *Mayoman* from Castlebar, Paddy Hegarty, an Irish Volunteer from Laherdane and Colonel Maurice Moore, a previous Inspector General of the Irish Volunteers.

Steadman's reports concluded with a list of political organisations, including branches and membership. For January 1919 the following organisations were listed:[12]

No	Name of Organisation	No of Branches	Member- ship	Remarks
1	Irish Volunteers	19	2,280	
2	National Volunteers	47	3,692	
3	U.I.L. [United Irish League]	53	3,966	
4	Gaelic League	16	649	
5	A.O.H. [Ancient Order of Hibernians]	32	1,661	
6	(I.A.A.)	5	302	
7	G.A.A. [Gaelic Athletic Association]	15	819	
8	I.N.F. [Irish National Foresters]	3	412	
9	Sinn Féin Clubs	68	6,613	
10	Town Tenants	4	182	
11	Gaelic Club	1	30	
12	Cumann na mBan	10	346	
13	I.R.B. [Irish Republican Brotherhood]	1	10	
14	I.T.G.W. Union [Irish Transport and General Workers]	12	2,741	

RIC County Inspector's Report on political organisations in County Mayo, January 1919.

In February, a new Sinn Féin club was formed at Irishtown, Ballindine Sub-District, while Irish Volunteer and Cumann na mBan companies were established at Islandeady. Steadman considered Islandeady a strong Republican area. It was to become the headquarters for the West Mayo Brigade. The RIC had identified Michael Staunton, Patrick (Paddy) Jordan, Mrs Ellen Tuohy and Paddy Cannon as leading opponents in the area. Their houses were raided in February, with seditious 'literature pamphlets' and 'a revolver and some ammunition' found in Jordan's house.[13] Jordan was subsequently arrested and handed over to the British military in Galway Jail on 20 February 1919. He went on hunger strike – losing 20 lb – before being released in the autumn. Important Sinn Féin Executive meetings were also held in Claremorris and Castlebar on 12 and 16 February in preparation for the forthcoming local government elections. Nevertheless, the overall impression Steadman created was one of a county firmly under RIC control. There was no need for alarm.

DI Owen Spellman was relishing the opportunity of beginning work in Claremorris. He stood up from his desk, strolled over to the window and looked out over the leafy avenue. Some locals were on their way home from one of the many public houses in the town. It was a source of annoyance to him, one he was determined to stamp out. In fact, one of his first court appearances took him to Ballinrobe where Mrs Margaret Conway, owner of St Colman's Hotel in Claremorris, had applied for a new alcohol licence. Spellman objected on the grounds that Claremorris already had forty-nine public houses and scarcely required another one. However, Sergeant Healey, one of Spellman's own constables, appeared in Mrs Conway's defence, stating that the licence would increase the value of the property and would be properly managed. Spellman was embarrassed and said his opposition was to drink and not to Mrs Conway. Judge Doyle KC granted the licence.[14]

As he went through the various files, DI Spellman could see times were changing, and that the daily duties of the RIC had been transformed by the seismic shift that had taken place in Irish politics over the previous decade – the split between Sinn Féin and the Irish Parliamentary Party and the different strands of nationalism they represented. This divide was epitomised in the falling out of two brothers, William and Patrick J. Doris of Westport. They were owners of the *Mayo News*, established in December 1892. The Doris brothers originally used the paper to argue for Home Rule. They constantly attacked the British government's policies on Ireland and sought support for the United Irish League, a group closely connected with John Redmond's party, of which William was the first Secretary.[15] William Doris was elected as the Irish Parliamentary Party MP for Mayo South in the General Election of December 1910. 'Please God,' he declared in his victory speech, 'I will never forget that I am the son of a poor man, elected mainly by the poor people of this constituency.'[16] The new MP moved to Westminster, leaving the *Mayo News* in the hands of his capable brother.

The Liberal Party had held the election of 1910 to break the power of veto the House of Lords held over the House of Commons; their victory was enshrined in the Parliament Act of 1911. The Lords had vetoed previous attempts to enact Home Rule. With their powers now limited it became clear that the Third Home Rule Bill, introduced to the Commons in 1912, would become law in 1914. Home Rule, however, was already part of an old world passing away. Sinn Féin, arguing for a greater degree of independence for Ireland, was beginning to attract younger supporters, leaving the more conservative elements in Irish society behind. The *Mayo News* began to drift towards Sinn Féin, demanding complete independence for Ireland. William Doris' days as an MP were numbered as support for the Irish Parliamentary Party began to slip away. Before too long, P. J. Doris and many other Sinn Féin supporters in Westport were to come to the attention of the new Resident Magistrate (RM) John Charles Milling. As an RM, Milling was at the forefront of the British government's attempt to resist those seeking to establish an Irish Republic. Milling believed Ireland's only hope for the future lay within the British Empire as it brought prestige, employment and opportunity.

As the night wore on DI Spellman pulled out copies of the Sinn Féin activist files. These had been compiled with the assistance of the RIC in Mayo, G Division of the Dublin Metropolitan Police and British military intelligence. There were files on Michael Joseph Ring

Colonel Maurice Moore, Inspector General Irish Volunteers prior to 1914.
Featured here as a colonel of the Connaught Rangers with whom he served in
Afghanistan, India and in the Zulu and Boer Wars, South Africa. (From: Moore,
Colonel Maurice. *An Irish Country Gentleman George Henry Moore*. T. Werner
Laurie Ltd 1913. Courtesy The National Library of Ireland)

from Westport, Michael Kilroy from Newport, Patrick Moylett, a
Ballina and London businessman, Thomas Maguire from Cross and
Colonel Maurice Moore of Moore Hall. The file on Colonel Moore
had particular local significance for Spellman. His constables had been
keeping an eye on the activities of the Colonel during his occasional
visits to Claremorris, Ballinrobe and Moore Hall at Lough Carra.

Moore had extensive military experience. He had completed
his officer training at the prestigious Royal Military Academy at
Sandhurst in England before serving with the Connaught Rangers
in Afghanistan, India, the Zulu War (1877–1879) and the Boer
War (1900–01). Initial support for the Irish Volunteers in Mayo was
opposed by a hostile United Irish League and Irish Parliamentary
Party. Colonel Moore became Inspector General of the Irish

Volunteers. He recorded his experiences in a series of articles for the *Irish Press* in 1938. His touring book recorded a visit to Mayo in April 1914:

> Saturday, April 18, 1914. I went from Dublin to Ballina, and next day I addressed a large meeting, after which 520 men were enrolled and a good Committee was formed. I promised to send more detailed information about organisation on my return to Dublin, and to send enrolment forms. In the afternoon I joined the Committee in a pleasant excursion to Enniscrone, where we enlisted some more Volunteers on the way, and talked over Irish history and traditions. I was much impressed by the eager and intelligent patriotism of these young men.
>
> On Monday, having wired to Castlebar in advance, I went to a parade in the Green; 120 men formed up at 8 p.m. The notice had been short, and men could not be warned in time. The companies drilled well, but the crowd on the Green encroached too much. The band was quite good.
>
> Tuesday, Westport, where Joe MacBride, a good old Nationalist, was in charge; Sergeant Formby, late Connaught Rangers, a first-rate man, is chief instructor ... On Wednesday I inspected 50 men at Newport, and had a talk with Pat O'Donnell, who is the most energetic Nationalist in the town ... The country people are eager to raise a corps, but cannot get an instructor at present – they have to come in three miles.[17]

The following August, Colonel Moore ordered 'The O'Rahilly', a senior Volunteer officer, to Mayo to conduct a tour of duty. On his return, The O'Rahilly submitted an account of his inspection at Castlebar:

> A Chara,
>
> Agreeable with Colonel Moore's orders, I went to Castlebar on Saturday, 11th inst., 10.30 train, and on arrival met Mr Ryan, the other Committee members not being available till Sunday.
>
> On Saturday met local people, and talked over matters with them ... On Sunday they had a tournament with all sorts of competitions, at which several thousand Volunteers attended

and gave displays. There were over 12,000 of the general public, and they made about £200 for the equipment fund ... Castlebar is to be the Regimental Headquarters. I found the spirit excellent, both as regards the immediate armament and the absolute permanence of the Volunteer organisation.

Mise do cara,

Ua Rathghaille [The O'Rahilly][18]

With the outbreak of the First World War in August 1914, the Home Rule crisis faded into the background. Encouraged by their leaders, tens of thousands of Irishmen in the UVF and the Irish Volunteers joined the British Army to fight for the 'rights and liberties of small nationalities' against 'the intolerable military despotism of Germany'.[19] On Fair and Market Days across the county, the British Army held recruiting parades. In Claremorris, Lady Oranmore of Castlemagarret led speeches encouraging the men to join up and do their bit in fighting 'the Huns'. The recruiting parades also featured rousing marching songs played by the Brass Band of the Kent Regiment.[20] However, Redmond's support for the war split the Volunteer movement. Colonel Moore was one of the few leading members of the original organising committee of the Irish Volunteers to side with Redmond in the split. As a result, Moore was never really trusted by the Sinn Féin Republican movement.[21]

DI Spellman reviewed Colonel Moore's file. The attention of the RIC on his routine was constant throughout 1917. Initially, the RIC believed Moore was canvassing as an 'Irish Partyman'.[22] On 22 February, reports reached County Inspector (CI) Steadman that Moore had arrived in Ballinrobe to 'ascertain the views of R.C. Clergymen as to his contesting Mayo South at [the] next election. He called on Rev Fr Healy P.P. Kilmaine on 18th inst. where he met also the Rev Canon D'Alton P.P. Ballinrobe.'[23] The RIC were also watching the local Sinn Féin movement. One report, on a meeting of the Dr O'Dwyer Sinn Fein Club, Ballinrobe, offered significant inside information:

all the Committee were present except James Shaughnessy. Martin Costello was in the chair. The Secretary reported the membership to be 326. The total amount in the hands of the

Treasurer is now £35. The Club is to be affiliated at once and endeavours are to be made to increase the membership as much as possible before next meeting as a good many of the country people have not sent in their names yet.

It was directed that prominent men in country villages be communicated with a view to getting them to collect as much money as possible in order that the Club will be in a sound financial position and to have the membership as large as possible. There was no date fixed for the next meeting.
John Ellis Con 57,658.[24]

Later that year, Moore returned to south Mayo where the local RIC were waiting to monitor and report his every move. Moore attended a Sinn Féin club meeting in Ballinrobe on 25 September. He was recorded by Constable John Ellis as having spoken to the meeting on their lack of organisation and then subscribed ten shillings to their fund.[25] It then emerged Colonel Moore had addressed a Sinn Féin meeting in Westport on 23 September and attended a Sinn Féin Executive meeting in Balla on 26 September. It appeared to the Mayo RIC that Moore had now 'definitely joined the Sinn Féiners'.[26] For the most part, surveillance was pretty mundane work for Spellman's constables. A report submitted by Constable C. Leary (No. 57,883) on 5 October 1917 is a good example:

I beg to report that Colonel M. G. Moore 'Sinn Feiner' arrived here on 24:9:17 from Westport and put up at Valkenburg's Hotel, he went to see Canon D'Alton that night at 9:15 p.m., and he remained with him till 10.20 p.m. On 25:9:17 he attended the funeral of the late Thomas F. Ruttledge at Hollymount, that night he attended a Committee meeting of Dr O'Dwyer Sinn Féin Club in the Town Hall and remained there from 9 p.m. to 10:30 p.m. On 26:9:17 he visited some of the leading Sinn Féiners in town and remained with Martin Costello for 1/2 an hour, he had a conversation with Patk McCormack in his office from 12:30 p.m. to 1 p.m. They discussed the Sinn Fein policy all the time. On 27:9:17 he visited John J. Hession Sec S. F. Club at 1:15 p.m. and remained with him till 1:30

p.m. On 28:9:17 he visited Thomas Walsh Abbey Street who is Treasurer of S. F. Club at 11:15 a.m. and remained with him till 11:45 a.m. On 29:9:17 he went into Mrs Murphys Main Street got a paper and returned to his Hotel, he remained there till 5 p.m. when he went down to Springvale for a walk and returned at 6:45 p.m. On 30:9:17 he left town on Valkenburg trap at 2 p.m. and went to a Sinn Fein meeting in Clonbur Sub. Dist. He returned at 7 p.m. to his Hotel and remained there for the night. On 1:10:17 he went to the Railway Station got the daily paper and returned to the Hotel and remained there almost all the evening, he went to post letters at 7:30 p.m. returned to the Hotel and remained there for the night.[27]

The final page on Colonel Moore's file showed that his efforts to become an MP came to nothing. Sinn Féin rejected his proposals and selected William Sears instead.

Although subsequently sentenced to six months' imprisonment for 'a seditious speech delivered at Bangor Erris', William Sears was a most unlikely revolutionary. A distinguished-looking man, much like Sir Roger Casement in appearance, he was from The Neale, where his mother still lived in 1919. Her house was later burnt to the ground by the Black and Tans. By 1916, Sears had become the successful owner of a provincial newspaper in County Wexford, the *Enniscorthy Echo*. He was an early member of Sinn Féin, founded by Arthur Griffith in 1905. A personal friend of Griffith, he served on the Sinn Féin Executive from 1908. His son, David, attended Patrick Pearse's Scoil Éanna in Rathfarnham and participated in the Easter Rising of 1916. After the Rising, William Sears was arrested as a member of Sinn Féin and imprisoned in England along with his entire staff of the *Enniscorthy Echo*. Sears' imprisonment turned an intelligent, articulate and influential businessman into a revolutionary. He was imprisoned at Frongoch in north Wales after the Rising. He would go on to serve two more jail terms – six months in Mountjoy in Dublin and a further stint at Ballykinlar internment camp in County Down. He went on hunger strike in Mountjoy and endured solitary confinement for a considerable period of time. It was this experience that left his health permanently weakened.[28] In spite of this, William

William Sears TD Mayo
South, 1918–1927.
(Courtesy The National
Library of Ireland)

Sears was to play a very influential role in events in Mayo over the
next few years. He was chosen as the Sinn Féin candidate for Mayo
South for the 1918 General Election because he was a member of
the IRB and considered to be reliable if the struggle against Britain
became protracted and difficult.

Having put aside all other files, DI Spellman now turned his
attention to the highest-profile case in Mayo, the murder of John
Charles Milling RM.

On the night of Saturday 29/30 March 1919, a snowstorm
accompanied by howling winds descended on Westport. Shortly
after 10 p.m., Kate McDonald, maid to the Milling family, wrapped
a shawl tightly around herself and stepped out of the front door. As
she did so she noticed two men lurking in the shadows near the front
sitting-room window. The weather being unpleasant, she paid the
men no heed and hurried on. A short while later, Milling entered the
sitting room to wind the clock as he was in the habit of doing before

John Charles Milling, RM for County Mayo, murdered by the IRB in Westport 29 March 1919. (Courtesy The National Library of Ireland)

retiring to bed. With the lights on in the house and the curtains open, Milling could not see the two figures outside in the dark as they drew their revolvers. A number of shots rang out. Milling lingered between life and death all through the next day until he finally passed away in the evening. He was tended to by his family, two local doctors and a specialist surgeon from Dublin. In spite of their utmost efforts the 46-year-old RM had lost too much blood.[29] This warm and caring family man left behind his wife, Lilla, and three children, Robert, Marjorie and Henry Desmond. The opening shots of the War of Independence in Mayo had been fired.

Archbishop Gilmartin of Tuam condemned the murder. 'If the perpetrator is not insane,' he wrote to Rev. Canavan, the Catholic administrator of Westport, 'he is a criminal of the first order, and it is the duty of all good citizens to do all in their power to bring to justice one who is an enemy of God, an enemy of society and an enemy of Ireland.'[30] The night Milling died a public meeting was held in the

Town Hall in Castlebar. A resolution was passed expressing 'utter abhorrence at the dastardly outrage'.[31] By Thursday 3 April, the British military had arrived in the town and the Royal Air Force (RAF), based at Castlebar, flew over the surrounding area continuously. In spite of a statement from the Westport Urban District Council regretting 'this foul stain upon their town', martial law was imposed. Lilla Milling lodged a claim for £5,000 at the loss of her husband. It was later raised to £6,000 and levied on the local ratepayers. Some, like Lord Sligo, attempted to exempt themselves from payment. The money to be paid became known as the 'Milling Tax'.[32] The money was paid by the County Council who sought to recoup the cost from Westport Urban District Council. The payment of the money was to become the centre of serious argument between Westport and the County Council for the next six years.

John Charles Milling had been appointed Resident Magistrate to County Mayo in 1915. He was a former District Inspector of the RIC in Belfast, where he had a reputation for impartiality in his treatment of both Protestant and Catholic communities. Milling had looked forward to his Mayo appointment. Westport was the place where he had grown up, his father, Oliver, serving as County Inspector of the RIC there. Milling's grandfather had also served as an RIC officer, awarded the Constabulary Medal for Gallantry during the Fenian Rising of 1867.

Milling was well known to Henry Tynan-Hinkson RM and his wife, Katherine, who lived at Brookhill, Claremorris. Katherine was an author. Her books, *The Years of the Shadow* (1919) and *The Wandering Years* (1922), tell of her time at Brookhill and offer valuable insight into the life of the privileged in Ireland both during and after the First World War.[33] She described Jack Milling, as he was known to the family, as kind and hospitable but easy to annoy when it came to the subject of Irish nationalism. The Tynan-Hinksons deliberately teased Milling by singing Jacobite songs.[34] Jack was 'always willing and eager to entertain his friends' when he would thrill them with stories of his time in Belfast, where he was often heard to say 'they have hard skulls in Belfast'.[35] But Jack Milling was also very forthright in his opinions, which led Henry Hinkson to warn him about 'the careless and imprudent things he was in the habit of saying publicly'.[36]

The RIC ABC by District Inspector J. C. Milling. The book became a basic requirement for RIC recruits. (Reproduced with kind permission of Raymond and Jane Shearer. Photograph Courtesy Neil Harrison Photography)

As an RM, Milling sat in the courthouses of Louisburgh, Newport, Castlebar, Balla, Kiltimagh and as far north as Ballina. He heard a wide variety of cases. Among those presented before him were robbery, assault, drunkenness, trespass, threatening and abusive language, no lights on a cart, non-compliance with the sheep dip order, use of false weights and measures, and poitín making. The fines he imposed for these cases ranged from one penny to one shilling. Milling was not an unduly harsh RM. In fact, a review of cases that came before him between 1915 and 1919 compared with those appearing before the new District Justices of the Irish Free State appointed in 1923 show he was much more lenient in dispensing justice. He frequently called on those appearing before him on drinking or fighting charges to join the army. However, the one area where he applied the law rigorously was the 'treason' of Republican ideas.

Joe Ring, Westport Company of the Irish Volunteers prior to 1919.
(Courtesy Michael Ring TD)

The Easter Rising took place from 24 to 30 April 1916. In the weeks that followed, Milling and the local RIC arrested and detained many of the leading members of the Irish Volunteers in Westport under terms of the Defence of the Realm Act 1914. Support arrived in the form of the 16th Lancers and the North Staffordshire Regiment who were based in Castlebar. In Westport, over thirty Volunteers and Sinn Féin supporters were arrested on the direct orders of Milling and DI Shore. This formidable team was also responsible for drawing up a list of Irish Volunteers to be deported to Frongoch in Wales and to other British prisons. Milling's experience as a former police officer combined with his dedication and thoroughness as an RM were invaluable resources to the British administration in neutralising the Volunteer movement in County Mayo. Among those imprisoned were Joseph Ring, Tom Derrig and P. J. Doris, editor of the *Mayo News*. There were two others sent to Frongoch whose whereabouts were to become highly significant on the night of 29/30 March 1919: Joseph Ruddy and Charles Gavin.[37]

The initial reaction of the British authorities to the Rising in arresting and imprisoning Irish Volunteers and Sinn Féin supporters was popular. The Rising was at first viewed with anger and disbelief by many Irish men and women who saw it as an act of disloyalty while thousands of their countrymen were dying in the trenches of Flanders. As Pearse and fellow prisoners were marched through the ruins of Dublin to Richmond Barracks in Inchicore, they were showered with abuse by hundreds of Dubliners angry about civilian casualties and the disruption caused to civil life.[38] The urban and district councils throughout Mayo sought to reaffirm their loyalty to John Redmond. The Rural District Council of Castlebar passed the following resolution:

> We ... register our deep regret for, and resentment against, the deplorable and insane action of a section of Volunteers in this country, who at the time of terrible crisis in her history, seized the opportunity to disrupt the country, to precipitate civil war, to discredit the Irish Party and the Irish leader, and to bring irreparable damage and disaster to the prospects of prosperity and progress.[39]

On 3 May 1916, a notice was posted outside Kilmainham Jail informing the public that three Irish Volunteers, Patrick Pearse, Thomas Clarke and Thomas MacDonagh, had been executed. The executions continued until 12 May, by which time fourteen Irishmen had been shot by firing squad at Kilmainham. Elsewhere, Thomas Kent was executed at Cork Detention Barracks on 9 May while Sir Roger Casement was hanged at Pentonville Jail the following August. The executions produced a powerful change in public opinion, leading to popular support for a revolution that united the political and military movements of Irish Republicanism effectively for the first time. The opportunity of Ireland existing as an independent country now lay in the hands of new generation.

Joe Ring and other Mayo Volunteers were released from prison at Christmas 1916. Back in Westport, Ring, Ned Moane and others set about rebuilding the Irish Volunteers. Ring's training of the Volunteers in Westport was a serious provocation to Milling and the RIC. The RIC file on Joe Ring, Officer Commanding (O/C) Irish Volunteers Westport Company, was extremely thorough. Compiled in November 1917, the RIC identified thirty-four of the leading Irish Volunteers in the Westport district complete with address, age, occupation and activities. They also identified eleven key members of the Fianna (Sinn Féin Boy Scouts) along with address, occupation and constabulary remarks on same. Many of those listed were to become leading members of the Irish Volunteers in west Mayo during the War of Independence.[40]

It was the intention of Milling and DI Shore to arrest 'active and locally prominent Sinn Féiners' including Joe Ring, Ned Moane, Willie Malone and Peter Kelly. However, a surprising intervention by the Undersecretary for Ireland and the commanding officer of the British Army in Ireland led to the Westport Volunteers remaining free, with the Westport RIC simply told to continue their surveillance of Joe Ring's company.[41]

Milling was subsequently drawn into a spiralling series of confrontations that saw the disintegration of British control in Mayo. With the RIC holding back, the Irish Volunteers grew in confidence and continued their public demonstrations of Irish nationalism. Éamon de Valera visited Castlebar on 19 January 1918 to review companies of Irish Volunteers drawn from across the county. For the young Mayo Volunteers, the presence among them of the only surviving commandant of the Rising was inspiring. The atmosphere was enhanced with the pipes and drums of the Bohola Marching Band. De Valera delivered a rousing speech from the steps of the courthouse to the cheers and delight of the crowd, stating 'that if the English were serious about peace, all they had to do was clear out of this country'.[42]

For Milling, de Valera's speech made conflict inevitable. The RM saw it as a direct challenge to British authority. On Thursday 14 March 1918, Ned Moane was arrested and charged with 'Illegal Drilling and Unlawful Assembly' before Milling at Westport courthouse. Joe Ring organised a noisy demonstration outside the court in support of Moane. The RIC drew their batons and waded into the crowd. A full-scale riot ensued with bricks, bottles and paving slabs thrown at the police who in turn inflicted many casualties on the Volunteers. The plate-glass windows of the town shops were smashed. Brodie Malone described the scene:

> When Mohane [*sic*] was brought back for trial in Westport, the Cuslagh Band turned out to give him a welcome and the RIC and military turned out. The RIC stood behind the band and the procession. Then the RIC charged and clogged hell out of the lads in Castlebar St, but the lads fought back and a lot of the police were hurted. Ring told the lads to get pick handles from outside the shops and he got a plant on him (from a cutter) under the ear which knocked him out, and Ring got 6 months for this. Willie Malone who was in the burnings in England in Liverpool, and is now in Brea was captured for that row also and Joe Walsh, who was afterwards killed, and another fellow. The Baton charges went on from Thursday. The lads from Cuslagh defended themselves with pipes, but the big drummer they couldn't get at for he was a big powerful man, and he defended himself with his drum. In the Courthouse we were shouting for Ned to give him heart. Then we tore up the paving to get ammunition for the fight and you could see the spikes being knocked off the padded helmets of the RIC.[43]

Moane was given one month in Sligo Jail. As a result of the rioting, Milling issued warrants for the arrest of William O'Malley, Joe Ring, Thomas Kitterick, Charles Gavin and William Malone. Appearing in court, Ring said: 'We are Soldiers of the Republic and refuse to recognise the Court.' Ring accused Milling of boasting publicly that he 'would give Ring a long rest', meaning he would jail him.[44] Milling ignored Ring and remanded the five in custody to appear in Castlebar court on 20 March. The proceedings in Castlebar saw the Westport Volunteers turn their backs on Milling to sing '*Amhrán na bhFiann*' ('The Soldiers' Song'). Milling described Ring and the others as 'street roughs' engaged in 'hooliganism' and 'blackguardism'. They received six-month sentences with hard labour in Sligo Jail. Another riot ensued, and with the crowd shouting 'Up the Irish Republic' and 'Up de Valera', the RIC drew their batons and charged. Milling was safely escorted away.[45] The people of Castlebar were not impressed with this riotous behaviour. The *Connaught Telegraph* blamed 'youngsters from Westport' for all the trouble. The editor claimed 'Conduct of this kind will not free Ireland but tighten the chains around her'.[46]

Obstruction to Milling's court sittings was not confined to Westport and Castlebar. In September 1918, Captain Stephen Donnelly of the Ballina Volunteer Company appeared before Milling on a charge of resisting arrest and assault on the RIC. Donnelly had been knocked unconscious in a riot between Irish Volunteers and the RIC. In the subsequent court hearing, Donnelly refused to recognise Milling's authority or that of the court. He was sentenced to five months' imprisonment, which he served at Sligo, Derry and Belfast jails.[47] The Bishop of Achonry intervened when another case involving Milling and riotous behaviour occurred in Charlestown in January 1919. Milling and the local RIC had identified twenty-two people responsible for undermining the court. Dublin Castle had actually advised Milling to drop the case.[48] In fact, such was the widespread resistance to Milling's court sittings, the British administration were beginning to consider him a liability.

In October 1918 Milling moved from Rosmalley into the town of Westport to a house on the Newport road. He believed living in the town might be safer as he had received a number of death threats. These had been followed by an arson attack on his boat during the summer. In January 1919 his close friend Henry Tynan-Hinkson died. Milling felt very isolated. 'They are working me like a Galley Slave. I have Belmullet and Ballina Districts and am always on the road. Ye Gods, who would be an RM ... I feel so lonely and I cannot bear this country now,' he wrote in his last letter to Henry's widow, Katherine.[49]

Milling applied for a transfer to County Antrim, but before it came through his 'unknown assailants' had struck.[50] His killing remained a mystery for many years. However, the RIC file on the event has recently come to light. It contains a list of witnesses and what they saw on the night of 29/30 March 1919 in Westport. There were also suggestions as to who the RIC wanted to interview further. The file also contains a series of notes from various members of the RIC senior command, including G. J. Smith, Assistant Inspector General of the Constabulary Depot at the Phoenix Park. In November 1919, as part of a police review into the case, senior RIC officers proposed holding an official inquiry under the terms of the Criminal Law & Procedure (Ireland) Act 1887, more commonly known as the Coercion Act. They believed putting witnesses on the stand might cause them to crack and reveal further vital information. The new District Inspector, Francis Maguire, did not agree. 'The holding of the inquiry would do harm to those witnesses named,' he said. 'It would place them in danger of being shot for giving information if it were ever suspected that they told anything to the Police. Coyne (No 4 Witness) is already watched by the Police as he is afraid owing to the detention of McLoughlin that he is suspected of giving information.'[51]

The main witnesses DI Maguire was worried about were numbered by the RIC one to six. A description of what they saw follows:[52]

Names of persons who should be examined	Evidence expected to be given
Martin Barry, 50yrs, Coal Porter.	When going home shortly before 11 pm saw two men on the road near Milling's house. He can describe them but cannot identify them. I expect this man would give information if he knew it.
William A. Stewart, 22 yrs, Bank Clerk.	When passing Milling's house shortly before the murder saw two men near the window through which the shooting took place. As he is a stranger in the Dist[rict] he could not identify them.
Kate McDonald, 30 yrs, Domestic Servant.	Was a domestic servant in Millings. She was going out on a message after 10 pm and saw two men near the window where the shots were fired. She states she did not know the men. She may be able to go further.
John Coyne, 23 yrs, Farmer's Son.	Saw 2 men crossing a wall on to the Castlebar Rd about 11 pm after the murder. Should have been committed. He believes them to have been two men named Ruddy + Gavin. The wall is at the rere [sic] of Millings House forming the base of an isosceles triangle having for its sides Westport Rd (where the murder was comtd) + Castlebar Rd where these men were seen. I think Coyne has told all he knows.

John McLoughlin, 21yrs, Labourer.	Was with Coyne when the latter saw the men crossing the wall but he denies seeing any person. He was taken to Dublin by the Police + detained without any good results. This man would swear anything rather than divulge any information, but in my opinion he can give none except what Coyne has voluntarily given.
Mrs James Kelly, 40 years, Housekeeper.	It is rumoured that this woman saw two men at Milling's House but she now denies it. If she saw the men she may be able to identify them but though she is religiously minded, am of opinion that she wouldn't say it on oath.

[Page 10] 'Inquiry under Sec 1. C[riminal]. L[aw] + P[rocedure] Act 1887 into the Murder of J.C. Milling RM'

Maguire's judgement in RIC documents can be called into question as it later emerged that he collaborated with the local Irish Volunteers, frequently passing on highly classified documents. On the basis of the witness statements, RIC senior officers recommended examining the following: Joseph Ruddy of Church Street, Belturbet, County Cavan, his parents and two brothers who had served in the Canadian Army. Ruddy was one of two men John Coyne saw climbing a wall at the back of Milling's house just minutes after the shooting. Ruddy was a Westport man from Quay Street, born in 1892.[53] In the 1950s, Thomas Heavey, a member of the West Mayo Flying Column during the War of Independence referred to two aspects of the Milling murder. He said it was rumoured in the town that DI Scott in Westport was having an affair with Lilla Milling, and that it was Scott who had killed the RM. Heavey discounted this story, claiming the IRB were responsible and naming Ruddy, Joe Gill and Joe Walsh as the men who carried out the operation. Heavey also said the other members of the IRA never talked about the killing.[54] The only name to appear in both the former IRA man's witness statement and the original RIC investigation file is Joe Ruddy.

Joe Ruddy had been in Frongoch detention camp with Michael Collins, Richard Mulcahy, Joe Ring and many other men who were to lead the IRA in the War of Independence. In late 1919 he gave his address as Belturbet, County Cavan. One cannot help but question

RIC District Inspector's whistle of J. C. Milling. (Reproduced with kind permission of Raymond and Jane Shearer. Photograph courtesy Neil Harrison Photography)

why he left Mayo so soon after Milling's murder. There is, however, no evidence of his being in that part of Cavan during the War of Independence. He may have gone under an alias or, after the RIC had tracked him down, moved to Britain. He returned to Westport in 1922 as a captain of the National Army and a member of the elite 'Ring's Own' force. It seems certain that he was involved in Milling's murder, but this cannot yet be confirmed. One of the other men named by Heavey was Joe Walsh. He remained in Westport, fighting with the West Mayo Flying Column. Walsh also became an officer in the National Army during the Civil War. Both Ruddy and Walsh were to go into action on the same day in 1922 against former comrades with tragic consequences.

The RIC also wanted to interview Charles Gavin and Batty Cryan in connection with the Milling case. Gavin had been seen climbing the wall at the rear of Milling's house with Ruddy. They were taking a route that would bring them through the convent grounds to Captain's Wood and out into the countryside. This was a route frequently used later on by Volunteer patrols to enter Westport unobserved. Gavin had also been in Frongoch with Ruddy. Undoubtedly, the two men knew each other very well. Batty Cryan later moved to Ballinrobe, County Leitrim. The local council was vehement in their denials that any member of the community had anything to do with the killing. But there was clearly local involvement as the RIC suspected John McDonagh, a leader of the local Fianna, of being a scout for those who killed Milling. This corresponds with an earlier incident in the town in October 1917, when Thomas Kitterick and Tom Derrig had attempted to steal a rifle from a Connaught Ranger, James Ralph. The RIC in Westport noted that there were many Irish Volunteers posted in various locations around the town that night acting as if they were scouts.[55] Sheridan, who lived next door to Milling, may also have known a lot more than he let on. His claim to have heard a single footstep on the street does not hold up as the night of the murder witnessed a terrible snowstorm and a single footstep would not have been audible.[56]

Milling's death was followed by the assassination of another Resident Magistrate, Alan Bell, who by coincidence had also served in Mayo. His death bore many similarities to Milling's. Both men were applying considerable pressure to the Irish Volunteers, Sinn Féin and their operations. Both men were also former District Inspectors of the RIC. Bell was investigating the attempt on the life of the Viceroy, Lord French, by an Irish Volunteer unit led by Dan Breen. He was also on the trail of the Dáil Éireann Bond Scheme organised by Michael Collins. Alan Bell was taken off a tram by members of Collins' notorious Squad and shot in the head in broad daylight in Sandymount, Dublin. Milling's death in Westport was suspected by CI Steadman to be an act of revenge by the local Irish Volunteers for his repeated jailing of their members. It could also be argued that Milling's killing was one of a number of assassinations ordered by Michael Collins and the IRB to eliminate members of the British law-and-order establishment who posed the most serious threat to the Irish Volunteers and the Sinn Féin movement. Collins wanted to warn others RMs and members of the RIC from being as zealous as Milling and Bell.

It is quite possible that Collins ordered Milling's murder through his IRB network to test out the British response. It was not to be the first time that Collins proposed to use Mayo as a testing ground for actions to be applied elsewhere. Milling's murder had all the hallmarks of the type of killing carried out by Collins' Squad during the War of Independence. It was both brutal and at close range. That Milling did not die immediately was due to the .38 revolvers used by the assassins. Collins' Squad had similar experiences, with a number of their first victims miraculously escaping death. The Squad later switched to a heavier calibre round, a .45, which was certain to kill the intended victim.[57] The shooting of such a prominent official as Milling could not have been carried out without the permission of the IRA General Headquarters (GHQ) or Michael Collins. Evidence suggests Collins' strategy was very effective. Milling's death had a profound impact on the course of the War of Independence in Mayo. The RMs in the county began to hand out more lenient sentences and even acquittals. It became impossible for them to even bring Irish Volunteers to court, sending them to Galway instead. The British court system eventually collapsed with the establishment of the Republican courts. In Mayo, CI Steadman's monthly reports grew more sparse in detail as the War of Independence turned against the British. Perhaps he was aware his reports were being read by the IRA and had to be careful about the content and people he named.

DI Spellman closed the files and returned them to the cabinet. It was well beyond the small hours. Yet he had gained a valuable insight into both the RIC and the Sinn Féin movement in Mayo. His first task would be to ensure he gained the upper hand in his own district of Claremorris. The constable on duty saluted as Spellman stepped out of the barracks and turned right heading towards the Imperial Hotel. As Spellman approached The Square in the centre of Claremorris all was quiet. It was not to remain so for long; the Irish Volunteers were beginning to muster their forces and discontent over land was growing.

'An Apprenticeship of over 700 Years':
Sinn Féin and the Mayo Volunteers, 1920

Christmas Eve 1919 saw a number of important Sinn Féin prisoners released from Sligo Jail. Among them were Conor Alexander Maguire, a solicitor from Claremorris, Martin Nally, a district councillor from Claremorris, P. R. Hughes, President of the Thomas Ashe Sinn Féin Club in Claremorris and Harry Bourke, a young playwright. Maguire had appeared regularly in the courts of Mayo to defend Irish Volunteers, Sinn Féin members or tenants arrested for cattle drives. His greatest achievement had been as Sinn Féin director of elections for South Mayo in securing the victory of William Sears. Maguire was also President of the Sinn Féin Mayo South Comhairle Ceantair (District Executive). As the released prisoners travelled by train through the dark countryside, bonfire after bonfire lit the way to south Mayo. They pulled into Claremorris Station well after dark. The crowd to welcome them was enormous. A band led a torchlight parade through the streets to the Town Hall where '*Amhrán na bhFiann*' was played. DI Owen Spellman, expecting trouble, had drafted in extra constables but they just stood by, taking notes on the participants and the proceedings. Speeches welcoming the heroes' return were made at The Square and all went home peacefully to celebrate Christmas in jubilant mood.

Maguire and his Sinn Féin comrades had been imprisoned for 'unlawful assembly ... with other evil disposed persons' to solicit contributions for Michael Collins' Dáil Éireann Bonds. They had refused to attend the court and were arrested at bayonet point by Michael Horgan, the District Inspector for Castlebar, accompanied by British troops in full battle dress. Conor A. Maguire, with blond hair and blue eyes, cut an impressive figure in the witness box as he challenged the right of the court to jail him and his fellow Republicans. He eloquently argued that the Irish people had used the British ballot box to choose a Republican programme at the General Election of 1918. He then proposed that 'Lord French, the Lord Lieutenant, in suppressing Dáil Éireann, had suppressed the Irish People and as the Editor of *The Times* of London has printed the Sinn Féin programme, he is as guilty as I am.'[1] The court argued that Dáil Éireann was an illegal organisation that had been proscribed by the British government. This was in addition to the banning of the Sinn Féin Party, the Irish Volunteers and Cumann na mBan the previous year.

The release of the prisoners on Christmas Eve 1919 was an important morale boost for what Sinn Féin officials felt to be the flagging spirit of the people after the landslide election victory the previous December. The British government periodically ordered the release of some Republicans held in jail. Earlier in the autumn, Joe Brennan, an Irish Volunteer officer from Claremorris, had been let out of Galway Jail. Prisoners released early could be rearrested and imprisoned at any time under the so-called 'Cat and Mouse Act'.[2] Paddy Jordan, another to be released, had immediately immersed himself in organising and training the Volunteers for attacks on the RIC and British military. For him, it would end in a desperate situation at a place called Kilmeena in west Mayo in May 1921.

On 3 January 1920, John Joseph Collins, journalist, auctioneer and renowned traditional Irish musician, stood at the corner of Castle Street and Market Street in Castlebar.[3] Collins watched as a gun carriage, carrying the Union flag-draped coffin of seventeen-year-old Private Heap, passed by. Heap had been killed accidentally as he jumped out of the dark to trick his friend Private Partington who was on guard duty at the RAF Aerodrome in Castlebar.[4] Heap and Partington were soldiers of the 2nd Battalion, Border Infantry Regiment stationed in Castlebar, Westport and Ballinrobe. The Infantry was supported by units of the Royal Army Medical Corps,

J. J. Collins, editor of *The Mayoman* and elected member of Castlebar UDC.
(Courtesy Thomas Collins KHS)

Royal Army Supply Corps, Royal Engineers, and Signals.[5] The British
military was to play an important role in supporting the RIC in
neutralising the Sinn Féin organisation and Irish Volunteer battalions
in Mayo.

Prior to 1919 British troops stationed in Mayo were third-line
reserve battalions, such as the West Kent Regiment, the Munster
Fusiliers and the Lancers. It was hoped a heavy British presence in
Mayo would guard against a German invasion during the First World
War. The British had a real fear of a German landing at Belmullet
in the summer of 1918, with DI Horgan reporting that the plan
was for Irish Volunteers to assemble on the coast and march inland,
drawing the RIC and British military away from the German landing
zone. Horgan maintained that his source insisted plans for a landing
were continuing despite many arrests and intensive questioning of
prisoners. The Volunteers were receiving instruction in machine
guns, signalling and field telephones.[6]

Lt Norman H. Dimmock, RAF, who flew missions from Castlebar Aerodrome. On 28 August 1920 Lt Dimmock's aircraft crashed, leaving him severely injured and killing his Observer, Major Henry Chads MC, 2nd Border Regt. Major Chads was buried with full military honours at the old cemetery, Castlebar. (Reproduced by kind permission of the RAF Museum)

After the war, the British replaced their younger, less experienced troops with battle-hardened soldiers who had seen action in the trenches of Flanders. Most of them were looking forward to returning home to Britain when instead they were posted to Ireland. The country was not considered a plum posting among officers of the British Army. As the War of Independence progressed, Sir Henry Wilson, Chief of the Imperial General Staff, became alarmed at the number of officers who when posted to Ireland submitted appeals not to be sent there.[7]

Some soldiers brought families with them to Castlebar, and at one point there were as many as eleven wives and fifteen children living in the barrack accommodation.[8] Life was not easy and there was some heartbreak as their time passed. On 14 June 1920, four-year-

J. J. Collins (seated second row, far left) and Castlebar Choral Society 1917.
(Courtesy Thomas Collins KHS)

old Fred Rainscar, son of Private Fred Rainscar, was chasing a puppy in Mrs Quinn's kitchen on Station Road. He slipped and fell into a large pot of boiling water. His mother wrapped him in a blanket and took him to Sergeant Major Cluley's wife. Although she nursed young Fred with great skill his injuries were too severe. He died the following afternoon from shock and extensive burns and was buried in Castlebar.

As J. J. Collins listened to the Border Regiment Band play the death march, the funeral cortège for Private Heap moved slowly on towards the railway station. Collins hoped there would soon be no more British troops on the streets of Castlebar. Collins was a man of great energy. He was a member of the Urban District Council (UDC) and the Board of Guardians and intent on seeking re-election in the coming local government elections. Collins was also owner and editor of a new paper, the *Mayoman*. Having previously worked as a journalist for the *Mayo News*, he felt Castlebar needed its own

Republican weekly paper. With financial support from friends, J. J. Collins set up the *Mayoman*. Printed by Chapman & Co. Athlone Printing Works, it was to become an influential paper throughout Mayo during the War of Independence. Even when Chapman & Co. was burnt to the ground by the Black and Tans, Collins managed to find an alternative printer in Castlebar.

The first edition of the *Mayoman* appeared on Saturday 24 May 1919, covering social, political, agricultural and sporting events from mainly west, east and south Mayo. Collins was not a man to observe parliamentary decorum when it came to the British. David Lloyd George was referred to as 'The Wobbling Welsh Wizard', 'The Welsh Juggler' and 'The Welsh Grasshopper'.[9] Collins' sarcastic opinion of British rule in Ireland was frequently voiced in his weekly editorials. A typical Collins editorial read as follows:

> Surely after an apprenticeship of over 700 years as hewers of wood and drawers of water we [the Irish] ought to be content in our servile state, and for the future desist from slandering, either at home or abroad those great and good masters who are keeping us under martial law ... and who are so considerately filling the jails with our men and women.[10]

A man of great intellect, Collins also demonstrated a keen ability to read political events and the tide of social change both in Ireland and abroad. For example, he saw correctly how the harsh treatment of the Germans by the Treaty of Versailles would lead to further war. 'Not the seeds of Peace but dragons' teeth have you [the Allies] planted,' he stated.[11] Collins was also instrumental in establishing the Town Tenant League in Castlebar. The League sought to provide better housing with land attached to enable poorer townspeople to acquire property with a supply of fresh food and dairy produce.

J. J. Collins, like many of his fellow councillors, was a committed Republican who believed that the time had come to establish a free and independent Ireland. The UDC meetings became antagonistic as the Republican Collins sought to outmanoeuvre Alexander Clendenning Larmine, a unionist who had given forty years of his life to public service as a councillor and Justice of the Peace. To his credit,

Larmine rarely rose to the bait and accepted times were changing. Larmine's main concerns were for the smooth running of the UDC on a solid financial foundation and for the safety of the Protestant population of the town and district as the War of Independence became more violent. The Castlebar UDC elections were held on 15 January 1920, using the Proportional Representation system. The town was divided into East and West Wards. Those elected were as follows:[12]

Castlebar Municipal Elections, January 1920 – East Ward		
Party	Seats	Candidates
Sinn Féin	2	1st Anthony MacBride, 2nd Anna Carney
Unionist	1	3rd A. C. Larmine
Labour	2	4th S.T. McCormack, 5th Pat Boland
Independent	1	6th Michael Horan

Castlebar Municipal Elections, January 1920 – West Ward		
Party	Seats	Candidates
Sinn Féin	2	1st Mrs Bridget Ryan, 3rd John Hoban
Labour	1	2nd Thomas Loftus,
Independent	2	5th Austin Lavelle, 6th Michael Horan
Independent Sinn Féin	1	4th J.J. Collins

County Inspector David Steadman was encouraged by the results. He noted in his monthly report for January 1920 that 'Sinn Féin and its coadjutors the Transport Union and the Gaelic League have made little apparent headway during the month. The Urban Elections proved a disappointment to Sinn Féin and showed its influence and power to be on the wane.'[13] While Sinn Féin did not achieve the success it hoped for, it is notable that the two women candidates polled extremely well, with Bridget Ryan topping the poll. Labour's turnout reflected the change in social structure taking place in Ireland.

J. J. Collins (back row, far right) with a traditional Irish music group, Castlebar.
(Courtesy Thomas Collins KHS)

In fact, the Castlebar O/C of the Volunteers, Michael McHugh, was main speaker at Labour election rallies – and under a red flag! First World War veterans, calling their party Comrades of the Great War, also fielded a number of candidates but failed to get any elected. The results demonstrated the changing times with Sinn Féin and Labour as the strongest parties. But the strong performance of the Independent candidates indicates not all were happy to support Sinn Fein or their programme.

The newly elected UDC concerned itself with issues like sanitation, water supply, finance and road surfacing to cater for the ever increasing motor traffic. Inevitably, political issues like allegiance to Dáil Éireann and non-cooperation with the British Local Government Board began to surface. It was to be people like J. J. Collins and his colleagues who were to articulate the vision for a 'new' Ireland. This leadership was fundamental in gathering public support for the Volunteers in the fight to come. This support, whether logistical, moral, financial or political, was robust enough even to withstand the condemnation of Archbishop Gilmartin of Tuam. J. J. Collins was the Archbishop's cousin and regularly printed his pronouncements in the *Mayoman*. Originally from Castlebar, Archbishop Gilmartin was raised by an aunt and uncle, Martin and Mary McHale, at Kileen near Ballyvary. He subsequently served as Vice-President of Maynooth and later as Bishop of Clonfert before being appointed Archbishop of Tuam on 18 May 1918.[14] The Tuam archdiocese was and remains extensive in territory. It stretches from Achill on the Atlantic Ocean to Moore Parish on the River Shannon, a distance of 120 miles.[15] Gilmartin's pastoral concerns and political connections were to place him at the heart of a number of peace attempts involving the British government.

The RIC District Inspector for Castlebar was Limerick man Michael Horgan. He was a committed officer who came from a family with a long tradition in policing. He deputised regularly for CI Steadman, and sometimes wrote the monthly RIC reports for Mayo. Horgan had J. J. Collins placed under surveillance and led many of the raids on houses belonging to Irish Volunteers and their supporters. As 1920 progressed doubts about these activities were to grow in the minds of Horgan and many other RIC men. In fact, hundreds of policemen who were not prepared to implement the aggressive retaliation ordered by Chief Secretary Sir Hamar Greenwood and Major General Sir Hugh Tudor actually resigned their posts. Constable Liam S. O Rioghbhardain, stationed at Murrisk, County Mayo, gave the following account of his resignation, along with those of Constables P. J. Lydon and O'Donnell:

> The resignations were handed to the Sergeant at Murrisk and he said, 'Three nice bloody cowards', and he dispatched me to Westport to Head Constable Allen, with the resignations. Allen was very enraged particularly as earlier in the day or the previous day he had outlined his idea of dealing with Sinn Féin and the patriotic movement. I arrived back to Murrisk with three replacements. Our arms were taken from us and we were brought to Castlebar. We were kept in what is now called

restrictive custody for three days in the Barrack in Castlebar
... Head Constable Allen and County Inspector Steadman
recommended our deportation.[16]

The beginning of 1920 was to see the War of Independence enter a
new and more violent phase in other parts of Ireland. If the Mayo
Brigade were to engage the RIC and British military in the tactics
now proposed by GHQ, a considerable phase of training and
reorganisation was required. In December 1919, the RIC estimated
the number of political organisations in the county as follows:[17]

No	Name of Organisation	No of Branches	Membership	Remarks
1.	Irish Volunteers	21	2,362	
2.	National Volunteers	41	3,496	
3.	Sinn Fein Clubs	70	7,107	
4.	Gaelic League	58	7,476	
5.	A.O.H. [Ancient Order of Hibernians]	33	1,143	
6.	A.O.H. (I.A.A.)	5	1,640	
7.	G.A.A. [Gaelic Athletic Association]	15	302	
8.	I.N.F. [Irish National Forresters]	3	412	
9.	Town Tenants	4	197	
10.	Cumm na mban	11	384	
11.	Gaelic Club	1	30	
12.	IT+GW Union [Irish Transport and General Workers' Union]	15	3,316	

RIC County Inspector's Report on political organisations in County Mayo,
December 1919.

Mrs Anne Zita Kelly (née Lynn),
Intelligence Officer, Cumann na mBan,
North Mayo. A native of Ballycastle,
Mrs Kelly lectured in first aid, carried
dispatches and ammunition, and assisted
the Republicans at the Glenamoy
Ambush during the Civil War. (Courtesy
Kilmainham Gaol Museum)

The Irish Volunteers in Mayo had grown in strength since the beginning of 1919. This was due to the conviction of its members and also to the support of Cumann na mBan members like Anita McMahon of Achill, Beatta Healy of Claremorris, Margaret Ford (née Conway) of Ballinrobe and the Kenny sisters of Crossard near Ballyhaunis. Women like these took enormous risks transporting and hiding weapons, delivering dispatches and administering first aid. Anita McMahon was later to be arrested while carrying dispatches of the West Mayo Brigade of the IRA. She was court-martialled and sent to Galway Jail. People like J. J. Collins, while not members of the Volunteers, were committed members of Sinn Féin, the Gaelic League and the GAA. CI Steadman reported that it was the Gaelic League and GAA that kept support for Sinn Féin strong. The link between all these organisations was the IRB. The same men ran all the nationalist organisations. Nothing now was permitted to pass in the county without their approval.

Cumann na mBan brooch made for the RDS, Ballsbridge Tattoo 1945. It was modelled on the original Cumann na mBan brooch worn on the uniform. (Brooch of Margaret Williamson. Photograph courtesy Bernadette and Margaret Quinsey)

The GAA provided a welcome distraction from violent events unfolding elsewhere. It also provided cover for the IRB organisers to meet in their attempts to plan a military campaign. The year 1920 was a good one for Mayo football. The county had lost the Connaught Football Championship to Galway by a single point the previous year. The venue for the 1920 final with Galway was the subject of an appeal by the Mayo GAA County Board. They felt Tuam was used as the location for the Connaught final too often. This benefited the Galway GAA financially to the detriment of other western counties. Confusion reigned over the initial final and a replay was held at Castlerea, County Roscommon. Mayo triumphed by 2-4 to 0-3. The Mayo goalkeeper, Dick Creagh of Castlebar, put in such a fine performance that even the Galway players congratulated him after the game.[18] While the Mayo footballers were demonstrating their skills on the field of play, plans were being put in place that were to transform the Mayo Irish Volunteers.

The Volunteers were initially organised in Mayo as a single Brigade with the O/C being Joseph MacBride TD of the Westport Battalion.

Michael McHugh of the Castlebar Battalion was Vice O/C with the Brigade Quartermaster being Tom Derrig of the Westport Battalion. Brigade Adjutant was Dick Walsh of the Balla Company. All the senior officers of the Brigade were members of the IRB. Nationally, the IRB had planned and carried out the Easter Rising. In its aftermath, however, the entire Supreme Council of Tom Clarke, Patrick Pearse, Thomas MacDonagh, Seán MacDermott and Eamonn Ceannt had been executed. The subsequent leader, Thomas Ashe, died on hunger strike in September 1917. It was his death and funeral that acted as the catalyst for a reorganisation of the IRB and subsequently the Irish Volunteers.

On the last day of the Sinn Féin Árd Fheis (Party Conference) on 25 October 1917, a Convention of the Irish Volunteers was held at Croke Park, headquarters of the GAA. The meeting was attended by delegates from the entire country and went on for over ten hours. The crucial decision to emerge from this meeting was the establishment of the Irish Volunteer Executive. Seven men from Dublin and three from each of the provinces were on the Executive. Mayo man Dick Walsh was one of the Connaught representatives.[19] A GHQ staff was then established from the Executive, with Richard Mulcahy as Chief of Staff, Michael Collins Director of Intelligence, Eamon Price Director of Organisation, Gearóid O'Sullivan Adjutant General, Rory O'Connor Engineering & O/C of the IRA in Britain, Eóin O'Duffy Assistant Chief of Staff, Seán Russell Munitions, Seán McMahon Quartermaster General, J. J. O'Connell Training, Emmet Dalton Operational Training, Seán Donovan Chemicals, Liam Mellows Purchases and Piaras Béaslaí Publicity. All members of GHQ were in the IRB. Along with men of outstanding resolve and initiative in Clare, Cork, Dublin, Longford and Tipperary, GHQ initiated and pursued the War of Independence.

The Irish Volunteers were initially independent of political control. Then, in 1919, Cathal Brugha, Minister for Defence, proposed that an oath of allegiance to Dáil Éireann be taken by the Irish Volunteers. This oath bound the Volunteers to the authority of the Dáil. The Volunteers were from then on known as the Irish Republican Army or IRA. Many in the Volunteers resisted the oath as they feared the intrusion of politics and politicians into the war effort. In Mayo, however, the oath was universally accepted, although the people continued to refer to the IRA as the Volunteers.[20]

In early 1920 the Mayo Brigade was divided into seventeen battalions based on the major towns of Ballina, Ballinrobe, Castlebar, Claremorris, Swinford and Westport. Each battalion was led by a commandant and made up of four to eight companies, each with 103 men. The smaller county towns, villages, parishes and townlands like Aughagower, Balla, Ballyhaunis, Ballyglass, Ballysokeery, Cong, Cross and Kiltimagh provided the companies. The company was the main tactical unit for the Volunteers. It was commanded by a captain, two lieutenants, a company adjutant and a company quartermaster. Included in the ranks were specialists who looked after explosives and weapons. There was also an intelligence officer who gathered any information on the enemy that might be useful, including names of enemy officers and men, regular patrols and social haunts.[21]

The official uniform of the Volunteers was dark green. The officers wore an open-necked tunic with shirt and tie and Sam Browne leather belt. The hats were either a peaked cap or slouch Boer hat with a Volunteer badge depicting a sunburst with the letters FF at the centre, meaning Fianna Fáil, a reference to the legendary Celtic warriors Na Fianna. This was surrounded by a circular band on which was inscribed *Óglaigh na h-Éireann*, meaning Irish Volunteers. The cap badge had been adopted from the Dublin Brigade. Previously, the Mayo Brigade cap badge featured the Cross of Cong. Tunic buttons were of brass and carried a harp with the letters IV for Irish Volunteers. In reality, few Volunteers could afford a uniform. Even if they did have one it was dangerous to wear it in public. Volunteer Companies began to adopt an unofficial uniform of casual cap, trenchcoat, leather leggings and a bandolier for ammunition. Officers were distinguished by shirt and tie with a Sam Browne belt worn over the trenchcoat. This form of dress made it easier to blend in with the local population and was more practical in the form of warfare that was to unfold. As 1920 progressed the Volunteers in Mayo had grown to such an extent that control from a single county brigade headquarters was no longer possible. Dick Walsh, Brigade Adjutant, was alarmed at the 'serious deficiencies' in the Brigade caused by the lack of special services.[22] The Brigade had been trained

Irish Volunteer Mayo Brigade cap badge. (Courtesy Abie and Annie Allen)

to fight a conventional war. Senior officers of the Mayo Brigade now required training in the new tactics devised by experience in the field and by GHQ.

After the Rising in 1916, many younger members of the Volunteers had been imprisoned in Frongoch, north Wales. Here, the future leadership of the Irish Volunteers had an opportunity to assess the military failure of the Rising. New tactics were devised in this so-called 'Republican University'[23]; the result was guerrilla warfare carried out by elite units called Flying Columns or Active Service Units. They were to be supported by a counter-intelligence network established by Michael Collins. The RIC were aware of the Volunteers' newly developed strategies. The Inspector General of the RIC included in his report for February 1920 a captured document entitled 'The Strategy that the Volunteer Force as at present armed and trained is likely to use in case it takes the field voluntarily'.[24] The document, in the possession of a Volunteer arrested in Dublin,

Chief of Staff Irish Army (1923–27) Peadar MacMahon, formerly Training Officer in Guerrilla Warfare to the Mayo Brigades 1920. (Courtesy the Military Archives, Cathal Brugha Barracks)

contained strategies and tactics 'likely to be employed' in smashing the 'enemy communications' network of 'Military Posts, RIC Barracks and Post Offices'.[25]

Mayo Brigade Adjutant Dick Walsh had read the newly proposed strategies for Volunteer activities. He saw the need for intensive training in Mayo. He approached Michael Collins who in turn dispatched Commandant Peadar MacMahon with the greatest urgency to Mayo. MacMahon, from County Monaghan, immediately set to work organising instruction classes for Volunteer officers in each battalion area. Each series of classes lasted ten days and included callisthenics, field drill and musketry. The officers then held similar classes for their companies.[26] One of the East Mayo Brigade officers commented: 'A man named McMahon came down from Dublin and started a class for officers. He stayed with us about a month. We all liked him and picked up a lot from his instructions.'[27] MacMahon received no pay for his work. There were efforts to organise a collection for him in some areas but he would not hear of it. The Chief of Staff, Richard Mulcahy, stepped in and organised a payment of £6 per week, £3 of which was for his keep. Although MacMahon was captured by the British in Dublin during Christmas 1920, the training he initiated was to transform the Mayo IRA.[28] MacMahon eventually became Chief of Staff of the Irish Army.

In order to facilitate the new tactics of guerrilla warfare, GHQ directed that new Brigade structures be established.[29] Up to mid-1920 it is evident that actions on the part of the Volunteers depended upon the initiative and bravery of individual officers. The case of Stephen Donnelly of Ballina was one such example. Initially, he established a company of Na Fianna Éireann (Sinn Féin Boy Scouts) in response to the events of 1916. The Fianna, like the Volunteers, met a number of times during the week for drill, training and lectures in premises secured by Michael Tolan, a tailor from Hill Street. Tolan was one of a number who were to be brutally tortured and murdered in the west by the RIC and the British military during the War of Independence. Na Fianna and the Volunteers met up on Sundays for a joint route march with tactical training.[30]

Donnelly was given a five-month jail sentence in September 1918 for holding a Memorial Parade for Thomas Ashe with Na Fianna in Ballina. He ended up in Belfast Jail with 600 other Irish political prisoners, including Tom Derrig, Ernest Blythe and Austin Stack. While there, Donnelly was introduced to a more formal military structure. Lectures were held in Irish by Blythe and others on military training and tactics. Life in prison was harsh. There were riots by the prisoners and beatings at the hands of the warders who often smashed their way into the political prisoners' block with sledge hammers. But there were lighter moments, too. Donnelly recalled the nicest smoke he ever had was a packet of Woodbine thrown into his cell while in solitary confinement by a Constable Patrick McNulty, who turned out to be from The Quay, Ballina. Donnelly also used to treat the other prisoners to a fine rendition of 'The Men of the West'.[31]

On release, Donnelly received a hero's welcome in Ballina. In his absence, however, Na Fianna had fallen away. Parents were unwilling to allow the younger boys to risk imprisonment. The older ones had

Captain Stephen Donnelly, North Mayo Brigade, Ballina Company *c.* 1920.
(Courtesy Barry Donnelly)

joined the Irish Volunteers. Donnelly did likewise and was made a
Section Commander. Under his command were Pat Kilduff, his old
schoolteacher, and P. J. Ruttledge, future TD for Mayo North.[32]
Donnelly's section was regularly out at night until 2 a.m., raiding for
arms, intercepting mail and monitoring RIC patrols.

Some of the Mayo Volunteer companies were trained by former
soldiers who had served in the First World War. This was the case
in Ballina, Claremorris and Aughagower. Some were trained by ex-
RIC men as in Kiltimagh. Others depended on British or United
States Army Manuals for guidance. GHQ eventually published a
manual called *Slí na Saoirse* (The Path to Freedom), along with a
bi-monthly journal called *An t-Óglach* (The Volunteer). The journal
contained articles on tactical training, weapons, explosives and the
construction of landmines and grenades. It also aimed at raising
morale by highlighting successes against the RIC and the British
Army. However well-intentioned, GHQ's lecturing of Volunteer

IRA officers: (l–r) Captain Pádraig Dunleavy O/C Claremorris Company and later O/C Tuam Battalion, Tom Mannion, Dr Mangan, Tom Nohilly and Tom Kilgarriff seated. (Courtesy Dominick and Mary Dunleavy)

companies on training and organisation for guerrilla warfare often came across as patronising, unrealistic and over-officious. An example of this was the planning of offensive operations against the RIC or British military. GHQ requested that all operations be cleared by them in advance. Dick Walsh said Volunteer commanders considered this order to be 'nonsensical, unnecessary and farcical'. It removed the command capability of officers in a locality and affected their ability to surprise the enemy. Also, if the plans were captured it would alert the enemy to the proposed action and place the lives of the Volunteers in serious danger of capture or death.[33] Consequently, this GHQ order was usually ignored.[34]

The men and women on the ground in Mayo were to learn more through the bitter experience of reality than through manuals. However, the training did develop a strong sense of *esprit de corps* among the young Volunteers. Discipline was good and senior officers led by example. Drinking was frowned upon by many officers like

Michael Kilroy of Newport, Seán Corcoran of Kiltimagh and Joe Brennan of Claremorris who were strict teetotallers. The people of Mayo were fiercely proud of their Volunteers and loved to see them parade at fairs and marching through localities on route marches.

During Easter 1920, Pádraig Dunleavy, O/C of the Claremorris Volunteers, gave orders for the income tax office to be destroyed in his absence. The raid did not happen. Dunleavy eventually raided the office himself and stole some books. He maintained he had 'to carry out the job at great personal risk, as the excise office was only a few doors away from the RIC Barracks'.[35] The Claremorris Battalion also attempted two other operations that did not work out. One was an attack on Cross RIC barracks to seize weapons. The other was a planned ambush on an RIC cycle patrol from Claremorris that had gone to Croagh Patrick for Reek Sunday, the annual pilgrimage on the last Sunday of July. The patrol failed to return by the same route and thus escaped.

At Cross, Pádraig Dunleavy, Harry Burke, Willie Kenny and Willie Hearney dressed in British officers' uniforms and drove to the village. The plan was to take the RIC barracks while most of the constables were at Mass. The Volunteers pretended to have a breakdown outside the barracks. Dunleavy claims he had arranged to meet up with Tom Maguire, O/C South Mayo Brigade, and a section of his men. On arrival, Dunleavy's men found Maguire was at Mass. Maguire, in his account of the incident, claims Dunleavy lost his nerve. The truth may never be known as both men were on opposite sides during the Civil War, which undoubtedly coloured their recollections. Whatever the case, it was a lost opportunity for the South Mayo Brigade to obtain urgently needed weapons.

In July 1920 General Eamon Price, Director of Organisation, arrived in Castlebar. Under the cover of the Annual County Sports held at the Asylum grounds, he attended a meeting of the senior Mayo Brigade officers to reorganise the Irish Volunteer structure in Mayo. The county was to be divided into four Brigade areas: North, South, East and West. The O/Cs for the various Brigades were chosen by GHQ. Brigade O/Cs were allowed choose their own senior officers. Tom Ruane (Ballina) was appointed O/C of the North Mayo Brigade; Tom Maguire (Cross) was O/C of the South Mayo Brigade;

Commandant General Tom Maguire, O/C South Mayo Brigade IRA 1920–21 and O/C Second Western Division IRA 1921–22. General Maguire was also TD for Mayo South 1921–27. (Courtesy Dr Seán Maguire)

Seán Corcoran (Kiltimagh) was O/C of the East Mayo Brigade and Tom Derrig (Westport) was O/C of the West Mayo Brigade.[36]

North Mayo was the biggest of the four Brigades. It started at Foxford and ran north of Lough Conn covering Ardacoole and Ross. It covered the Nephin Mountains and took in Erris. It also included Ballina and further east, 7 miles beyond Enniscrone in County Sligo. The South Mayo Brigade was also vast and took in Balla, Ballyhaunis, Irishtown and Ballindine. It went west to Lough Corrib including Shrule, Kilmaine, Cross, Cong, Clonbur, Ballinrobe, Hollymount and Claremorris. It also included Partry, Tourmakeady, Lough Mask, Lough Carra, half of Ballintubber and Ballyglass.[37] Commandant Tom Maguire established his headquarters at the homestead of Margaret Forde (née Conway) near Ballinrobe. Her husband, Seán, had been the previous O/C before Maguire took over.[38]

The East Mayo Brigade covered Kiltimagh and northwards towards Foxford. It took in Straide and turned east at Swinford until it reached the Sligo border. It also included Ballaghaderreen, Kilkelly, Charlestown and Frenchpark. Ballyhaunis was placed in the East

Mayo Brigade area because of its vital railway link to Dublin and direct access to GHQ. The West Mayo Brigade ran adjacent to the South Mayo Brigade from parts of Connemara, north to Louisburgh, enveloping Clew Bay with the towns of Westport, Newport and Mulranny. It also included Achill Island. In the east it included Castlebar, Ballyhean and half of Ballintubber.[39]

Almost as soon as the Brigade commanders were appointed they became hunted men and went on the run. British military intelligence was well informed and stated in a report that Commandant Tom Maguire 'has more than once escaped arrest by both the Military and Police by the skin of his teeth'.[40] British surveillance on Maguire continued, as this report from March 1921 indicates:

> On the night of the 11th March last, Maguire attended a Meeting of rebels at a Stable situated in Lord Oranmore's demense at Castle MacGarret, Claremorris; making the usual fiery speech of the Sinn Fein 'stump' orator, in which he stated that Mayo would be surpassing the deeds of the South. He congratulated Ellis Staunton, who was present (since arrested) for the re-organisation of the Claremorris Battalion of the IRA.[41]

Maintaining security was to be difficult for the Mayo brigades. Most commanders became very cautious and told very few of their real intentions. With the establishment of a new command structure, the Volunteers now turned to the most serious problem facing them, the lack of arms and ammunition. The Volunteers raided the houses of country gentlemen and soldiers home on leave. Tom Kitterick, Quartermaster West Mayo Brigade, remembered finding 300 rounds of dumdum ammunition in Burrishoole Lodge where a British Army officer, Lieutenant Good, lived. These dumdum bullets had been banned by the Hague Convention of 1899. Nevertheless, Kitterick admitted using them due to a shortage of other ammunition. He recalled how they made a terrific crack as they went through the air.[42]

In the autumn of 1920 the Mayo brigades began to look to Britain to import arms. This enterprise was first entrusted to Dick Walsh. All such arms 'collections' had to be approved by GHQ. Dick Walsh travelled with Michael Collins' authorisation to a Neil Kerr in Liverpool. Kerr was in charge of arms acquisition in the north of England. Walsh was astonished to find out that his two weapons consignments for Mayo had been sent to Cork on Collins' orders. In all probability these were the weapons that armed Tom Barry's Flying Column. All the money for these purchases had come from Mayo.[43] The four Mayo brigades felt aggrieved and protested vigorously but to no avail. Ernie O'Malley recorded what men of the West Mayo Brigade told him of attempts to secure weapons and the conflict that emerged with GHQ. According to Dr John Madden, an IRB man and member of the West Mayo Flying Column:

> Dick Walsh brought Lee-Enfield rifles from England before the Tan War, but like a bloody fool he reported to [Michael] Collins who said to him 'God you're a Godsend, you've just arrived at the right time. They're planning a big thing down in Cork and I'll guarantee to get the rifles back for you.' Dick handed them over and we never got them back, nor did we get anything in exchange for them. Kitterick brought rifles to Maam Cross and he had arranged for a car to meet him but the man wasn't there. But there was an RIC Sergeant on the station. What are you waiting for asked the sergeant, come on I'll give you a hand. There was a big trunk of stuff and the Sergeant helped Tom [Kitterick] to carry it out. Kitterick also spent a night with the Auxiliaries in the Skeffington Arms Hotel in Galway, drinking, and they helped him to bring out his load of stuff from the QMG, which he had with him.[44]

Finally, it was Charlie Hughes and Myles Hawkshaw, both merchants and Volunteers from Westport, who provided the West Mayo Brigade with the money to buy twelve .303 Mark III Lee-Enfield rifles.[45] Hawkshaw was also Vice-President of Sinn Féin in the Westport district.[46] Kitterick arranged the purchase and sent Pat Fallon with Dick Walsh as an assistant but also to prevent the third weapons consignment falling into the hands of GHQ. This third attempt by the Mayo brigades to procure arms was unknown to GHQ. Walsh, Fallon and a Joe Goode made for London. They established contact with the IRA there and through Joe Browne, John 'Blimey' O'Connor and the Carr brothers, a consignment of pistols was sent to Mayo through

Liverpool. Walsh and his team then turned to Manchester and met up with a man from Ballaghaderreen called Anderson. It was through this contact that the essential rifles were delivered. The Liverpool IRA had many Mayo men on active service and it was they who ensured safe passage for the arms to Ireland. Walsh also went to Sheffield where a man called Benson from Boyle, County Roscommon, put him in touch with a principal of a Christian Brothers' School. The principal allowed the school to be used as a storage depot for the arms and ammunition destined for Mayo. Walsh even brought some Parabellum pistols back to Ireland in a cheap travelling bag. All told, Walsh succeeded in getting about 400 rifles, automatics and revolvers back to Ireland. He even managed to establish contacts in the Birmingham Small Arms Company, although he suspected the weapons he secured from there were stolen.[47]

The incidents relating to Dick Walsh's efforts in Britain demonstrate just how difficult it was for the Mayo brigades to obtain weapons. Evading both the British and their own GHQ required some ingenuity. Procuring weapons was exhausting and dangerous work. It was only by turning to their own network of Mayo men and women in Britain that they eventually succeeded in obtaining the sufficient rifles and ammunition required to begin offensive operations. Dick Walsh had great respect for those in Britain who helped him: 'A great many of those people had been out of Ireland for 30 or 40 years. A large number of them were born in Britain of Irish parents. I would certainly say that those people deserved the gratitude of the Irish people at home.'[48]

Dick Walsh and Tom Kitterick were threatened by GHQ with court martial for going through 'unofficial channels'. GHQ sent orders to IRA units in Britain to arrest Walsh. GHQ was politely told by the IRA in Britain that this was unacceptable and the order would not be carried out. Walsh's activities made him well known to the RIC and on one occasion he was lucky to escape with his life:

> I had arranged an interview with a man named Fitzgerald who was attached to our QMG's. staff. I went down to his place that evening. It was down in that portion of Parnell Street opposite Dominick Street [Galway]. I was going in the side door and

I got a hold of the handle and pushed it in front of me and I was aware of a man pulling it from me in a very rough way, and when I got inside the door, which was a swing door, I got a thump in the face. I looked up and saw that it was an Auxiliary. I turned and tried to get out but discovered there was another man behind me who also hit me. The two of them used me as a punch-ball for about ten mins. At last I got away and as I came out the door I was hit again and just outside the door were two more Auxiliaries with drawn revolvers in their hands. The last fellow that hit me drove me as far as the centre of the road where I fell. I looked back and saw these two fellows with revolvers in their hands waiting for me to get up. I had the good sense to stay where I was and not to rise, and while this was happening, a crowd of people were gathering. A number of them were dealers in Dominick Street and some from Parnell Street. They commenced denouncing the Auxiliaries and sympathising with me. I decided to let the crowd surround me and get between me and the two men at the door with drawn revolvers, and when I was satisfied that I was covered by the crowd, I ran up Dominick Street. I entered a house which was a Bar and the name was Reilly. I was covered with blood, and the barman washed my face and cleaned the wounds, etc and he got a piece of sticking plaster for the cuts.[49]

Walsh bore the strain of all this activity until the Truce. On his return to Balla in the summer of 1921 he suffered a near complete physical and mental collapse due to the constant pressure he had been under. Dick Walsh was lucky to recover after a number of months of expert care in Castlebar Infirmary. A man of great strength and energy, he still had a great deal to offer Mayo.

The possession of these weapons, particularly the .303 Lee-Enfields, seriously improved the combat capability of the West Mayo Brigade. Lee-Enfield rifles increased the range, accuracy and intensity of fire of troops in combat. During the First World War, German infantry coming up against British troops armed with Lee-Enfields for the first time suffered so many casualties they believed they were under machine-gun fire.

The Volunteers in Mayo also had a number of short- and long-barrel Mauser rifles. Kitterick thought these rifles were useless as rapid fire made the sights fall off.[50] The German Mausers were some of the weapons landed by Erskine Childers on board the *Asgard* at Howth, County Dublin, in July 1914. Some of the other rifles held by the Volunteers were very old. Brodie Malone of Westport had a Martini-Henry.[51] This was considered the rifle of the British Empire. It had first seen service in the Zulu War in South Africa in 1879; its major disadvantage was that it had no magazine. The Volunteers also had a mixed assortment of revolvers and automatics such as Webleys or Colts. Among the most favoured was the Mauser automatic pistol nicknamed 'The Broomhandle' or 'Peter the Painter'. However, single- or double-bore shotguns were the most common weapon held by the Volunteers. Ammunition was always in short supply. Volunteers frequently made shotgun cartridges but most of these failed to work because they were damp or ill-fitting. Raiding for weapons was useless as they had all but dried up by 1920, the RIC having collected the weapons throughout the county. Sean Gibbons viewed all this raiding for shotguns as pointless. 'We did make some gun-powder and filled cartridges with buckshot, but I never believed in it. I never favoured it, and could see no point in having any member of a Flying Column armed with anything else but a rifle, revolver, a bomb [grenade] and a bayonet.'[52]

However, it was going to take a little more than weapons for the West Mayo Brigade to evolve into the successful fighting unit it was to become. The road to eventual victory was to be a painful one. Casualties were not always due to combat with the British or RIC. Tommy Heavey recalled how Volunteer Jim Duffy from Prospect was killed accidentally as members of the West Mayo Flying Column were cleaning their weapons at the kitchen table of one of their safe houses:

> Jimmy [Flaherty] had cleaned my Parabellum and I stuck back the magazine. There was another empty gun on the table: and Jimmy picked up mine, pulled up the bolt action and pulled the trigger and poor Duffy died within a quarter of an hour. We buried him at night and we made a coffin at night near Islandeady. We buried him somewhere near that place.[53]

Patrick Marley was another Volunteer who lost his life in the same way. The dead Volunteers were buried secretly but were later reinterred with full military honours in 1922.[54] Joe Baker, of the West Mayo Flying Column, said of these incidents: 'The lads were quite shocked at this unfortunate happening and for many of them it was their first experience of being directly concerned in a death. However, most of us took the view that this was only the beginning, the forerunner of several casualties, fatal and otherwise, and we had to be prepared for whatever the future held.'[55]

The arrival of the Black and Tans and the Auxiliary Division of the RIC in the summer of 1920 was to introduce appalling bloodshed to the west. This in turn gave urgency to the Mayo brigades' efforts to strike back. The new formations of the RIC were to engage in a campaign of terror throughout the countryside, which included burning of homesteads, looting, beatings and even the murder of innocent civilians. However, prior to the arrival of the Tans, Mayo was to face a crisis that was to tear at the very fabric of its civilised society. This crisis had been bubbling up for generations, but in 1920 it finally erupted, bringing chaos, distress and violence in its wake. The land of Mayo itself was to be the prize, and there were few prisoners taken in this struggle.

3

'For the Sake of the Republic': Chaos, Murder and the Republican Victory of 1920

On the evening of 28 March 1920, the Vestry Committee for Kilcolman and Crossboyne (Claremorris) Church of Ireland met at the local parish hall. The mood was sombre as they discussed the death of one of their former parishioners, Alan Bell RM. Shot in broad daylight in Dublin by members of Michael Collins' infamous assassination Squad, Bell was fondly remembered in Claremorris where he had served as an RM until late 1914. Rev. Jackson, Chairman of the Vestry Committee, wrote to Mrs Bell to express 'the deepest sympathy in their bereavement and detestation they felt at the cruel and cowardly murder of Mr Bell whom they all liked and respected'.[1]

The same week as the Vestry Committee meeting, the *Mayoman* reported the beginnings of unrest among tenant farmers on large estates in south Mayo and north Galway. There were arrests of four men at Carrickgloon near Ballinrobe and another fifteen at Kilmaine for driving cattle and other livestock. Further trouble occurred in Irishtown and Claremorris. The British military managed to restore order but only temporarily. This strife over land was a surprise to many, with up to 70 per cent of tenants having purchased their holdings by this time under the terms of the various Land Acts introduced since

1870. However, many small farms were uneconomic and prices during the First World War were extremely high. Subsistence was no longer acceptable to farmers who wanted to improve their own standards of living and educate their children so that they could remain in Ireland instead of emigrating. There were also many labourers who wished to obtain some land of their own and bring some stability to their precarious way of life.

The 1916 Proclamation, read by Patrick Pearse outside the GPO, had inspired many with its vision of hope:

> The Republic guarantees religious and civil liberty, equal rights and equal opportunities to all its citizens, and declares its resolve to pursue the happiness and prosperity of the whole nation and all of its parts, cherishing all of the children of the nation equally and oblivious of the differences carefully fostered by an alien government, which have divided a minority from the majority in the past.[2]

This vision was reiterated by the first meeting of Dáil Éireann on 21 January 1919:

> We declare in the words of the Irish Republican Proclamation the right of the people of Ireland to the ownership of Ireland, and to the unfettered control of Irish destinies to be indefeasible, and in the language of our first President, Pádraíg Mac Phiarais, we declare that the Nation's sovereignty extends not only to all men and women of the Nation, but to all its material possessions, the Nation's soil and all its resources, all the wealth and all the wealth-producing processes within the Nation, and with him we reaffirm that all right to private property must be subordinated to the public right and welfare.[3]

Declarations like these encouraged poorer tenants to seize the land of the large estates that they now viewed as their own, including larger estates that the Congested Districts Board had been supposed to sell off before being interrupted by the First World War. The Congested Districts Board had instead rented most of the land under their control to ranchers who were able to make a tidy profit from the British Army's demand for beef during the war years. The ranchers usually did not live among the local communities. Their cattle brought little economic improvement to the areas in which they were located. In the meantime, tenants looked on with desperation as their children faced emigration instead of remaining in Ireland and building a future on a decent-sized farm.

As early as June 1919 the Mayo TDs were urging the Dáil to act with more urgency on the land question. Joe MacBride, TD for West Mayo, suggested the establishment of an Agricultural Bank to facilitate the acquisition of land by the young men of the country.[4] The Dáil took MacBride's advice. On 20 August, William Sears, TD for South Mayo, made his first Dáil contribution after his release from prison. Sears supported the Minister for Agriculture, Robert Barton, on the establishment of the Agricultural Loan Bank. MacBride, aware of the poor circumstances of many seeking to buy land, suggested that the requirement of a 25 per cent deposit was too high. He thought the bank should lend 100 per cent of the cost. However, the Dáil became distracted by de Valera's mission to the United States of America to seek recognition for the Irish Republic. Many TDs were also rearrested. This led to serious disruption of Dáil business and the land question languished.

By October 1919 Dr Crowley, TD for Mayo North, was asking Minister Barton for information on the progress of the Agricultural Loan Bank. Crowley argued that while the Dáil had granted £1,000 for the expenses of Agricultural Loan Bank officials, little else had been done. He was facing men looking for loans to buy farms of up to 120 acres that were coming up for sale. Crowley expressed grave concern that the land that was becoming available in Mayo was being bought up by wealthy ranchers and graziers with poorer tenants having no chance of purchase. The pressure exerted by the Mayo TDs reflected their first-hand knowledge of the need for urgency on the ground in averting a crisis. Arthur Griffith, Acting President of the Dáil in de Valera's absence, assured them that the Agricultural Loan Bank would be established within three months.[5] The bank, however, was not established until the following year; in the interim, Mayo was to face disorder and violence verging on social disintegration.

Events were to aid the breakdown of law and order. In early 1920 the RIC, aware of the IRA's plans for a more active campaign against outlying RIC barracks, began to withdraw their constables from vulnerable remote areas into larger towns. This left large sub-districts of the countryside without an RIC presence. CI Steadman reported later: 'As repeatedly pointed out the closing of police stations has proved a most disastrous and dangerous expedient and which the lack of men, of transport, and of effective military cooperation have only added to the mess.'[6]

Those holding on for the long-promised sale of the estates could wait no longer and in sheer frustration began to take matters into their own hands. Steadman began to express concern that inaction on the part of the Congested Districts Board 'in splitting up the grass lands in its possession was causing unrest in places'.[7] This was the first indication that pressure was beginning to build. There were some local efforts at addressing the grievances before they came to violence, with a Fr Carney establishing an arbitration court in The Neale. Steadman stated that Carney was opposed by his parish priest and that hardly any of the parishioners took him seriously.[8] Steadman's reports were usually well informed, yet before too long there would be many who were only too willing to listen to Fr Carney.

By Saturday 10 April 1920, the *Mayoman* was carrying the front-page headline 'Western Land Hunger'. The article described how 'the fight for the grazing land is developing to an alarming extent all over South Mayo, Galway and South Roscommon. Cattle drives were occurring in many areas.' Such drives involved large groups of men and women breaking down the walls and fences of an estate or farm and making off with the cattle or sheep. The animals were usually kept or sold at a nearby town on market day with no questions asked. Sometimes, the animals were left to wander the roads and starve.

In south Mayo drives took place in Cong, Cross, Kilmaine, Crossboyne and Ballindine. Those arrested were brought before magistrates on Wednesday 7 April 1920. The first case to be dealt with concerned an incident at Lacafinny Farm near Cong. It belonged to a Mrs Clarke who lived in England. Sergeant Goulden and Constable Moran witnessed fifty to sixty men driving a horse, twenty cattle and thirty sheep from the 403-acre farm. Conor A. Maguire, solicitor for the defence, argued that Sir Henry Doran of the Congested Districts Board had visited Cong five years previously and told the men that they would not receive any land until Lacafinny Farm was sold. The First World War had delayed the sale and the men of the area, Maguire stated, naturally thought they had been forgotten about. They took the action to draw the attention of the authorities to their plight. Maguire told the court he had gone to Ballinrobe to speak with the agent of the farm, Mr Crawford. A sale had been agreed and a valuation was being undertaken. Maguire asked that no punishment be inflicted as negotiations would soon be closed. Maguire's defence of the accused went far beyond pure legalities. In many of the cases he represented, Maguire worked hard to arrive at a just solution to the dispute before appearance in court. It led to a high success rate in many of his cases. This format was to become widespread as the soon-to-be-established Republican courts received the official sanction of Dáil Éireann. Maguire was one of the key advisers to the government in their establishment.

The judges decided that a settlement rather than imprisonment was sufficient; although, given that cattle driving was still an offence, the defendants were bound to the peace by payment of recognisances of £10 each. In fact, in all the five cases heard that day only one person received a term of imprisonment – and this was until 'the rising of the Court'.[9] The judges had been extraordinarily lenient when one considers that two years earlier a defendant would be jailed for between two and six months for a similar offence.

Archbishop Gilmartin of Tuam was not quite as understanding as the judges. In delivering his sermon in Tuam Cathedral on Sunday 4 April, he had issued a prophetic warning: 'Violence begets violence and it will end in bloodshed'. Gilmartin was in favour of an equitable division of land. Nevertheless, 'if you take the law into your own hands and act unjustly, there will be a reign of violence and no one can say where it will end'. The Archbishop concluded with an appeal for the people to keep the law during these awful times for the good of their country and the honour of Christianity.[10]

The Archbishop was ignored. The drives continued and the end of April saw more than fourteen men appear in court in Castlebar for cattle drives in Ballyhaunis, Hollymount and Ballindine. The

Ballindine drive saw Gilmartin's fears of mob violence erupt for the first time. The incident occurred at Luke Ryan's farm of 240 acres on 15 April 1920. It was witnessed by Sergeant Mullen of the RIC who arrested seven men from Irishtown. On arriving at Ryan's, the Sergeant cautioned the large crowd not to proceed any further. A number of threats were made from individuals in the crowd. 'We'll have land or die,' went up one shout. 'If Mr Ryan gives us land there will be no violence,' said another. The mood of the crowd turned ugly, with calls of 'pull him out' and 'kill the informer'. Ryan's labourer, Kirrane, was set upon and badly beaten with a stick. Four men, including the ones who had beaten Kirrane, went in to see Ryan. They emerged and read a statement in which Luke Ryan agreed to sell the land. Constable Fitzpatrick corroborated Sergeant Mullen's account of what happened.

The defending solicitor, Fitzgerald, argued that no offence had been disclosed. The men had gone to Ryan as they were entitled to do and he had agreed to give up some land. Ryan said there was no intimidation and requested the case be adjourned.[11] He was clearly in fear for his life and considered his personal safety more important than the land. Of the sentences handed out that day, two were jailed until 'the rising of the Court' and bound to the peace for twelve months. All others were sentenced to one month in jail and bound over to sureties of £20 or another month in jail plus £10 sureties. The judges clearly believed such behaviour could not go unchallenged and that an example had to be made. However, the sentences did not have the desired effect as tenants became increasingly desperate. The concerns of their TDs were being realised.

While the number of cattle drives increased, the IRA also became more active. On Saturday 3 April 1920, 182 recently evacuated RIC barracks were burned along with attacks on over 100 tax offices throughout the country. Tax books and documents were all destroyed. These attacks were ordered by GHQ to commemorate the 1916 Rising. Dublin Castle was totally unprepared. It was General Nevil Macready's first crisis on taking up his new command as O/C of British forces in Ireland.

In Mayo, Deergrove RIC barracks near Castlebar was destroyed by fire. Cloontumper barracks was also burned.[12] Fr Paul McLoughlin, parish priest of Islandeady, condemned the attacks in his Sunday sermon. In response, the British military carried out some raids in the district but nothing was found. J. J. Collins referred to the British military's activities as 'The Grand Imperial Circus'.[13] They also raided Dick Walsh's home in Balla but failed to apprehend him. Walsh was now on the run and would remain so until the Truce in July 1921. *The Times* editorial remarked on Easter Monday 5 April that it was evident the Republican movement had become a serious menace to British authority and that the (British) government had to devise better methods of combatting them.[14]

While mayhem reigned in the countryside, the towns were witnessing unprecedented organisation. Branches of the Town Tenant League were established in Castlebar, Claremorris and Ballinrobe. The Town Tenant League aimed to secure fair rent and fixity of tenure for those renting property in towns. They also aimed to purchase land close to the town that could be used for the common purpose of guaranteeing a supply of fresh milk, butter and vegetables for those less well off. Mr Coghlan-Briscoe, General Secretary of the League, was invited to Castlebar in early May 1920. During the course of the meeting his main emphasis was to support tenants being ousted from long-rented properties by rent-raising landlords and house grabbers. This problem arose where a buyer offered the landlord a higher price for a sale while the existing tenant could not afford either an increase in rent or a higher sale price. The Castlebar Town Tenant League secured the purchase of Blackfort Farm of 87 acres to provide milk for the town. There was some disquiet from the poorer members of the League who were expected to provide the stock – in 1920 a cow cost an expensive £30 to £40. Dan Hoban asked: 'Was the Farm to be for a certain class of people?'[15] Rents for grazing 'milch cows' on Blackfort Farm were set at twelve shillings per month from May to October and seven shillings per month for the rest of the year.[16] At these prices poorer tenants could not afford to use the land. It appeared that the 'new' Ireland might only be for those of a certain standing in the community.

While the Town Tenant League sought equal rights for town-dwellers, cattle drives increased in number and violence throughout the countryside. The RIC and British military arrived at Clooncondra near Ballyheane on 24 April to arrest seven men who were charged with unlawful assembly, driving cattle, attempted eviction and assault on the 30-acre farm of Matthew Reilly. Those charged appeared before Colonel Meldon RM at a special court in Castlebar. They were remanded on bail of £20 and sureties of £10 each until the petty sessions the following week. In the meantime, Sir Henry Doran of the Congested Districts Board wrote to the Mayo Farmers Association to make it clear that profits made by the Board would be deducted from the eventual cost of the farm when offered for sale, thus making it cheaper to the eventual buyer. Doran was reacting, all be it belatedly, to the accusations that the Congested Districts Board had deliberately delayed the sale of the estates in their care to make large profits from rents to cattle ranchers. The delay of the sale of the estates stretched back over ten years. Doran appears to have had a case to answer. For the tenants and rural poor, it was too little too late. Their hunger for land intensified. Sinn Féin still lacked extensive control at local level and the absence of the RIC left a dangerous power vacuum that was being filled by large groups from local communities who at last felt they had some form of control over their own destinies. The Mayo Farmers Association passed a resolution calling for the speedy sale of land as the only resolution to the hunger for land in Connaught.[17]

As unrest on the land festered, Sinn Féin was busy preparing for the local government (county council) elections to be held on Friday 4 June 1920. J. J. Collins rowed in behind the party, an editorial on 15 May attacking the British MPs at Westminster:

> loud mouthed and aggressive when it was a question of handing out self-determination to the peoples occupying God's earth that happened to be under the political government of England's enemies but it was a horse of a different colour when it came to a question of equal rights for people like ourselves, for the Indians and Egyptians, tyrannised and military-ridden by England.

Collins was attempting to motivate opposition to any candidates other than Sinn Féin in the coming elections. The strategy was effective as most of the non-Sinn Féin candidates withdrew before the elections were held. With the local government elections looming, the land crisis in Mayo took centre stage.

Prior to 1920 Sinn Fein's Standing Committee of Arthur Griffith, Joseph Plunkett, W. T. Cosgrave and Austin Stack had identified ranch grazing farms as a legitimate target for cattle driving. However, thay had also maintained that activists had to differentiate between ranchers on untenanted land and small farmers in their localities. This was an important distinction as the Sinn Féin leadership did not want the Republican movement to be used as a means of 'sorting out' local grievances among small farmers, tenants and landless labourers.[18] On the ground such subtle distinctions were irrelevant as cattle drives continued and intimidation of local small farmers began to mount.

In a case of five Hollymount tenants arrested for intimidation and coercion the defendants agreed to bail of £20 and being 'bound to the peace' for six months but refused to give any undertaking to remove their animals from the farm of Michael Kelly, which that they had taken over. Kelly had been harassed, his turf burned, a shot fired into his home and his cattle driven off. The British courts and the RIC were evidently losing their hold on the county. However, Sinn Féin had yet to demonstrate whether a new Irish state could replace it effectively.

Dáil Éireann was aware matters were spiralling out of control and issued a statement through Brian O'Higgins, TD for West Clare, in mid-May. He encouraged people who believed they were justly entitled to land now in the hands of others to file a claim with the registrar of the district courts: 'It must be clearly understood that anyone pressing forward a claim/dispute/threatening letters etc in the name of the Republic does so in the knowledge that he/she is acting in defiance of the peoples' elected Representatives and to the detriment of the National Cause.[19]

Similar letters were issued by de Valera and other TDs to their constituents. In Roscommon, Fr Michael O'Flanagan issued a statement summarising Sinn Féin's strategy for taking control of the crisis in the west of Ireland. Land was considered the only way to make a living in some counties and the state had a duty to provide young Irish men and women with a livelihood. However, in a serious attempt to rein in the chaos of cattle drives and the growing violence, Fr O'Flanagan also pointed out that a man's right to life was more sacred than the right to property. Fr O'Flanagan also stated that where the land was not being used to support the majority of the people then the people had a right to bring about a change in ownership, by force if necessary. He concluded by issuing a warning: 'People must, for the sake of justice, and even for their own interest, see that no acts of cruelty or injustice be perpetrated in their midst.'[20]

Conor A. Maguire, now a Land Commissioner for Sinn Féin, was asked for his advice on solving the chaos in the west. Maguire told the Dáil they had two choices. They could use the IRA to suppress the land agitation or they could establish land courts and implement land distribution that had been delayed for too long by the Congested Districts Board.[21] Arbitration courts were already in existence in some parishes, for instance Fr Carney's court in The Neale. Kevin O'Sheil was sent to Connaught by Sinn Féin to formally establish the Republican court system. Griffith told O'Shiel that 'he took the gravest view of the western outbreak, and said that if it was not immediately dealt with, it could wreck the entire national movement'.[22] O'Sheil worked very closely with Mayo men Conor A. Maguire, P. J. Ruttledge and P. R. Hughes. Together they succeeded in calming the situation and establishing an effective justice system. It was not easy and it took the involvement of the IRA to enforce the courts' decisions when unpopular judgements were passed. Maguire later reflected on the establishment of the Republican courts:

> It is not easy to understand how we were allowed so easily to get away with it in the critical months when we were steadily establishing the Courts and gradually undermining the British system ... The Courts were carried out with a quiet dignity and great seriousness. There was not much ceremony. Sinn Féin was determined everyone who accepted their jurisdiction was given a patient hearing and a fair deal ... Kilmaine, a South Mayo case put the whole system to a searching test.[23]

Maguire was referring to the Fountain Hill Farm case, which was heard in Ballinrobe on 22 May 1920. Art O'Connor TD and Kevin O'Sheil BL sat as arbitrators. Commandant Tom Maguire's Volunteers provided security for the locality and in the courtroom. Such courts as established by Dáil Éireann were considered illegal by the British government and any participants could be arrested and

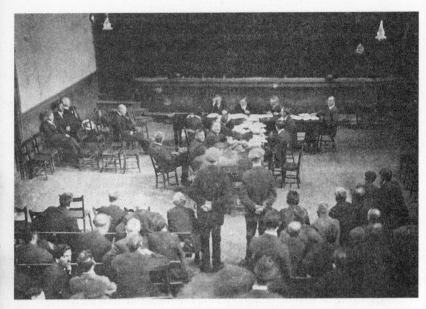

Republican Court, Westport 1920. Top table, centre (l–r): John O'Boyle, Mayo County Council; Conor A. Maguire, Chairman, Mayo County Council; Ned Moane, West Mayo Brigade IRA. At the solicitors' table: J. C. Garvey (prosecutor for the Crown in the Clogher Murders case) and John Gibbons. Two IRA policemen stand in the centre aisle, one being Seán Gibbons. (With kind permission of the Capuchin Archives. Copy of an image from *The Capuchin Annual* 1969, courtesy The National Library of Ireland.)

jailed. The details of the case saw nine tenants from Kilmaine lay claim to a farm at Fountain Hill rented by Mr Hyland and Mr Murphy from the Magdalene Asylum, Galway. Conor Maguire appeared for the claimants. Fr M. Healy stepped in at the last moment for Hyland and Murphy as their solicitors had withdrawn. Maguire argued that the nine men had insufficient land to sustain their existence while Messrs Hyland and Murphy had 24-acre home farms in addition to their rented holdings of 250 acres at Fountain Hill. The claimants gave evidence to their miserable living conditions and said that some in their families were forced to emigrate. Healy, the parish priest, said that this crisis would not have arisen if the Congested Districts Board had released the hundreds of acres under their control in the area.

However, the current rent charged to Hyland and Murphy was £264. If they lost the land they expected compensation of £4,000. The court decided to inspect the lands and reserved judgement until then.

After carrying out an inspection of the lands, the court decided in favour of Messrs Hyland and Murphy. The nine claimants refused to accept the judgement and kept possession of the land. They stormed out declaring 'it was no S[inn] F[éin] Court' and 'worse than the British'. Commandant Maguire was in sympathy with claimants and told them to remain in possession of the land until he told them otherwise.[24]

O'Sheil contacted Cathal Brugha in Dublin who ordered him to use the IRA to implement the decision of the court. Three of the nine claimants were arrested by Maguire's men and held on an island in Lough Corrib. This acted as a deterrent to the others who removed their stock and repaired the fences they had damaged. The Fountain Hill case was crucially important for Dáil Éireann and the Republican movement. It prevented disunity among the various classes of people supporting Sinn Féin. It also unified the Irish Volunteers and the new justice system in support of the Irish State. The decisions of the court were now accepted, sometimes reluctantly, by the people of the county and the nation in general. Mayo was an example of a revolution from the bottom up, the dire needs of the people pressurising Sinn Féin into providing a social and political solution. Republican courts followed in Ballyhaunis, Castlebar, Claremorris, Hollymount, Swinford and Westport.

This robust intervention was to come too late for two Mayo men living in Clogher-Lynch just south of Castlebar. The men concerned were Michael O'Toole and Martin Ferragher. The 52-year-old O'Toole was married with nine children and had worked as general manager on the estate of Mr James Fitzgerald-Kenny JP for twenty-six years. Martin Ferragher also worked for Fitzgerald-Kenny as a coachman. Fitzgerald-Kenny had refused to sell any of his estate to local tenants and farmers seeking to buy grazing land. The RIC had mounted extra patrols in the district for a number of years. The locals had then resorted to a boycott. With a large family to support, Michael O'Toole could ill-afford to boycott his employer and so continued working on the estate. Both O'Toole and Ferragher were warned by locals not to undertake any extra work outside the Fitzgerald-Kenny demesne. On Saturday 29 May, O'Toole helped a nearby neighbour plant oats. It was the last day's work he ever undertook. Driven to sheer desperation at Fitzgerald-Kenny's intransigence, some locals gathered to take out their revenge upon O'Toole and Ferragher.

That Saturday night, O'Toole and Ferragher went to A. J. Downey's Pub in Clogher. On the way home, near the post office at Knockboy, they were confronted by a group of about twenty masked men. A third man with O'Toole and Ferragher, Henry Kelly, was ordered by the group to go home. The masked men then set upon O'Toole and Ferragher, who resisted fiercely. The two men were savagely beaten and dragged over a wall to a nearby wood. Ferragher managed to escape but O'Toole was tied to a tree and subjected to a sustained attack of shocking brutality. His assailants beat him with the brass pipe of a spraying machine, rocks and sticks. His body was then cut loose and remained at the foot of the tree until it was found the following morning by his wife, Mary. She could scarcely recognise the body as that of her husband. One of her sons went to the Fitzgerald-Kennys' house for help. Mrs Fitzgerald-Kenny drove to Balla and returned with Dr O'Boyle. While O'Toole was being beaten to death, Ferragher, after breaking loose, had staggered home to his brother and sister's house where he lived. He drifted into sleep induced by concussion. Ferragher was attended to by Dr O'Boyle and brought to the County Infirmary in Castlebar where he died on 17 June from injuries sustained during the attack. The details of both inquests were published in full by J. J. Collins in the *Mayoman*.[25]

Sergeant Murphy and Constable Grehan from Balla RIC barracks gave evidence before John Kelly JP at the inquest held in Castlebar as to what they encountered upon arriving at Clogher. At the post office near Knockboy they found large splashes of blood on the road, the wall and on the grass leading to a tree 20 yards into the wood. It was there they found Michael O'Toole's body. His hands were stretched out in front with his legs gathered up underneath him. There were several deep wounds on his head, hands and body.

The county was in deep shock at O'Toole's murder. The public reaction was best summed up by Archbishop Gilmartin of Tuam, who wrote to the priests of the Clogher-Lynch district:

I feel bound to express my sympathy with you and your good people in the horror you must all experience at the ghastly murder of Michael O'Toole ... an innocent man, with a wife and nine children, and engaged in lawful employment ... But trampling on the express Commandment of God, 'Thou shalt not kill', the culprits in this case have descended to a depth of savagery which I did not think possible in Mayo or in any part of Ireland.[26]

The RIC and military combed the district but few people would speak to them. By Monday, however, four arrests had been made. They included Jeremiah Bourke, twenty-nine years old, 5 foot 5 inches tall with brown hair and blue eyes; Pat Coleman, fifty-two years old, 5 foot 6 inches with grey hair and blue eyes;[27] and brothers James and Pat Gill. The men appeared before A. C. Larmine JP at a special court sitting in the old RIC jail in Castlebar. A fifth man, James Gorman, was arrested the following week. All five were held on remand at Sligo Jail awaiting a hearing on the case.

The hearing to establish a prima facie case was delayed on two occasions while clothing was being analysed for forensic evidence. Finally, on 14 August 1920, Jeremiah Bourke, Pat Coleman, James Gill, Patrick Gill and James Gorman were brought before Colonel Meldon RM in Castlebar. The court at Castlebar heard the background to the case and the long dispute of the people of Clogher with the landlord, Mr Fitzgerald-Kenny. The RIC told how there had been constant trouble in this district between 1913 and 1917. They had to provide escorts for the ladies of the family to and from their church at Carnacon.

The case against Jeremiah Bourke provided the strongest evidence of involvement in the double murder. On conducting a search of Bourke's home, Constable Daly found bloodstained socks, a shirt, vest and overalls. Bourke could not account for how his clothes had arrived in such a state. The bloodstained clothing was sent to Dr Robert Bronte of York Street, Dublin, for analysis. Constable Daly continued his search of the district and in the house of Pat Coleman found a new pipe for a potato-spraying machine. The prosecution believed this was central to the case as the old one had been found on the road near the scene of the murder. Coleman could not say what had happened to the old one.

Bourke also provided an account of his movements that day that brought Pat Coleman and Pat Gill into the story. The three had met with a group of others at Downey's Pub earlier in the day. Together they talked at length over a couple of bottles of stout. James Gill, in his statement, claimed he was also in Downey's but had stayed only a few minutes. All the accused claimed they left the pub early in the evening and went to bed between 11 p.m. and 11.30 p.m. O'Toole and Ferragher, meanwhile, left the same pub at 11.15 p.m. having stayed only three quarters of an hour. A quarter of a mile from Downey's the two men met their assailants and, ultimately, their deaths.

Charles Bewley put up a strong defence for the accused. In Jeremiah Bourke's case, the forensic analysis offered by Dr Bronte had revealed human blood on just one item of clothing, the overalls. The amount of blood was small, just a few drops. According to the RIC, Bewley argued, the amount of blood at the murder scene should have meant the assailants were saturated in it. This was not the case for Bourke's clothing. In Pat Coleman's case, Bewley stated that there was nothing strange in his inability to account for the old pipe that had been replaced. For the others accused, Bewley argued the RIC case amounted nothing more than their presence at a pub at least four to five hours before the murder. There was nothing to connect them to the attack at Knockboy Wood.

John Garvey, for the Crown, argued passionately for all of the accused to stand trial for murder. He also appealed to the community of Clogher to speak out in support of the wife of Michael O'Toole and her nine children now left without a father. Yet silence was what met the police in the course of their investigation. Whatever the result of this case, Garvey said, he 'hoped the guilty one would be afflicted with an awful conscience'.[28] Garvey picked out Jeremiah Bourke and Pat Coleman for special attention as he believed he had the greatest chance of success with the evidence in their case. His strategy succeeded. Bourke and Coleman were returned to Sligo Jail to await trial for the capital offence of murder. James and Patrick Gill and James Gorman were discharged.

The conclusion of this case is shrouded in mystery. On 7 October 1920, Bourke and Coleman were released from Sligo Jail on the orders of Colonel Meldon RM.[29] There was no court appearance and no explanation for the release. Subsequently, at a court hearing before Judge Doyle KC at Castlebar, Mrs O'Toole was awarded £1,800 with £90 interest as compensation for the loss of her husband. John and Bridget Ferragher, brother and sister of Martin Ferragher, were awarded £850 with £17 10s interest for their loss. The hearing was attended by the Clogher-Lynch landlord, Fitzgerald-Kenny, who gave a moving account of the loss of Michael O'Toole to his family.[30] This would suggest a deal was done behind the scenes to settle the case. A new Irish Republic would not have relished the prospect of hanging two citizens if found guilty in one of their first high-profile murder cases.

The prosecution's case was also plagued with problems. The British court system had collapsed in Ireland in the summer of 1920. DI Horgan, who was leading the investigation, had also resigned, much to the surprise of all, in early August. A solution may have been brokered by the landlord Fitzgerald-Kenny, himself a lawyer in Mayo. The compensation awarded, while nowhere near atoning for the shocking events at Clogher, would have provided some security for the O'Toole and Ferragher families. The use of a financial settlement was a solution used in another Mayo murder case in the same year. In this case, Michael Kilgallon, a thirteen-year-old boy from Bohola, was found by his mother and sister dead on the road outside his home in a pool of blood. He had been stabbed through the heart. The case was investigated by the Irish Volunteers and a court held at which Seán Corcoran, O/C of the East Mayo Brigade, was president. The court returned a verdict of manslaughter against a local boy called O'Malley. The boy was exiled from Ireland and his father was ordered to pay £300 to the Michael Kilgallon's family as compensation for his loss.[31] The Clogher murders remain unsolved to this day. The true extent of the RIC's detective work will only come to light when the file on the murders is revealed.[32] While the RIC investigation into events at Clogher was being carried out, momentous political events were occurring across the county.

On 12 June 1920, J. J. Collins congratulated the electorate of Mayo on securing the independence of their country by returning an exclusively Sinn Féin County Council in the local government elections. There were some notable successes, with the imprisoned Martin Nally of Claremorris topping the poll. Also returned were Joe Brennan and P. R. Hughes. The nation had chosen an independent Republican government in December 1918. Now, in June 1920, the people were again choosing to strengthen the Sinn Féin Republican government by electing Sinn Féin officials to run their towns and counties.

The local District Councils met on Monday 14 June 1920. All District Councils elected were now Sinn Féin Councils. The meeting of the Castlebar Council provided great drama as the new Council set about re-establishing their honour. In 1916 a resolution had been passed by the that condemned the Rising as 'insane' and 'deplorable'.[33] The new Chairman, Michael Lavelle, publically ripped the 1916 resolution from the minute book. The resolution was read aloud and the names of those who voted for it recorded by John Hoban who then put a match to the document. There was a burst of applause and loud cheering as the views of the past were consigned to ashes. Honour was deemed to be restored.

The first meeting of the new Republican County Council was held on Monday 21 June 1920, signalling the transfer of power to the people of Mayo after centuries of British administration. The elected representatives were as follows:[34]

Mayo County Council, Elected Representatives June 1920			
P.J. Ruttledge Ballina North Mayo	John Judge Foxford North Mayo	Edward Moane Westport West Mayo	Thomas Jordan Kiltimagh East Mayo
William Coyne Ballyhaunis East Mayo	John McIntyre Charlestown East Mayo	John O'Boyle Kilmeena West Mayo	James Morris Knock East Mayo
Michael Lavelle Castlebar West Mayo	Oliver J. O'Connor Kilkelly East Mayo	Michael Staunton Islandeady West Mayo	Martin Nally Claremorris South Mayo

Seán Corcoran Kiltimagh East Mayo	Patrick Corrigan Achill North Mayo	Michael Gleeson Ballinrobe South Mayo	Dr John A. Madden Belderrig North Mayo
John Munnelly Belmullet North Mayo	M. McAndrew Bangor Erris North Mayo	Thaddeus Walsh Westport West Mayo	Patrick Jordan Turlough Castlebar West Mayo
Thomas Maguire Ballinrobe South Mayo	Michael Keaveney Ballina North Mayo	Thomas Ruane Kiltimagh East Mayo	Eamonn Gannon Ballina North Mayo
Patrick Hegarty, Lahardane North Mayo	Patrick Waldron [Absent] Cong South Mayo	John Healy [Absent] Claremorris South Mayo	Conor A. Maguire Claremorris South Mayo
Tomás MacCathmaoil Swinford East Mayo	John Corcoran Ballycastle North Mayo	Matthew Lally Tourmakeady South Mayo	

Eamonn Gannon stood and the assembly went quiet. He proposed, seconded by Michael Gleeson, that one of Mayo's brilliant young lawyers, Conor A. Maguire, be elected Cathaoirleach (Chairman) of the first independent Republican County Council of Mayo. Gannon said: 'In him [Maguire] they would have a young man in whom they could place the highest confidence and who would be a credit to Mayo and Ireland.' There was tremendous applause as Maguire rose to take his place at the head of the assembled councillors and guests. It was a deeply symbolic moment. 'It is not speech making that is required now but good work in securing Irish independence and carrying out the decrees of the Irish Republic,' Maguire said.[35]

After a standing ovation lasting a number of minutes, Maguire asked all present to stand and take an oath of allegiance to Dáil Éireann. It was put in English so that all present would understand it. Eamonn Gannon was elected Leas-Chathaoirleach (Vice-Chairman). The Council then got to work with some urgency. Committees on Finance, Law & Dáil, Proposals, the County Asylum, Agriculture,

Conor Alexander Maguire of Claremorris. Chairman of the first Mayo Republican County Council, elected June 1920. (Courtesy Mayo County Council and Tom Campbell Photography Castlebar)

Milk Commission, Tuberculosis, Technical Schools, County Infirmary and University Scholarships were established. Some of the councillors quipped that they would have to take up residency in Castlebar permanently to attend all these committees.

The month of June 1920 was one of unprecedented celebration throughout the county. There was a general feeling of empowerment, that the people had at last seized control of their own destiny. Most of Mayo felt deeply that after the suffering of the Great Famine, eviction and failed risings their time at last had come. In his editorial of 19 June, J. J. Collins, in a confident act of defiance, boldly described Lloyd George as 'the greatest political trickster of his age, an over-rated poltroon afraid of his own shadow where high class Tories stand in the light'. Subsequent events were to show Lloyd George was far from 'an over-rated poltroon' but instead one of the most skilled and cunning politicians Ireland was ever to face.

In the meantime, the IRA had grown in strength and had begun to make its presence felt. DI Michael Horgan, prior to his surprise resignation, had compiled the County Inspector's report for June in the absence of Steadman. Horgan reported that 'on the whole matters have become worse'. He pointed out that people were afraid to report anything and that he was sure the amount of intimidation had increased. Balla railway station, for example, had been robbed of petrol drums, but the staff did not report it until the local police heard about it casually. Horgan put this down to fear or sympathy or both. Raids by 'Sinn Feiners' had also resulted in the robbery of twenty shotguns in the Swinford district. An RIC cycle patrol had also been ambushed on 30 June and deprived of their one firearm, a revolver.[36]

Horgan also pointed out that Sinn Féin courts were no longer secret tribunals. They were held in the open and fully reported in the local press. Those presiding announced that decisions of their Republican courts would be enforced by 'the military forces of the Irish Republic'. *An t-Óglach*, the Irish Volunteer paper, was now widely distributed. Local railway staff refused to man or drive trains carrying the military or ammunition. Horgan finished with a warning that current forces available were not sufficient to cope with the situation.[37]

By August, CI Steadman was all but admitting that the RIC had lost control of the county. To remedy the situation, he called for increased police numbers, the reopening of closed RIC barracks, improved equipment and transport. Steadman concluded by calling for closer cooperation between the RIC and the British military, coupled with closer distribution of forces to enable common action.[38] The British command was to respond favourably to most of Steadman's requests. The summer months saw the arrival of additional British troops, better transport and increased numbers for a dwindling RIC force. The winter of 1920/1 was to see a more aggressive British policy throughout Ireland. The time of the Black and Tans and Auxiliaries had arrived, and Mayo was not to escape the onslaught lightly.

4

'Demons': Tans, Auxiliaries and the Counter-Terror Strategy

The clock on the mantelpiece chimed the half hour. It was 11.30 a.m. on Friday 23 July 1920. The Prime Minister, David Lloyd George, looked at those assembled in the Cabinet Room, 10 Downing Street, London. Before him were the most senior politicians and military commanders of the British Empire. Among the politicians were Andrew Bonar Law, Conservative Party leader and Lord Privy Seal, Austen Chamberlain, Chancellor of the Exchequer, Winston Churchill, Secretary of State for War, Arthur Balfour, Lord President of the Council, Sir Hamar Greenwood, Chief Secretary for Ireland, Walter Hume Long, First Lord of the Admiralty, Field Marshal Viscount French, Lord Lieutenant of Ireland, Lord Birkenhead, Lord Chancellor and Sir James Craig, leader of the unionist community in the north of Ireland. The military men included Sir Nevil Macready, O/C British forces in Ireland and Major General Hugh Tudor, recently appointed 'police advisor' to Dublin Castle administration but in effect O/C of the RIC. There were also a number of legal and civil servant advisors.[1] This conference was to determine the course of British policy in Ireland leading up to and beyond the Treaty. It would have major repercussions for the men, women and children of Mayo and indeed the whole country of Ireland.

William Evelyn Wylie, the legal adviser, proposed two options for dealing with the deteriorating situation in Ireland. The first was

'Martial Law of the most stringent kind.' He felt this 'was abhorrent, and afforded no solution of the problem' as 'once lifted, the feeling of bitterness and hatred among the Irish towards Britain would intensify and conditions would return to the present strife'. The second option, Wylie suggested to the Prime Minister, was a settlement with Sinn Féin. He said the Sinn Féiners were 'not committing outrages through blood-lust but had convinced themselves that this was the only way to focus the eyes of Europe on their cause'. Wylie concluded by stating: 'If the Government attempted to bludgeon the Irish people, no good could possibly result, and Ireland would still remain a thorn in the side of the Empire. But if the Government played straight, within two years Ireland would be one of the strongest partners within the Empire.'[2]

General Tudor then spoke about the RIC, admitting it would cease to function in a few months. Tudor did, however, hold out hope for the RIC if it were reconstituted as a military organisation. He informed the Cabinet that he had already recruited 500 ex-officers and a number of ex-soldiers to make up for the resignations in the RIC. Tudor believed that given the proper support it would be possible to crush the 'present campaign of outrage'. To implement his plan, Tudor argued for restrictions on travel, compulsory identity cards and the imposition of fines on districts where murders occurred or the seizing of livestock if payment was refused. He also requested the sending of all prisoners to Britain to do hard labour, purging the Post Office of 'traitors' and refusing Cardinal Mannix, the Archbishop of Melbourne who was on a Peace Mission, entry to Ireland.[3]

Tudor assured the Prime Minister that he could control the situation in Ireland if enough men were available. He appealed for the recruitment of 'Temporary Cadet Officers' from England to enable him to raise the numbers required in Ireland. Up to mid-1920, the IRA had engaged in terror tactics to achieve their ends. RIC men and British soldiers had been boycotted, beaten, intimidated and shot. RIC barracks had been set on fire when evacuated and some attacked directly. Lloyd George decided that the most effective response was to implement a counter-terror strategy. Winston Churchill, who always had a liking for 'Special Forces', proposed the development of two distinct corps. One, formed from ex-enlisted soldiers, became known as the Black and Tans. They would supplement falling numbers and would be integrated into the RIC as constables. They eventually numbered 12,000. The second force, the Auxiliary Division, was to be formed exclusively from former British Army officers. The Auxiliaries, or Auxies as they were popularly known, became an elite and much-feared force throughout Ireland. Auxiliaries received pay of £1 a day, double that of the Tans, and had an eventual strength of 1,500 men. General Tudor was personal friend of Churchill. This friendship ensured strong support for the counter-terror strategy in the British Cabinet.

The Black and Tans, or Tans as they became known in the west of Ireland, were posted to the existing RIC barracks throughout the country. The name derived from their uniforms that were a mix of British military khaki and RIC dark green, a combination that came about due to a shortage of complete uniforms. Their arrival was part of a general shake-up of the British administrative, military and police structures in Ireland. This was implemented to counter Michael Collins' effective undermining the power of Dublin Castle.[4] As part of this reorganisation General Sir Nevil Macready replaced Lieutenant General Frederick Shaw as O/C of British forces in Ireland, and Sir Hamar Greenwood, a Canadian, was appointed as Chief Secretary of Ireland, in effect head of the British administration.

The Assistant Undersecretary, Alfred Cope, stated that the Republican courts were 'doing more harm to the prestige of the British Government than the assassinations'. As regards General Tudor's scheme for putting down murder, he 'doubted whether it would be effective, and felt that any suppression now would come back like a boomerang on the Government'.[5] Sir John Anderson, the Joint Undersecretary, argued caution. He believed Tudor's confidence came from the way in which the campaign of murder in Limerick city had been suppressed. Anderson was sure this was because of an exceptional RIC officer and could not be applied in each county. Anderson feared martial law would end the British civil administration of Ireland, turn power over to the military and ensure there was nothing to work with when the fighting was all over.

The Prime Minister listened intently to the arguments for and against further military measures in Ireland. He then asked if the 'inconveniences' as suggested by General Tudor would create the desired atmosphere whereby a settlement could be reached with Sinn Féin? Tudor assured the Prime Minister it would. Sir James Craig was asked for his views as he had not attended previous meetings. Craig 'did not think there had been sufficient energy in dealing with Sinn Féin'. Craig suggested a small committee of three or four to work out an effective plan for Ireland. It was proposed that Sinn Féin would be offered an amended Home Rule Bill granting dominion rule for the south and west of Ireland with control of finance and internal administration. Control of the army and navy was to be left to the Imperial government. Wylie said this would not be accepted by Sinn Féin and a new offer would have to be made that appealed to the 'imagination' of Irishmen.[6] One wonders if this suggestion was the origin of the concept of the Irish Free State or Saorstát Éireann?

The Cabinet conference adjourned for lunch and reconvened at 3.30 p.m. Sir James MacMahon, Joint Undersecretary, was of the view that repression would fail and would drive moderates into the hands of the opposition. MacMahon also stated that the Roman Catholic Church had always been opposed to a Republic. MacMahon differentiated between the 'real' Sinn Féin movement and a small number of 'extremists' who carried out the violence. MacMahon was then asked 'why if so many of the leading lights in the Sinn Féin movement were prepared to accept Dominion Home Rule, they stated they would accept nothing less than a Republic?' His reply: 'they did this on the principle of a man who wished to sell a horse and stated that he required £100 when in reality he was prepared to accept £70.'[7]

The end of the discussion saw MacMahon state that the majority in the south of Ireland would accept Dominion Home Rule with control of customs and excise, a small contribution to the Imperial exchequer and command of the army and navy remaining with the Imperial government. The Catholic Church, MacMahon added, 'would accept such a scheme with glee'. The real crux for Lloyd George was if Dominion Home Rule was granted to the south, would the new Irish government be able to put down the 'assassins'?[8] MacMahon believed it would.

This Cabinet meeting demonstrated how experienced the British were in both diplomacy and military matters. Lloyd George was well satisfied as it broke up. He would allow General Tudor to implement his counter-terror measures through the Auxiliaries and the Black and Tans. This would serve to weaken the extremist elements in Sinn Féin. If the policy failed, the government would have Dominion Home Rule to offer, which would guarantee an Irish government favourable to Britain and its neighbour in Ulster. This option would have the backing of the Roman Catholic Church and the support of the general population who were likely to be worn down after months of violence. Mayo was to be among the many counties weary of violence, but rather than being suppressed by General Tudor's strategy, opposition increased and the IRA grew in strength and prestige as operations against the RIC and the British military began.

For the west of Ireland, the change in British policy meant the appointment of a Divisional Commissioner for the counties of Galway and Mayo. These two counties were viewed as one police and military district. Richard Francis Raleigh Cruise was appointed Divisional Commissioner (DC) for Galway-Mayo on 10 November 1920. A Meath man, Cruise was forty-two years old and stood 5 feet 9 inches in height. A former mathematics teacher, he had joined the RIC in 1902 and had served extensively throughout the country. Cruise was a man of considerable 'zeal, energy and efficiency'. Among his many achievements was the introduction of fingerprinting to police work in Ireland.[9] Cruise was to become a formidable and dangerous opponent of the IRA in the west.

The task of the Divisional Commissioner was to identify the leading IRA and Sinn Féin organisers within his area. He was then to liaise with the British military in a coordinated strategy designed to eliminate the IRA threat. Cruise began using intelligence from the remaining experienced RIC men who had not yet resigned. These 'bitter enders', so-called by the IRA because they would fight to the finish, had a deep knowledge of their districts; they knew all the Volunteers by sight and also their homes and training areas. In addition, Cruise gathered intelligence from civilians throughout Galway and Mayo. He visited homesteads with parties of Tans and military to intimidate 'suspects'. Others were arrested and interrogated, sometimes with considerable violence, in order to gain the information required. Some gave information freely. Of invaluable support to Cruise were the talents of British military intelligence who established a headquarters at Dominick Street in Galway. A Captain Keating was the O/C. Patrick Coleman from Ballina referred to them as 'The Murder Gang'.[10] They were well named. One of their key officers was a Captain Harrison of the 17th Lancers whose cap badge was a skull and crossbones with the regimental motto of 'Death or Glory'. Irish Volunteers Joe Togher from Galway and Patrick Coleman were both interrogated by Captain Harrison.[11]

DC Cruise also had additional battalions of British troops at his disposal. The 2nd Battalion of the Argyll and Sutherland Highlanders arrived in Claremorris and Swinford on 19 July 1920 after marching from Enniskillen in County Fermanagh. Their war diary relates the sight that greeted them in Claremorris:

> all ranks were depressed at the state of the camp. It consisted of unfinished and unfurnished huts, no roads, a few drains. Royal Engineer material was lying all over the place, in fact the campsite resembled a shell stricken area in France. Headquarters, B and D Companies settled down as best they could in Claremorris where their duties were guards and escorts to convoys. Training was almost impossible as duties absorbed all available personnel. During the next two months many incidents occurred but none of a serious nature, perhaps the most interesting was the raiding of the Town Hall in Claremorris, where a Sinn Féin Court was found to be sitting. Several arrests were made and large quantities of seditious material were found.

Special activities of the 2nd Battalion included the commandeering of all arms and ammunitions in the possession of civilians on 20 September, searching all mails in the Battalion area on 1 October and the searching of all trains entering Claremorris on 4 October and all traffic on 10 and 11 October. Many arrests were made, the most important being that of the adjutant of the Sinn Féin Battalion in Swinford with incriminating documents on his person.

Armistice Day (11 November) was observed in Claremorris. The Claremorris detachment paraded on The Square in the town where

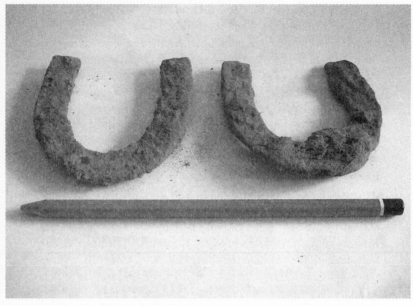

Boot metal recovered from former Argyll and Sutherland Highlanders Camp Claremorris, County Mayo. (Author's photograph)

the minute's silence was observed. The populace was given warning of the Parade on the previous day and turned out in large numbers who were generally, with a few exceptions, respectful and seemed to appreciate the ceremony. Following the assassination of fourteen British officers in Dublin (21 November 1920), orders were received on 23 November to arrest all officers of the IRA and detain them pending instructions regarding their internment. By the following evening thirty-six had been arrested in Claremorris and Swinford areas and by the end of the month fifty were held.[12]

With the Black and Tan, Auxiliary and British military reinforcements, DC Cruise set out to neutralise the IRA in Galway and Mayo. This was to be achieved by the use of mobile patrols of RIC and troops. The British Cabinet was worried about handing over complete authority to the military in Ireland. They were afraid of a repeat of the mistakes made following the 1916 Rising. As a result, the military never achieved the full autonomy they looked for in the field of operational control. However, the Black and Tans and the Auxiliaries were a different story. In Mayo and throughout the rest of the country, they were to act with impunity and with great brutality. Their actions were excused, dismissed and covered up by their commanders and the British government as they were seen as an essential element in the war against the IRA and Sinn Féin.

The Tans first made their presence felt in the west on 24 July in Tuam, County Galway. The *New York Times* led with the headline: 'Gunfire and flames rage in Irish town; Troops and Police Sack Tuam following the killing of two Constables.'[13] The IRA had ambushed an RIC patrol returning to Dunmore from the Galway assizes. Constables Carey and Burke were killed as they removed a barricade thrown across the road. In response, an RIC convoy including a large contingent of Black and Tans from Galway went on the rampage and burned Tuam Town Hall, which had been the venue for the first local Republican court the previous week. The RIC also set fire to at least four other shops and threw a hand grenade into the house of J. Casey, the Republican court registrar. Numerous shots were fired into several other houses, with Nohilly's on the Dublin road 'riddled with bullets'.[14] Nohilly had two brothers in the IRA. The homes targeted all had connections with the IRA or Sinn Féin. Tuam's Head Constable intervened to save the life of one of the locals as the Tans were going to shoot him. The events in the town that night caused deep outrage. They also set the blueprint for Tan and Auxiliary activity in the west.

Black and Tan patrols would travel through the countryside firing indiscriminately at locals in the fields, often wounding or killing them. The presence of children made no difference. John Connor was standing in a field with Michael Kenny and his daughter near Gallagh, Tuam, when a lorry of Tans opened fire on them. Bullets splattered the earth around them, wounding Connor in the hip.[15] A typical Tan raid involved arriving in a village or town with considerable gunfire. They would continue firing at homes and breaking windows. They would then select particular houses for closer inspection. The doors were usually broken in and the homes ransacked and frequently looted. Inhabitants were beaten, interrogated and sometimes shot and murdered. Usually the raiding party departed with prisoners. On occasion furniture was piled up outside and set alight while the house was blown up with grenades or burned.

General Sir Hugh Tudor with Black and Tans (right) and RIC Constables (left) photographed on The Square at the RIC Depot, Phoenix Park, Dublin during 1920. (© RTÉ Stills Library, Cashman Collection)

On 1 September, members of the East Mayo Brigade of the IRA ambushed an RIC cycle patrol en route from Ballaghaderreen to Frenchpark, County Roscommon. Two RIC constables died, one of them Mayo man Edward Murphy. Also shot dead was Captain Tom McDonagh IRA. Black and Tans who arrived after the ambush threw his body into the back of their truck and returned to Ballaghaderreen. It was then placed on public display in the town square before being removed to the barracks. That night the townspeople were traumatised as prominent businesses were blown up and set alight by Black and Tans armed with grenades and tins of petrol.[16]

The Volunteers, now known as the IRA, began to intensify their activities throughout the autumn of 1920. In south Mayo, Tom Maguire's brigade burned out Kilmaine, Partry, Shrule, Cong and Ballindine RIC barracks after these posts had been evacuated. In the North Mayo Brigade area, Bangor Erris, Ballycastle, Ballycrory and Kilcummin RIC barracks were burned out.[17] There were more serious attacks, too. On 22 August, the East Mayo Brigade carried out a daring raid on Ballyvary RIC barracks while most of the garrison was at Mass. Seán Corcoran's men seized 20 rifles, 25 revolvers, 5,000 rounds of ammunition and a few boxes of hand grenades. At Swinford, military stores worth £1,200 en route to British Army detachments in Mayo were burned in their railway wagons. The North Mayo Brigade launched a successful attack on Enniscrone Coastguard Station on 2 September 1920. Patrick Coleman described the assault:

> Shortly after joining my other comrades we opened the attack by Paddy O'Beirne and Paddy O'Connell jumping the wall and disarming the sentry while we were rushing the building. At this stage a Mrs Livermore, wife of the Chief Coastguard who must have seen the disarming, opened a window and started screaming at the top of her voice. She could nearly be heard in Ballina, 9 miles away. This roused the rest of the garrison and some of them opened fire as we were rushing in to the attack. One had the heel of his boot shot off although we were rushing straight at the building. The shot must have come from an angle. We dashed around the corner to a side entrance which was open and surprised a Coastguard cooking fish at a range. The sizzling of the fish must have partly drowned the screams as we got him by surprise. We forced him with another coastguard up the stairs in front of us and disarmed the remainder of them. We then collected the arms and the ammunition ...
>
> I went to Enniscrone to get a car to remove the stuff and, while on my way there, I heard two voices on the road, one of them asking Chief Coastguard Livermore, who was returning from the town, 'Was he needed at the station as he heard some shooting and thought there might be some shot or wounded.' Livermore replied, 'There is no one required at the station,' and the voice said, 'Your station has been captured.' Livermore said 'Impossible' and walked on towards the station which he entered to find our boys in full possession. I crossed to find who owned the other voice, questioned him to find he was Dr Michael Coolican of Ballina. I asked the Doctor why he told Livermore about the shooting and the capture of the station and his reply was, 'I am a Doctor and thought I might have been some assistance to either side.' I suggested that he should

go home until called for, which he did. His uncle was the Crown Solicitor.

I got the car, loaded up and proceeded to Carralavin, Bonniconlon. On the way we picked up two guides, Tom Loftus and Anthony Kerrigan, who took us to the arranged dump where we placed the stuff (about 14 or 15 rifles), the same amount of revolvers and a quantity of ammunition. The rifles were Canadian Ross pattern [.303 calibre round].[18]

RIC raids became more pronounced in response to the increased IRA activity. Known members of the IRA, Sinn Féin, priests and religious began to receive death threats in the post informing the receiver to 'Prepare for Death'. Such threats were a Mayo tactic of old going back to the Land War, but the Tans adopted it to good effect. Among the first to receive one was Pádraig Dunleavy, O/C Claremorris. He kept it as a talisman for the rest of his life. Shortly afterwards, Dunleavy was sent to north Galway by GHQ to rebuild the brigade that had been decimated by recent Auxiliary action. He was replaced in Claremorris by Commandant Joe Brennan who was then arrested, court-martialled and jailed for eighteen months. Among others who received death threats were Rev. Br Ward, Acting Superior of the Christian Brothers, Westport, and the parish priest of Balla. Br Ward's death threat was the most menacing, perhaps written by persons in an intoxicated state.

To the Head Christ Brother from Head Officer Westport
Sir,
If you the school any more you will be bulleted with bombs, yourself and your followers we will take ye out and shoot ye agin the wall, like a Dog, and burn the place to ashes.

We never do anything of the likes with sufficent cause and so bad we will do to the nuns if they do not obey the order.[19]

Before the worst of the terror, Archbishop Gilmartin of Tuam made an appeal to the people: 'We are living in a very terrible time and the only policy at present is one of restraint.' 'Shooting, counter-shooting and raiding people's houses was the gospel of the devil,' he stated. The

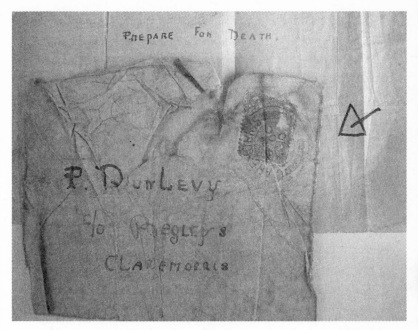

Death threat received by Captain Padraig Dunleavy O/C South Mayo Brigade, Claremorris Company, IRA, 21 October 1920. (Courtesy Dominick and Mary Dunleavy)

Archbishop called for a 'Truce of God'.[20] Gilmartin had written to Sir Neville Macready following the burning of Tuam but with little success. Macready had simply stated: 'I fear that the occurrence may be one of those which is due to the natural inexperience of our young soldiers, coupled with the fact that in this country it is so difficult for them to distinguish between friend and foe.'[21] Macready wrote a second time, saying the police were 'incensed at the calculated and cold-blooded murder of their comrades' and that as there was no military involvement, he was handing on Gilmartin's concerns 'to the relevant authority'.[22]

It was clear to the Archbishop from reports coming in from the parishes that a carefully coordinated campaign of counter-terror was now at work in the west. Gilmartin must have agonised over what was happening to the innocent civilians in his diocese. A man committed to peace, he drew anger and criticism from both Sinn Féin

Dr Thomas Gilmartin,
Archbishop of Tuam.
(Courtesy Tuam Diocese
Archives)

and the British in his attempts to stop the violence. There are few
other bishops in Ireland who managed to implement such a varied
approach on many different levels in order to bring about a truce.

On 30 October 1920, the *Mayoman* was published in heavy black
mourning bands. It carried a photograph of Terence MacSwiney,
Lord Mayor of Cork. He had died at Brixton Jail in London on the
previous Monday morning at 5.40 a.m. after seventy-four days on
hunger strike. The account of MacSwiney's death was very emotional.
It was related through the testimony of Capuchin priest Fr Dominic
who had attended the Lord Mayor and his family during his last
weeks of life. The paper also featured a letter written by Archbishop
Gilmartin to *The Times* of London about 'evidence of the frightfulness
to which the people of this district have recently been subjected'. The
Archbishop was seeking to bring public pressure to bear on the British
government by writing publicly and placing the responsibility for
the reign of terror squarely on the British Cabinet. The Archbishop
referred specifically to the Black and Tans who had arrived in north
Galway during the first week of October. Among the incidents

outlined by the Archbishop were searches of houses and arrests in the dead of night, men stripped and scourged, brutal floggings, and police firing repeated volleys from moving lorries at workers in fields and at houses. 'I could mention many other instances of barbarity and of reckless and criminal firing by the auxiliary police, but I think I have said enough to give the English people a sample of what is being done in their name.' Mayo was soon to receive its share of the terror. In early November, Kevlihan's and Murphy's homes in Shrule were burned to the ground by the Tans.[23] The British public were appalled at the accounts of the violence carried out by the Auxiliaries and the Tans as reported in the press and raised in parliament. However, the County Inspector for Mayo, David Steadman, was delighted with the progress of the counter-terror measures:

> I beg to report that the dread of reprisals combined with a more active cooperation of the military in these parts with the Police is exercising a very salutary effect and if quietly and systematically continued will thrash the bottom out of the Sinn Féin movement in a short time. People generally are beginning to see whither the Sinn Féin programme is dragging them and to what dangers and troubles it exposes them and would for the most part gladly welcome a return to the old Status quo with the feeling of safety and security that accompanied it. Sinn Féiners never counted on it being possible that reprisals would ever overtake them and they had become much exercised in mind and body at the very suggestion of the application to themselves of a little of their own ointment. That it has seriously crippled Sinn Féin prestige and power already there is no room for doubt ... Loyal people, on the other hand, let down so often to their cost, pin no faith to Government promises and protestations and simply sit on the fence watching developments until it is seen what way the cat is going to jump ... A healthy sign of the times is that the dread of reprisals in the event of anything untoward happening in their locality is making people generally exercise their influence to prevent anything occurring in their midst that would likely bring such in its train. This is a rather novel feature of Irish psychology.[24]

Steadman was right to a point. Communities throughout Mayo were living in terrible fear of the violence that would come in the wake of IRA operations in their areas. However, the Tans had already demonstrated that they did not need the excuse of IRA operations in order to apply terror. For a time, the RIC strategy worked, but with the arrival of arms and ammunition the IRA was to have the means to take on those who terrorised their communities. The British counter-terror strategy had merely increased the level of violence, as predicted by a number of Lloyd George's Cabinet advisers.

The RIC intelligence network in Mayo was effective. There were enough long-serving RIC men still in the county to continue to identify existing IRA, Cumann na mBan and Sinn Féin members. This intelligence was supplemented by people giving the RIC valuable information, people who saw themselves as assisting the powers of justice against the intimidation of the IRA. An example of IRA intimidation was the beating of ex-British soldier Frank McGinty in Shraigh on 29 October 1920. David and Michael Henry, Patrick Reilly and Patrick Heneghan punched and pistol-whipped McGinty, inflicting nine wounds over an inch long to his head alone. The men were arrested and court-martialled for attempted murder. Surprisingly, they were acquitted of attempted murder but found guilty of 'wounding with intent'.[25] The RIC also put people under pressure through interrogation to reveal information. Among those who assisted the RIC were a post office worker, an ex-RIC man, farmers, an IRA man and a parish priest, one Rev. Fr John Flatley of Aughagower.

Fr Flatley was connected to the highest levels of the British government. He had become firm friends with Walter Hume Long, the First Lord of the Admiralty, who as Chief Secretary for Ireland in 1905 had spent a good deal of time touring the west. Their first meeting was in the middle of a howling gale as Long's touring motor pulled in to Leenane. Fr Flatley was a prolific writer and it was through the power of his pen he gained influence with Chief Secretaries in securing many benefits for his parishioners.[26] Long was a Conservative-Unionist MP descended from landed gentry in Wiltshire and County Wicklow. He wrote a prophetic letter to Fr Flatley in September 1918, in which he expressed sorrow 'that the

(L–r) Rev. Fr John Flatley, Walter Hume Long and an unknown man. (Photograph from Robinson, Sir Henry KCB, *Memories: Wise and Otherwise*, Cassell and Company Ltd, London, New York and Melbourne, 1923. Courtesy The National Library of Ireland)

feeling against England has never been so bitter as it is at this moment, and that there is no prospect of any reconciliation ... Of course any idea of Dominion Home Rule is unthinkable. I am satisfied that the bulk of the English people would fight rather than concede a demand which would make Ireland really an independent country.'[27]

Two years later, in November 1920, Fr Flatley wrote to Long. He was concerned that the Congested Districts Board policy of assigning freed land from Lord Sligo's estate to certain Westport families involved in intimidation would be 'utterly ruinous to peace and quiet social life in this parish for a period to which it would not be easy to place a limit'.[28] Sir Henry Doran, head of the Congested Districts Board, opposed any form of discrimination in the distribution land. The Board worked on the principle that the longest-serving tenants on the estate to be divided should be the ones to benefit in a redistribution of land. Long asked Fr Flatley to reveal the names of those engaged in the intimidation. On 27 January 1921, Fr Flatley wrote to Captain Siltzer, Long's Assistant Private Secretary, naming many of those involved in the alleged intimidation in the Westport district. His letter was to have serious consequences for certain families in Westport.

Dear Sir,

In reply to your of the 24th inst, I am prepared to give to Mr Long, the names of the parties, I consider it would be highly objectionable to give land to, in view of the future preservation of peace & good conduct, in this parish. I am also prepared, to give the grounds of my objections, which are fully known to government officials, who have a knowledge of the district. They are as follows,

Owen Hughes, Manus Kane, & Patrick McDonnell all well known to the police, as actively engaged, some years ago in swearing in members of a secret agrarian Society. Of this Society, which was responsible for many outrages in the parish, Owen Hughes was president, Manus Kane was Secretary, & Harry Hughes was Treasurer. Their crimes are beyond number. A principal object was, to secure to & Charles Hughes, a draper in Westport, & brother to Owen Hughes, the exclusive custom at his shop, of the people of this parish of Aughagower. In furtherance of this object, certain women of this parish, cousins of the Hughes, patrolled the streets of Westport on market days, to spy upon any of the parishioners, who want to do business in any shop but Hugheses, & to denounce them to the society, for daring to do so. The parties guilty of this misconduct were, Mrs Lavelle (widow), Mrs James Touhay, & Mrs Walter Heneghan, & Charles Hughes is now on the run

For denouncing this conduct in the Church, on several occasions, the heads of the society made many unoffichial [*sic*] attempts to interfere with me, & to injure me; mortally killed all the fowl one night of the people who refused to lessen their contributions to my support; wrote shocking false statements to the Archbishop on several occasions, cut the tail off my calf, upset my stacks of oats (70 st).

It is known to the police, that on several occasions, Hughes & the Society interfered with the course of justice, in private cases, by supplying witnesses to give false evidence, or by engaging to get up riots, to prevent the auction of cattle, seized under decrees for rent issued by the County Court Judge. This was notorious in the case of The Crown, at the prosecution of Constable Finn against Hoban, & in the civil case of the Westport District Council against the purchaser of Lord Sligo's wards, whose name I forget. The police could supply the names of the seven false witnesses, in the Court. Hughes himself was the primaful [*sic*] witness in the District Council case ... The principal workers amongst those, who can be disclosed as the unofficial members of the Society & who did most to promote its objects, were Hubert the son of Edwd Reid of Creggandarragh, John the son of John Cusac[k] of Mace, John Foy of Aughagower.

It must not be understood that the above is at all, a complete list of the evil deeds of the Society. It is far indeed from it, & gives but a faint idea of the terror they infussed [*sic*] into the minds of the people of the parish, & by which they drove people to crime, who if left to themselves, would never think of committing such.

I remain

Yours faithfully

John Flatley PP[29]

Fr Flatley, who must have known that naming people this way would endanger their lives, had no time for secret societies or militancy of any kind. This led him to oppose the IRB, the IRA and other societies concerned with freeing the tenants of landlords. However, he also challenged the British when he viewed them to be guilty of killing innocent civilians, putting pen to paper on 4 Decemer 1920 following the death of a young man named Thomas Lyons from near Westport:

To Rt Hon Sir Neville MacCready

Commander of the Forces in Ireland

Rt Hon Sir,

As Parish Priest of the young man Thomas Lyons, lately shot at Knappagh, by a military party, under circumstances entirely unjustifiable, I beg to enter my most serious protest. When every possible allowance is made, for the requirements of self protection by the military, in the present unfortunate condition of the country, there remains nothing to be said, in justification of the action, that was taken in this case. He was alone, & being at great distance from the road, & in clear surroundings, the military party could have experienced neither difficulty or danger, if a little patience had been used, to secure his capture. Whilst the fact, that neither arms, ammunition, or any seditious literature were found on his person, goes to show, how rash was the act of the military. And, though they could not be acquainted with the important circumstance of his general excellent character, notably his careful abstention from all antisocial, or even political associations, the shooting of such a man, is certainly calculated to cause a very bad feeling, against all government action.

This case, with all its surroundings, appears to me, to be one for liberal compensation to his family, & compensation to be measured, not merely by the material loss of one true breadwinner, but such as would largely tend, to the assuagement of the latter shock, it has caused to his aged father & sister. Such compensation by the Government, would too, have the excellent effect, which no one could desire more earnestly than I do, of allaying much ill feeling in the district, against the military forces. And, I hope, I may rely on your assistance, in furtherance of the proposal.

I remain

Rt Hon Sir

Yours obdt servant

John Flatley PP[30]

Fr Flatley, however naive, was clearly motivated by a sense of justice. It did not matter to him whether those people carrying out such unjust activities were secret agrarian societies, the IRA, RIC or British military. He continued writing his letters into the spring of 1921. By doing so, he was to place his own life in mortal danger along with those he had named in Westport, including his own curate, Fr McHugh.

Meanwhile, RIC raids on known IRA and Sinn Féin families continued. The Tans were supported by the Auxiliaries' E Company in Boyle, D Company in Galway and another company in Sligo. In December 1920 the British military raided Hoban's in Castlebar. They could not find the father so they took his son, saying 'you'll do instead'. He was stripped and whipped in Eglington Street RIC barracks in Galway with a cat o' nine tails. Fr O'Malley from Castlebar wrote about the poor conditions in which the prisoners were kept in Galway Town Hall. He informed Archbishop Gilmartin that there was one room for seventy-three men and they were given no exercise. The prisoners had to sleep on the floor. Some were seriously ill.[31] Numbers for arrests and imprisonment are difficult to arrive at, but according to the Mayo newspapers there were over 150 arrests between September 1920 and March 1921. But if the numbers of arrests noted by the Argyll and Sutherland Highlanders was around 50 in November alone for Claremorris and Swinford districts, then the overall number is more likely to be above 200.

The 'legal' underpinning of all this activity was the Restoration of Order in Ireland Act passed in August 1920. Under the terms of this Act, the RIC and British military were granted strong powers that included the replacement of trial by jury with trial by court martial and the replacement of coroner's inquests by military courts of inquiry. Prisoners from Mayo were held initially at Ballina or Castlebar RIC barracks. There were a number of reports of maltreatment in Castlebar. At his court martial, Joseph Henry of Swinford claimed he had been tortured for nine weeks at Castlebar. Henry had been caught with IRA intelligence documents relating to the movements of Mayo men in the RIC. Anthony Gaughan of Bunnawillin also said he was maltreated at Belmullet and also Castlebar where prisoners' sanitation consisted of a half-full bucket for communal use. They had

Prisoners at the Curragh Camp during the War of Independence.
(Private Collection)

to use handkerchiefs to block out the smell. The cells were freezing, with broken windowpanes ensuring prisoners were exposed to rain and wind.[32]

After initial interrogation at Castlebar, prisoners were moved to Galway Town Hall or Eglington Street RIC barracks while they awaited trial by general court martial at Renmore barracks, Galway. Other Mayo prisoners were sent to Sligo Jail and then transferred to Belfast for court martial. The more senior ranking IRA officers like Paddy Hegarty were imprisoned in England. Hegarty, from Lahardane, was a senior officer in the North Mayo Brigade and a member of Mayo County Council. His house was raided by the Tans in July 1920 and his family, including his sister, subjected to terrible treatment.[33] Hegarty was sentenced to two years' imprisonment with hard labour. While serving his term in Liverpool, he learned of his father's death after yet another severe beating by Black and Tans on Christmas Day 1920.[34]

Other Mayo men and women were imprisoned in Galway Jail or at internment camps in Ballykinlar, County Down, or in the Curragh, County Kildare. The *Mayoman* carried an account of conditions in

Captain William O'Keefe, Staff Officer South Mayo Brigade and Manchester ASU, IRA, 1919–21. National Army Officer Transport, Limerick. Resigned August 1922 and remained neutral throughout the Civil War. (Courtesy Celio Burke (née O'Keefe))

Ballykinlar by Mr John Rice of Clonegal, County Carlow, who was released on parole in March 1921:

> The food is bad, the beds are bad and the sanitary conditions are bad ... itch, mumps and scabies are raging in the camp. Three days a week the prisoners are provided with bacon for dinner, the sight of which is almost calculated to provoke nausea. The men seldom touch it ... Two water-soaked potatoes are also 'dished up' ... The beds are composed of three hard planks, covered by a mattress which weighs about 11 pounds. Three light blankets added to this constitute the whole bedding. The huts, our informant compared to cattle sheds, cold and damp. At night a chilling wind adds to the general discomfort. The camp, which is divided into two parts, now contains about 1,600 men and will hardly contain any more.[35]

Those who managed to evade capture went on the run in other parts of Ireland or sometimes in Britain. William O'Keefe's family ran a

War of Independence medal with Cómhrac bar of Captain William O'Keefe, South Mayo Brigade, Claremorris Company and Manchester ASU, IRA. (Courtesy Celio Burke (née O'Keefe))

cycle works in Claremorris. He described how IRA dispatches were hidden inside the handlebars or the saddle post and delivered to the various companies around the South Mayo Brigade. O'Keefe did not fancy spending his time in a prison camp and so left for Britain. He ended up in Manchester where he joined an IRA Active Service Unit. The unit was formed mainly from men working at the Ford Motor Company, Trafford Park. O'Keefe soon linked up with other Mayo men. Among them was Jack Finnan, who had laid the block floor for St Colman's Roman Catholic Church, Claremorris, in 1910. Together, they engaged in burning barns and warehouses and trying to procure arms for dispatch to Ireland.[36]

While violence became more widespread the County Council tried to maintain a sense of governance and stability throughout Mayo. It was a very difficult task. The main priorities for the Council were structural, educational and political. Lack of finance became a serious problem as the Council failed to recoup £2,000 from the British War Department for the damage to Mayo's roads caused by constant British military traffic. An initial payment of £94 10s was received in August but that was all.[37] In November, the Council carried out a threat not to make good the damage to the roads as the War Department had not paid the outstanding bill for repairs. The resulting impasse did more to hamper the British than the IRA in terms of wear and tear on its vehicles on poor Mayo roads. The financial crisis was compounded by the County Council's refusal to recognise the British Local Government Board. This was the body that issued grants to county councils and reviewed their financial books and statements. For Mayo County Council to recognise the Board's authority would be to recognise Britain's authority to govern Ireland. The Council held firm and a stand-off ensued whereby no grants were forthcoming.[38]

The Council was also shocked to discover that the previous County Council had paid the 'Milling Tax' that had been levied on Westport UDC after the murder of John Charles Milling RM. So angry were the members of the current Republican County Council that they voted to prosecute the old County Council before a Republican court.[39] This decision was never carried out. The Westport UDC failed to pay its share of the tax and at one point owed the County Council £5,429 9s 4d. The dispute was not resolved until the summer of 1923.[40] The Council also established an educational committee to support young talent through scholarships. A special levy of one penny was also added to the annual amount paid by ratepayers to support the teaching of Irish. All Council officials were expected to speak Irish and those who did not were ordered to learn it by undertaking a special course. The Council issued a restriction on reporters in that its public sessions could only be printed in Irish. The County Secretary, M. J. Egan, learned to write his name in the old Gaelic script and signed off the minutes, written in English, with his name in Irish:

M. Mac Aodhagáin, Rúnaire.

Politically, the County Council maintained its allegiance to Dáil Éireann in spite of the many challenges it faced. Nothing expressed this more definitively than the Council's reaction to the resolution received in December from Galway County Council 'suggesting the desirability of negotiating a truce between the armed forces of the

British Empire and the armed forces of the Irish Republic'. Chairman Conor A. Maguire proposed a counter-resolution: 'We consider that in the present crisis the making of Peace with England should rest with Dáil Éireann. We deprecate the interference of bodies of individuals in a matter which should solely concern the people's elected representatives and we refuse to be stampeded by either terrorism or false promises and we hereby reaffirm our allegiance to Dáil Éireann.'[41]

In the meantime, Archbishop Gilmartin continued in his condemnation of violence and killing. On 9 December 1920, he wrote to the Secretary of State for War, Winston Churchill, urging him to use his influence to secure a peaceful settlement.[42] Churchill replied that 'the murders of the police and military must stop. Until they stop there can be no recovery and things will go from bad to worse.' Churchill concluded with a statement of hope about the introduction of Home Rule for the south of Ireland in the Government of Ireland Act 1920.[43] Gilmartin wrote back to Churchill regretting that the Secretary of State was not more encouraging. He proposed that if Churchill were to suspend all military and auxiliary police operations for a month to six months then the IRA would observe the truce. The Archbishop continued: 'then the elected representatives of the Irish people would have an opportunity to lay their demands before the British Cabinet'. Gilmartin was very hopeful of a lasting agreement emerging. In concluding his letter he singled out one armed force for special mention. 'The Auxiliary Police are exercising terror & torture unchecked & still the spirit of Sinn Féin is as strong as ever.' A blunt PS added: 'It is only right to add that nobody here takes the Home Rule Bill seriously.'[44] That ended the communication with Churchill! However, the Archbishop continued his appeals for peace through a number of contacts that were to bring his ideas to the Cabinet tables of both the British and Irish governments right up to the months before the Truce in July 1921.

In the 'Relatio Status', the official report on the Diocese of Tuam to Pope Benedict XV for 1920, the Archbishop informed His Holiness in no uncertain terms of the behaviour of the Black and Tans and the Auxiliaries:

Si quis de condicione materiali Dioeceseos dicere vult, milites Brittani et alii mercenarii ab Anglis missi maximas in nos iniurias ac damna intulerunt. In hac Dioecesi mercenarii Britanni octo saltem cives causa inaudita trucidaverunt, aliquot cives vulneraverunt, multas domos incenderunt, passim felis ac scorpionibus ita utebantur ut Dei sola miseracordia multi alii mortem vitare possent. Quae facta sunt postquam quidam mercenarii armati Brittanorum necati sunt vel vulverati: hoc omne genus agenda nos publice condemnavimus.[45]

[Speaking of material matters the Diocese would wish to let it be known that the British Military and their mercenaries sent by the English have caused much injury and damage. In this Diocese British mercenaries murdered at least eight people, without due process, they injured others and burnt down many homes. They struck like scorpions, at random and it is only thanks to God's mercy that many others were not killed. It is true that after this armed British mercenaries were killed and wounded. We have publically condemned all actions of this kind].

By December DI Owen Spellman of Claremorris had proved his worth to the RIC senior command. Spellman had concentrated specifically on putting the local IRA out of action. He was highly successful, arresting thirteen members of the Claremorris Company. Six had already been court-martialled and sentenced to imprisonment at Ballykinlar camp, County Down.[46] Another seven were held in very overcrowded conditions in Galway Town Hall. Among them were Tom Ruane and Joe Brennan. Ruane, who worked in Brett's Store, was charged with possession of a Lee-Enfield rifle and 120 rounds of ammunition. Brennan was charged with possession of receipts for Dáil Éireann Bonds and the War Fund. He was also charged with reading the Sinn Féin Manifesto in public. Ruane was found not guilty and released while Brennan was given an eighteen-month sentence without hard labour.

For the successful operations of his policemen DI Spellman was promoted and sent to Waterford on 1 December 1920, where

Police Museum, Belfast

Charles Wilkins, District Inspector, Claremorris RIC, 1921–22 (front row, second from left). (Courtesy The Police Museum, Belfast)

he eventually assumed command of all RIC forces in the city.[47] Spellman's departure was part of an overall restructuring of the District Inspectors of County Mayo at the end of 1920. DI Wilkins took command at Claremorris and DI Donnellan at Westport. Both of these officers were to distinguish themselves by achieving major successes against the Mayo IRA. Two other officers were to bring the reign of terror to new depths. Both were Irishmen. The first was DI White, a Catholic from Roscommon stationed at Ballina. A former officer in the Royal Field Artillery, his men were to develop a culture of torture and murder. The second RIC officer to become notorious was DI Fuge, a Presbyterian from Waterford, who was stationed at Newport. He was a former lieutenant in the British Army. He led his men on some truly terrifying raids. Ned Lyons, O/C Newport IRA, was captured and tortured to such a degree that his health never recovered. He died a few years later. Lyons' capture was to bring about the promotion of one of the most formidable opponents the British and RIC would ever face in the War of Independence in Mayo, Michael Kilroy.

As 1920 came to an end, the RIC and British military in Mayo had good reason to ring in the New Year with good cheer. Many officers of the IRA had been arrested, court-martialled and imprisoned. Sinn Féin's organisational effectiveness had been seriously affected with many of its officials also interned. A new batch of Black and Tans arrived in Mayo in December along with four Crossley Tenders and five Ford motor cars. This was in addition to the one Crossley and two Ford cars the Mayo RIC already held. These new vehicles were to be 'a valuable asset' in increasing the mobility of the RIC throughout the county in 1921. The RIC were not, however, naive enough to think the IRA was defeated, CI Steadman warning 'Sinn Féin is not going to abandon its hold without a struggle and that it is preparing a new offensive as a counter reply to the more recent more vigorous action of police and military.'[48] The construction of barbed-wire defences for RIC barracks continued 'as rapidly as possible'.[49] A serious confrontation with the Mayo IRA was expected.

British continued their counter-terror strategy throughout 1921 while simultaneously seeking a settlement behind the scenes. The Dáil continued with its establishment of the new Irish State. This became increasingly difficult with many TDs in jail or abroad in the United States. For the IRA's GHQ, the involvement of areas other than Cork, Tipperary and Dublin in larger operations was crucial to success and to easing the pressure on these beleaguered counties. In Mayo, the training was completed and enough arms and ammunition had been gathered. It was now time to strike. No GHQ manuals could prepare Commandants Tom Maguire or Michael Kilroy for what was to follow, only the bitter experience of battle itself.

On 9 January 1921, the RIC, led by Head Constable Wray, raided Beckett's saw mill on Shamble Street, Ballina. They captured Patrick Coleman along with a large quantity of arms and ammunition. The RIC were apparently acting on information received as they knew exactly where to look for the weapons – in a pit under a saw bench. For Coleman it was the beginning of a nightmare. He was taken to the RIC barracks and interrogated a number of times. DI White and Sergeant O'Brien with two others 'questioned' him first.

IRA cap badge. Based on the Dublin Brigade of the Irish Volunteers, this cap badge replaced all regional versions to become the official symbol of the IRA. The Irish Volunteers officially became the Irish Republican Army in 1920 after Cathal Brugha, Minister for Defence, proposed that the Irish Volunteers take an oath of allegiance to Dáil Éireann. (Courtesy Thomas Smith)

They used the revolver belonging to a Sergeant Armstrong who had been shot dead the previous July by an IRA squad in Knox Street. Armstrong's death had caused great outrage in the town. The Cavan man had been well liked and had been close to retirement. He left behind eleven children. Coleman was present the night Armstrong was killed, which might explain why his treatment at the hands of the RIC was so savage. He was dragged out to the barracks yard at 2 a.m. and placed before a firing squad. He was told to name others in the local IRA or he would be shot. A mock execution followed where DI White discharged two barrels of a shotgun. Coleman fainted as he thought he had been shot. He came to in his cell, looked up and saw the chimneys of the Imperial Hotel. 'This isn't heaven anyway, because the chimneys looked more like Hell,' he recalled. Next evening Coleman was interrogated by Captain Harrison of

British military intelligence using a small automatic pistol. DI White returned to the cell and shouted at Coleman, 'you white-livered f....r, if you weren't going to be shot tonight I'd burn the skin off you with this lamp'. Coleman related the subsequent events of that night to the Bureau of Military History in 1957:

> At about midnight I was ordered out of the barracks and placed in the middle of three cars. We moved off past the railway station out the Pontoon road which crosses the line at Rehins, about a half a mile from the town. I was ordered out of the car. The night was not fully dark and I was placed in charge of a man who was in civilian clothes, as were the rest of the party (the usual attire for the Murder Gang). As all the others had faded into darkness I decided to jump on my escort and if possible make a run for it. I had my hands over my head and started to edge towards him; he spotted it and said, 'Coleman, if you come any closer I'll give it to you in the guts.' Shortly afterwards a number of them came back and ordered me to double down a narrow country road which led to Ballinahaglish Graveyard. I started to run at top speed down this road and fire was opened on me. I was hit by a bullet which struck me in the right thigh and this knocked me on the road. I got up again and started to run towards the old school when I noticed a black mass on the road. This was the first car of the convoy and was drawn across the road to bar my escape. Fire was opened on me from the car. I then saw what they were about to do and wheeled sharply to run back when I received another bullet in the right shoulder. I turned and jumped the ditch with a wire fence on top. I shall never know how I managed to do so.
>
> I headed towards the Pontoon road, crossing the railway line and the road and dropped into a marshy field and made my way as best I could through flooded fields in which I was nearly drowned as I fell several times through the loss of blood. I was making for a house which was on hilly ground; it took me a long time to reach this house on account of climbing the hill. I got to the door and knocked without reply. I went a short distance away and lay down for a short time. I then got

up and rushed at the door, which went in with me, where I
fell on the floor in the kitchen. I saw a man standing over me
with a hurricane lamp and I recognised him as John Reape of
Cloonturk ... He got me strips of cloth, helped me to strip and
get into bed where I made the tourniquet for the thigh wound
but could not do anything for my shoulder. As the bedclothes
were soaked in blood I told him to burn all the clothes which
he did. I then asked him to get me a priest.

At this point, Reape took Coleman to an outhouse and covered him
with hay. Coleman continued his story: 'a man's hand pulled the hay
from around my face. I then recognised him as a Ballina man named
Paudge Sweeney ... when he saw the state I was in he started to cry
and produced a bottle of brandy of which I took a good slug ... I was
brought to Frank Curran's of Gortoher who put me up in his own bed
and sent his wife and children to Ballina. Curran was a Volunteer.' A
Dr David Rowland of Ballina came to dress Coleman's wounds, but
'as there was no anaesthetic he gave me plenty of brandy during the
operations. The Doctor said I was very lucky as both bullets had gone
right through ... Dr Crowley at Ballycastle who dressed my wounds
again told me, after examination, that one of the bullets had just
missed the femoral artery.'[50]

Coleman was blessed not only to have escaped but also to have
survived his wounds. DI White was seriously concerned at Coleman's
escape. An RIC statement was issued to the press on 12 January to
the effect that Patrick Coleman had revealed under questioning that
he would lead them to an IRA arms dump at a farmhouse. Coleman
then used the opportunity to make a dash for liberty. Fire was opened
on him and he was seen to fall after being hit in the leg.[51]

The RIC account would appear plausible enough. Coleman
was afraid and took an opportunity to make a break for freedom.
However, other accounts of terrifying brutality in Ballina offer strong
support for there being a culture of extreme violence and murder by
the RIC under the leadership of DI White. In February 1922, the
Western People reported the claims made at the Ballina court sessions.
What transpired was a litany of shocking accounts of incidents against
Mayo men and women at the hands of the Black and Tans, Auxiliaries

and military. Many have ridiculed these accounts as attempts by people to make money out of non-existent injuries. Neverthless, the accounts given in court that day under oath and at other court sessions in Mayo are confirmed independently in the newspapers. They are also confirmed in contemporary witness statements collected by the Tuam diocese, private letters and statements to the Bureau of Military History in the 1950s, among other sources. One such account from February 1921 was recorded by Rev. Fr McDonald, parish priest of Newport, the RIC district under DI Fuge's command. It makes extremely disturbing reading:

> I was roused from sleep by a woman knocking loudly at my door. She told me that Crown Forces had just wrecked her brother's house, and had so beaten and trampled on her brother that she was not sure if he was still alive. She begged me to come with haste. When I came, I found the man thrown on a bed in a neighbour's house and two women who had towels and water were washing away the clotted blood and trying to stop the wounds from which blood was still flowing. The condition of the man appalled me. His head was swollen and his hair was matted with blood. His face was so disfigured with wounds that I could not recognise his features. Blood was still coming from his mouth. His entire body had been so kicked and crushed that he was writhing with pain and begged those beside him to turn him now on one side and again on the other. In the course of 28 years which I have spent ministering to persons who were dying from disease or from accident or from injury I have never seen anything to approach in frightfulness the condition of that man that Sunday morning. And all for absolutely no cause. He is an inoffensive industrious fellow, about 40 years, and not married. A delicate sister lives with him. This woman struggled wildly to come to his relief but was held back by one of the raiding party who actually put his revolver in her mouth. She was as paralysed by this brutal act that when the Party withdrew she could not close her mouth.
>
> The Party next proceeded to a house which was also occupied by an unmarried man named P. Lyons [The man's

name may have been Thomas Lyons, brother of Ned Lyons, O/C Newport IRA] and his sister. They accused this man of being a Sinn Féin Magistrate. They dragged him out of bed and kicked him on the floor. They took down pictures and smashed them on the floor strewing the room with broken glass. They took a table lamp and swung it at him and broke the oil container of it on his head. They took his sister's sewing machine from off its stand and dashed it to pieces on the floor. They then took the man by his two feet and dragged him on his naked back over the shattered glass and metal. They next made him stand up and followed him drawing kicks at him forcing him to run barefooted over the splintered glass from corner to corner of the room. After that they took him to a small room at the end of the house and put him into his sister's bed. When they had confined him there, they went out into his stables and brought in his horse and a cow and forced them into the narrow room where the man was lying. They then secured the door and went outside and banged stones through the window at the horse and the cow to madden them and to force them to trample on the prostrate victim. I came there a few hours later and saw the wreckage all over the house and the fresh horse manure in the bedroom.

They invaded four other houses in that district that morning. Their savagery was superlative. Their language was laden with filth. All the infamy could not be related, but it was like an orgy of demons on the morning of the Lord's Day.

The purpose of the whole fiendish thing was a calculated effort to exasperate the people of a peaceful district which through the efforts of Parochial clergy has been free from crime.[52]

There are simply too many accounts to discount the counter-terror strategy unleashed by the RIC under Lloyd George's instruction in July 1920 to believe that the Tans and the Auxiliaries were simply rogue elements. Not all RIC District Inspectors permitted their men to engage in this behaviour, but enough did so to shock even the Prime Minister. At a Cabinet meeting on 29 December 1920, Lloyd George, with General Macready's support, confronted General Tudor over the level of drunkenness among the Auxiliaries and the poor quality of RIC officers. General Macready said he 'did not think it possible to have the police more disciplined; they had no code to work under, and the officers were not the standard of men to enforce discipline'. Tudor defended the RIC, saying 'their discipline was very fine; they were entirely under the control of their officers'. Lloyd George impressed upon Tudor the importance of a disciplined police force.[53] It made little difference to the situation on the ground in Ireland as the violence continued. Patrick Coleman's account is of significant historical importance as he names the individuals involved, describes the events as they began to unfold and also because he survived an attempt to murder him. Michael Tolan, of the Ballina IRA, was not to be so lucky. DI White would make sure there would be no one to tell tales a second time.

The IRA in Mayo had been a long time in training. They watched as the RIC carried out their campaign of terror throughout their county. The IRA would appear to have been slow to react directly against the RIC. This would suggest the IRA in Mayo were either afraid or demonstrated considerable discipline in not engaging in random acts of retaliation. Subsequent events would demonstrate there was no lack of courage among the Mayo brigades. The time was approaching where the IRA would have their opportunity to face the RIC and the British military in action. Their early experiences were to be painful but they were to learn quickly. The existence of the Republic hung in the balance.

Commandant Tom Maguire was a very cautious man and for good reason. He had been on the run for many months and had more than once escaped arrest by the British military and the RIC. Thus as the time for the IRA to take the field of battle drew near he revealed his true intentions to very few. One evening in early March 1921, as light began to fall, a group of men assembled at Forde's home near Ballinrobe. Commandant Michael O'Brien struck a match and lit an oil lamp. The light slowly illuminated the faces of Commandant Tom Lally and Captain Paddy May, senior officers of the South Mayo Flying Column. As Commandant Maguire placed a map of Partry on the table before his officers, they looked at each other with the knowledge that their war was about to begin.

5

'Desire for Revenge': Ambush – The Road to Victory

On the evening of 28 February 1921, DI McNeill of Castlebar concluded the County Inspector's report for Mayo in Steadman's absence. He was a worried man, with several 'cases of anticipated ambushes where rebels were seen lying-in-wait ... reported during the month'.[1] The RIC were also searching for the IRA's newly acquired weapons and ammunition. In early February, the RIC had raided the homes of Pat Lambert, Martin Geraghty and Jack McDonagh. All of them were members of the West Mayo Brigade and on the run. Some of the family members were seriously maltreated in an attempt to extract information, but the police found nothing and were none the wiser as to the location of the local IRA arms dump.[2] These raids were to mark a significant shift in RIC behaviour in Westport. DI Maguire, who had cooperated with the IRA, tipping them off in advance of raids and passing on RIC intelligence documents, had just been moved to the RIC depot in the Phoenix Park so that his superiors could keep a closer eye on him. His replacement, DI Peter Donnellan, was to pursue the IRA with deadly force. While Westport was the focus for increased RIC activity, IRA Commandant Tom Maguire was ready to strike in south Mayo.

On Monday 7 March 1921, a Crossley Tender of the 2nd Battalion Border Regiment left Ballinrobe for Castlebar. On board were two officers, Captain Chatfield and Lieutenant Craig, fifteen other ranks and a Royal Army Service Corps driver. The Border Regiment were experienced and well-trained soldiers. In order to keep the soldiers busy the officers had entered the Battalion in many sporting competitions. Their boxing team had won the Fifth Division Cup at the Curragh in 1920. The football team, meanwhile, were beaten by the 1st Battalion Wiltshire Regiment in the final of the Army Cup (2-0). Military training also continued. The newly formed Machine Gun Platoon came second among all British regiments in a competition in September 1920.[3] The Machine Gun Platoon was then based at the RAF Aerodrome, Castlebar. The Border Regiment was certainly no pushover.

Tom Maguire's men lay in wait 1 mile north of Partry village at Kilfaul. The IRA column was composed of the Srah and Ballyglass Companies. They were armed with some rifles but mostly shotguns. The IRA took up positions on both sides of the road while Maguire assigned Martin Conroy as marksman to pick off the driver. Another man was detailed to throw grenades while the others were to lay down fire once the ambush was on. Conroy succeeded in hitting the driver and the vehicle came to a halt. Captain Chatfield was hit in the knee and severely injured. Corporal Bell was badly wounded and Privates Warlde and Southworth were also hit.[4] The Volunteer throwing the grenades forgot to pull the pins out and they failed to explode. A number of soldiers took cover behind the lorry and returned fire. Hopelessly outnumbered by an IRA column of up to sixty men, the soldiers retreated towards Ballinrobe after a brief exchange of fire. The others around the cab of the lorry surrendered after a short, sharp engagement.[5] One of the Volunteers picked up an unexploded grenade with the intention of throwing it among the prisoners. Maguire stopped him. The Commandant described the scene immediately after the ambush: 'Rushing out upon the road, I reached the lorry. There was a young soldier there apparently dead, with his head hanging over the side. When he felt someone near him he looked up nervously. He was bleeding from the face. Opening the eyelids he gazed at me with anxious brown eyes, and I returned the stare.'[6]

Maguire and his men had carried out the first attack on the British military in Mayo since 1798. He and his Brigade staff had reconnoitred the ambush position beforehand. They had chosen their men well, anticipated events and carried out the attack successfully. From now on Maguire's Column had to be ever more watchful as the RIC and British military were determined to catch up with them. The British wounded were attended to by Commandant Michael O'Brien. After the IRA withdrew, the wounded were taken to the County Infirmary in Castlebar in a car owned by a civilian, Mr Lewis, who happened upon the aftermath of the ambush. That night Lewis' car was set alight and destroyed by the IRA while parked in his garage at home in Castlebar.[7] Corporal Bell died of his wounds on Tuesday 12 March.

The reaction to the ambush was predictable. Scores of RIC and British military searched the district making arrests. Later that night, a farmer was shot dead in his home at Srah. Dublin Castle issued a statement declaring the victim to be 'Thomas Horan, aged 45, farmer, Ballinrobe district ... having been killed, apparently, by a shotgun'.[8] The use of word 'shotgun' was cynical, as it gave the impression the wound was either self-inflicted or carried out by the IRA. Rev. Fr O'Malley, a local parish priest, wrote to Archbishop Gilmartin about the ambush and its aftermath. He said he had come upon the scene of the attack after the IRA had gone. The soldiers, clearly in an agitated state, roughed him up and pointed revolvers and rifles at him. They blamed him for the ambush. The priest said he was in real fear for his life. Fr O'Malley wanted to go to the lorry where the wounded men were stretched out in order to anoint them. The officer told him to stay away. He then described how Horan, who was actually closer to sixty years old, had been shot with a rifle by the RIC; the Dublin Castle account was a complete misrepresentation.[9] Horan fell into the fire when shot and had to be pulled out by his daughter, Mary. He suffered a dreadful open head wound and lay dying in his daughter's arms for a number of hours.[10] A British officer arrived and sent for a doctor, but the wound was too severe and Horan died that evening. Fr O'Malley believed Horan was killed because he had placed a claim for fowl looted by the British military while searching in his village six weeks earlier, and had thus brought himself to the attention of the

RIC.[11] Like so many innocent victims of the War of Independence, Thomas Horan was easy prey for those seeking revenge.

Many people were not happy with the manner in which the IRA fought the War of Independence. They believed ambush tactics were not the practices of 'civilised' warfare. The criticism directed at the IRA did not sit easy with Michael Kilroy, O/C West Mayo Flying Column:

> We had heard so much previous to this from many British propaganda sources of the cowardice of the Volunteers in shooting at British Forces from behind fences that the taunt affected us very much. We felt it was up to us to vindicate ourselves. No man, least of all an Irishman, likes to be called a coward. We would make our slanderers swallow their ridiculous and ill-founded accusations and attack the enemy in the open, with the advantage of numbers in the open.[12]

Archbishop Gilmartin certainly had strong words to say about recent ambushes:

> What is called the IRA may contain the flower of youth, but they have no authority from the Irish people, or from any moral principal, to wage ambush war against unequal forces, with the consequences of terror, arson, and death to innocent people. I have been accused of strengthening the arm of the [British] Government by such pronouncements as this, but my answer is that I must give my people moral guidance, even though corrupt politicians turn the preaching and the Gospel to corrupt ends.[13]

There is little that is civilised about warfare. Once battle is opened it must be pushed to a conclusion. If the IRA in Mayo or in any other county had engaged the British Army and RIC in conventional military tactics it would have been annihilated. The British and many of the RIC had serious military experience. They had just endured a war that had seen the introduction of poison gas, flame-throwers, tanks, aircraft and concentrated artillery bombardments. The IRA

War of Independence Medal of Commandant P. R. Hughes, Claremorris Battalion, IRA, and lid of a box of gelignite explosive with ammunition including dumdum round for a Luger pistol. (Courtesy Brendan Hughes)

had neither the men nor the material to engage in this sort of warfare, and any attempt to do so led to disaster. The only chance for the IRA was to choose its ground, its moment and use the element of surprise. This is how Commandant Peadar MacMahon had trained the Mayo brigades. The tactic of ambush would tilt the odds in the IRA's favour.

With the ambush at Partry as inspiration, the West Mayo Flying Column was also seeking contact with the RIC or British military. Michael Kilroy of Newport had been promoted to O/C of the Flying Column, which was formed with Volunteers from Castlebar, Newport and Westport. They soon opened their account. On the moonlit night of 22 March 1921, Sergeant John Coughlan and three constables from Westport were on a cycle patrol near Carrowkennedy. Turning off the Westport to Leenane road, they dismounted to walk up a steep incline on a boreen to Oughty. As they reached the top of the rise, they were confronted by Kilroy, Brodie Malone and Joe Ring. The rest of the column was nearby but was not involved in the firefight that occurred. Kilroy and Malone were armed with Mauser automatic pistols or 'Peter the Painters'. 'My bullets were only .32 – shining and clean nickel – that had not the stopping power of a heavier lead bullet and would only sting and annoy if you did not hit some vital part of the body,' Kilroy recalled.[14] Both IRA and RIC opened fire simultaneously. Ring and Malone managed to wound one constable and take him prisoner. Kilroy described those frantic moments: 'I had a terrible buzzing in my ear, as a result of a near miss by a bullet that must have almost got its mark ... I was in a desperate hurry and wondering what was holding up that hunk of lead I expected. The breadth of the road, a matter of nine feet, only separated us.' One policeman in attempting to leap a fence had knocked himself out and Joe Ring disarmed him. Two other policemen had also jumped over the fence. Kilroy ordered them to out on the road:

> The furthermost of the two, about five yards away, was slow in coming out, so I hurried to him and kept the light shining on him. His revolver was attached to him by a lanyard. It was lying on the ground, at full cock, with his hand open and just over it. I felt he was going to grab it and fire at me. He looked very wild and aggressive, and took no notice of my repeated orders ... I threatened to fire but it had no effect on him, so I did fire, as I thought, along his ribs ... 'I am done now,' he said, and walked out on to the road. I regretted this very deeply afterwards.[15]

Sergeant Coughlan, the man Kilroy had shot, died shortly after the firefight.

This first operation, though small, was a great boost to the morale of the Flying Column.[16] Four days later, in the early hours of Saturday 26 March, the RIC in Westport set out from their barracks to inflict severe retribution on the town and district of Westport. Homes and businesses of IRA families were specifically targeted. Among them was Charles Hughes, whose name had been given to Captain Siltzer the previous January by Fr Flatley of Aughagower. Hughes, Chairman of the UDC, had his home and business blown up with grenades, and his furniture piled high in the street and set alight. Also destroyed in a similar fashion was the pub and grocery shop of Thaddeus Walsh, Chairman of the Rural District Council. Other families to face the destruction of their homes were John McDonagh, John McGreal and Patrick Kitterick. Families in the surrounding district, too, faced a night of terror, with homes in Carrowkennedy, Carrowbawn and Drummindoo burned to the ground or wrecked.[17] The fact that the wrecking of Westport took place four days after Sergeant Coughlan's death shows it was well planned and organised by the local RIC under DI Donnellan. For many years they had sought to deal with the

Westport IRA. They were sure this night had taught the West Mayo Brigade a valuable lesson. However, rather than having a punitive effect, the destruction only increased the resolve of the IRA to deal a knockout blow to the RIC. While events were gathering pace in west Mayo, the east of the county saw increased RIC and British military activity.

On the night of Good Friday 25 March 1921, a party of armed and masked men, claiming to be members of the IRA, attacked the house of Rev. Fr O'Hara, parish priest of Kiltimagh. They attempted to gain access to the house and fired a number of shots through the front door. O'Hara was singled out for this attack because he had gone to the British military camp at Claremorris to complain about the treatment meted out to young men in Kiltimagh a few days earlier. A group of young men had been kicked, punched and marched out of the town at bayonet point to a bridge and forced to jump off it repeatedly into the freezing water below. One of the town curates was also arrested and brought to Claremorris that night. The bishops and priests of the Achonry diocese condemned the outrage and were 'convinced beyond any shadow of reasonable doubt, that the perpetrators of the crime were servants of the Crown'.[18]

On the night of 29 March 1921, Constable William Stephens, a Black and Tan, was seriously wounded in Ballyhaunis. Shot in the back and legs, he died of his wounds in Galway Hospital.[19] Two days later, in the early hours of 1 April, armed and masked men called at the home of Volunteer Michael Coen at Lecarrow just outside Ballyhaunis. His cousin, also Michael, saw fifteen men, some with flashlights, get out of a car and lorry and walk up the boreen from the main road to Coen's house. The young man was dragged out of the house and severely beaten. He was then subjected to a horrendous death. A bayonet was used to cut his throat through to the windpipe. Both sides of his chest and his two feet were also stabbed. His body was left alongside a ditch 120 yards from his home where his father found him at 5 a.m. the next morning. Dublin Castle issued a statement saying Coen had been killed in Dunmore, County Galway. Sergeant John O'Sullivan of the local RIC actually called to the house the following morning, and saw Coen's body laid out on the kitchen table. O'Sullivan subsequently gave evidence at the Ballinrobe Quarter

Sessions on 27 October 1921 regarding Michael Coen's injuries. He said Michael had been subjected to a great deal of violence.[20]

The killing in east Mayo was not quite finished for 1 April. Later on, Commandant Seán Corcoran, O/C East Mayo Brigade, and Commandant Maurice Mullins were walking uphill from Crossard crossroads, about 6 miles north of Ballyhaunis. Just ahead of them, a combined cycle patrol of RIC and Argyll and Sutherland Highlanders were carrying out a search on Curley's homestead. The *Western People* printed the following account of the events as recalled by Constable Bernard Fitzpatrick at Mullins' court martial:

> The district inspector with a party of men went into the house [Curley's] to search, and witness [Constable Fitzpatrick] was ordered to remain on the road outside. While the search was in progress he saw two civilians coming along the road towards him, each pushing a bicycle. There were two members of the Argylls and another Constable with witness. When he saw the civilians approaching he took his bicycle and called on one of the Argylls to come with him. They then mounted their bicycles and went to meet the civilians, who when he saw them first were walking together. They appeared to be conversing then. When he approached them both were advancing, one about ten yards in front of the other. Witness passed the first man and told the Argyll to take charge of him. He told the second man to halt. The man drew a pistol from his pocket and fired at witness. Witness then fired his revolver at this man. Heavy fire was then opened on the witness and his comrade. He took cover and looked in the direction from which the fire came. He did not see the parties but saw the flashes about 200 yards away. The firing lasted about 10 minutes, and when it ceased he saw men running away. They appeared to be scattering left and right. He then went up to the man who he shot, and he appeared to be dead. Deceased had a Colt automatic in his right hand. The pistol contained four live rounds. The district inspector came up then and gave the order to retire. He then went up to the prisoner in charge of the Argyll and asked him his name. He said it was Mullins and that he came from Larganboy.[21]

Johnny Grealy, an East Mayo Brigade officer, also mentions of the presence of other IRA men who opened fire on Constable Fitzpatrick and the soldier from the distance in his accout of Corcoran's death. All other sources, including local accounts, say Corcoran and Mullins were alone when they confronted the RIC and troops in a shoot-out.

For DI Charles Wilkins of Claremorris, the killing of Seán Corcoran was a major victory. It was the first death of an IRA commander in Mayo. Corcoran had planned and led the storming of Ballyvary RIC barracks. He had also made an attempt to blow up Ballaghaderreen RIC barracks using a beer barrel filled with gelignite before his men were discovered by passing civilians and had to abandon the attempt.[22] His Brigade cooperated considerably with the Sligo, Roscommon and North Mayo Brigades. Much of his life since 1916 had been spent in prison, having been sentenced to terms in Frongoch, Sligo, Dundalk and Lincoln jails for Irish Volunteer activities. The effectiveness of Corcoran's Brigade, however, had been hampered by an internal split that came to a head in dramatic circumstances during the Truce.

Constable Bernard Fitzpatrick was awarded the Constabulary Medal for his actions. DI Wilkins received a Favourable Record Citation.[23] For the people of Mayo, Seán Corcoran's death was keenly felt. The funeral witnessed a huge crowd pay their respects at Kiltimagh. The RIC removed the tricolour from the coffin as it left the church. Nevertheless, the British military on duty that day stood to attention to salute the coffin as it passed en route to the Kilkinure Cemetery just outside the town.[24] The County Council were deeply shocked at Councillor Corcoran's death. They considered his early demise a great calamity not only to the County Council but to the Irish nation. They tendered to his afflicted parents and sisters their wholehearted and sincere sympathy in their bereavement.[25] While the East Mayo Brigade had just suffered its first major casualties, the North Mayo Brigade was facing threats from a variety of sources.

Just after midnight, on 3 April 1920, an RIC search party entered the village of Bonniconlon near Ballina. A dance was in progress in the local hall and the RIC suspected some IRA commanders were present. Four RIC constables who remained behind guarding the lorry outside the town came under heavy fire from a grove of trees nearby. Constable Hawkins, a Black and Tan, was hit in the hip. DI White, keeping a cool head, withdrew his men from the village to support those under fire. The IRA dispersed and the RIC consequently found a quantity of ammunition while searching the grove. DI White of Ballina was given a 'Favourable Award for gallant conduct'.[26] A few days later, Commandant Tom Ruane received the following letter from GHQ. It had been written by Thomas Moore, a post office worker from Ballina:

> Sir,
>
> My ambition for some years past was to join the RIC but having defective vision and cannot get along without Glasses I have abandoned the idea and decided to offer my services in a different way.
>
> I am at present employed in a branch of the Post Office and my position brings me from town to town. I work where messages are sent and received and judging from the way Police messages were dealth [sic] with some time ago in Castlerea I think my services would be useful.
>
> I could devote all my spare time to detective work If I would be trusted with sutch [sic]. I have a good carrickter [sic] and was never joined in any Political Society. All I require is a little instruction and I will prove worthy of any spare time position you give me.
>
> Trusting you will see your way to employ me.[27]

A typed GHQ note accompanied this handwritten letter: 'Do you know this man, and what do you know about him? You should make inquiry at once and let me know without the least delay. I am making a similar inquiry in Roscommon. If you find out other of his previous places, please send me a note of them.' It appears that even at this late stage of the War of Independence some people saw themselves as having a more certain future by serving the Crown rather than the Sinn Féin Irish government. It also demonstrates how difficult it was for the IRA in Mayo to operate effectively with people from their own county working against them. With offers such as Thomas

Alexander Boyd
North Mayo Brigade,
Ballysokeery Company,
IRA, 1921. (Private
Collection)

Moore's, the RIC were continuing to strengthen their intelligence network throughout Mayo.

Such intelligence led to the arrest of Michael J. Tolan on Friday 15 April 1921. He was taken to the RIC barracks on Knox Street [now Pearse Street] in Ballina. Tolan, a tailor, was also an IRA recruiting officer in for many years. Prior to his capture he had been on the run for a considerable time. We can be sure he received a rigorous 'interrogation'. Unfortunately for Tolan, his IRA comrades were to make matters even worse.

On Saturday 16 April, Constables Moore and Davis were on foot patrol at 9.45 p.m. when they were ambushed at the lower end of Bridge Street, Ballina. Moore was shot through the spine while his fellow constable was hit in the groin and hand. An RIC rescue party brought a severely wounded yet conscious Constable Moore back to the barracks. Shortly after 10.30 p.m., a heavily armed force of RIC and Tans swept through the town bringing utter destruction in their wake. Rifle and revolver shots interrupted by grenade explosions continued until 5 a.m. In Knox Street, T. O'Connell's,

E. P. McLoughlin's, Hanley's, Shanley Bros. and Miss Hennigan's were hit. In King Street it was M. Beirne's, Moylett Bros., Hanley's and Callan's. In Bridge Street D. Molloy's, P. McAvock's, John Roland's, M. Corcoran's, P. Beirne's and James Murphy's were targeted. In all, sixteen of the town's major shops and businesses were wrecked. Homes throughout Ballina were also scarred with bullet holes and the streets strewn with broken glass.[28] For Tolan, too, that night must have been dreadful. As the RIC took two badly wounded friends back into the cover of the barracks, they had Tolan in the cells to answer questions as to who had carried out the ambush.

Michael Tolan was visited by his mother and sister shortly after his arrest. They brought with them his shoes, as he had tried to escape arrest in his bare feet the day he was captured. He was also visited by a Miss O'Hara, a family friend, the day before he was taken away from Ballina. She gave him a green overcoat to go over his grey sports coat. It was to be the last time Michael Tolan was seen alive by his family or friends.[29] While events for Tolan were taking a turn for the worse, the South Mayo Brigade was now facing a serious crisis of its own.

Beatta Healy, a member of Cumann na mBan, cycled over the railway bridge in Claremorris. She continued down James Street and into the countryside. Her journey took her out past Hollymount to Tom Maguire's headquarters at Forde's homestead near Ballinrobe. Hidden in the handlebars of her new bicycle was a dispatch from GHQ. It had been sent over a month previously, on 15 March. Maguire would not be happy with the delay. Commandant Maguire opened the letter and had to sit down. He could not believe what he was reading: 'Information is in our possession showing that John Walsh, Thomas Brennan, and Martin Burke, wrote and addressed the following letter to David Lloyd George, Prime Minister of England.'

> Sir,
>
> We, the undersigned, beg to say that the following are the leading Sinn Féiners in this locality:–
>
> Dick Hegarty, Brownstown
> Eddie Manning
> John Macken

Martin Walsh, Kilvandooney
Peter Shelly, Ballygarris
John McDermott

Manning is their Magistrate and in the interests of peace and justice, it would be a charity to place those blackguards under restraint and have them deported from this part of the country, for its simply terrifying to see how they are acting, raiding out houses, going about threatening people to come to their courts, etc.

The letter had been written on 2 November 1920. The GHQ note continued:

From further information in our possession it would appear that the RIC have made the following notes in this case:

Hegarty is a farmer's son, 25 years, a Sinn Féiner though not active, was constant associate of John Cullina, a leading S.F. who left Ballygarris for Longford about 12 months ago.

Edward Manning farmer's son, about 23 years. Appointed S.F. magistrate and acted as such at a court held at Raheen, fining some publications for alleged breaches of licensing acts.

Martin Walsh farmer's son of Kilvandoney, reputed to be a local S.F. Registrar of Arbitration Courts, Has shown some activity as S. Feiner, but not prominent. His house was searched but nothing incriminating was found.

Peter Shally Farmer's son, 27 years, fairly active as S.F. but taking no leading part.

John McDermott Farmer's son, 27, not a prominent S.F. Not regarded as quite sane.

John Macken Farmer's son, 22 years, was a candidate for RIC about a year ago, but owing to family disabilities was not recommended, character good, but now an S.F. has not taken any active part in it.

The letter concluded: 'In view of above, can you submit a report at once in regard to the writers of the letter. They are obviously marking down the men for punishment.'[30]

Maguire had his men investigate the case immediately. The results were sent to GHQ on 21 April and detailed what happened to the members of Sinn Féin who had been identified in the letter intercepted by GHQ. Maguire said the information 'conveyed to the enemy' was correct. Hegarty, Manning and Macken had been arrested in January while Walsh and McDermott were both on the run. Shelly was not mentioned. Of the men who wrote the letter, Maguire said Walsh and Burke, from Brownstown, were farmers, almost sixty years of age and anti-Republican. Maguire thought them to be the accomplices of Thomas Brennan, an ex-RIC man, while the local people considered them to be dangerous.[31]

GHQ responded to Maguire on 6 May, noting that the O/C 'made no suggestions for dealing with the persons who wrote the letter'. The dispatch continued:

> I would like to have the following further points dealt with:
> 1. Have the men (letter) been called on by any representatives of ours and have they been given a chance of explaining?
> 2. Would it be practicable to place them under arrest with a view to discovery of the real instigator of the thing?
> 3. What punishment would you suggest, if found guilty? (Fine, destruction of property or anything else)
>
> My first dispatch to you on this matter was dated 15 March. When did this reach you? Your reply was dated 21 April and reached me on 2 May. The length of time taken in this matter is simply appalling.[32]

This demonstrates the sometimes overbearing nature of GHQ and the manner in which the brigades outside Dublin were treated. Maguire was very proud of the fact that no spy was ever shot in his Brigade area during the War of Independence. He was a man of few words and probably judged correctly that revealing too much to GHQ would bring even greater problems or a dilemma which he dare not contemplate. For GHQ, the exchange of letters with Maguire became a point of discussion involving Gearóid O'Sullivan, Richard Mulcahy and Michael Collins. Eventually, Collins resolved the problem, stating:

Leo Whelan's painting of IRA GHQ staff. Seated (l–r): Michael Collins (Intelligence), Richard Mulcahy (Chief of Staff), Gearóid O'Sullivan (Adjutant General), Eamon Price (Organisation), Rory O'Connor (Engineering & O/C Britain), Eóin O'Duffy (Assistant Chief of Staff), Seán Russell (Munitions), Sean McMahon (Quartermaster General). Standing (l–r); J. J. O'Connell (Training), Emmet Dalton (Operational Training), Seán Donovan (Chemicals), Liam Mellows (Purchases), Piaras Béaslaí (Publicity). (Photograph courtesy the National Museum of Ireland. Background to painting: Mulcahy, Risteárd. Leo Whelan's painting of the IRA GHQ staff, 1921. *The Irish Sword*, Vol. XXVII, Autumn 2010, No. 109 pp. 274–5.)

> I suggest we could come to an agreement on the basis of paragraph 3 of my minute of 6th. Make suggestion that intention on part of guilty was a serious one and fine them £50 each. It would be more serious if they gave away information on the Bde Comdt. I would suggest that discretionary power be as to the amount levied.[33]

This discussion at GHQ shows Michael Collins could be quite balanced and discerning with regard to those considered to be 'cooperating' with the RIC. While the senior officers of the IRA were discussing 'paragraph 3 ... minute 6th', Tom Maguire had led his

South Mayo Flying Column into action that involved an ambush at Tourmakeady followed by breathless pursuit and engagement across the Partry Mountains. The events of this day were to witness courage, tragedy and the makings of a legend.

On Monday 3 May 1921, an RIC supply patrol of a Ford car and Crossley Tender set out from Ballinrobe to Derrypark RIC barracks on the west side of Lough Mask. The route was to take them through the village of Tourmakeady. Waiting for them was Commandant Tom Maguire's Flying Column. The IRA had received news of the patrol from Patrick Vahy, who worked at Bermingham & Co. where the RIC collected their provisions. As the IRA took possession of the village early in the morning, Mrs Billington, the postmistress, saw Maguire giving instructions to the different sections of the Flying Column. She asked Volunteer Jack Ferguson, 'Who is the man giving the orders?' Ferguson answered, 'Michael Collins.' 'Do you think Mr Collins would like a cup of tea?' she asked. 'Mr Collins' did have a cup of tea![34] All the villagers were rounded up and taken to an unoccupied house.[35] They were kept under guard until the IRA withdrew from the village.

The Flying Column was divided into three sections. The first section, led by Commandant Michael O'Brien, was at Fair Green. The second section, led by Commandant Tom Lally, took up position at the junction opposite Hewitt's Hotel. The third section, led by Captain Paddy May, lay in wait at Drumbawn Gate. Of this last section, only Michael O'Shaughnessy had a rifle. The rest were armed with shotguns.[36] Once in position, the men of the Flying Column simply rested and enjoyed the glorious sunshine of early May.

Around 1 p.m., the Ford car, driven by Constable O'Reagan and accompanied by Sergeant John Regan and Constables Oakes and Flynn, drove into a volley of shots from Captain May's section. O'Regan was shot through the head and died instantly as the car crashed into Drumbawn gateway. A brief exchange of fire followed. O'Reagan and Oakes were now dead while Sergeant Regan lay mortally wounded. Constable Flynn survived by feigning death.[37] The IRA collected the weapons from the car and then heard firing from Fair Green. O'Brien's section had opened up on the Crossley Tender, killing Constable Power. The police managed to get out and return fire. Constable Morrow had his arm badly injured as he lay under the lorry giving covering fire to his comrades. Morrow later had to have his arm amputated. The RIC made it to Hewitt's Hotel, a solid stone building. Maguire and his men had neither the time nor the equipment to lay siege. The RIC defended their position well and drove off three IRA men posted at the junction with rifle grenades.[38]

Maguire's men split up, with some of the third section heading through a wood to the lake and turning northwards. They came under fire from the RIC at Hewitt's but managed to escape without casualties. This group met with Michael Costello at Srah; he led them through a gully in the Partry Mountains to Goat's Hotel on the Ballinrobe to Westport road.[39] Meanwhile, Maguire regrouped the remaining two sections and headed west for the Partry Mountains. He was to be criticised for leaving Hewitt's unoccupied when taking over the village. However, Maguire did not have enough men to hold Hewitt's Hotel. He clearly expected a serious fight and had all his men focused on the initial point of contact with the RIC. Maguire's action was well planned with both RIC vehicles allowed to enter the ambush position over a distance of 300 yards before fire was opened. A more serious mistake was not ensuring the telephone at the post office was put out of action before leaving. To have disconnected it prior to the ambush might have alerted the RIC in Ballinrobe that something was afoot. It had then been forgotten in the heat of the firefight. With the village in their hands, the RIC quickly called Ballinrobe, informing them of the ambush and calling for reinforcements. The chase was on.

Two lorries of Border Regiment troops arrived at Tourmakeady under the command of Lieutenants Ibberson and Smith before 3.30 p.m. A further detachment of twenty men with two Lewis guns under Lieutenant Craig headed for the northern end of the Partry Mountains at Gortbunacullin to cut off any attempt by the IRA to escape via Srah. Ibberson was enraged by what he found in the village. 'Although decorated for my part in the fighting ... believe me, I realise that what ruled my actions that afternoon was anger and desire for revenge, (this latter, in any case, being an unpraiseworthy quality) at seeing the bodies of those simple men of the RIC loyal to their uniforms, stretched out on the ground at Tourmakeady.'[40]

The RIC men were not to be the only casualties at the village. Before Lieutenant Ibberson arrived, a young IRA man, Padraig Feeney, had cycled out from Ballinrobe to try to reach Maguire's Flying Column. He arrived too late and was captured by the RIC and detained in Hewitt's Hotel. Accounts differ as to whether Feeney was 'shot attempting to escape' or was simply taken out and executed.[41] The pattern already established in such situations would seem to lend itself towards Feeney being shot as a reprisal. He was not the first and certainly would not be the last unarmed IRA or RIC man shot in such circumstances in Mayo.

Lieutenant Ibberson called for assistance from Border Regiment headquarters at Castlebar and from DI Donnellan's RIC garrison at Westport. Lieutenants Ibberson and Smith, 300 yards apart, then cleared the wooded area near Tourmakeady and began to rise up into the mountains. Ibberson later said he found himself with just two of his original detachment. The others never came out of the woods. Strangely, in another account of the events, Ibberson said his men were with him on the mountain when they first opened fire on the IRA column.[42] This may have been to cover up the embarrassment of his men going to ground in the woods.

Ibberson, now minus his officer's tunic and puttees due to the heat of the day, climbed up onto the Partry Plateau. A keen cross-country runner, he had no problem catching up with the IRA men. He continued across the mountain and eventually saw Maguire's men below him. Picking out the IRA commander, Ibberson fired his .303 rifle and hit Maguire in the arm. Commandant Michael O'Brien ran to help the wounded Maguire to cover. Incredibly, O'Brien then emerged a second time to recover a weapon dropped where Maguire was first hit. Ibberson then heard one of Lieutenant Craig's Lewis guns opening up. Encouraged, Ibberson charged his rifle with eight rounds and closed on the Column. The IRA did not open fire on the advancing British officer as he looked like Michael Costello, the Volunteer who was leading Captain Paddy May's section across another part of the mountain. Ibberson called on the men to surrender. O'Brien went for his rifle. Ibberson reacted quickly and fired, killing O'Brien and wounding Maguire in the shoulder with the same bullet. It was the seconds it took for O'Brien to cease attending

Maguire and reach for his rifle that cost him his life. Maguire always maintained it was the fact that Ibberson had taken off his officer's tunic that enabled him to get so close. Seeing O'Brien killed, the IRA opened up fire on Ibberson. Hit at least seven times, his rifle shot out of his hand and his bandolier torn from his back, he was, astonishingly still standing. Ibberson had more than demonstrated his courage and decided to pull back. Covered in blood, he staggered down the mountain, reaching a cottage where a farmer loaded him onto a cart and brought him to Lieutenant Craig's position at Gortbunacullin.

Lieutenant Smith's detachment had meanwhile captured two men, one armed with a shotgun, in the mountains during their sweep. The prisoners, Patrick King and Philip Hallinan, were repeatedly kicked and punched back down the mountain to Tourmakeady. They were then set upon by RIC constables, with Hallinan knocked unconscious by a blow to the chest with a rifle. Prodded by bayonets he came round. The prisoners were brought into a wood by two officers and were ordered to remove their boots, kneel down and prepare for death. They were questioned about the ambush. King and Hallinan maintained the British officers withdrew a short distance as if tempting them to escape, thus offering the soldiers a chance of shooting them. Eventually, they were dragged by the hair and thrown into a waiting military lorry and taken to Ballinrobe RIC barracks. They were in a sorry state, battered, bruised and bloody. They were placed in the guardroom and a doctor was called to attend to their wounds. He said they would get over it. After the doctor departed, the men were again subjected to prolonged assault in an attempt to get information from them. After a week in Ballinrobe, King and Hallinan were sent to Renmore barracks in Galway for court martial. They were released after two months on 18 July, having been acquitted.[43]

Meanwhile, reinforcements had arrived from Castlebar. Lieutenant Craig's rifles and Lewis guns kept Maguire's Column pinned down while troops attempted to close the gap between the two forces. Commandant Lally said he was ordered to take over at this stage, as Maguire was 'suffering from shock and in a very weak state'. Maguire's men had a commanding position with the high open ground sweeping away from them towards the British below. The IRA did enough to hold off their attackers until after dark.[44] Eventually, as darkness fell, the British officers sounded their whistles and recalled their troops.

Lally knew the British would be back. It was decided to save the Column at all costs. Leaving their weapons on the mountain along with the body of Michael O'Brien, the Column descended via Derassa and spent the next few days filtering through the boreens of south Mayo through Ballyglass, Robeen and back to the Ballinrobe district. Maguire was carried on Lally's back to the house of Bridgie Lally and given first aid. The following morning a double egg flip mixed with whiskey helped to revive the commandant.[45]

A search of the Maamturk Mountains planned by the British was extented to include Partry. Involved were the 17th Lancers, 2nd Battalion Suffolk Regiment, 2nd Battalion Border Regiment and 2nd Battalion Argyll and Sutherland Highlanders with RAF support in the form of a two-seater Bristol F2 aircraft. The British found twenty shotguns, three German rifles, a Lee-Enfield rifle, two revolvers and a large quantity of ammunition when they returned to the scene of the fighting.[46] It was much too dangerous to permit Maguire to remain in the house. Derassa, however, was a maze of gullies, streams, trees, ditches and small fields – ideal for concealing the wounded man. For those few days following the ambush, he was hidden in a dry stream bed under the cover of gorse bushes. In desperate pain while listening to troops searching the surrounding fields with an aircraft assisting overhead, he must have had an anxious time. Maguire said if the Column had been beaten at Tourmakeady he would not have survived his wounds. The victory gave him the will to live. Judy Joyce from Derassa ensured the injured man received care and nourishment throughout the week, regardless of the consequences if she were to be caught.[47] Maguire's luck held and by the following Saturday he was in the Ballyglass area receiving urgent medical treatment. The courage and support of the people of south Mayo had saved their commandant.

Archbishop Gilmartin of Tuam and Monsignor Dalton, parish priest of Ballinrobe, 'called to the local RIC Barracks to express their deep sympathy at the loss of men of excellent character'.[48] Reprisals were carried out with Padraig Feeney, Michael O'Brien and Tom Maguire's family homes being burned out or ransacked. Tourmakeady

Celtic cross headstone on the grave of Commandant Michael O'Brien, Vice O/C South Mayo Brigade IRA, Cong Cemetery, County Mayo. (Author's photo)

Co-op was also destroyed along with O'Toole's and a house at Drumbawn gate. There was also one more RIC casualty: Constable Tommie Hopkins of Leface, Ballindine in south Mayo.

In early May 1921, Constable Thomas Hopkins was at home on leave from police duties in County Tyrone, where he had been assigned after completing his RIC recruit training at the RIC Depot in the Phoenix Park in March 1920. The 21-year-old was on the way home from Ballindine where he had visited a neighbour. The local IRA Company lay in wait for him. Thomas Hopkins' brother had been beaten over the head with an iron bar to prevent him escaping to warn of the ambush. Constable Hopkins stood no chance, and on reaching a hill a quarter of a mile from his father's home he was captured, blindfolded and shot in the head and chest by his assailants. The execution-style killing was quite unusual for the IRA in south Mayo. Given the RIC's terrorising of civilians and captured Sinn Féin and IRA Volunteers, all IRA Brigades had received a GHQ order for RIC men to be shot on sight. Nevertheless, Dick Walsh, former Adjutant of the old County Mayo Brigade, had to travel the county personally and show individual officers the written order as they would not believe it. His thoughts on the GHQ order reflected the general attitude among most Mayo commanders towards summary executions: 'The RIC contained many decent men whose relations with the people were generally good and there were also RIC being used for Intelligence purposes. The indiscriminate killing of RIC would get a lot of our people against us. Shooting RIC during an operation was a different matter.'[49]

According to British military intelligence documents from the 5th Division, 'a certain captured dispatch written by Maguire during his activities in the Partry Mountains, revealed the fact that he probably organised, or ordered, the brutal murder of Constable Thomas Hopkins'.[50] Maguire, however, was wounded and hidden among the scrub in Derassa, totally isolated from his command structure. Nevertheless, with young Feeney murdered and homes burned out, there were a number of reasons why another senior officer or individual members of a local IRA Company might have acted independently of Maguire. The shooting of Constable Hopkins gave the Black and Tans of south Mayo a serious warning – desist from reprisals or face death. It may also have been carried out to lay down a marker as to what awaited other Mayo men who might dare to join the RIC during this period. Constable Hopkins' shooting has since been dissociated from the events at Tourmakeady but there is little doubt that the events at Leface on the night of 7 May were part of the aftermath of the battle. The deaths of both Feeney and Hopkins demonstrate the cruel nature of the War of Independence.

That Tom Maguire survived his wounds further increased his stature. While recovering in the care of Dr Maguire from Claremorris, the commandant was selected to run as a candidate for the second Dáil. Two ambushes and one running battle across the hills of Mayo ensured his victory. Ironically, Sir Hamar Greenwood, the Chief Secretary for Ireland, inadvertently enhanced Maguire's reputation when he reported the events at Tourmakeady to the British Cabinet, stating Maguire had a 200-strong force in the field.[51] It was clearly inconceivable to the British that a Flying Column of around fifty men could ambush, fight and evade well-trained British forces far superior in number. The British certainly considered Maguire a force

The .303 ammunition pouch of Constable Thomas Hopkins, RIC, who was shot dead while on leave at Leface, Ballindine, County Mayo, May 1921. (Courtesy Bridie Hopkins and family)

to be reckoned with. Lieutenant Ibberson also achieved considerable recognition for his part in the engagement. He was taken to the King George V Hospital in Dublin where his injuries were treated and he was subsequently awarded an MBE for his bravery. In war, a country needs its heroes. There can be no doubting the bravery of Maguire and his men. Inexperienced in warfare, they had given a highly effective account of themselves, inflicting defeat on the British military and the RIC while evading capture. Such a run of victories inspired those who were facing increased British military pressure in other parts of Ireland.

In the days before the ambush at Tourmakeady, the *Mayoman* published an interview Michael Collins gave to American journalist Carl W. Ackerman of the *Public Ledger*, a newspaper in Philadelphia. Part of the interview was quite enlightening:

Collins says 'We have got them beaten – practically so, and it is only a question of time until we shall have Ireland cleared of Crown forces.' 'The question is how long can you continue the fight,' I asked. Collins smiling, confident and cheerful, retorted: 'We have been fighting for 750 years for Irish independence, and I see no reason why we cannot go on for a long time still, but, seriously we are going on until we win. That is the simplest answer to your question.'[52]

The victories of the South Mayo Flying Column at Kilfaul, Tourmakeady and Partry strengthened Collins' claims. IRA resistance was spreading across the country. For Maguire, the events of Partry were to stay with him a lifetime. He was bitter with Ibberson for removing his officer's tunic and puttees, as it allowed him to get very close to the Column's position and kill Michael O'Brien. For General Tudor, O/C of the RIC, Maguire's victory and the inability to apprehend him was a strong message that his counter-terror strategy was failing. In fact, his strategy had strengthened IRA resolve and determination. It had stirred up more trouble than he could have possibly imagined. Nevertheless, events in west Mayo were to offer some hope that the IRA could be defeated.

Kilmeena, Skerdagh and Rumours of Spies: May 1921

The West Mayo Flying Column had spent the spring of 1921 attempting to ambush the RIC or British military patrols. This Flying Column was a combined unit of Newport, Westport and Castlebar IRA Companies. The actions they were to face would forge them into one of the most effective Flying Columns of the War of Independence. The fighting in west Mayo was the culmination of years of confrontation between the RIC and the nationalist movement in that part of the county. For generations the ancestors of these men had grappled with the local RIC in the hills, streets and courthouses of Mayo. Between May and July 1921 this mutual animosity exploded into violent and bloody fighting in the struggle for the ultimate victory.

As dawn broke at around 6 a.m. on Thursday 19 May, the West Mayo Flying Column moved into position for an ambush on the main Westport to Newport road at Kilmeena. Michael Kilroy O/C was hoping his Flying Column would finally see some action. About two weeks earlier, a planned ambush at the Big Wall, midway between Castlebar and Westport, had been discovered when an RIC patrol spotted IRA scouts on a hilltop. The RIC halted and turned back for Castlebar. Another group of IRA men from the Islandeady Company had been ordered to cut a trench across the main Castlebar to Westport road at Clonkeen. This would have cut off the RIC patrol from any reinforcements when the ambush at the Big Wall had begun. The RIC came upon these IRA men in the act of digging the trench and opened fire, killing cousins Thomas O'Malley and Thomas Lally. Two others, James McNulty and Frank O'Boyle, were captured.[53] Kilroy hoped for better success at Kilmeena.

Kilroy's plan was to draw out the RIC from their barracks so he sent out three sections to stir up trouble in Castlebar, Westport and Newport the night before the planned ambush. The Castlebar section returned without incident. The section sent to Newport consisted of four men led by Captain Jim Moran. Moran decided to carry out a sniping attack on the RIC barracks. Just as the IRA were in position, RIC Sergeant Francis Butler was returning to barracks from his home nearby. The IRA had been aware that Butler was one of five particular RIC men who had carried out shocking treatment of civilians in the Newport district.[54] He was shot and badly wounded from a distance of 300 yards. It is unlikely the IRA knew who the Sergeant Butler was at that range. It was just coincidence. He died the following day.[55] In response, the RIC attacked and burned down Michael Kilroy's home and his workshop. His brother, John, also had his home and business in the town of Newport destroyed. Kilroy's wife had to throw herself over her baby son Peadar as the bullets shot the plaster off the walls of the house prior to it being set on fire.

The IRA section sent to Westport consisted of approximately eight to ten men. It was led by Brodie Malone and included Tommy Heavey and Joe Baker. They did not engage in any military activity that night and at dawn had reached a house at Carraig about 5 miles from Kilmeena. They did not return in time for the ambush for reasons that have never been properly explained. Their absence, along with that of their eight Lee-Enfield rifles, was to leave the Flying Column facing a near catastrophe.

At Kilmeena, the main Flying Column consisted of twenty-two riflemen and sixteen armed with shotguns. They also had some hand grenades. Kilroy placed the main attacking sections beside the Dance Hall, facing west, at the crossroads on the main Westport to Newport road. It was just south of Knocknaboley railway bridge. Occupying fields belonging to Cummins and O'Grady, the IRA men lined up along a ditch parallel to the road about 30 to 40 yards distant. On the right flank, Kilroy placed Vice-Brigadier Ned Moane, Michael Staunton and Jack Connolly on top of Knocknaboley Hill. This spot was 150 feet high and dominated the area to the north of the IRA position. On the left flank, Kilroy posted Johnnie Gibbons and Butch Lambert on the hilltop opposite the home of Fr Conway, the parish priest of Kilmeena. This spot was 400 yards from the ambush position and covered the southern approaches from Westport. However, these men were poorly armed, with Gibbons possessing only four rounds of ammunition for a revolver and Lambert with a single-shot Martini rifle. The main part of the Column was also separated from both flanks by two roads running perpendicular, west to east, on either side of their position. Kilroy felt the flanks provided adequate cover as they had over a mile of road under observation.[56] Dr John Madden was posted 250 yards to the rear of the main Column beside a small quarry.

There was a lot of traffic on the road early in the day. There was a meeting at Fr Conway's house, 300 yards south of the ambush position. The IRA had been ready to open fire a number of times only to discover a car passing was not RIC but filled with nuns or clergy. As the day was warm and sunny, many of the men drifted off to sleep while they waited through the long morning and into the afternoon. Tommy Kitterick, the Quartermaster, set off with Captain Jim Kelly to raid Mrs Cummins' farm yard just below the ambush position on the same side of the road. Kilroy saw Kitterick and Kelly at work on the white Wyandotte chickens. 'How those two young smiling officers could lower themselves to such a slaughter was a surprise to many,' he recalled.[57] While Kitterick and Kelly busied themselves preparing a large chicken stew for the hungry men, the Column watched traffic passing on the road. Mr Cummins began walking up and down the road, hands clasped behind his back, as if he were inspecting the IRA positions. Kilroy instructed Paddy Cannon from the Castlebar Company to go down and threaten him to move off. Cummins did not loiter long after that.[58]

At around 3 p.m., just as Kitterick was ready to serve up his chicken stew, a lorry filled with RIC men suddenly came into the ambush position travelling from the Westport direction. It took the IRA completely by surprise. Nevertheless, they still managed to open fire and discharge two volleys into the vehicle before it disappeared over Knocknabollia Bridge. No other RIC lorry appeared before the Column. They must have thought it was an easy day's work. The action, however, was only about to start. DI Peter Donnellan, who was in charge of the RIC patrol, had just completed a course in anti-guerilla warfare run by the British 5th Division at the Curragh.[59] Kilroy's men were unfortunate enough to find out just how effective those tactics were to be.

The first lorry stopped 200 yards beyond the bridge. Approximately ten RIC men jumped out and doubled back to the bridge. The ditch and wall were high enough to give them complete cover from Ned Moane's position on Kilroy's northern flank. From the bridge, the RIC opened fire on the IRA in the ditch with rifles and a Lewis gun. This machine gun fired 600 rounds per minute. Moments later, a second Lewis gun opened up from the railway bridge near the parish priest's house. This second group of RIC were from two other lorries that had halted on hearing the initial firing. There were more than twenty RIC men in this group under DI Donnellan's direct command. The IRA were caught in a murderous crossfire and almost immediately began taking casualties. Captain Seamus McEvilly, hit across the stomach, was the first to be killed. The injuries were terrible, with men suffering head wounds, shattered tibia, torn calves and shredded toes. The IRA returned fire, killing Constable Harry Beckett, a Black and Tan, and wounding Head Constable Potter. This managed to hold back the RIC for a considerable period of time.

After about a half an hour, the RIC men managed to outflank the IRA on both sides. Kilroy, keeping a cool head throughout, ordered

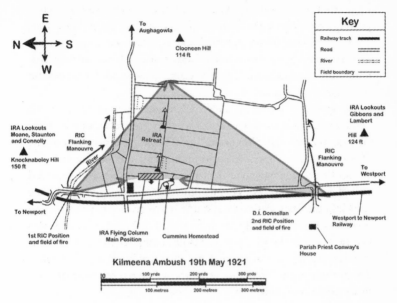

Kilmeena Ambush, Thursday 19 May 1921. (Courtesy Eoin Brennan)

his men to fall back to a second ditch 75 yards to the rear. Those on
the northern end of the IRA position were totally exposed to RIC
fire as they retreated for cover. The IRA at the southern end were
more fortunate, as a natural fold in the ground ran along a ditch on
the crest of a hill leading to the rear. This afforded invaluable cover as
they too fell back. By now, the RIC had begun to use rifle grenades.
For IRA men facing their first experience of combat this must have
been terrifying. The flanks were unable to repel the RIC pressure and
Donnellan's men succeeded in outflanking the IRA's second ditch.
Kilroy then ordered a full retreat with the intention of regrouping at
Aughagowla.

At this point John Collins was shot through the heart and killed.
He died in the arms of Kilroy's cousin Patrick O'Malley, who said an
Act of Contrition in his ear.[60] Kilroy borrowed a rifle from his cousin
and put down some accurate fire on the RIC, which enabled some of
his men, including Kitterick, to escape with their lives. Kitterick and
Kelly had been trapped in Cummins' farmyard.

Several of our men had fallen already with the first blast; sod ditches were cut in pieces and retreat from the first fences to fences in the rear began ... Kelly and I managed to get back to the ambush point where our wounded men were being taken away. Several were lying on the field, apparently dead, but we were unable to get any of them, due to the heavy crossfire. What was left of our main body endeavoured to prevent the enemy from advancing up the two by-roads on our left and right flanks and thereby getting on our rear. With our wounded men we began to retreat, whilst others fought a rearguard action. We fell back on Kelly's of the half-parish at my father's old home. The enemy, if they had any initiative, could have wiped us all out that day, but the rearguard kept them at bay.[61]

The RIC reached the house of a tailor named Flynn to the rear of the IRA position and opened fire again with the machine gun. Commandant Paddy Jordan of Castlebar came out into the open with Kilroy and together they put down covering fire to enable the surviving men to make a break from the second ditch over the crest of Clooneen Hill and away. Jordan and Kilroy came across a group of badly wounded men 150 yards from the second ditch: ·

We came across Paddy O'Malley broken leg and Thomas Nolan wounded in left knee slightly and shot through the right calf. His shin bone was broken and paralysis had set in. Also present was a chap called Pearse [Pierce], who was unwounded but would not leave his pal Tom Nolan. The wounded could not be moved any further and Jordan decided to remain with them ... I was then in desperate hurry to get away ... I heard the enemy shouting and cheering. Evidently they had advanced to the first fences we occupied, and come upon our dead and wounded companions.[62]

Kilroy felt bad leaving the wounded behind, but to take them would slow the others down and expose them to further machine-gun fire. Paddy Jordan remained with them for a little while and then made a break for the hill top. Open to fire from both flanks, the bullets cut up the ground all around him. Jordan was eventually shot down by a bullet to the head.[63] He was barely alive when captured. He died a few days later at the King George V Hospital in Dublin. That evening, as the survivors made it to Aughagowla, the list of casualties became apparent. Those who had been killed were Captain Seamus McEvilly and Thomas O'Donnell of Castlebar, John Staunton of Kilmeena and John Collins of Westport. Wounded and captured were Paddy Jordan, Paddy O'Malley of Newport who had a broken leg, Thomas Nolan of Castlebar who had been wounded in both legs, Paddy Mulloy of Tiernaure, Newport and John Cannon from Westport. Dr John Madden was already at work with Nurse Lottie Joyce tending to the wounded who had escaped. Some of the local women also gathered to assist. Mrs Kelly (then Miss Gallagher), Brigid Kelly and Mary Mulchrone were among them. Jimmy Smyth's feet were so badly injured that Dr Madden had to amputate some of his toes. Hughes from Castlebar had a flesh wound in the arm and John Chambers' knee was disjointed.[64]

Kilmeena had been a disaster for the West Mayo Brigade. The ambush had exposed both their lack of tactical awareness and shortage of adequate weapons and ammunition. The positioning of the Column left it exposed to outflanking from both sides. The outlying scouts on north and south of the Column had proved ineffective. The Column also lay in the ambush position for nine hours. It is more than possible that someone reported their presence, enabling DI Donnellan to prepare a tactical counter-strike. Kitterick said: 'We were very depressed after our defeat and the stories we heard en route did nothing to help for we heard that the Tans had pitched our dead and wounded into lorries; covered them with tarpaulin and danced on them through the streets of Westport.'[65] Sean Gibbons believed it would have been a disaster of overwhelming proportions if not for Kilroy's keeping the RIC back.[66] It had been a terrifying baptism of fire. Nevertheless, most of the Column had managed to escape. Kilroy was to learn valuable lessons for the future operation of his Column.

For the RIC, Kilmeena was a stunning victory. RIC senior officers were delighted with the success. DI Peter Donnellan was awarded the Constabulary Medal 'for gallant and meritorious service.'[67] For the RIC, the aftermath of the battle also resulted in a success that they had not dreamed possible.

Constabulary medal of
DI Peter Donnellan, RIC
Westport. Awarded
for action at Kilmeena
Ambush, 1921.
(Courtesy The Police
Museum, Belfast)

While Kilroy was evacuating his wounded on horseback to
Skerdagh at the foot of the Nephin Mountains, the IRA men
captured at Kilmeena were taken to Castlebar RIC barracks. They
were subjected to intensive questioning. One of them, Dubliner
John Pierce, chose to speak to the Divisional Commissioner, Robert
Cruise, in private. What he revealed stunned even Cruise. Pierce
handed the entire West Mayo Flying Column and some of its most
ardent supporters to Cruise on a plate. This is his statement:

> The information of John Piers [Pierce] of Westport in the Parish
> of Westport and the County of Mayo who says on his Oath
> that I am 18 years of age and my mother and brothers live at 4
> Sherriffs Place North Wall Dublin. I was at the Artine [Artane]
> Industrial School for five years and in January 1919 I came
> down as an apprentice to Pat Malone tailor Westport. I learned
> my trade in Artine. On 17 April 1921 myself & Johnny Collins

were walking out across the hill at Corrig about two miles
out from Westport when we saw seven fellow[s] together in a
hollow. They all were armed and we went over and asked to join.
I knew they were the IRA. The leader of them was Kilroy and
the others were Ainsworth (Westport) McDonagh (Westport)
Pat Lambert (Westport Quay) Naughton (Westport) Tommy
Heavey (Westport) Staunton (Mills Street Westport). It was
about 5 p.m. We stayed until 6 p.m. and came home, and joined
them at Curvy next evening. I was given a shotgun and Collins
a rifle and we both got riding breeches and leggings from
Kilroy. We remained with this flying column moving around
for a fortnight watching various roads. We slept in outhouses
and got fed from farmer's houses. After about fourteen days
we joined up with another flying column now in which there
were twenty. The leader was Jordan but Kilroy took command
and Jordan was second in command. I remember Guss Reilly,
Swift, and Dolly Chambers all of Castlebar, and Pat Cannon
Islandeady and Ainsworth of Castlebar were in the second
lot. I heard them talking of the capture of the military officers
near Castlebar a short time before and that they let them go.
From that on we lay in ambush, twice looking out for police
or military and nothing happened. The first place of ambush
was at Brackloon wood thre[e] miles from Westport on the
Louisburgh road. We remained there between 12 and 3 p.m.
The next place was at the High wall 4 or 5 miles from Castlebar
on the Westport road there were at least 70 there Kilroy was
in command. He has command of Westport, Newport and
Castlebar. We arrived at 6 a.m. and stayed there until night.
Nothing passed – the intention was to attack police or military.
Joe Ring, Bruddie Malone, and Thomas Kitterick and Johnny
Gibbons were there in addition to those in our column and a
lot from Newport I did not know. Willie Joyce (Westport) and
Paddy and Johnny Duffy from Cloonkil and Jimmy Flaherty –
an ex-soldier who worked with Kearney (Westport) – were also
there. Ned Hogan – who was working at a farm of O'Donnell's
on the Ballinrobe road was there. All these were armed and there
were bombs. This day I speak of is the day the two fellows were

killed between our ambush and Castlebar. Part of the Westport and Castlebar columns stayed together and the rest scattered. On the 8th May we were in Owenwee in houses I was in Kerns and Bruddie Molone, Thomas Ketterick and Joe Baker went into Westport leaving for it about 6 p.m. and they came back late that night – I was in bed. Next day they told us that three of them bombed the police from the Railway bridge the three were together when they were telling us. Some of the men said it was wrong because there might be reprisals in Westport. On the 13th May we had parties on the High road, the Quay road and the Mill road – about 70 in all – we were to attack a patrol eleven police were seen going up to the station but they were not seen coming down. Kilroy was in command and Jordan was there – Ring was second in command. I was also at Clogher on 22nd April when the police attacked us, and there were no casualties on either side. Joe Baker, Jim Flaherty, Paddy Duffy, Johnny Duffy, Willie Joyce, Mike Staunton, Tom Ainsworth, Johnny Collins, Ned Regan, Pat Lambert, McDonagh, Tom Basquil, and Bradly (Murrisk) were there. On last Saturday on 14th May we were at Cashel and the next night we all went to Confession at Gerraghty's Bunrobber. Father McHugh came out from Aughagower that Sunday night he was sent for. The Castlebar Crowd were with us and we were in all about 30. Johnny Collins and I were uneasy about shooting at police and he asked Fr McHugh about it and was told as long as he got the orders he was not responsible that it depended on the intention he had at the moment. He knew we were a flying column and we all Received the Blessed Sacrament the next morning from Father McHugh at Geraghty's house. He did not advise me to leave the column. On yesterday 19th about 30 of us lay in ambush from 7 a.m. until the police came at 3 p.m. Before that about five cars passed from Newport – priests and Nuns. Kilroy was in charge and Paddy Jordan second in command. The two Ainsworths were there also McDonagh, Tommy Heavey, Johnny Collins, Pat Lambart, Martin Naughton, Guss Reilly, Swift, Dolly Chambers, Pat Cannon, and there were also strangers to me there. We were all armed and there were bombs we got food during the day from a cottage near the scene – a thatched house. I was asleep when the firing started and when I awoke up I fired four shots. I did not see anything or aim at anything. I heard Kilroy give an order in two or three minutes to retire into the next field and I did so and I lay there and then ran across another field and over another bank and lay there till the fight was over and I was taken prisoner. Johnny Collins was killed next me early in the fight and I could hear groaning from others who wer[e] wounded.[68]

Speculation has continued as to whether Pierce turned informant or whether he was a spy all along. Given that DI Maguire of Westport was passing intelligence to the IRA at the time of Pierce's arrival, it is likely he would have known if Pierce was a spy. What is certain is that Pierce was seen travelling throughout the district in the back of a Crossley Tender with the RIC for a number of days following the battle at Kilmeena. He gave the RIC detailed and valuable information regarding the haunts of the Flying Column. Pierce then disappeared and was never seen again.

As a direct result of Pierce's statement, DC Cruise, backed up by the RIC and British military, paid a visit to Dominick Gereghty's of Bunrower and Fr McHugh of Aughagower on Saturday 21 May. Gereghty was forced to sign a statement that Mass and confession had been given to the IRA in his house by Fr McHugh. Cruise next visited Fr McHugh. The priest, deeply shaken, feared he was going to be killed. Cruise also visited Archbishop Gilmartin, and handed him a copy of Pierce's statement. The Archbishop also received a letter from General Macready concerning the behaviour of his priest.

The parish priest of Aughagower, Fr Flatley, saved the life of his curate Fr McHugh through his contacts in the British establishment, writing that evening to Sir Henry Wilson, Chief of the Imperial General Staff, General Macready and Archbishop Gilmartin. Next day, the IRA from Westport held up the Dublin train and confiscated the mail bags. In the process of censoring the mail, they discovered Fr Flatley's letters to Gilmartin and the British military command. Both priests were now in a desperate situation, Fr McHugh in fear of the RIC and Fr Flatley, unknown to himself, at risk of being convicted as a spy by the IRA. Kilroy held a Brigade Council to discuss Fr

Flatley's letters. Tommy Heavey said Fr Flatley should be shot as a spy as he was corresponding with Dublin Castle. Much to Heavey's disappointment, his opinion was not accepted.[69] Fr Flatley was left in peace. Had the IRA known about Fr Flatley's previous correspondence with Walter Hume Long the situation might have turned out very differently. Fr McHugh, for his part, began to conform to the political leanings of the Archbishop and was also left in peace. The behaviour of the priests of Aughagower demonstrates the common divide among many diocesan clergy. Older priests tended to be more conservative and anti-Republican whereas the younger priests were much more likely to support the IRA and Sinn Féin.

While the drama concerning the priests of Aughagower was playing out, Kilroy had managed to billet his men at Lower Skerdagh. Time was not on their side. The RIC were still on their trail and at 5 a.m. on 23 May a patrol led by DI Munroe of Newport discovered their whereabouts. (Munroe was new to the command, his predecessor at Newport, DI Fuge, having been transferred to Limerick city.) A furious firefight developed as the IRA retreated into the mountains through Glenlara.

DI Munroe was wounded and Constable Joseph Maguire killed as the RIC pressed the IRA further.[70] Kilroy again seized the initiative, laying down accurate fire to keep the RIC at a distance as his men grouped together and headed for escape. One IRA man, Jim Browne from Kilmeena, was shot through the stomach and killed. Kilroy picked six men to act as a rearguard. Peadar Kilroy, son of Michael, referred to the rearguard as 'The Magnificent Seven'. They included Tom Kitterick, Paddy Cannon, Seán Connolly, Johnny Gibbons, Captain Jim Moran, (John) McDonagh and Michael Kilroy.[71] While the firing continued, one RIC constable succeeded in roping a farmer's horse. He galloped to Newport to call for reinforcements. Strengthened in numbers, the RIC and British military began to move into the Nephin Mountains in an extended line. They raked the hillside with machine-gun fire but the IRA were deep under cover of the heather. The troops settled down in the area for a long stay. After dark, Kilroy infiltrated British lines and led his men back down to MacDonald's farm, where their wounded had been. The family gave them salmon. This small IRA group under Kilroy then made for Glenisland, avoiding British lorries now scouring the countryside with searchlights.[72] At one point Dr Madden fell into a bog hole up to his neck in an attempt to escape a British patrol! Eventually, after a few days of 'cat and mouse', Kilroy gave the RIC and British troops the slip, and met up again with the Westport and Newport men near Aughagower. Word was sent to the Louisburgh Company to join them. Kilroy's West Mayo Flying Column was still in the field and ready for action once more.

While the West Mayo Flying Column were fighting for their lives, elections under the Government of Ireland Act 1920 took place in all parts of the country. The original Mayo constituencies had been redrawn. North and West Mayo were grouped together, South Mayo went in with South Roscommon. East Mayo was now linked with South Sligo.[73] Elected for North and West Mayo were Joseph MacBride (interned), Tom Derrig, Patrick J. Ruttledge and Dr John Crowley (on the run). They were the only names to be nominated. For South Mayo, William Sears (in jail) was returned, with Commandant Tom Maguire (on the run and still recovering from his wounds) elected to Dáil Éireann for the first time. Dr Francis Ferran (in jail) and Thomas O'Donnell were elected for East Mayo.

The elections reaffirmed the partition of Ireland achieved through the Government of Ireland Act. One hundred and twenty-four Sinn Féin TDs became the Second Dáil, 42 of them being in prison at the time of the election. It is also worth noting that there were five women TDs: Mrs Pearse, Dublin County; Mrs O'Callaghan, Limerick East and City; Miss Muriel Mac Sweeney, Cork City; Countess Markievicz, Dublin South; and Dr Ada English of the National University. The TDs of the second Dáil would vote on the Treaty that concluded the War of Independence. This vote would tip the country into civil war. 'Ireland has spoken and the world is listening,' Michael Collins wrote, 'and in view of the unanimity of this latest verdict of the people's will, the end of this seven-century struggle cannot be far off.'[74] There was one last chapter to be written in the long struggle, that of Carrowkennedy, County Mayo.

CARROWKENNEDY: JUNE–JULY 1921

On Thursday 2 June, the West Mayo Flying Column was billeted around the townland of Claddy, near the Westport to Leenane road. In mid-afternoon news reached O/C Michael Kilroy that an RIC patrol of two Crossley Tenders and a Ford car had stopped at Carrowkennedy. The RIC formed a work detail from men cutting turf nearby to fill in the main road, in which the IRA had dug trenches. The patrol, led by DI Edward Stevenson, then went on its way to Leenane. Stevenson was a former British Army officer with the prestigious Black Watch Regiment. He had been wounded on the Western Front in France in October 1918. Although assigned to Belmullet RIC barracks, he had been drafted into Westport to assist in the hunt for Kilroy's men. Sergeant Francis Creegan, who had fought at Kilmeena, was with Stevenson. He was considered an inoffensive man who had even let IRA men pass on 'unnoticed' during RIC raids. The two Crossley Tenders were carrying a considerable amount of ammunition and grenades. Stevenson's patrol also carried a Lewis machine gun, the type that had proved so successful against the IRA at Kilmeena.

Kilroy knew that the patrol would have to return as his men had destroyed Erriff Bridge, making the road impassable. Woken from their sleep, the Column grabbed their equipment and made for the main road. The forty-five to fifty men were organised into three main sections and then subdivided into small units of six men under the command of a more experienced officer. This was to prevent the panic that had occurred at Kilmeena when intensive fire was returned by the RIC. The Westport men, commanded by Vice-Brigadier Brodie Malone, formed one section. Vice-Brigadier Ned Moane, Joe Baker, Joe Duffy, Tommy Heavey, Paddy and Johnny Duffy, Jimmy Flaherty, Batty Cryan, Jack McDonagh and Jack Keane, the latter a skilled marksman, were among their number.[75] They were placed on high ground 120 yards from the road. Taking advantage of a stone wall, the IRA men removed stones to make loopholes as firing positions. Dr John Madden was further on their right.

The second section was made up in the main of Newport men, including Commandant Joe Doherty, Captain Jim Moran and

Rick Joyce. They were positioned further west, extending from the end of the first section's position along a wood to the main road.[76] The third section, from the Louisburgh Company, were ordered to cross the road and hold a hill above the junction to Drummin. The sections were to hold fire until all vehicles were within range of the entire Column. Kilroy had learned a great deal from Kilmeena. He handpicked marksmen to take out the drivers of both vehicles. He also assigned men to pay particular attention to any machine-gunners, who could not under any circumstances be allowed into action.

On discovering the Erriff Bridge destroyed, the RIC patrol retired to Darby Hastings Pub for some refreshments. The weather was very warm and the stop-off was an unexpected surprise for Stevenson's men. Having quenched their thirst, the twenty-man patrol headed back towards Westport; the West Mayo Flying Column were in position and hungry for revenge. The Ford car broke down and was being towed by the second lorry as they drove back through Carrowkennedy. Gus Delahunty, a civilian from Westport, had been commandeered to drive his own car as part of the patrol. Stevenson, who had not followed 5th Division anti-guerrilla warfare directions, was driving the first lorry when he should instead have been in the back of the second vehicle with his men.[77] This exposed him to increased risk and separated him from his men, weakening the command structure. His Crossley Tender had some armour plating welded to the front and sides.

An IRA scout signalled the approach of the RIC patrol at Carrowkennedy around 6.30 p.m. The IRA eased off the safety catches of their rifles. Jimmy O'Flaherty, an ex-Connaught Ranger, lined up his sights on DI Stevenson in the leading lorry. At the last second Stevenson looked up to the high ground to his right almost as if he sensed something was about to happen. He never heard the bullet that killed him. It went straight through the centre of his forehead. The first lorry lurched forward and stopped in the middle of the road. Chaos ensued for the RIC as bullets rained down from on high.

The IRA's second section opened fire on the second lorry killing the driver. The lorry coasted to the edge of the ditch on the side of the road where it came to a halt. The men in this lorry jumped out the back and ran 20 yards for the cover of a small bridge and ditch. Commandant Joe Ring ran across the road to get behind the RIC. Seeing his haversack, they opened fire, narrowly missing him. Ring made for the hillock 150 yards to the west. From here, he kept the RIC pinned down. Constable William French, a Black and Tan and war veteran, attempted a flanking movement on the main IRA position. Jimmy O'Flaherty identified French as being in command and brought him down. French, badly wounded, fell back into the ditch by the bridge. He was to remain there for over two and a half hours. This finished any offensive action by this RIC detachment.

Pinned down by the bridge and with inadequate cover, the RIC from the second lorry made a run for widow McGreal's house, leaving their wounded behind. The Louisburgh men had been unable to get into position adequately before the firing opened, which allowed the RIC from the second lorry to reach the house and hold up there. Tommy Heavey maintained 'this could not have happened had the section covering the Drummin Road under Jack Connolly held their ground. Whatever happened, this section pulled out of the fight, ten men in all, and the Westport men with Paddy Cannon had to finish the job on their own'.[78] Meanwhile, Gus Delahunty, the civilian, dived out of the Ford car and under the small bridge on the road. Frightened out of his wits, he remained trapped there until the action ceased. With one RIC detachment pinned down in the widow McGreal's, the IRA were now free to concentrate on the first lorry.

Kilroy described what happened as the RIC from the first lorry attempted to counter the IRA ambush:

> The enemy pushed and kicked out the Lewis gun from the rear of the lorry. Several men followed it on the flat, like Salmon jumping. They knew they could not rise their back, head or any part of their body. When they landed on the ground, they had about a two foot, six inch sod fence to protect them. Under this cover, the machine gun was set up. There was a burst let up into the air to frighten the supposed rabbits. Then a poor fellow tried to level it across the fence at us, but that was all. Suddenly, there was too much lead in his head. Another comrade pushed him aside and started the same game. This second man had

scarcely caught the gun until he also was dead. Then a third man made a like effort and met with the same fate.[79]

Three RIC men were killed as they tried to get the Lewis gun into action. No other dared try it. The shooting of the IRA was so accurate that to provide a fraction of an inch as a target meant death. At this stage, the RIC had lost DI Stevenson and Constables Sydney Blythe, James Brown and John Doherty. The remaining men in the lorry were led by Sergeant Creegan. Attaching a grenade launcher to one of the Lee-Enfield rifles, they began firing at the IRA. Brodie Malone's section were beyond range, but the grenade fire did prevent them closing the distance with the RIC. For the next two hours both sides exchanged rifle fire. They also traded insults, with the IRA firing stones to conserve ammunition. The IRA then broke into song with 'Kelly, the Boy from Killanne', a rousing battle tune recalling the 1798 Rising in County Wexford.[80] It was punctuated by the odd discharge of a Lee-Enfield rifle. Each IRA man had on average fifty rounds of ammunition for his rifle. Fearing they would soon run out, Kilroy decided the stalemate had to be broken. He ordered a detachment to flank the lorry and put it out of action. Tommy Heavey was 'volunteered' to take part:

> Following some discussion it was decided to send two parties to attack the lorry at close quarters from front and rear and, if necessary, charge with the bayonet. I was one of the unfortunate possessors of a bayonet and so was Johnny Duffy. Cautiously, I proceeded, covered by Joe Baker and Jack McDonagh, until I came within stone's throw of the back of the truck, the tail-board was down.
>
> I could see at an angle into the vehicle. One figure lay still, the arm of the other could be seen. I fired two or three rounds into the vehicle and I noticed Duffy was firing also. Suddenly there was an explosion in the tender and almost immediately a white handkerchief fluttered. I still lay in cover but stopped firing. Duffy, on the other hand, fired more rapidly than ever. I knew he was thinking savagely of the treatment his mother had received a few weeks earlier at the hands of the RIC. As

it turned out, the hand of which held the flag of surrender aloft was the hand of the man who had viciously buffeted Mrs. Duffy to try to wrest information from her. He was Sergeant or Head-Constable Creegan. At last all the firing ceased and our fellows converged on the truck ... Only Creegan, Constable Cullen and an English Tan were alive.[81]

The IRA came down from the hillside and surrounded the lorry. Kitterick, the Quartermaster, stepped up and looked into the back of the lorry:

a dreadful sight met my eyes. It seemed that in the course of firing a grenade one of the occupants was struck by a bullet, thus dropping his rifle and releasing the grenade in the lorry. Half his head was blown off, another man's hands were gone and the complete woodwork of a Lee-Enfield rifle had been blown into the legs and stomach of another man, whom I recognised as a policeman named Creegan – a man who had done me a good turn previous to this during a raid on Westport Workhouse.[82]

The machine gun had three dead men around it. One of them, Constable John Doherty, lay on his face in a pool of blood. The IRA men were so shocked at the sight they left him where he was.[83] Doherty's case was particularly tragic. With twenty-five years' service in the RIC, the Roscommon man had been due for retirement. The patrol was to be one of his last duties. Sergeant Creegan, still fully conscious and bleeding heavily, was in a terrible condition. The IRA men went to nearby elderly widow Sammon's cottage. They asked her to allow them bring Creegan into her home. When she refused, the IRA men took the front door off her house and used it as a stretcher to carry Creegan up to the second lorry. Also wounded were Constables Dowling, Allen, Bollie, Upton, Collick and Fitzgerald.[84] Sergeant Creegan and Constable French died during the night. Constable Dowling died shortly afterwards.

Jack Keane went up to McGreal's house with one of the wounded Tans in front of him as a shield. He called on the RIC in the house to surrender or at least send out the woman and her children. They

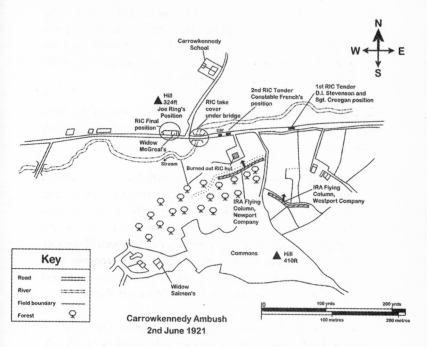

Carrowkennedy Ambush, Thursday 2 June 1921. (Courtesy Eoin Brennan)

refused. O'Flaherty, who had taken possession of the Lewis gun (which he named 'Mrs Lewis'), fired a burst at McGreal's house. After this, the RIC surrendered. Some of the IRA men's accounts speak of them coming under fire from McGreal's when they were attending to the wounded at the second lorry. Kitterick shouted to them that if they opened fire again the wounded would be shot. After the surrender there was some argument over what to do with the prisoners. The Tans among the RIC were particularly nervous. Malone wanted to shoot them all on account of the terror campaign they had waged in west Mayo. Kilroy refused, saying, 'Oh, sure our nature isn't hard enough.'[85] Kilroy then sent Head Constable Hanlon off to Westport by bicycle to bring medical assistance for the wounded.[86] Throughout the entire engagement the IRA had suffered no casualties.

Kilroy moved fast as enemy reinforcements were expected at any time. All RIC were searched for documents. Captured weapons were gathered. It was an impressive haul, yielding twenty-eight Lee-Enfield rifles, one Lewis gun, boxes of hand grenades, thousands of rounds of ammunition plus pans for the Lewis gun. On the body of DI Stevenson was a revolver with an inscription from Sir Edward Carson, the unionist leader. The revolver had been a gift to Stevenson's father, who was Chief Constable of Glasgow.[87] Pockets now bulging with grenades and ammunition, and, some with two rifles slung over their backs, the IRA headed east for Aughagower. This was a trick, Kilroy laying a false trail for the British military to follow. After twenty minutes or so, the Column turned west for Pat Joyce's of Durless, a remote part of the mountains behind Croagh Patrick. As they tracked their way across the Mayo countryside, the plumes of smoke from the burning Crossley Tenders were visible for some time. As Tommy Heavey and his IRA comrades marched away from Carrowkennedy they were satisfied that Kilmeena had been avenged.[88] The West Mayo Flying Column was now bristling with weapons, and with 'Mrs Lewis' for company they were now more than a match for any RIC or British military unit attempting to engage them.

The British did not actually venture out to the ambush position at Carrowkennedy until the following day. Kilroy's ruse seemed to have worked as the military and RIC, backed up by aircraft, searched east towards Tourmakeady. However, their intelligence was good, and after a bad start they were never more than a day behind Kilroy's Column. Commandant Chaplin of the British Army Galway Brigade and DC Cruise of the RIC travelled to the Westport district to conduct operations personally. A Royal Navy destroyer sailed in to Killary Harbour while an additional Auxiliary company was stationed at Leenane to prevent any escape south to Connemara. Kilroy's men were now in serious trouble, and for the next month led the British military and RIC on a chase through north, east and finally back to west Mayo.

While billeted at Derrymartin village under the shadow of Nephin Mountain, Jack Leonard, Kilroy's brother-in-law, took the now famous photograph of the West Mayo Flying Column.[89] It is unquestionably the best contemporary photograph of an IRA

Medals of Volunteer Michael Hastings Westport Company, IRA. (L–r): the War of Independence Commemorative Medal and the War of Independence Medal. (Courtesy Michael Hastings)

Column ever taken. It shows them brimming with confidence and armed to the teeth after their victory at Carrowkennedy. With the British on their tails they moved on continuously with local IRA Companies providing scouts, and local women in cottages providing rashers, eggs, and brown bread washed down with tea. Sometimes, there was the odd drop of poitín – when Kilroy was not looking! From Laherdane it was across Lough Conn at Pontoon and south to Bohola, Kiltimagh and Balla. Finally, on 2 July, Kilroy's men were at Tonlagee, back near Carrowkennedy. They could see Very lights (flares) in the night sky as British troops closed in. Kilroy hid the weapons in an arms dump and then dispersed the Column. The men retained only their revolvers. Kilroy, Ned Moane, Tom Kitterick and Gibbons headed west for Connemara via Glenlaur. On the way they had a close call with a party of Auxiliaries but managed to evade them. The Column escaped capture and awaited a recall for further action.[90]

While Kilroy and his men were recovering from the action at Kilmeena, the North Mayo Brigade finally caught up with the notorious DI White, ambushing him on the night of Tuesday 24 May

West Mayo Brigade Flying Column IRA pictured on the slopes of Nephin Mountain, 20 June 1921 at 11.45 a.m. The photograph includes: back row (l–r): Commandant Michael Kilroy, QM Tom Kitterick, Comdt. Ned Moane, Capt. John Gibbons, Joe Walsh, Paddy J. Cannon, Pat Lambert, J. Kelly, Comdt. Josie Doherty, Comdt. Brodie Malone, Jim Rush, Comdt. Joe Ring; middle row (l–r): M. Naughton, J. Hogan, J. Harney, Dan Sammon, Jack Keane, J[ack]. Connolly, Rick Joyce, Pat McNamara, Willie Malone; front row (l–r): Dan Gavin, Tommy Heavey, Johnny Duffy, John McDonagh, Comdt. Paddy Kelly, Jim Moran, Jimmy Flaherty, Batty Cryan, Michael Staunton; lying in front: Dr John Madden, Medical Officer. Inset: top (l–r) Comdt. Paddy Duffy, Joe Baker; bottom (l–r): Michael Gallagher, Tom Ainsworth. (Photography by Jack Leonard. Reproduced with kind permission of Anthony Leonard, The J. J. Leonard Collection of Historic Photographs)

as he drove home with his wife from a visit to a friend outside Ballina. Although hit in the shoulder, DI White managed to accelerate and escape. His wife was shaken but uninjured. The IRA were convinced White was wearing body armour. They could not believe his good fortune was down to their inaccurate shooting. The RIC surprised a group of IRA men at Bunree the next day, fatally injuring eighteen-year-old James Howley.[91] White did not remain in Ballina long after

Captain Micheál Ó Cléirigh, IRA, *c.* 1921. Sent to assist with the reorganisation of the North Mayo Brigade IRA in 1921.

the attempt on his life. He rightly believed the IRA were getting too close for comfort.

On 18 June 1921, the *Western People* reported a gruesome discovery in a bog on the road between Ballina and Foxford:

> The partly decomposed body of a young man was found in Shraheen bog near Foxford. There was a large wound in the side of his abdomen. He was wearing a heavy greenish coloured overcoat with a light grey sports coat underneath in the pockets of which were found two linen collars marked JJ Murphy draper Ballina, a black tie and a tooth brush.
>
> The military have viewed the body, gave an order for reburial, which was carried out on Tuesday under the Superintendence of Mr Thomas Callaghan RO: A military inquiry in lieu of inquest is to be held. No trace of man's identity has yet been discovered. The body was party eaten by rats or dogs.[92]

Michael Tolan, Ballina Company IRA, had been found, and it was apparent he had endured an horrific death. His body was interred by poor law authorities in the 'Strangers Plot' in Leigue Cemetery, Ballina. The British military held an inquiry into the cause of death but the results were not published.[93] For now, Tolan was to lie in an unmarked grave, but he did not rest in peace. The day after his body was interred, Eamon Gannon, O/C North Mayo Brigade, along with a number of his staff, were captured in an RIC raid. Volunteer Tom Nealon was killed, Pat Bourke wounded and Bartley Hegarty, Anthony Farrell, Mr Loftus with his son Tom captured.[94] The Adjutant wrote to GHQ outlining their losses:

> A Chara,
>
> The Bde Vice Comdt has commanded me to give you a detailed list of losses this week owing to the Flying Column having been attacked. Five of the men were taken prisoner who lost 3 service rifles, 82 rounds 303, 1 Colt Automatic and 22 rounds of stuff for same, documents which were also taken were of no importance.
>
> The men taken were the Brigade Commandant, No. 4 Battalion Comdt who was Flying Column Comdt, No 3 Batt Comdt who was Column Adjutant, Company Captain in No 3 Battalion & private. The Vice Comdt is in the unfortunate position of not knowing much with regard to working the Brigade as he says the Comdt always kept things to himself & did all the work & beyond the fact of appointing him Vice Comdt he never had a Bde meeting for some months So that we don't know where he stands with the work or how he has reported to GHQ. The Vice C will be grateful for a report on the matter + also if he is to take charge as Commandant.
>
> Adjutant
>
> P.S. is there any quicker method of despatch than by Despatch couriers? I mean is there any covering address used by post + one that we could use. Same as is used in the Boycott Stunt?[95]

This level of confusion in the North Mayo Brigade would continue for some time. GHQ appointed Captain Micheál Ó Cléirigh as

Captain Stephen Donnelly (front row, middle), North Mayo Brigade, Ballina Company, IRA, 1921. (Private Collection)

Brigade Adjutant to reorganise them. While that reorganisation was taking place, the IRA were to demonstrate just how ruthless they could be. On 1 July a cycle patrol of seven constables was ambushed 6 miles southwest of Dromore, County Sligo. Constables Thomas Higgins and John King were taken prisoner as the North Mayo Flying Column withdrew into the Ox Mountains near Glenesk.[96] The RIC and British military followed in hot pursuit, and at one point were within half a mile of the Column. IRA Commandant Matt Kilcauley described what happened when interviewed by Ernie O'Malley in the 1950s:

> We had two RIC prisoners with us. One of them was King who had led the RIC and the Auxiliaries on several previous raids and who knew most of us. When we were being fired on we asked what we would do with our prisoners. So we had a short Council of War and we decided to shoot them. We gave them a short few seconds in which to say their prayers. King pleaded

hard for mercy. He made all kinds of promises and we would
have liked to let the other RIC man go free. He was younger.
He pleaded hard and he cried and again pleaded with us. The
others would have heard the shots.[97]

Events in Mayo took an even more sinister turn when the body of
Anthony Foody, an ex-RIC Sergeant, was found at Carralavin near
Ballina. The ex-Sergeant had been shot dead and a placard placed
around his neck with the message: 'Revenge for Dwyer and The Ragg'.
Edward Dwyer, Adjutant of the 3rd Tipperary Brigade IRA, had been
shot dead in his home by masked and armed men in October 1920.
The IRA suspected Foody, who was on active service with the RIC
in Bouladuff, of being involved in Dwyer's death. This type of IRA
killing was to become all too common in Mayo in the months ahead.
In the meantime, peace moves continued. Much to the surprise of the
IRA brigades, but surely to the relief of the civilian population, two
important notices appeared in the national press on Saturday 9 July
1921. The first was issued by the IRA GHQ:

GENERAL ORDER

To Officers Commanding All Units

In view of the conversations now being entered into by our
Government with the Government of Great Britain and in
pursuance of mutual understandings to suspend hostilities
during these conversations, active operations by our troops will
be suspended as from Noon, Monday, July Eleventh.

RISTEARD UA MAOLCHATHA

[Richard Mulcahy]

Chief of Staff[98]

The announcement of the Truce caught many IRA units by surprise.
Kitterick's attitude was the position of many in the Mayo brigades:

The Truce to us was bewildering and we did not know what to
make of it. None of us took it that the war was over for long and
assumed that the peace would be only temporary.

However, we were glad for the respite – glad to get home to see our people and to get proper rest and regular meals once again to fall asleep without a 'gun' in our hand.[99]

A second statement was issued by Éamon de Valera.

PROCLAMATION

Fellow-citizens,

During the period of Truce each individual soldier and citizen must regard himself as a custodian of the nation's honour. Your discipline must prove to the most convincing manner that this is the struggle of an original nation. In the negotiations now initiated your representatives will do their utmost to acquire a just and peaceful termination of this struggle, but history, particularly our own history, and the character of the issue to be decided are a warning against undue confidence.

An unbending determination to endure all that may still be necessary, and fortitude such as you have shown in all your recent sufferings – these alone will lead you to the peace you desire.

Should force be resumed against our nation, you must be ready, on your part, once more to resist. Thus alone will you secure the final abandonment of force, and the acceptance of justice and reason as the arbiter.

EAMON DE VALERA[100]

Peace had come unexpectedly. De Valera was preparing the people for the need to resume conflict should it be necessary. For the civilian population the Truce brought great relief and jubilation. In Ballina, curfews were lifted by the RIC and the Auxiliaries held an impromptu open-air concert for the public at Barrack Hill. The Auxiliaries then held a mock wake, complete with candles, to allay fears of any resumption in hostilities. Next morning, everyone awoke to find the Auxiliaries had departed. Life, for now, was returning to normal. On Sunday, celebrations continued with traditional Mayo bonfires lighting the night sky. However, it was mainly children who celebrated. The public believed 'it was yet premature to give way to undue optimism as to the outcome of the peace negotiations'. Nevertheless, during 'the day on Sunday one noticed round the town enjoying a welcome relaxation some young men who for a considerable time past have been compelled to absent themselves from their homes'.[101] The young men and women of the IRA, Cumann na mBan and Sinn Féin were beginning to return home to their families after years of struggle. War was temporarily suspended.

In Newport, Michael Kilroy stood in the ruins of his home and business destroyed by the Black and Tans. He looked around aghast. The building had been completely gutted. He hoped the Truce would hold as there was a lot of rebuilding to be done, but Kilroy was not optimistic. His brigade would need new recruits and intensive training to be ready if war were to be resumed. With the threat of a resumption of hostilities hanging over them, the other Mayo brigades also attempted to reorganise. None of them expected they would soon have to fight each other instead of the British military and the RIC.

6

'The Year of Destiny': Truce, Treaty and Descent to Civil War

On the morning of Saturday 9 October 1921, a large crowd gathered under overcast skies at Kingstown Harbour [Dun Laoghaire] in Dublin to watch an Irish delegation depart for London. They were travelling over to negotiate a treaty with the British government. The negotiations, which were to last from 11 October to 6 December, were the result of preliminary talks between Éamon de Valera and David Lloyd George the previous July. Members of the press called for Arthur Griffith, Eamonn Duggan, Robert Barton, Erskine Childers and George Gavin Duffy to stand together for photographs. In jubilant mood, the Irish delegation, or plenipotentiaries to give them their proper title, obliged, much to the delight of the crowd. Michael Collins, another member of the delegation, was not present. He would travel across the next day, joining up with the delegation at Hans Place, in the fashionable area of Knightsbridge, London. In the crowd looking on was Patrick Moylett from Tooreen, Crossmolina, in County Mayo. Moylett understood better than most the monumental task facing the delegation. During October and November 1920 he had undertaken secret negotiations with the British at Arthur Griffith's request.

Patrick Moylett had emigrated to London as a teenager with only twenty-two shillings and sixpence in his pocket. He found work as a porter with the Great Eastern Railway at Houndsditch.[1] Showing great determination and business acumen he eventually went into partnership with his brothers, opening shops in Ballina, Ballyhaunis and Galway. Patrick's passion for Irish independence led him to join the IRB. His shops were targeted by the Black and Tans who bombed and looted them more than six times. In January 1921, his brothers in Ballina were forced to parade around the town with a Union Jack, kneel, kiss it and then burn a Republican flag. Patrick wrote a letter to *The Times* of London detailing the violence. It was published, much to his surprise, on 30 April 1921, together with an editorial referring to his considerable courage and character.[2] As a result, Moylett became a target for the Galway Auxiliaries who dispatched their O/C Jock Burke and intelligence officer Captain Harrison to Dublin with orders to track down and kill him. They were spotted in Dame Street on 17 June 1921. After an exchange of fire with the Dublin IRA on Stephen's Green, Harrison left Ireland for good.[3]

Moylett's approach to the British government was arranged through John Steele, London correspondent of the *Chicago Tribune*. It led to six meetings with C. J. Phillips of the Foreign Office and resulted in a presentation of 'Sinn Féin's Proposals for Peace'. Those proposals are crucial to understanding the subsequent events of the Treaty negotiations between the Irish and British representatives in Downing Street in late 1921. The proposals presented by Moylett in October and November 1920 contained some astonishing revelations:

(1) The Dáil Éireann should be allowed to meet on the distinct understanding that –

    (a) Attacks on the police and soldiers instantly cease.

    (b) At the meeting no reference be made to the existence of any 'Irish Republic'. From the point of view of the British Government the meeting would merely be that of representatives of Ireland referred to by the Prime Minister in his speech in Parliament on the eve of recess (22 August).

(2) The only 'business' of the meeting would be to receive and answer an invitation from the British Government to nominate representatives to a conference called by the British Government for a settlement of the whole Irish question. Sinn

Féin's idea of the conference is that it would consist of one or two members representing Ulster, one or two representatives Sinn Féin and (say) five others representing England, Scotland, Wales and possibly the two Dominions specially interested in the Irish question, viz Canada and Australia. Sinn Féin professes confidence in the success of such a conference.

In the course of the meetings with Moylett, the British Prime Minister, Lloyd George, also stipulated:

(a) Separate treatment for Ulster
(b) No risk to military security of the British Isles in time of war
(c) No evasion by Ireland of some equitable liability in the matter of Imperial finance

The proposals were agreed to by Arthur Griffith, Acting President of the Dáil while de Valera was in the United States. Phillips' view of his meetings with Moylett led the British to believe the terror of the Tans and the Auxiliaries was winning the war. He wrote to Lloyd George:

From the conversations I got a very clear impression (on evidence too long to quote here at length) that the Sinn Féin leaders realise quite well the hopelessness of their attempts to carry on the struggle on present lines and are seeking a plan by which they may at the same time end the present crisis, save their own faces as far as possible and checkmate the extremist section among their followers.[4]

Anxious for a response to his proposals, Griffith sent a message through Steele to Philip Kerr, Lloyd George's Private Secretary, saying he was quite confident he could 'deliver the goods if the British Government will do their part.'[5] Griffith's efforts were thwarted by Michael Collins, whose Squad struck on Sunday 21 November, killing twelve British Secret Service officers. The Black and Tans retaliated just a few hours later, killing fifteen and wounding fifty civilians at Croke Park on a day that would become known as 'Bloody Sunday.'[6] Griffith was arrested in the subsequent round-up by the British military. A reporter from the *Irish Independent*, McQuerney, broke the news of Moylett's peace attempts. The result was distrust among the Sinn Féin moderates of the British and Lloyd George in particular. With Griffith in jail, the Republican movement was now being run by Collins. One cannot help but wonder if Collins sent the Squad into action that day not just to eliminate the British intelligence network in Dublin but also to sabotage any chance of peace at that stage in the war. As if to reinforce the IRA's capability, Tom Barry's West Cork Flying Column struck on 28 November, wiping out an RIC patrol of eighteen Auxiliaries. Griffith's proposals, delivered through Moylett, demonstrated to the British that many in Sinn Féin accepted an Irish Republic could not be achieved. In addition, the partition of Ulster from the rest of the country looked to be a fait accompli. The subsequent six months, during which time the Mayo Flying Columns went into action, undoubtedly strengthened the hand of Dáil Éireann and the position of the committed Republicans within Sinn Féin.

De Valera returned to Ireland at Christmas 1920, following a eighteen-month trip to the United States. His decision to send both Griffith and Collins to negotiate with Lloyd George and to opt out himself mystified many. Griffith and Collins represented the two different wings of the Sinn Féin movement, those who sought a compromise with Britain and those in favour of military action to ensure the establishment of an independent Irish Republic. If a deal with the British had to be done, it was with these two wings of the movement. De Valera's decision to stay in Dublin was a serious mistake, with repercussions of enormous magnitude. Many believe it was during the July talks with Lloyd George that de Valera became aware a Republic was impossible. He could not shoulder the responsibility of bringing that reality home to the Irish people. The composition of the Irish delegation to London was chosen with this reality in mind.

Patrick Moylett was not happy with the composition of the delegation. He believed Collins should have remained in the background. He also was worried about the presence of four ex-British Army officers among the delegation – Erskine Childers, Robert Barton, John Chartres, Assistant Secretary to the delegation and suspected member of British intelligence, and David Robinson,

The Moylett family: (l–r) Patricia, Molly, Patrick senior, Frank, Florence (neé Simons, wife), Betty and Patrick junior. Patrick Moylett senior, from Ballina, acted as Arthur Griffith's secret emissary and was sent to London in October and November 1920 to present Sinn Féin proposals for peace at an early stage in the War of Independence. (Courtesy Anne Butterly and Susan Moylett)

Childers' valet. It was these men who were 'charged with the heavy responsibility of bringing peace and honour to Ireland'.[7] As the mail boat sailed out of Kingstown Harbour it passed a British destroyer at anchor. The menace of its presence was not lost on the delegation. War would resume should the Truce break down. It was a fear that played heavily on the delegation's minds. The Treaty they signed and their intentions for the future of Ireland would be debated ever after.

As the Truce continued, the IRA prepared itself for what it believed was an inevitable return to war with the British. Richard Mulcahy, Chief of Staff at GHQ, used the lull in military operations to reorganise the IRA thoroughly. In Mayo, brigades were merged into divisional areas. Tom Maguire, now a Commandant General, was placed in command of the 2nd Western Division, which took in south and east Mayo along with parts of north Galway and south Roscommon. His division had 24 senior officers and 2,420 men rising to 3,507 by the end of 1921. Michael Kilroy, also a newly promoted Commandant General, was given command of the 4th Western

Division covering north and west Mayo along with Connemara. Kilroy was able to draw on a strength of 22 senior officers and 2, 288 men rising to 3, 721 by December 1921.[8] Recruitment and training intensified with special camps being established. Mayo commanders withdrew their forces deep into unpopulated areas and away from the prying eyes of the RIC and the British military. Maguire held two training camps, one at Clydagh near Headford and the other on the estate of Colonel Beddington at Ballycurrin on the shores of Lough Corrib. Maguire said the camps were well run and discipline was tight. The IRA lived with the knowledge that they might have to resume the war at any moment.[9] Michael Kilroy also established a training camp in the Nephin Mountains, 8 miles northeast of Newport. The RIC were aware of these camps but could not identify the exact locations due to their remoteness.[10] Not all commanders showed the same discretion. In east Mayo, the Argyll and Sutherland Highlanders reported 'the Sinn Feiners underwent intense training openly and defiantly especially in the Swinford area where three companies were drilled and equipped'.[11] IRA GHQ also ran training courses for senior and junior officers that involved bomb making.

The routine for training camps involved long hours with an emphasis on discipline. The following is a 'Scheme of Training' implemented in the 2nd Western Division:[12]

No 1 Camp	
Out of Bed:	6.00 o'c
Parade:	6.30 to 7.30
Breakfast:	7.30 to 8.45
Rifle and Revolver Practice:	8.45 to 9.45 am
Manoeuvres:	10.00 to 12.00
Bayonet Drill:	12.00 to 1.00
Dinner:	1.00 to 2.30
Bomb [Grenade] Throwing:	2.30 to 3.30
Scouting and Engineering:	3.45 to 5.00
Recreation:	5.0 to 7.0
Lectures:	7.15 to 8.0

Supper:	8.0 to 9.0
Gaelic Class:	9.0 to 9.30
Bed:	10 o'c (Rosary in Irish) By order O/C Brigade.

GHQ also used the Truce to increase intelligence gathering. Formal report forms were to be filled in by the local IRA intelligence officer and returned to GHQ no later than ten days after the month to which they referred. The 2nd Western Division intelligence report for August 1921 read:[13]

Western Division Intelligence Report August 1921
'Óglaigh na h-Éireann [Irish Volunteers]

1. Brigade: South Mayo, August '21.

2. Enemy Regular Troops:
    1.   Brigadier General Chaplin, Galway.
    2.   Captain Chatfield, Ballinrobe, Border Regiment.

Ballinrobe	200 Border Regiment	Capt Chatfield Lt Gronow Lt Craig Lt Smith
Claremorris	240 Argyll & Sutherland Highlanders	Capt Stewart Major Ritchie Capt Johnson Lt Anderson

3. Enemy RIC

		Station
Divisional Commissioner	Cruise	Galway
County Inspector	C. Steadman	Castlebar

District	Station	Strength		D.I.
		Sgt	Men	
Claremorris	Ballinrobe	6	31	DI Peacock
	Clonbur	2	14	" "
	Claremorris	5	25	DI Wilkins
	Holymount	2	16	" "
	Balla	2	15	" "

4. Enemy RIC Auxiliaries
Nil

5. Other Enemy Stations

Jail	Governor
Internment Camp	Commandant
Coastguard Station	O/C

6. Enemy Agents (Special) All Suspects Included
Nil

7. Enemy Officials

County Sheriff	
County Sub Sheriff	T.F. Ruttledge, Westport.
Crown Prosecutor	John Garvey, Ballina.
Lieutenant of the County	Lord Sligo, Westport.
Clerk of the Crown & Peace	M.V. Calligan, Ballina.
R.M.	Capt Holmes, Tuam, Kilmaine, Bohola.
J.P's	Richard Sweeney, Claremorris.

9. Others
Tax Collectors
Land Commissioners
Local Government Board Inspectors

10. Enemy P.O's and Telegraph/Phone, Railway Station

P.O.	Claremorris	Mr Johnson	
P.O.	Ballinrobe	Mr Ganley	'Friendly with the enemy'
P.O.	Holymount	Mr Greer	'Friendly with the enemy'
P.O.	Claremorris	Mr Fegan	'Neutral'
P.O.	Ballindine	Mr Kelleher	'Sound'
P.O.	Balla	[Blank]	'Sound'

11. Notes on Enemy Social Institutions

12. Special Notices/Remarks
Policemen's wives most dangerous. Seeking and getting information from civilians.

This intelligence report, compiled by Director of Intelligence for the South Mayo Brigade, is relatively sparse on detail compared with reports from other Brigades. In fact, reading the local papers would have supplied more information than was given here. The report was an improvement on the previous month's, which was severely criticised by GHQ as being in a 'ragged condition and not signed or initialled'. GHQ continued to be critical of the intelligence it was receiving from south Mayo, requesting enemy officers be named in full, that comments from the local intelligence officer should accompany the report and that the Brigade should attempt to infiltrate the local Golf clubs and Hunt Dance where British officers socialised.[14]

GHQ also began to collect information on the weapons held by the IRA. By September 1921 the Mayo Brigades were still short of weapons and ammunition.[15] While Kilroy's West Mayo Brigade was the best equipped, both the South and North Mayo Brigades had lost weapons to the British military.

Mayo Brigades Munitions Report September 1921

Mayo Brigades Munitions Report September 1921.				
Weapons	South Mayo Brigade	East Mayo Brigade	West Mayo Brigade	North Mayo Brigade
Rifles				
Lee Enfield	14	12	46	15
Martini	1	4	1	5
7.9mm Mauser	1	4	2	2
Howth Mauser		4	2	5
RIC Carbine		3		
Shot Guns				
Double	1	71	50	191
Single	1	67	15	285
Pistols				
Peter the Painter		1	4	2

Parabellum	1	1	3	2
.45 self ejecting	11	19	22	20
.38 self ejecting	3	7	5	2
.32 self ejecting	3	4		
Grenades				
Time Pattern	15	42	43	86
1st Class	15			
2nd Class				
Ammunition				
.303	200	306	1,000	650
7.9 mm	7	45	150	25
Shot gun cartridges 12 bore	300	820	300	600
Revolver .45	250	10		
Revolver .38	350			
Peter the Painter			30	3
Parabellum			20	5
Explosives		5,871 lb		100 lb
Exploders (Detonators)		3		20 electric 60 other
Fuse		90 ft		
Machine Guns				
Sub Machine Gun			1	
Lewis Gun			1	

While allowing for a tendency among Quartermasters to keep some material hidden in order to ensure they would receive supplies from GHQ, it is evident the Mayo Brigades were very short of weapons and ammunition. If war were to break out again they would not be able to take the field adequately as the British had promised much greater involvement from their military than had previously been experienced. Also, the wide variety of weaponry in use by the IRA made uniformity in training difficult. The IRA throughout Ireland had only 3,300 rifles and 5,000 shotguns available to its Volunteers. Michael Collins would have been supplied with this information prior to his departure for the Treaty negotiations; it would have had an influence on his efforts to secure peace.

The attention of GHQ on the Mayo Brigades was part of an effort to transform the IRA's military structure from a guerrilla army to that of a standing army. GHQ's focus on Mayo was also due to the outcome of an inquiry conducted in August and September 1921 by two GHQ officers, McNeill and Chadwick. Their brief had been to investigate a serious split in the East Mayo Brigade that had culminated in a shoot-out among some officers from the East Mayo and North Galway Brigades.[16] The trouble began in the summer of 1920, when the Kiltimagh Company of the IRA raided the local railway station and seized barrels of petrol under the orders of their senior officers, Captains Thomas Ruane and Johnny Walsh. Commandant Seán Corcoran, Brigade O/C, ordered the return of the petrol. Ruane refused, claiming it was for Pat Walsh and A. Cleary who had always placed their cars at the disposal of Volunteer business.[17] Corcoran immediately suspended Ruane and Walsh from duty and held a court martial that August. Commandant Michael McHugh, O/C Castlebar, was the President of the court. Corcoran's decision was upheld and Ruane and Walsh ordered to apologise. They refused and were subsequently dismissed from the IRA.

This rupture was further compounded by the involvement of Captain Eamon Corbett. On the run, Corbett was a member of the South Galway Brigade who arrived in east Mayo in the summer of 1920. He assisted Corcoran in planning and carrying out the raid on Ballyvary RIC barracks in August 1920, 'displaying considerable ability and courage'.[18] Corbett accused the East Mayo Brigade Adjutant, Joe Sheehy, of cowardice. Corbett also maintained that Fr Denis O'Hara, the highly respected parish priest of Kiltimagh, had an assurance with the local RIC that if no active operations were carried out by the IRA, the town and local people would not be interfered with. Corbett said Sheehy knew about this arrangement and used his senior position to prevent operations by the local IRA. The accusation caused a serious division in the Brigade. Corbett was expelled from east Mayo and warned by the Kiltimagh Company not to return. In spite of GHQ appearing to support Corbett's claims, there is no evidence to suggest such an 'arrangement' was in place between the Tans and the IRA in Kiltimagh. In fact, arrests in the area had been widespread. There had even been an attempt on Fr O'Hara's life and an incident where a group of men from Kiltimagh were forced to jump repeatedly into a river at bayonet point. In the wider district there were the murders of Paddy Boland and Michael Coen and the killing of Seán Corcoran. Boland, from Cloongownagh near Toureen, had been captured on 27 May 1921 by Argyll and Sutherland Highlanders. He was then bayoneted and shot. His body was then mutilated.[19] The area certainly was not at peace during the War of Independence.

During August and September 1921, GHQ held the court martial of Joe Sheehy. The opinion of the investigating officers regarding Sheehy was damning:

> J. Sheehy while being efficient from the point of view of writing reports and carrying out routine duties he has a most unsavoury influence in the Brigade and especially in Kiltimagh, and appears to us as to have used his Republican Army position to further the private interests of his employer to the detriment of the Brigade. It would be better if he were removed from the IRA altogether. He has been ordered to hand over all money and papers relating to the IRA.[20]

The report of McNeill and Chadwick referred to the poor munitions situation, saying the East Mayo Brigade had only six Mauser rifles and twenty rounds of ammunition. They also recommended the proper formation of Republican courts as the local IRA were getting involved in land disputes. Only one decision of a local Republican court had been carried out; the remainder were ignored because they did not suit the contending parties. They also stated that Thomas Ruane from Kiltimagh wished to be reinstated as an IRA officer but they did not believe this would be in the best interests of the Brigade.

Finally, it was the view of these two GHQ officers that as soon as the East Mayo Brigade was properly trained and armed it would give a very good account of itself. They mentioned in particular an ex-RIC constable, Tom Carney, who was training the IRA in grenades and musketry and was anxious to prove himself.[21]

After the investigation by GHQ, Corbett was reassigned as a transport officer to the 1st Western Division commanded by General Michael Brennan. However, on 11 October 1921, Corbett returned to Mayo to the house of Walter Sheridan near Straide, which was a North Mayo Brigade area. The East Mayo Brigade found out Corbett was nearby and surrounded the house he was staying in. Commandant Boyle, the North Mayo Brigade O/C, ordered the East Mayo men out of his area. Corbett also got word to his commanding officer, Commandant Reynolds, in Galway, who immediately travelled up to Kiltimagh with his intelligence officer, P. Fahy. Rescuing Corbett, the three men made for the railway station in Kiltimagh. While standing on the platform Corbett was recognised by some local Volunteers. They drew their revolvers with one of them, Dan Sheehy, opening fire. Corbett returned fire. A local woman, Ms K. Comer, was nearly killed in the exchange. As a result of this incident, the entire Kiltimagh Company of the IRA was suspended from duty. The Adjutant General of the IRA, Gearóid O'Sullivan, was also annoyed at the 'unseemly conduct' of the Galway officers entering the Mayo area of operations without permission. The East Mayo Brigade O/C, Liam Forde, claimed Corbett was in league with the Ruanes of Kiltimagh and the source of all the trouble in east Mayo. He also insisted that a shot had been fired at an escaping prisoner called Benson and Corbett was vain enough to think it was fired at him![22] Infighting like this had seriously reduced the effectiveness of the East Mayo Brigade. It became the focus of intensive training courses organised by GHQ in the autumn of 1921, with forty-five officers retrained at each of three camps held at Oldcastle House, Meelick and Swinford.[23]

There was also an unfortunate postscript to the Seán Corcoran story. In July 1921 the Brigade Adjutant requested financial assistance from GHQ to help Corcoran's aged parents and five sisters. It being a matter of great urgency, the Adjutant hoped a substantial grant would be made. Michael Collins attempted to have it dealt with by

Prisoners' Dependents' Fund. He also did not want the family put in an unpleasant position by the request for assistance being investigated locally. Eventually, a cheque for £100 was sent to the Corcoran family. The family, however, returned the cheque uncashed.[24] The memory of Commandant Seán Corcoran was not for sale. With the reorganisation of the East Mayo IRA now set in train, attention turned once more to disturbing events in the north of the county.

On 12 October 1921, a few days after the departure of the Irish delegation to London, Gearóid O'Sullivan, Adjutant General of the IRA GHQ, received a letter from Micheál Ó'Cléirigh of the North Mayo Brigade relating events concerning Michael Tolan:

> A Volunteer named Michael Tolan, a private in 'A' Company 1st Battalion, was arrested by local forces on 18 April last & detained in Ballina Barracks until 7 May, he was handed over on the latter date to an escort of Galway Police who returned to Galway that evening but the prisoner did not arrive. The local D.I. wrote to P. J.Ruttledge TD on 27/9/21 as follows: 'I am informed by my authorities that owing to the transfer & absence on sick leave of some of the members of the auxiliary police force who are concerned in the case it has not been possible as yet to complete inquiries into the matter.' A week or so after Tolan was removed from Ballina the body of a badly decomposed man was found in a bog about eight miles from Ballina by crown forces, they brought the remains to League (a graveyard one mile from Ballina) & buried him in an 'unknown' mans Plot & from inquiries made we believe it is Tolan. We desire disinternment, hold a post-mortem examination which will probably establish his identity owing to certain deformities & and also inquest. If there is identification we wish to have a public funeral with full military honours, we await your immediate advice.[25]

An initial refusal by the Adjutant General to permit a post-mortem and funeral with full military honours was overruled by General Richard Mulcahy. The North Mayo Brigade were told to go ahead with public funeral if they were sure the remains were Tolan's, although GHQ pointed out that a very full and detailed statement from the doctors would be important. GHQ then asked why the case had not been reported earlier. The probable answer is the disruption caused by the capture of the O/C of the North Mayo Brigade, Eamon Gannon, on 25 June 1921. Dr John Madden was promoted from West Mayo to take over the North Mayo Brigade in Gannon's absence. It was his leadership that initiated an investigation into Tolan's death. Dr Madden told GHQ that P. J. Ruttledge, TD for Mayo West-North, had reported it to Desmond Fitzgerald, Minister for Publicity, and Arthur Griffith months previously but nothing had been done. The Adjutant General at GHQ noted this was untrue so far as he was aware.[26]

In November 1921 the body of Michael Tolan was exhumed and an autopsy carried out by Drs Crowley and Ferran, both TDs. Dr Crowley gave the following evidence at the Ballina Quarter Sessions on Friday 3 February 1922:

> It was the body of an adult male. He should say that the cause of death was the two bullet wounds which they found in the head. The feet were missing, and he thought severed off. From the jagged appearance of both bones he should imagine that the feet had been crushed by blows of some blunt instrument. The feet were not in the coffin nor was the right arm. Some of the lower bones of the left forearm were also missing, as were also five teeth. The formation of the thigh bones pointed to the fact that the deceased must have suffered from some deformity of the feet.[27]

The body was formally identified by Mr Phelim Alfie Calleary, intelligence and engineering officer of the 1st Battalion Ballina Company IRA. Volunteer Michael Tolan had died a lonely, violent death at the hands of the RIC. His killers were never brought to justice. Mr Fitzgerald-Kenny, solicitor in the case for Tolan's mother, had letters relating to the RIC's investigation into the case but would not produce them in court.[28] The IRA in Ballina buried their comrade with full military honours. The first anniversary of his death was commemorated as a public holiday in north Mayo. Michael Tolan was at last permitted to rest in peace.

Captain Stephen
Donnelly (left) and
unknown senior
officer, North
Mayo Brigade Flying
Column, IRA, 1921.
(Private Collection)

On 20 November 1921, almost a year after Bloody Sunday, a
Republican celebration rally was held at the Fair Green, Ballyhaunis
in east Mayo. The meeting was chaired by William Coyne, local
solicitor and now Chairman of the County Council. Conor Maguire
had resigned from the post as he was on the run and working for
Dáil Éireann elsewhere.[29] In attendance were General Sean MacEoin
TD, Commandant General Tom Maguire, William Sears TD,
Tom Derrig TD and Dr Michael Waldron, President of the South
Mayo Republican courts. General MacEoin, the famed blacksmith
of Ballinalee, had made his reputation with his Flying Column in
County Longford. He was later captured, jailed and sentenced to
death. Collins organised an escape attempt that almost succeeded
in freeing MacEoin from Mountjoy Jail. He was eventually released
during the Truce, partly because of his humane treatment of
Auxiliaries after the ambush at Ballinalee in February 1921.

William Coyne spoke of the trauma through which Ireland had
just passed, saying no one wanted to go back to those days. But,
he continued, if it was necessary they would be ready to fight to

the last man, for they would have nothing but a Republic, and the whole Republic. MacEoin thanked the rank and file of the IRA who had done the fighting. It was to them the people should be grateful. He also encouraged the audience to have confidence in their representatives negotiating in London.

The crowd was next addressed by William Sears. He pointed out that such a meeting could not have been held a year ago or it would have ended up like the massacre at Croke Park. The crowd fell silent as Sears recalled the atrocities carried out against the Mayo people over the previous year: 'Here in Mayo old age was no protection, and over in Partry the scum of [Hamar] Greenwood went into the house and shot an old man's brains out. They were afraid to meet the IRA and so waged their war on women and children.' The crowd shouted 'Shame, shame'. Sears went on: 'They [the crowd] knew what happened poor Boland, whose body was mangled after he had been killed, and Coen and the others. No one could tell all the civil population had suffered at the hands of these monsters who went round at night.' Sears continued, recalling Tolan's death and the cover-up organised by the British officers at Foxford. He then added: 'If they were a revengeful people they would prepare a list of war criminals, and if they had that list they would place on the top of it the men who killed the cripple in Ballina.' Sears pointed out MacEoin and Maguire and said it was thanks to them that there were not a dozen more crimes like Coen's. Reaching the climax of his speech, Sears stated boldly, 'smashed at Ballinalee and routed at Tourmakeady, Lloyd George was not alone beaten on the field but he was beaten bankrupt'. The crowd cheered and cheered. Victory was theirs and they loved every moment of it.[30]

The meeting continued with a sober warning from Tom Maguire. He asked for young men of military age and physical fitness to join the ranks of the IRA. The one thing all those present should keep before their minds was an Irish Republic. Tom Derrig then addressed the crowd and the rally ended with the singing of 'The Soldiers' Song'.[31] Within a month, William Coyne and William Sears were to find themselves supporting a Treaty that proposed the establishment an Irish Free State, thus ending the Republican dream. Tom Maguire and Tom Derrig were to face pressure to row in behind those in favour of the Treaty.

Alex Boyd, North Mayo Brigade, Ballysokeery Company, IRA, and Connaught 220 Yard Dash Champion, 1921. (Private Collection)

William Sears' speech that day in Ballyhaunis, and his use of the words 'scum', 'monsters' and 'war criminals' in describing RIC activities, was unintentionally to lend powerful support to a killing spree of ex-RIC men returning home to Mayo after their disbandment. There were to be no war crimes trials in east Mayo, just the implementation of rough 'justice' and the murder of innocent people. In an interview with Ernie O'Malley, Johnny Griely, an officer of the East Mayo Brigade, identified a British officer called Anderson of the Scottish Border Regiment at Claremorris as being responsible for the death and horrific mutilation of Michael Coen and Paddy Boland.[32] The South Mayo Brigade intelligence report for July 1921 also identified a Lieutenant Anderson of the Argyll and Sutherland Highland Regiment stationed at Claremorris during this period. It therefore appears that the British military rather than the RIC were to blame for the shocking mutilation of two young IRA prisoners. The presence of an RIC sergeant at the claims court in support of Coen's family would further indicate the RIC were not responsible for the deaths and were anxious to distance themselves from those terrible events. This made little difference to the IRA men who were to take a terrible revenge once the Anglo-Irish Treaty was in place.

Connaught Champion 220 Yard Dash 1921 Gold Medal of Alexander Boyd, North Mayo Brigade, Ballysokeery Company, IRA. (Private Collection)

The Treaty between Great Britain and Ireland was signed at 2 a.m. on the morning of 6 December 1921. De Valera was in a 'towering rage' when he found out later that evening.[33] He felt that as President of the Dáil he should have seen the concluding document before it was signed. The division of opinion among Republicans on the Treaty began immediately. Dr Kathleen Lynn, Mayo woman, doctor and Sinn Féin activist, was less than pleased. In her diary she noted:

> 'Peace' terms but such a peace! Not what Connolly & Mallin & countless others died for. Please God the country won't agree to what Griffith, Barton, Gavan Duffy, Duggan & Mick Collins have put their names to, more shame to them, better war than such a peace. Council meeting from 10 to 4, we did good work, however. It is terrible how many who should know better seem quite pleased with terms.[34]

Dr Lynn had been Chief Medical Officer with the Citizen Army during the 1916 Rising. She was imprisoned in Kilmainham Jail along with Countess Markievicz and was there when the leaders of the Rising were executed. Republicans like Dr Lynn were never going to be convinced by a Treaty that required an oath of allegiance to the British Crown. Nevertheless, news of the agreement was received with genuine relief and happiness in Ireland. King George V was 'overjoyed to hear the splendid news' and issued a royal proclamation ordering the immediate release of over 5,000 interned Irish prisoners. Among them were many Mayo men and women who would now be coming home for Christmas. The release of the prisoners had been an issue of great concern in Mayo, with the County Council petitioning de Valera to withdraw the Treaty delegation from London at a pivotal point in the negotiations pending their release.[35] On 10 December, the *Mayo News* described the agreement as 'A Treaty of Peace' and 'a victory of sacrifice'. Archbishop Gilmartin of Tuam, perhaps more aware of the dangers that lay ahead, simply said: 'I consider the basis of settlement quite satisfactory, the negotiators deserve the profound thanks of both nations.'[36] Arthur Griffith summed up the importance of the Treaty for those who supported it by stating: 'These proposals do give Ireland control of her own destinies. They put our future in our own hands – enable us to stand on our own two feet ... In short, we have won the struggle of centuries.'[37]

The Dáil met to debate the Treaty on Wednesday 14 December. They would continue until the Christmas break began on Thursday 22 December, resuming in early January 1922. If a vote had been taken before Christmas the Treaty would have been defeated. The break gave the pro-Treaty camp time to mobilise strong support from the Catholic Church, newspapers and the business community who feared a return to violence and also the coming to power of a Republican party with a strong social agenda. The Mayo TDs had to decide where they stood.

Tom Maguire was unable to travel back to Mayo for Christmas and so remained in Dublin. He was still recovering from his wounds when he contracted a serious bout of flu. While convalescing in the Exchange Hotel, he received a call that two priests were waiting for him in the Gresham Hotel. On arriving, Maguire met with Canon

D'Alton, the parish priest of Ballinrobe, and Fr Martin Healy from Kilmaine.[38] Both priests had attended meetings of their local council, using their positions to promote acceptance of the Treaty on the instruction of Archbishop Gilmartin.[39] Canon D'Alton had spoken quite bluntly at Ballinrobe, declaring 'Those opposed to ratification [of the Treaty] were only fit to go into the asylum ... If the Treaty is thrown out this country practically disappears.'[40]

Letters were dispatched from Ballinrobe calling on the Mayo TDs 'to vote for the Treaty in the interests of our long suffering country'.[41] Another letter arrived from Fr Flatley, the parish priest of Aughagower, who had also chaired a meeting that secured a pro-Treaty resolution.[42] Maguire did not respond to the letter he received from D'Alton, hence the Canon's personal visit to Dublin. Neither the letters nor the visit could change Maguire's mind: he would vote against the Treaty along with most of his fellow Mayo TDs.

Mayo County Council held a two and a half hour meeting *in camera* on 30 December to discuss the Treaty. Conor A. Maguire and Thomas Ruane proposed the Council should take no action on the Treaty before Dáil Éireann had come to a decision, and also that it should issue a statement expressing hope for unity.[43] There was unanimous agreement among the Mayo councillors.

The *Mayo News* declared 1922 to be 'The Year of Destiny'.[44] Some of the Mayo TDs made substantial contributions to the Treaty debate. William Sears addressed the Dáil on 4 January. His address was pragmatic, and focused on the clear advantages for Ireland in accepting the Treaty:

> I would like to give it as my opinion that if this Treaty is rejected this assembly will be guilty of as great an act of political folly as is recorded in history. The plenipotentiaries that we sent over to London were selected by the President himself, and confirmed by this Dáil. There are no men in the Dáil superior to those, if there are equals, in political foresight and judgment (hear hear). For two months they contended with the ablest diplomats of the world, and they succeeded marvellously, in my opinion ... We did not expect them to bring home a Republic, but this Treaty will put us on the shortest road to the completest independence of the country ...

I will refer to some of the solid material advantages already in the Treaty, and see whether there is any compromise in our accepting them. For the first time in 700 years the English army is to march out of Ireland. I see no compromise in that. There have been withdrawals in history, as we know, and I never knew a withdrawal of the kind to be considered a compromise. We get charge of our own purse, and our own internal affairs. Is there any compromise in that? If the delegates brought home the Republic there are some gentlemen who, I think, would insist that England should surrender half her fleet as well ... If, twelve months ago, the Minister for Defence was marching out to battle he must have two objects – one, to drive the English army out of Ireland, and a second, to guard and see that there was no further invasion. If someone then told him that the British Army was being turned out without firing a shot, would he not say: 'Well, then I will devote all my energies to guarding against another invasion'? Surely he would not say: 'Leave them there; I would rather have the pleasure of putting them out myself.' And if anyone came and said: 'You will have an opportunity of equipping an Irish Army,' surely he would not have refused it.

Deputy Seán T. O'Kelly very rightly said here that whether this Treaty is accepted or not the fight for the complete independence of Ireland must go on. Certainly it will. And we have the opportunity of helping the nation towards that ideal. If, instead of entering on a disastrous war, we took charge of the schools and universities of the country, then we would be taking steps to preserve that ideal ... I will admit with regard to the Gaelic ideal, that whether it is in a Free State or Republic, as long as we have powerful British influences on our flank, it will be a terrible uphill fight to spread the Irish ideal. We can do that if, instead of the two parties in this Dáil wrangling with each other, they combine to advance the Gaelic ideal; then they would be doing better work for the country more than you could re-stage a battle ...

I say: 'God speed the Diehards.' Let them fight on, but do not let them step in the way of our country gaining the material benefits she is so badly in need of. We are entitled to that. It is all very well to speak of the flame, but the candle must be kept going too. Now I say this Treaty is a victory for the Irish Republican Army. This Treaty is the fruits of efforts of the most gallant band in history who fought against fearful odds here and suffered; and it is the fruits of the victory of the most patient and heroic people on God's earth – the Irish people – and they want to consolidate what has been gained, and when the day comes to make another advance. I share the hope of the Minister for Foreign Affairs that, with a stronger Ireland, we will be able to bring about further achievements without another devastating war; and that we shall evolve and rise to greater heights; and that our status will grow, too. I am convinced that Ireland will yet see the fondest dreams of Tone and Pearse realised to the full.[45]

William Sears' impassioned speech imbued with appeals for reason and calm undoubtedly convinced some of those who were wavering in their decision to support the Treaty.

The pro-Treaty side had the Treaty Articles to present a picture of the new Irish Free State. The Republicans, on the other hand, struggled against the overwhelming influence of the Catholic Church, the business community and the newspapers. The Mayo newspapers, the *Mayo News* and the *Connaught Telegraph*, took a pro-Treaty line. The *Western People* was a little more balanced, publishing some anti-Treaty articles and letters. In general, however, the anti-Treaty camp proved unable to get their message across. Few people placed importance on what Pearse, Clarke or Connolly might have thought, as admitted by anti-Treaty TD for Mayo West & North, P. J. Ruttledge. His primary concern was about a Treaty 'negotiated' under threat of 'terrible and immediate war' by Lloyd George. Ruttledge instead called for 'Peace with honour'.[46]

Many of those who supported Griffith and Collins had no difficulty taking the proposed oath of allegiance enshrined in article four of the Treaty. That oath called on TDs to 'swear true faith and allegiance to the Constitution of the Irish Free State' and to 'be faithful to his Majesty King George V, his heirs and successors'.[47]

Thus in conscience the pro-Treaty supporters were able to accept the oath as their loyalty was to the Irish Free State. For committed Mayo Republicans like Ruttledge, Derrig, Maguire, Dr Crowley and Dr Ferran, however, this was too much of a compromise in their beliefs. They had already taken an oath to the Republic of Ireland and stood for election before their people as Republicans. Ruttledge said whether it was faithfulness or allegiance, those taking the oath were still slaves to a master.[48] Tom Derrig exemplified the anti-Treaty side of the debate for the Mayo TDs when he addressed the Dáil on 6 January, the eve of the crucial vote on the Treaty:

> I cannot vote for this Treaty because the unity of Ireland is not secured; and I can't see any prospect in the future that we can get Ulster in. In the second place, I feel, while it is absolutely necessary that we should take a step forward in the direction of securing control of the Government, that we might also take a step backward; and I feel that in accepting this Treaty we are taking a step backward. I feel that we are going over the cliff and giving away the sovereignty of our country. Professor O'Rahilly[49] says that we will regain it by constitutional evolution; the Deputy for Carlow says that the Constitution will develop a Gaelic State; I contend that within the British Empire we cannot have a Gaelic State because the whole tradition of our people will have to be moulded in an Imperial way. The interpretation of this Treaty is also to be interpreted to safeguard the strategic interests of the British Empire.
>
> There are a number of articles in the Treaty which are very vague and I think we cannot look upon it as a Treaty. We are told that a Constitution must be drafted; and this Constitution must be legalised by the British Parliament. In my view there can never be an Irish Constitution until Irish unity is first secured ... There has been a good deal of talk about the material advantages in this Treaty. Lord Birkenhead has already written in the American Press; and our people are under the impression that the English Government has agreed under the Treaty to pay for the damage done in this country for two years. Lord Birkenhead and Winston Churchill have asserted that under

the Treaty England has us economically in the hollow of her hand – a most illuminating statement ...

While I believe that the Treaty would confer great material advantages on this country and that there might be a serious effort made to develop the Gaelic State I realise that we have completely lost our position before the world. After all, this movement is not the Gaelic State. This movement ought to be based on the traditions of the men of 1867 and 1916: and I think these are the ideals we ought to stand for. I came up here with an open mind; the mandate I got from my constituents was to try and do whatever I could to bring about an agreement; I am afraid now that there is no chance of substantial agreement ... To my mind the alternative to this agreement can be got; the only alternative that I can see is rejection ...

Finally, I don't believe that we can be in a better position in five years' time than at present; we had attained a magnificent position throughout the world; the position throughout the world does not demand that we should make a peace now that they did not think fit and proper. I have great faith in Gandhi and his 250 million people, and in Egypt; I don't think the Deputy from Cork is right when he says the Free State is responsible for the movement in these countries; I think it is the Irish Republic is responsible for them. If this question is brought before the country it is not alone that it will cause a split in the country but in the ranks of the army; and I earnestly ask every Deputy here to do what he can to preserve the integrity of the Army. Whatever we do with this Treaty let us do the best for the country.[50]

Thus the members of the great Sinn Féin movement had come to the parting of the ways. The fateful vote was taken on at 8.35 p.m. on Saturday 7 January 1922. The result was sixty-four votes for the Treaty with fifty-seven votes against. Griffith and Collins had pulled off a victory, but one that was to have enormous cost. Mayo TDs Dr Crowley, Tom Derrig, P. J. Ruttledge, Tom Maguire and Dr Ferran voted against the Treaty. Only two Mayo TDs voted for the Treaty, Joe MacBride and William Sears. As the months rolled on the divisions in

Sinn Féin were to become increasingly bitter. This was mirrored in the IRA, which eventually split into two distinct groups. The pro-Treaty IRA became Provisional Government troops and later the National Army. They were led by Michael Collins, Richard Mulachy, Gearóid O'Sullivan and Eamon Price and operated from Beggars Bush Barracks, Dublin. The anti-Treaty IRA were led by Rory O'Connor and Liam Mellows. They eventually seized the Four Courts in Dublin as their headquarters. The IRA in County Mayo were generally united against the Treaty, with the exception of a small contingent behind Joe Ring in Westport and a unit in Kiltimagh under Thomas Ruane. Division over the Treaty in Mayo would manifest itself in the County Council. The conflict in the County Council would reach its climax with a visit by Michael Collins to Castlebar in early April 1922. Before that, however, the County Council attempted to rebuild the damage inflicted by two years of neglect and war.

After the Truce was declared in July 1921, the County Council began to operate without interference from the RIC and the British military. The list of urgent tasks awaiting their attention was long. The first job was the abolition of the workhouses, which had an awful association in Mayo folk memory with the Great Famine in the 1840s. The Council agreed on a comprehensive scheme that would see all workhouses in the county close. All 'inmates' were transferred to the County Home at Castlebar. Hospitals attached to the workhouses at Ballinrobe, Claremorris and Westport were to be closed and patients transferred to a Central Hospital at Castlebar. Ballina and Swinford were to retain District Hospitals along with a small Fever Hospital at Belmullet. The Council also laid down the regulations for running the new system as directed by the Local Government Department of Dáil Éireann. One of the new developments was to have ominous consequences for young women in particular. As part of the new scheme, the Council addressed the issue of 'Unmarried Expectant Mothers and Unmarried Mothers'.

> It need hardly be pointed out that the presence of this particular class would be a stigma on the status of the Central Home. The Committee should consider how the following suggestions can be made practicable –

(a) Transferring these undesirables to some provincial or national institution, where their maintenance will be paid for, as far as possible, by their own labour, e.g. laundry work, basket-making, sewing, knitting, etc.

(b) Utilising the present Magdalene Asylums.

(c) Allowing such cases a small pension for maintenance in their own or friends' home during the period of incapacitation from work.[51]

The language used by the County Council indicated the dark future that awaited such women. It is a tragedy that one of the first actions of the 'new' Ireland was to initiate a system of enslavement for girls and young women who happened to become pregnant outside marriage, often through no fault of their own, and to subject them and their children to a long period of further abuse and rejection, hidden away from society.

The next major task facing the County Council was the repair and renewal of the road network. The stand-off with the Local Government Board under British control had starved the Council of the necessary funds to carry out essential work. With the Truce came surprising developments. The British War Department paid £1,800 to the Council for the damage done by British forces to the roads in the county. There was also time for levity in the more relaxed atmosphere of the Truce. The County Secretary, M. J. Egan, read out a letter received from the local District Inspector. DI Mahon requested the use of the courthouse for an RIC New Year's Dance. Egan could hardly be heard amidst the roars of laughter from the councillors, especially when he added that they would all be invited as special guests. The request was turned down, with the councillors suggesting that Mahon resubmit his application in Irish.[52]

Christmas 1921 saw the welcome return of more than fifty IRA prisoners to Ballyhaunis, Claremorris, Castlebar and Westport. They were welcomed with torchlight parades and accompanied by marching bands. Some other prisoners only made it home in early January. Patrick Coleman was one of seven prisoners who arrived home in Ballina on 14 January 1922. Coleman and his comrade A. Farrell were met by a huge crowd. A procession led by the Irish

Captain Micheál Ó Cléirigh (left) and unknown senior IRA officer of the North Mayo Brigade *c.* 1921. (Private Collection)

National Foresters and the Ancient Order of Hibernians marched to the Central Hotel. Bonfires lit up the night sky as the assembly partied late into the night. Brothers Paddy and Bart Hegarty from Laherdane and County Councillor Eamon Gannon who arrived home from jails in England the following Monday were given a similar reception.[53]

The end of January 1922 was a period of peace throughout the county. All hoped for a resolution to the split over the Treaty. There were great signs of hope. The British military had begun to evacuate their barracks. The Argyll and Sutherland Highlanders pulled out of Swinford and Claremorris on 23 January. They crossed to Liverpool late that night aboard the SS *Kerry*.[54] The Border Regiment remained until February. Large public auctions of military huts, stores and the very best of officers' mess furniture and silver took place. The married soldiers' families left Castlebar on 3 February. James Street RIC barracks in Westport was evacuated on Monday 12 February and handed over in an official ceremony the following day. The barracks in Castlebar were officially handed over on 12 February with the 2nd Battalion Border Regiment travelling by rail to Dublin the following day. After centuries of occupation the British were finally gone from the plains and mountains of Mayo. It was a staggering achievement for an Irish Parliament, a guerrilla army and a committed people. Curiously, there were no major celebrations. People were more worried about their immediate future. The distant thunder was drawing ever closer.

While politicians and soldiers busied themselves with the affairs of the new Irish Free State, those who had suffered in the War of Independence sought to rebuild their lives. Part of that process led them to the claims courts, which took place at the Mayo Quarter Sessions between October 1921 and January 1922. The claims were heard by Judge Charles Francis Doyle KC, a Limerick man who had been appointed to Mayo in 1910.[55] Over three months, Judge Doyle listened as men, women and children came before him with truly horrific accounts of what had happened to them. They represented every aspect of Mayo society, including farmers, shopkeepers, labourers, politicians, soldiers and policemen. They told of sadistic torture, pitch-capping, beatings, shootings to maim or murder, homes burned out or wrecked, produce looted and farm animals shot. Others were dependants of those killed by Crown forces or by the IRA in ambushes. Families had lost fathers, sons and brothers. Women and children were traumatised. Some died prematurely due directly to the violence. Most of the responsibility for this lay with the RIC and the British military. Many of those who claimed compensation in the courts were ridiculed and slandered, as others maintained they were out to make money from the state.

Charles Hughes of Westport claimed £6,500 for the loss of his business and home. Judge Doyle awarded him £3,257 11s and 9d for premises and £500 for personal effects destroyed. This was the exception rather than the rule, with most people in Mayo being awarded from £100 to £1,000 depending on the details of the claim. The British military and the RIC claimants received preferential treatment from Doyle. Their average award was in the region of £3,000, with money also being lodged in trust funds for children of RIC men killed in action against the IRA. Lieutenant Ibberson, who fought in the Partry Mountains, was awarded a generous £6,350 as he argued his injuries would prevent him continuing to serve in the Army. Ibberson in fact went on to reach the rank of Major before retiring in 1948. Thomas Lyons of Newport, whose brutal treatment was reported by Fr MacDonald, claimed £900 but was awarded £2,000 on the grounds that he was 'a physical wreck and had lost the sight of his left eye'.[56] He died a few years later.

The total amount of the claims lodged, including claims lodged up to September 1922 when the National (Free State) Army entered Mayo, was in the region of £250,000.[57] This was a colossal amount of money that was to be paid by the ratepayers of the county. Realising that the cost of the claims, at nearly £30 million nationally, would bankrupt the new Irish Free State, an arrangement was reached with the British government in January 1922. The British accepted responsibility for Cork, Limerick, Clare, Galway, Sligo, Roscommon, Leitrim, Tipperary, Louth, Wicklow and Mayo.[58] The British government, aiming to facilitate a 'resumption of normal civil life in Ireland', wanted settle the claims as quickly as possible.[59] The Provisional Government, on the other hand, went to great lengths to test the validity of claims, employing medical experts, architects, engineers, land valuers etc. Mayo councillors took exception to this hard-nosed approach, arguing the Provisional Government should pay the claims lodged as a national measure.[60]

The Provisional Government became concerned that the British, in settling claims quickly, would settle at high cost. In order to prevent this, Alfred Cope, Lloyd George's man in Dublin Castle, was brought in to find a solution. He proposed that awards and payments should be the same for each county. There would be a sifting of claims by trained men. Some cases would be recommended for immediate payment while others would require further inquiry. Investigators were authorised to settle cases on the spot up to £1,000. This had been whittled down by the Irish Ministry of Finance from £2,000. In cases over that amount the investigators were to submit recommendations to the Shaw Commission.[61]

In July 1922, Churchill, now Secretary of State for the Colonies, wrote to the Provisional Government expressing concern that the delay in the payment of claims by the Irish Free State was causing 'apprehension and hardship' among those awaiting settlement. He emphasised that His Majesty's Government could not divest themselves of a duty to see that such claims were met equitably and as promptly as the situation allowed.[62] By March 1923 the work of the Shaw Commission was still ongoing. New legislation was required as there was concern that the Criminal Injuries [Ireland] Act 1920 was British legislation and did not apply to Ireland. Constant questions were asked by TDs as to when claimants could expect to be paid. In fact, the Free State Government brought in an amendment that proposed to award government bonds and stock in lieu of money for the claimants.[63] The amendment was luckily defeated but the claims settlements dragged on. What is almost certain is that many never received the full amount to which they were entitled, leaving them in difficult circumstances and with shattered lives to rebuild. Some received only a fraction of the amount awarded by Judge Doyle whereas others received nothing at all. The Quarter Sessions at which the initial claims were lodged created an impression of thousands of pounds being awarded. It was far from the truth. The withholding of financial resources was becoming part of Provisional Government policy as the anti-Treaty IRA now faced the wrath of the Griffith, Collins and Mulcahy.

The Mayo IRA were almost to a man anti-Treaty. GHQ knew this and refused to pay them or send weapons and ammunition, fearing it might be used against them in a fight that was looking increasingly likely. Michael Kilroy received a rebuff from Richard Mulcahy when he wrote looking for financial assistance in October 1921. Mulcahy told him to organise a collection and look to the people of Mayo for payment.[64] This left the Mayo IRA in difficult financial circumstances. It also meant they could not pay the shopkeepers who had equipped them and provided food during the autumn and winter training camps. The Mayo IRA realised a confrontation with GHQ might be looming. What were to become the Mayo Republican brigades now urgently required armaments. Acting decisively, the East Mayo Brigade raided Charlestown RIC barracks on 16 January 1922 in a clear breach of the Truce. The British government had begun concentrating RIC constables and weapons in a number of the more fortified RIC barracks throughout the county. The attack was audacious and violent, resulting in the wounding of Sergeant McGovern and the severe beating of three constables. The raiders carried off twenty-three Lee-Enfield rifles and twenty-five revolvers, which were distributed among the East and North Mayo Brigades. The raid was investigated by Commandant Seán Walsh, liaison officer for the district.

In order to ease the evacuation of British troops and the disbandment of the RIC, liaison officers had been appointed by both the British military and IRA. Any breach of the Truce was to be investigated by them. Brigadier Emmet Dalton, Chief Liaison Officer, operated from the Gresham Hotel in Dublin. In Charlestown, Seán Walsh faced an uphill task as, unsurprisingly, none of the locals would talk to him. At Joe Ring's suggestion he visited ex-Captain Ruane of Kiltimagh. Ruane blamed the O/C East Mayo Brigade, Liam Forde. Walsh felt Ruane was prejudiced against the East Mayo IRA and discounted his information, especially when it emerged the Kiltimagh Company had again raided the railway station and seized two wagons containing rifles, ammunition and equipment around the same time as the Charlestown raid.[65] Walsh eventually tracked down the Vice O/C of the Ballaghaderreen Company of the IRA as being responsible for the Charlestown incident.[66] As Walsh was conducting his investigation, Joe Ring was more concerned about the conditions his former Volunteers were facing.

Commandant Joe Ring, O/C Westport IRA, had been appointed liaison officer for Galway the previous August. Ring was highly respected and gained a reputation for thorough and balanced investigation. He also retained a strong interest in the condition of his former company in Westport. Concerned that they were short of money for food and clothing he petitioned GHQ for funds to ease their hardship, stating that the matter was very urgent. Ring suggested '£10 a week would be sufficient to keep these men from absolute starvation'.[67] Ring also kept in regular contact with Michael Collins, sending him intelligence reports on the situation in the west. Collins received good information on Mayo from many contacts. In preparation for the forthcoming General Election in June 1922, Seán Cawley wrote a report for Collins on 'The Political Outlook in Counties Roscommon, Galway and South Mayo'. He said that all the business people and farmers were behind the Treaty, but that young people, especially in Mayo, were 'undoubtedly divided'. Cawley added that the anti-Free State movement was gaining ground and that women believed England would be afraid to declare war if the Treaty were rejected or a Republican party elected.[68] This may explain why women under thirty years of age were not granted the vote until after the General Election. The Republicans, aware of the level of anti-Treaty support among young women, were seriously concerned that plans to permit women over twenty-one to vote were being delayed by Arthur Griffith. The issue was hotly debated in the Dáil on 2 March 1922. Griffith, supported by Collins, argued that the voting register could not be completed in time, claiming it would take eight months. The Republicans argued the Representation of People Act allowed three months as adequate time for compiling a voting register.[69] A Dáil vote was taken with the Republicans defeated by forty-seven votes to thirty-eight. Women over twenty-one did not get the vote in the Irish Free State until April 1923. Events in Mayo, however, were soon to move beyond raids and intelligence reports, and into the realm of bloodletting and revenge.

Seán Cawley had reported to Collins that 'Truce Volunteers exercise a certain amount of intimidation'.[70] The Volunteers who joined the IRA during the Truce were known to veterans as 'Trucileers'. They had not known combat and so felt they had a lot to prove. East Mayo was about to see just how much some Volunteers felt they had to prove, as from March 1922, when the British government disbanded the RIC, many former constables returned home to Mayo. An IRA killing squad, perhaps remembering the words of William Sears TD the previous November referring to the RIC as 'war criminals', sought to take out their own form of 'justice'. They first struck on 4 March at Swinford, attempting to kill ex-Sergeant John O'Dowd. The assassins wounded O'Dowd and killed his wife as she held up a chair and stood between the attackers and her husband in an attempt to save him.[71] Two nights later, on 6 March, the killers struck again. This time they attempted to murder an employee of the Congested Districts Board, Patrick Cassidy. A local doctor operated on him immediately and extracted four bullets.[72] Cassidy was removed to Galway Hospital where it was thought he would be safe. However, a little over a week

Sergeant Tobias Gibbons, RIC, from Westport, County Mayo. Murdered along with Sergeant John Gilmartin and civilian Patrick Cassidy on the night of 15 March 1922 in Galway city. All three men were shot repeatedly in their hospital beds. (Courtesy Toby Gibbons)

later, Cassidy was killed by masked assassins in the hospital. That same night, 15 March, two ex-RIC sergeants, Tobias Gibbons from Westport and John Gilmartin, were murdered as they lay in their beds at St Bride's Hospital, also in Galway. Gibbons was shot eight times, including twice in the face.[73] One would have thought that all this killing would have satisfied their lust for blood. Unfortunately not. On the night of 6 April, commandeering two vehicles, the assassins drove to Ballyhaunis and picked out the homes of three ex-RIC men. Cranny was shot dead in his bed, Butler was seriously injured in his kitchen and evacuated to a Dublin hospital the next morning.[74] The third, a man called Flynn, was not in when the assassins called and he left town the next morning. There was a final murder on 23 May, ex-RIC Sergeant Walshe shot dead while on a visit to his wife and child in Newport.

Why were these men killed? The Treaty had been signed and ratified by both British and Irish parliaments. It was now surely time for peace. Some maintain the RIC men had been guilty of some atrocity during the War of Independence. Patrick Moylett claimed

Gilmartin had been involved with Auxiliaries in the killing of a young man with a bayonet near Moycullen.[75] Gibbons had been stationed at Tuam when it was sacked by the Black and Tans. Gilmartin and Gibbons had also both been awarded the Constabulary Medal. Their RIC files, however, do not state why the awards were made, which is a little unusual. Joe Ring carried out a thorough investigation into the murders at the two Galway hospitals. However, since the files on the investigation into the murder of Gilmartin and Gibbons have disappeared, it is speculation at this point as to the identities of the perpetrators from east Mayo.[76]

Sean T. Ruane of Kiltimagh suggested O'Dowd had been shot because he said he would reveal which locals were giving information to the RIC during the War of Independence. Ruane also said O'Dowd knew his would-be killers but refused to identify them and that none of his attackers gave any worthwhile service during the War of Independence.[77] The civilian, Patrick Cassidy, was a Congested Districts Board official involved in the redistribution of the landed estates. This is most likely to have been the reason for his death, rather than the suggestion that he informed the RIC as to the whereabouts of Seán Corcoran, O/C East Mayo Brigade. There is also the belief that Cassidy had identified Boland from Toureen as an IRA Volunteer for the RIC. This was based on a supposed eyewitness account from a young girl called Nolan. Boland, however, was murdered by the British military from Claremorris, not the RIC. In any case, the RIC would not have needed to identify Boland as he was already known to their constables in Ballyhaunis. What is certain is that Cassidy could identify the men who tried to kill him on 6 March. It was a risk those men were not prepared to take, and so they murdered Cassidy to silence him forever. Unfortunately, the file into Cassidy's murder, along with those of Sergeants Gilmartin and Gibbons, vanished many years ago.

The Treaty brought about a general amnesty for those on both sides who had engaged in warfare, assassinations and murder. The ex-RIC men in Mayo were killed at the hands of self-appointed executioners. There were many other ex-RIC men murdered in a similar fashion throughout the new Irish Free State. The local IRA commanders condemned the killings, calling them 'abominable'.[78]

One who escaped death was ex-Constable Owen Hannon. His frightened mother wrote to the Chief Liaison Officer describing a midnight raid by armed and masked men looking for her son on 19 March 1922. The men broke up the house and terrorised the woman looking for any information that might tell them her son's whereabouts.[79] Another RIC man, ex-Sergeant Jerry Kirby who had served in Claremorris, returned home to Listowel. He wrote a long letter to Captain William O'Keefe from Claremorris requesting a reference to testify he was not involved in any Black and Tan activities while serving in Mayo during the War of Independence. Ex-Sergeant Kirby was living in fear of being shot by the local IRA in Listowel. Finally, Former Divisional Commissioner of the RIC for Galway-Mayo, Robert Cruise, wrote to Walter Hume Long from Canada, where he had emigrated to begin a fruit business at Kamloops in British Colombia. He was concerned about the manner in which ex-RIC men had been treated after they were disbanded. Many, he argued, were not being awarded their full pensions. Long wrote to the British government outraged at the irresponsible decision to permit retired constables, with no protection, to be 'butchered' on returning to their families.[80]

Law and order in Mayo was once again breaking down. Behind it was the split in the County Council along pro- and anti-Treaty lines. The County Council had actually done its very best to prevent division after the Treaty was passed by the Dáil. Nevertheless, this became increasingly difficult as the months wore on, the pro- and anti-Treaty camps within the Council seeking to implement the policies of their respective Free State or Republican administrations in Dublin. The seizure of the Four Courts on 14 April by the anti-Treaty IRA Executive led by Rory O'Connor ended any hope of a peaceful outcome. The County Council Chamber at the courthouse in Castlebar became main theatre of conflict between the leaders of the Free State and Republican camps in Mayo. A dangerous power vacuum emerged across the county. Free State and Republican leaders encouraged an undermining of the authority of the other. This saw some young IRA commanders and Volunteers implement their own 'rule of law' at the point of a gun in small rural communities.

Senior Officers of the National Army visit the Curragh Camp in 1922. (L–r: Colonel R. Dunphy, Commande in Chief Michael Collins, Major General Emmet Dalton, Commandant General Peadar MacMahon and Commandant General D. O'Hegarty. (Courtesy the Military Archives, Cathal Brugha Barracks.)

Michael Collins visited Castlebar on 1 April 1922 after first stopping off to a hero's welcome in both Ballyhaunis and Claremorris. The date of his arrival was significant, as it was the first anniversary of the death of Seán Corcoran, O/C of the East Mayo Brigade. Collins, hoping the anniversary might encourage unity, was due to address a large election rally in The Mall. The forthcoming General Election would give the Irish public their first real chance to express an opinion on the Treaty. During the night, railway lines from Sligo, Ballina and Claremorris were ripped up and roadblocks put in place by Republicans attempting to disrupt the rally. Telegraph wires were also cut, leaving the press with no means of communication out of the county. In spite of this, people took to running through fields to avoid Republican IRA roadblocks in an attempt to get to Castlebar in time to hear Collins speak. He addressed the crowd from a large elevated platform in front of the Bank of Ireland and the Imperial Hotel.

Collins was supported by the entire Mayo pro-Treaty camp, including TDs Joe MacBride and William Sears and parish priests Macken of Claremorris and Colleran from Achill. Present also was Mayo County Council Chairman, William Coyne, Anita McMahon, Cumann na mBan and Colonel Moore of Moore Hall, former Inspector General of the Irish Volunteers. Collins received a tremendous ovation on his arrival. The atmosphere then grew tense as Republicans interrupted and shouted him down. Collins responded by saying he hoped the people of Mayo would not support the men who tried to murder people by tearing up the railway lines that morning. That was the Black and Tan method, but the Green and Tans were not going to be any more successful than the others![81] Fifteen minutes into his speech, a lorry made its way slowly through the crowd towards the platform. On the back of the lorry was Thomas Campbell, a solicitor from Swinford and member of Mayo County Council. Campbell began to challenge Collins and the two became embroiled in a heated exchange encouraged by the opposing groups in the crowd. Collins managed to resume his speech, saying: 'The English had deprived Ireland of freedom, of prosperity, language; robbed Ireland of the things of the mind and the spirit which mattered. After the lapse of so many centuries Ireland had recovered the power to get back what she lost ... now freedom is freedom, no matter what you call it. It is a fact not a title.'[82] Campbell pointed at Collins and shouted: 'The faithful subject of King George.' Collins glared at him and said: 'Your conduct is worthy of your record. You took good care to be in jail when there was danger.'[83] Such was the nature of the insults traded by those on opposing sides of the Treaty.

The Republicans in the crowd, mostly officers in the West Mayo Brigade, made a move towards the platform as if to remove Collins by force. Alex McCabe, TD for East Mayo-Sligo, produced a revolver, at which the IRA officers produced theirs. A dangerous impasse ensued. Charlie Byrne, a member of Collins' Squad known as 'The Count', got himself into a confrontation with some of the Republican officers. He was next seen, revolver in hand, running from The Mall pursued by Willie Malone, Paddy Duffy and Tommy Heavey of the

West Mayo Flying Column. Shots were exchanged and Byrne ducked into the Commercial Hotel in Spencer Street. A Mrs Fogarty was wounded in the shoulder. Byrne was arrested and held in Castlebar barracks by Kilroy's men where he was later court-martialled and acquitted.[84] Collins' men had long memories, and as a result of what happened to Byrne some of the Mayo Republicans were to receive rough treatment at the hands of the Squad when they were captured by the National Army during the Civil War.

Collins retired to the Imperial Hotel for a reception with the Mayo pro-Treaty Committee. That night Joe Ring was arrested in Westport by IRA officers and charged with recruiting for the National Army. He was held in Castlebar Jail where he immediately went on hunger strike. Ring was released on 13 April, returning to Westport as a conquering hero. Delivering a defiant speech at The Octagon, he said that 'it revived his exhausted spirit to see the overwhelming majority of people registering their solemn protest against an act of despotic militarism'.[85] The commandant was protected by a special bodyguard, which was the beginnings of a National Army Unit called 'Ring's Own'.

For Collins, his experience in Castlebar left a bitter aftertaste. He longed to settle accounts with the Mayo IRA. The following month, Collins sent a message to Winston Churchill. He indicated that the Provisional Government had decided to fight the Republicans and thus requested 10,000 additional service rifles, guns, mortars and ammunition. Collins proposed 'to deal firstly with outlying areas like Drogheda and Castlebar and leave the Republicans in Dublin undisturbed'.[86] Churchill, however, felt that the Provisional Government should be put to the test. At this point, the British Cabinet believed Ireland was in 'a process of rapid social disintegration'. He therefore proposed Collins should deal with Dublin first and the additional weapons would then be gladly supplied to enable the Provisional Government to undertake operations on a larger scale in the country districts.[87] Castlebar had Churchill to thank that the eighteen-pounder guns that shelled the Republican Four Courts were not first used to pound the Mayo capital into ruins. As Collins was preparing for inevitable confrontation with the Republicans matters came to a head in Mayo County Council.

County Council meetings became increasingly resentful as the pro-Treaty camp sought to frustrate the Republicans plans. Issues came to a head over a Republican proposal to impose an extra levy of sixpence on the ratepayers to pay the wages of the IRA. By April 1922 both Maguire and Kilroy's men were very short of money. They had not been paid by GHQ due to their anti-Treaty stance. Divisional Adjutant Christie Macken sent GHQ details of the debts incurred by the IRA to drapers of £1,200 and grocers of £2,200. Travelling expenses amounted to £200.[88] The sum of £3,900 was eventually sent by GHQ to Kilroy's 4th Western Division 'for the strict purpose of clearing off the debts reported from that area'.[89] It was accompanied by a request for receipts to be signed by an officer and countersigned by the Divisional Commandant. To prevent any confusion, Macken alone was to be responsible for the payment and collection of receipts. Mulcahy also discussed with Macken pay rates for a proposed IRA full-time strength of 200 men for the Division with the rest being stood down.[90] Kilroy was then accused by the Minister for Defence Richard Mulcahy of misappropriating the funds. In his defence, Kilroy published the list of names of those who received the money in the Mayo papers on 22 April 1922.

The correspondence between Kilroy and Mulcahy became the centre of debate at the County Council meeting on 27 April. The pro-Treaty camp, led by Chairman William Coyne and supported by a Local Government Department official, a Mr McGrath, declared a levy of sixpence imposed by the Council for maintenance of the IRA to be illegal. Hostile exchanges followed throughout the debate with Republican Dick Walsh being accused by John O'Boyle of being 'on the green hills far away' during the Tan troubles. O'Boyle, in full flow, then rounded on Thomas Campbell, telling him not to act the hooligan as he had done on The Mall in Castlebar during Collins' visit. 'Dáil Sassanagh' ('West Brit'), Eamon Gannon from Ballina shouted back.[91] The Republicans, exasperated by the Chairman's refusal to accept their decisions, attempted to replace him with Mr Keaveney, a Republican. Coyne refused to accept this decision, and as Keaveney walked towards the Chairman to take his place, the meeting was declared 'no longer in order' by McGrath. The infuriated Republicans said McGrath, who was not a member of the County

Michael J. Egan (left), Mayo County Council Secretary 1919–24 with P. J. Bartley, Mayo County Council official. (Courtesy Micheline Egan)

Council, had no right to take such action. They continued with the meeting as the pro-Treaty camp departed. The Secretary, M. J. Egan, gathered his papers and walked to the door only to be prevented from leaving by two IRA officers 'who compelled him to return'.[92] Egan then confronted Keaveney, the new Chairman, saying he was working only because he was compelled to do so. The Chairman told Egan 'he must in future obey the orders and rulings of the majority of the Council and as they were responsible for his salary he, on his part, must be responsible to them.'[93] The Republicans then passed a unanimous resolution advancing £2,000 as payment to the IRA and the recently formed Irish Republican Police.

By the end of April, GHQ was still withholding funds from the anti-Treaty IRA for payment of troops. The Republican Four Courts Executive ordered the anti-Treaty IRA to 'visit' Bank of Ireland branches throughout the country to withdraw the money that they were owed. The Bank of Ireland was where the Provisional

Government had invested its funds. In Mayo, a total of nearly £10,000 was taken from Bank of Ireland branches at Ballina, Ballinrobe, Claremorris and Westport. Receipts from the Four Courts Executive were politely handed over by armed men to the respective bank managers.[94] The bank raids were just another step on the descent to madness, encouraging greater lawlessness as institutions of the state were undermined.

Agrarian unrest once again reared its head. On the same day Collins was in Castlebar, Anne Horkan was shot dead and her sister, Katie, seriously wounded when their house at Grallagh near Straide was raided in an attempt to force them off land that their father had recently bought. One of the raiders, Patrick Gallagher, was also shot dead in the incident. Anne Horkan lived just long enough to give a description of her attackers.[95] On 30 April 1922, Mary MacSwiney TD was the main speaker at a Republican election rally in Castlebar.[96] In a highly charged atmosphere, chaired by Michael McEvilly, father of Seamus MacEvilly killed in action at Kilmeena, the Republicans emphasised the cost of their sacrifice in the cause of Irish freedom. McEvilly drew partly on the example of the 1916 patriots but also spoke of the hardship of life as a Volunteer in a flying column over the past three years. MacSwiney said the Dáil had established the Republic in 1919. It could not be undone by a splinter group. Addressing the majority in the Dáil who had gone with the Treaty, she said they had sacrificed the north of the country and were guilty of treason. MacSwiney regretted the division and bitterness among former friends, but she saw the shedding of blood as inevitable. MacSwiney finished her address with a solemn warning: 'every drop of blood that had already been shed, or that will be shed in civil strife over the Treaty will be on the heads of Mr Collins and Mr Griffith and their supporters. No Treaty is worth Civil War and those who won the Republic are determined the Republic shall not be subverted.'[97]

The meeting was followed by a concert at the Town Hall and a reception at the courthouse. The situation in the country was now like a tinderbox. Any flashpoint between pro- and anti-Treaty military forces could ignite a civil war. The Mayo newspapers began to ridicule the Republican position with the majority anti-Treaty County Council accused by the *Mayo News* of wanting to establish 'a little

Republic of Mayo' based on communism. The word 'Bolshevik' also began to be associated with Republicans in the papers.[98] A correspondent identified only as 'South Mayo' wrote in the *Western People*: 'To assert that any sensible Irishman went to London to get a Republic is mere eyewash, hogwash and the veriest balderdash for they might as well look for holy water in an Orange Lodge.'[99]

The antagonism between the two camps had now gone beyond the trading of insults. On Sunday 30 April, Thomas Ruane, now a Captain in the National Army, was shot in the hand in a row over a recruiting poster for pro-Treaty forces. Two weeks later, a Commandant Simmons accompanied by three GHQ officers visited The Neale, Cross, Shrule and Kilmaine in south Mayo on a recruiting drive for the National Army. The officers retired to an evening meal with Canon D'Alton, Fr Brett and Fr Healy. Captain Gorman, a Republican officer of the 2nd Western Division, arrived and demanded the National Army officers submit to arrest. Simmons refused and a dangerous stand-off ensued with press arriving expecting an outbreak of hostilities. General MacEoin of the National Army dispatched the Rolls-Royce armoured car, 'Ballinalee', from Custume Barracks Athlone to raise the temperature even higher. Eventually, Commandant General Maguire allowed Simmons to leave the area and peace was restored.[100]

The County Council met again and scrapped the proposed sixpence levy. At last aware they were heading for a precipice and taking the county with them, both pro- and anti-Treaty camps managed to display some semblance of civility and pulled back temporarily from the edge. W. T. Cosgrave made a last attempt to win over the County Council by forwarding £11,000 for the relief of unemployment in the county and £3,176 for the maintenance of the Mental Hospital.[101] The moves were not enough to calm the mood in the county as unrest continued. In Castlebar, Commandant James Chambers proclaimed martial law in the districts of Cornacool, Derrycoosh, Kilfea, Rahins and Snugboro near Castlebar as agrarian unrest continued.[102] The standing of the IRA was tarnished by the court martial of three officers from Castlebar, Captain James Hughes, Lieutenant Pat Ainsworth and Lieutenant Anthony Clarke, for carrying out a series of drunken robberies throughout the Castlebar rural district. The

Rubicon was finally crossed on Sunday 28 May, as James and Honoria Kelly, a married couple, stood outside their house in Sonnagh near Charlestown. They got into a row over the Treaty with a neighbour, Michael McIntyre, son of anti-Treaty County Councillor, John McIntyre. Mrs Kelly made some comment to McIntyre who turned and fired a shotgun at her. Mrs Kelly was hit in the face, neck and chest and died within fifteen minutes. Michael McIntyre was immediately arrested by the local IRA.[103] Mrs Honoria Kelly, aged forty-seven, an innocent mother and civilian, was thus the first victim of the Civil War in Mayo. Killed because of her stance on the Treaty, she died in her husband's arms with her daughter helplessly looking on.

The final throw of the political dice was made at the General Election on 10 June 1922. TDs elected were to take their seats in the third Dáil, the Constitution of which was published only on the morning of the election. The results for de Valera's anti-Treaty camp were disappointing. They won only thirty-six seats. Griffith and Collins' pro-Treaty camp did better, winning fifty-eight seats. The pro-Treaty camp also received the support of Labour with seventeen seats, the Farmers' Party with seven, Independents six and Unionists four.[104] The following candidates were elected for County Mayo:[105]

General Election Results 10 June 1922.
TDs Elected for Mayo Constituencies

Mayo West-North		Mayo South-Roscommon South	
Dr John Crowley	Anti-Treaty Re-elected Unopposed	William Sears	Pro-Treaty Re-elected unopposed
Thomas Derrig	Anti- Treaty Re-elected Unopposed	Tom Maguire	Anti-Treaty Re-elected unopposed
Joseph MacBride	Pro-Treaty Re-elected Unopposed	Daniel O'Rourke	Pro-Treaty Re-elected unopposed
P. J. Ruttledge	Anti-Treaty Elected for the first time unopposed	Harry Boland	Anti-Treaty . Re-elected unopposed mortally wounded Civil War

Mayo East-Sligo	
Frank Carty	Anti-Treaty Re-elected unopposed
Alexander McCabe	Pro-Treaty Re-elected unopposed
Seámus Devins	Anti-Treaty Re-elected unopposed KIA Civil War
Dr Francis Ferran	Anti-Treaty Re-elected unopposed Died while imprisoned at the Curragh on 10 June 1923.
Thomas O'Donnell	Pro-Treaty Re-elected unopposed

Mayo had overwhelmingly voted for anti-Treaty Republican candidates. Buoyant with this support, the Republicans on the County Council ousted pro-Treaty Chairman William Coyne and installed P. J. Ruttledge as the new Chairman by seventeen votes to nine. The move was engineered by Tom Maguire and Michael Staunton.[106] Unfortunately, the time for politics was at an end.

With the Treaty and the Irish Free State Constitution secure, the presence of the armed Republican headquarters in the Four Courts was an obvious challenge to the Provisional Government's authority. The assassination of Sir Henry Wilson in London by Reggie Dunne and Joseph O'Sullivan of the London IRA, along with the kidnapping of Provisional Government General 'Ginger' O'Connell by the Republicans brought matters to a head. Churchill, threatening to use British troops to attack the anti-Treaty Four Courts Executive whom he blamed for Wilson's death, forced Collins into firing the opening salvos of the Irish Civil War.[107] On 28 June 1922, Dublin was rocked by artillery fire as the National Army, using eighteen-pounder artillery on loan from the British, opened fire on the Republicans in the Four Courts. Ireland was now at war with itself. Mayo was to be no different. The Civil War would bring bloodshed and chaos to an already weary people.

7

'To the Bitter End': Civil War

Commandant General Edward Cooney was perched on the turret of the armoured car 'Ballinalee' as it drove down the Ballyhaunis road to Claremorris. With its Rolls-Royce engine smoothly ticking over and Vickers machine gun at the ready, the armoured car led a convoy of troops into the town. Coming to a halt in The Square, Cooney and his officers jumped down on to the roughly cobbled street. They were immediately swallowed up by the crowd, who cheered, hugged and kissed them and welcomed them as liberators. It was Sunday 23 July 1922: the National Army had arrived in Mayo.

After getting his breath back, Cooney, as Quartermaster for Western Command, organised Brigadier General Lawlor's head-quarters in the Imperial Hotel. Other ranks were billeted in different hotels and in the homes of those with spare rooms. The following night, as Cooney sat by a turf fire in the Imperial Hotel, he wrote to General MacEoin:

> Dear Sean,
>
> We wired Athlone today to send down a train with provisions & petrol for us. Get Comdt. Finnigan to send on about 30 p[ai]rs Boots also a good supply of cigarettes. The principal things short in the town here are Baking powder, sugar, and

cigs. However, when you are sending food supply you can send some of all stuff needed: such as Bacon Bread or flour some Bully-Beef etc. I need not enumerate all these. This last is for the Army. Well we are having a great time. The receptions we are getting in every town is something to write home about, and seems to be increasing as it goes on.

The Intelligence is top-hole the people make it their business to let us know all the know. How is the Mrs also 'The Duffy'. Do tell them all I was asking for them. I suppose you don't be in Ballymahon at all.

We have just heard they [the Republicans] are after Burning out Ballinrobe. They are flying before us like hell so far. We gave Kit McKeon [Republican commander from Athlone] a shot of a machine gun arriving at Ballinlough we could not keep near him after that he led the retreat at a great pace. We ought to get in touch any time now.

Goodbye now for the present. Make them keep the train service going down this way.

Is mise

E. J. Cooney

P.S. There was about one hundred girls getting tea for the troops here last night after they marched in. You could not imagine how delighted the people are and they are all enquiring after for you. The Expeditionary force is keeping temperate and generally a credit.[1]

Brigadier General Anthony Teasdale Lawlor was chosen to head the National Army's campaign in the west. His forces were to become known as Claremorris Command. The 24-year-old from Dalkey, County Dublin, had joined the British officer training corps for infantry at Trinity College. Lawlor subsequently served with the 73rd Squadron of the RAF during the First World War. He was hospitalised in July 1918 and later promoted to Second Lieutenant.[2] Demobbed in October 1919, Lawlor returned to Ireland and joined the IRA. He became a close friend of General Seán MacEoin and was

Colonel Lawlor (front centre without cap), National Army, O/C Claremorris Command August–December 1922. Pictured here as O/C Curragh 1953. (Courtesy Reggie and Fintan Darling)

in command of the shelling of the Four Courts at the outbreak of the Civil War.[3] Lawlor chose Brigadier Generals Cooney and Simmons as his senior officers in Mayo. Simmons had already been active in recruiting for the National Army in Mayo during the Truce. Lawlor's force was equipped with Lee-Enfield rifles, Lewis machine guns and a plentiful supply of ammunition and grenades. They also had the support of Rolls Royce, Lancia and Whippet armoured cars. While the infantry were occasionally transported by truck and rail, they usually had to resort to the age-old necessity of foot slogging from village to village.

Facing Lawlor, and once again defending their county, were Republican Commandant Generals Tom Maguire, O/C 2nd Western Division and Michael Kilroy, O/C 4th Western Division. As British troops began pulling out of Ireland in the spring of 1922, their military intelligence had continued to monitor Republican commanders who were opposed to the Treaty. Maguire was actually seen in a positive light: 'Thomas Maguire, leader of the Republicans in the Ballinrobe area, is apparently not an extremist; he rules his area justly, and stops profiteering by the shopkeepers.'[4] The cost of living in south Mayo created great hardship for ordinary people in late 1921, with Claremorris enjoying 'the unenviable reputation of being the dearest town in the county'.[5] Prices remained high with the outbreak of Civil War as the Provisional Government blockaded the west of Ireland. Food supplies were extremely short and the danger of an outbreak of disease ever present. In fact, Erris was hit by typhus the following year. Ballina, as a port town, became a vital link with the outside world for Republicans. Joseph Murphy chartered the boat SS *Esperanto* to beat the blockade. The ship delivered 56 bags of mail, 107 parcels and much needed supplies to the town on Monday 17 July 1922.[6]

Michael Kilroy was viewed by the British as a serious threat: 'An ardent Republican. Dangerous, clever & unscrupulous ... Age 35. Dark eyes. Pale & sallow complexion. Square build. Height 5' 9". Active appearance.'[7] Kilroy was a Republican idealist with a strong pragmatic streak. He was the most effective Republican commander the National Army faced in the west throughout the Civil War. A military innovator, Kilroy ordered the building of armoured cars to supplement those already captured from the National Army as well as a factory to manufacture grenades. One of the armoured cars, named 'Queen of the West', was designed by Thomas Moran. It was constructed using a cylindrical boiler from a hotel in Mulranny. Joe Baker said its nickname '*Fág an Bealach*' ('clear the way') was more commonly used.[8] After its capture by the National Army, it was renamed 'The Girl I Left Behind'.[9] Kilroy provided inspirational leadership that saw his column swell to 700 men, 100 more recruits than he could provide weapons for. Such numbers flocking to the Republican colours raises questions about the standing of the Provisional Government among the people of Mayo at this point in the Civil War.

The Republicans referred to the National Army as Free State Forces or simply Staters. The Provisional Government and National

Army referred to the Republicans as Irregulars or sometimes Bolshies.[10] This attempted association with Lenin's Bolsheviks would strike fear into the hearts of many middle- and upper-class Irish families, securing their allegiance to the fledgling Free State. Under Maguire and Kilroy, the Republicans equipped a number of columns that were usually named after their commanders. Dr John Madden was based in the west and north of the county, with Tom Carney's column in the east near Kiltimagh and Frank Carty's operating from the Ox Mountains. Each column was to contain thirty-five men, including engineers, signallers and machine gunners. They were then subdivided into a number of five-man sections each led by a non-commissioned officer.[11] The field of operations for Republican units was much greater than in the War of Independence. This made it very difficult for Lawlor's troops to catch up with the Republicans who were always on the move.

There were relatively few casualties in the early stages of the conflict. East Mayo saw the first National Army and Republican soldiers killed. On 29 June, Captain Willie Moran, O/C Bohola, was ordered to arrest Vice-Brigadier Thomas Ruane of Kiltimagh on account of his recruiting men for the National Army. Ruane, in keeping with his fighting spirit, resisted arrest. In the ensuing struggle he fired a shot, hitting Moran. Captain Moran staggered out into the street where he collapsed and died. He was just twenty years old. Martin Lavin, a Republican Volunteer, returned fire and fatally wounded Ruane. Ruane passed away on 5 July at the Castlebar Infirmary.[12] Both men had devoted their young lives to their country and had survived the Tan war. They had died at the hands of their own countrymen and their deaths were just the beginning. On 4 August, Commandant Patrick Moran of Tom Maguire's 2nd Western Division was killed in action at Kilkieran in north Galway.[13]

In west Mayo, Michael Kilroy was forced to evacuate Westport after a successful seaborne landing by National Army forces led by Brigadier General Joe Ring on 24 July. They first captured the Coastguard Station at Rosmoney, freeing some ninety men who had been held prisoner by the Republicans. Ring then landed his men at the Quay in Westport. He was supported by an armoured car that was nicknamed 'The Big Fella'. The Republicans, taken completely by surprise, set fire to

(L–r): Seán Walsh and Tom Carney, Republican officers, East Mayo Brigade, IRA, pictured during the Civil War 1922. (Courtesy Paraig Walsh)

the barracks and withdrew. Ring's troops, now known as 'Ring's Own', put out the fire and also defused a mine placed at the entrance to the barracks.[14] Kilroy had also ordered the burning of Castlebar barracks and the post office. The barracks were set fire to but the townspeople, led by Fr Prendergast, chased off the Republicans as they attempted to burn the post office just after midnight. It was a courageous act by the unarmed civilians, one of whom, named Quinn, was wounded by Tommy Heavey, an officer in Kilroy's Active Service Unit.[15] The saving of the post office was much applauded by the local press.[16] In the south of the county, Maguire ordered Ballinrobe barracks to be burned before retreating further west into his home territories around Cross, Kilmaine and Shrule. There were no clear battle lines between the Republicans and the National Army, and the military situation remained chaotic for much of the Civil War period. The first real contact in County Mayo between the National Army and Republican forces occurred on Thursday 3 August, at Bracklagh, near Kilroy's stronghold of Newport. A Sergeant Lally and Private Deasy of the National Army were killed with Republican Edward Hegarty also losing his life.[17]

Skirmishes, ambushes, sniping, blowing up railway lines and bridges became the norm for Republican columns. In response, Lawlor garrisoned the main towns of Mayo, which included Ballina, Ballinrobe, Castlebar, Claremorris and Westport. He then employed military drives from the various barracks to round up Republicans. It was a tactic borrowed from the British military and failed to have the desired success. The fighting was even more desperate than during the War of Independence. A deserter from the National Army told Republican officers of the 4th Western Division how 'Free State soldiers extract the lead from the casing of a .303 bullet, put in ground glass and then put back part of the lead.'[18] In return, the Republicans used 'dumdum' or exploding bullets. Either type of ammunition inflicted agonising wounds. It also emphasised the hatred some held for the enemy in this conflict. Not all felt this level of animosity, as it was hard to fight former comrades. Some men, like William O'Keefe of Claremorris, remained neutral, refusing to take up arms against friends. O'Keefe had initially joined the National Army but resigned when he saw what the Civil War entailed. These neutral officers formed an association and attempted to broker a ceasefire in the conflict.

Others, like Tom Maguire, could not fight with the same vigour as they had against the British. Years later he recalled:

> You could not bring yourself to want this sort of warfare. There was a different feeling altogether. The British were the enemy, the old enemy; there was a certain pride in having the ability to attack them. That feeling was entirely absent in the Civil War. It was very disheartening. We knew the Free State Army comprising 50,000 newly recruited mercenaries would not hesitate to shoot us, but that made it no easier for us to pluck up enough anger to really fight them. You were in doubt too about approaching houses where before you had been welcome. How are they taking the situation, you would wonder? The people themselves are disheartened. When I heard of the deaths of people on the Free State side like Griffith, Collins, Seán Hales, I could not be glad. You felt these are people who fought the British and now they are gone. Britain is really the victor.[19]

August was a difficult time for the Provisional Government, the *Western People* solemnly reporting how 'Ireland has suffered an almost irreparable loss in the death of Mr. Arthur Griffith, President of Dáil Éireann, which occurred with tragic suddenness on Saturday last [12 August]. He has fallen in sight of the Promised Land, and the country is poorer by his loss.'[20] General Michael Collins issued a statement hoping 'that as he [Griffith] lived his life for the good of Ireland his death may be the means of bringing an enduring peace to this country'.[21] By Tuesday 22 August, Collins himself was dead, killed in a Republican ambush at Béal na Bláth ('Mouth of the Flowers') in County Cork. A group of young Mayo men were with Collins' convoy that day. They had been on their way to Dublin to join the new Civic Guard police force when they were commandeered to remove any obstacles that blocked Collins' route.[22] The country was stricken with grief. Richard Mulcahy, Chief of Staff of the National Army, urged his troops not to blemish their honour by cruel acts of reprisals. 'Ireland, the Army serves – strengthened by its sorrow'.[23] Mrs Ryan, Chairperson of the Castlebar Urban Council, and J. J. Collins travelled to Dublin to attend Michael Collins' funeral.[24]

Expressions of grief were not extended to all who lost their lives in the Civil War. Mayo County Council was now back in the hands of Provisional Government supporters after P. J. Ruttledge, Ned Moane, Paddy Hegarty and other Republican councillors left to join their flying columns. The Council marked Griffith's death with a resolution that stated: 'We wish to convey to Mrs Griffith, to Dáil Éireann and the Irish Nation an expression of our condolences in the irreparable loss they have sustained and pray God to give his noble spirit Eternal Rest.'[25] The motion was passed in silence. Michael Staunton, a Republican councillor, then proposed that an expression of sympathy with the relatives of the late Harry Boland be added to the resolution for Griffith's family. The Chairman, William Coyne, ruled this out of order. Staunton, supported by a Mr Lally, next proposed a separate resolution for the relatives of Harry Boland, only to be ignored again.[26] Harry Boland, TD for Mayo South-Roscommon South, had been mortally wounded by National Army troops during a raid on the Grand Hotel in Skerries, County Dublin on 31 July. He was unarmed and died in St Vincent's Hospital two days later.[27]

On the evening of Saturday 25 August, a detachment of National Army troops discovered a Republican column hiding out in Brize House on the Claremorris to Balla road. Reinforcements arrived and an assault on the house was carried out with the aid of a Lancia armoured car. Inside the building, belonging to John McEllin, were Kit McKeon's Longford column and three west Mayo Republicans, Brodie Malone, Paddy Cannon and Tommy Heavey, who had just escaped from Custume Barracks in Athlone. They had been captured in the battle for Cooloney in County Sligo in July. A Republican scout spotted the armoured car speeding up the drive and ran to alert the others. According to Heavey:

> The bullets began to fly. It was a large two-storied house with a basement. Malone and I made a dash for one window to jump out of it but a burst of Machine-Gun fire came through us. We tried to open the window then but Brody Malone was hit in the left arm and the left thigh. I dragged him away from the window. The front door was closed. I brought him to the basement. The Column returned the fire from the upper windows. An armoured car plastered the windows from the outside. It was pitch dark now for we were waiting for the darkness to start out [to get away]. After an hour and a half we surrendered. They came to a window which was over our heads in the basement: and they threatened to bomb us. Malone did not want to surrender. Our outposts got away. The Staters were in a vile temper. There was a Sergeant Ellis who was very bad who was pushing us around. I [was] told then that there was a man who was severely wounded. An Officer came out of the armoured car and announced to us that Mick Collins was killed. They took us into Claremorris to a bare room in a house. They threw us all in together then. We had no sanitary arrangements, no beds. Next morning they drove us all to Athlone.[28]

McKeon evaded capture as he had been out reconnoitring some enemy positions. Nevertheless, the event was a major success for Lawlor's men, with 13 Republicans captured alongside 8 Mauser rifles, 2 Lee-Enfield rifles, 1 Thompson machine gun and 600 rounds of ammunition.[29] Malone was given basic medical care before being left to endure prison with a bullet in his leg for the next year and a half. He shared a cell with Johnny Gibbons. Later, they were charged with robbing the Bank of Ireland at Westport and imprisoned in Sligo Jail. Both had served in the West Mayo Flying Column. They were locked up in their cell for twenty-three hours a day throughout their incarceration.[30] By the end of August Provisional Government troops had occupied all major towns throughout Mayo. This mirrored the ascendancy they had gained across the country, seaborne landings at Cork and Tralee helping to oust the Republicans from their stronghold of Munster.

Ballina had been taken from the Republicans on Saturday 29 July 1922. Lawlor's troops occupied the workhouse as their headquarters, and twenty Republicans were immediately arrested in the town. The main Republican forces, led by Kilroy and Ruttledge, withdrew to the Ox Mountains and based themselves in Bonniconlon.[31] The majority of people in Ballina were delighted to see the National Army in control. Their celebrations would not last long, with the Republicans returning in force on the morning of Sunday 10 September. They chose their moment well as most of the National Army garrison were attending the funeral Mass of Lieutenant Moran, who had been shot dead by one of his own men in a row over lodgings at his father's house in the town. A Republican column of 150 approached Ballina, led by the recently captured armoured car 'Ballinalee' that they had renamed 'The Rose of Lough Gill'. Racing through Ardnaree and across the Ham Bridge they fired on the stunned sentries. P. J. Ruttledge was in the turret of the armoured car. Joe Baker of the West Mayo Flying Column was accompanied by Micheál Ó Cléirigh and Phelim Calleary. They rode into action behind the turret of the armoured car.[32] The streets of the town became lethal for civilians as both Republicans and National Army troops began firing on each other. A niece of Mrs Cafferty was shot dead as she crossed Bridge Street. A son of Mr Francis Walsh was also wounded as he sat in his window reading a newspaper.

Joe Baker and his men then went through back gardens to attack the Moy Hotel. Arriving at the back door they called on the Free State troops inside to surrender. Hearing no reply, they tossed in a grenade and then stormed the building. The National Army troops had run out the front door only to be captured by more Republicans coming up the street.[33] The armoured car then covered a detachment who placed a mine at the front of the post office. The resulting explosion was deafening, with the shockwave shattering the windows of most shops and houses in King Street (O'Rahilly Street) and John Street (Casement Street).[34] Henry Hewson, the chief clerk, was thrown down the stairs, lumps of the ceiling collapsing on top of him. Miraculously, he escaped severe injury. The post office clock stopped at 11.30 a.m., marking the time of the assault. The Republican troops then isolated the Imperial Hotel, forcing the surrender of National Army soldiers inside. P. J. Ruttledge was almost killed by a sniper as he passed the Jackson Memorial Font on Bury Street (Pearse Street). Malachy Gereghty, a 26-year-old returning to Dublin from the Crossmolina Fair, was then shot through the head as he attempted to take cover near the dispensary:

> His brother, who was with him at the time, was ... unaware of the serious injuries Malachy had received. He crouched under the wall, and in a few minutes when he looked around it was only to discover that his brother was dead. The shock he received made him almost hysterical and he sobbed bitterly with his Rosary beads in his hands. 'My only brother!' he cried. 'Isn't it awful?'[35]

The last stronghold to be taken was the workhouse, which was overwhelmed with relative ease. In all, the Republicans had captured fifty men of the National Army garrison along with rifles and ammunition. With the town in their hands, the Republicans set about obtaining much-needed supplies. The unfortunate Moylett Brothers were raided and much of their stock lifted. Kilroy, who was in command of the attack on the town, was surprised to see Dr John Crowley TD among the released Republican prisoners who had been held in the workhouse. Some Republicans remained in the streets and were served with cans of hot tea.[36] Many others, however, quenched their thirst in the local public houses. Baker put it delicately when he recalled: 'There was far too much dilly-dallying around the town and when we finally got under way it was well into the evening. We divided mainly into two groups. Most of the Ballina fellows went towards the Ox Mountains, others of them came with us, i.e. with Michael Kilroy's group [along the north coast].[37]

On the same day that the Republicans retook Ballina, Mayo County Council expressed profound regret and sorrow on the death of Michael Collins in letters to W. T. Cosgrave TD, General Richard Mulcahy TD and Mrs Sheridan, a sister of Collins living at Bohola.[38] However, the grief expressed at the loss of national figures such as Griffith and Collins was soon to be surpassed in Mayo by the death of one of its own real heroes, Brigadier General Joe Ring. It would bring home to people the real cost of civil war.

Lawlor, furious at the defeat in Ballina, organised a determined counter-strike against the Republicans in north Mayo. He established a strong battle group with troops from Claremorris together with Joe Ring's unit from Westport and reinforcements from Athlone. In Ballina they were joined by a further unit commanded by Commandant General Simmons. Joe Ring viewed his last sunrise on the morning of Thursday 14 September, as Lawlor's battle group led by 'The Big Fella' armoured car pulled out of the town and headed for Bonniconlon. The Republicans, aware of Lawlor's approach, withdrew from the village and took up positions at Drumsheen. This road led to a Republican stronghold deep in the Ox Mountains beside Lough Talt. As the National Army closed in on the Republicans they encountered obstacles and road mines. A firefight then began, which was to last for three hours, the 'The Big Fella' taking on the Republican 'Rose of Lough Gill', the two armoured cars slugging it out all through the day.

It was during this initial engagement that Joe Ring moved forward to call on the Republicans to surrender. While crossing a ditch he looked down to see a Republican Volunteer with a rifle lying underneath him. It was too late. Ring took the full force of the shot fired at him.[39] As the report of the rifle echoed across the Mayo hillside the body of one of its most respected commanders lay dead. Ireland had lost another of its talented, committed and bright young minds. Lawlor was also wounded, along with three others. The Republicans fell back to Lough Talt where the fight continued. Their

Brigadier General Joe Ring, National Army, Claremorris Command, Westport Battalion (standing on road, far right) pictured with National Army officers and troops beside 'The Big Fella' armoured car, August 1922. (Courtesy Michael Ring TD)

headquarters at Gleneask was taken. The Republicans continued to pull back and at Mullany's Cross the two armoured cars fought it out again until the driver of the National Army's 'The Big Fella', Sergeant John Ingram, was shot in the head and killed. General Lawlor was again wounded, this time in the foot. The Republicans then melted away. The National Army took shelter in nearby Tobercurry. They had captured 14 rifles with 5,000 rounds of ammunition and some mines.[40]

Joe Ring's body was brought back to the Ballina barracks before being transported the next evening to St Mary's Church, Westport.[41] On Saturday 16 September, he made his last journey out to Aughaval Cemetery surrounded by the people amongst whom he had lived his thirty-one years. The warmest tribute to Joe Ring was received in a letter to the Ring family from Michael Staines, commissioner of the new Irish police force, the Civic Guards. It was clearly written by a man who knew the Brigadier General very well: 'His loss is a stunning blow to me, with whom his personal relations were of the closest kind, and I find it difficult to realise that the fearless and impulsive, generous and warm-hearted friend of long standing has passed out of my life forever. May he rest in peace.'[42]

The Provisional Government began to pursue the Civil War with a ruthlessness that was unparalleled by the British in the War of Independence. It would be carried out under the 'legitimacy' of Irish Free State law. The support of the Roman Catholic Church and the newspapers would also be pivotal. Their programme was initiated with the gathering of the third Dáil on 9 September 1922. Just before he was elected President of the Dáil, W. T. Cosgrave faced a grilling from Cathal O'Shannon, Labour Party TD for Louth-Meath. O'Shannon questioned Cosgrave about the illegal detention of thousands of Irish men and women in jails. He also raised questions about the lack of detail offered by Cosgrave on the course of action the Provisional Government was to pursue:

> The Executive has the power of life and death over the whole population of Ireland. We must know, therefore, what is the policy of that Executive on these questions; otherwise, of course, we will be only getting into greater chaos. We want to know the relations between the Army and the Government. We do not know what are the relations between the new Executive and the Army, or whether the Army forces in the country are going to be responsible to this Dáil or not.[43]

Cosgrave replied with generalisations; there was no hint of the horror to come. O'Shannon continued to probe, questioning the position of the Civic Guard, the dual roles of responsibility held by government ministers who were also in the military, and finally whether a code of conduct for the military existed or not. He said the stories emerging from the many detention barracks throughout the twenty-six counties of the Free State were 'a disgrace to any Irish Government'.[44]

On 12 September, William Sears, TD Mayo West-South, proposed a motion in the Dáil approving the government's actions – past or present. He spoke of a reign of terror implemented by the Republicans and claimed Michael Collins had been torn from the platform in Castlebar. Sears argued the pro-Treaty party had attempted peace at every turn. After a lengthy debate, which again lacked detail about the future intent of Cosgrave's government, the Dáil passed Sears' motion of support by fifty-four votes to fifteen.[45] The Dáil never got the necessary detail it requested from Cosgrave. The President, however, through the Emergency Powers Act, got the 'legality' for the actions that were to be taken by his government, the National Army and the now infamous Criminal Investigations Department at Oriel House. They were to engage in a war without mercy against the Republicans and their cause.

Before the Civil War entered its deadly final stage, there were some attempts to achieve peace. Archbishop Gilmartin visited Islandeady on 30 September to confirm over 200 children in the parish. Present also were the parish priests from the Republican strongholds of Newport, Kilmeena and Westport. The Archbishop picked his place well as Islandeady had been the former headquarters of the West Mayo Brigade. Archbishop Gilmartin appealed to the Republicans to cease their armed opposition to the legitimate government of the country. The government, he claimed, had 'got a clear mandate from the people to function within terms of the Treaty'.[46]

Within a week Gilmartin received a letter from Count Plunkett, who argued that the Archbishop's appeal for peace was undermined by unsound arguments. According to Plunkett, the last election had been based on a seriously defective electoral register. He also noted that the Provisional Government had been slow to call the Dáil together despite repeated requests, and had instead attacked the Republicans thus forcing a Civil War upon the country. In perhaps the most damning part of the letter, Plunkett stated:

> Under cover of England's borrowed Artillery these quasi-Irish 'Ministers' set up, not DAIL EIREANN, the Parliament of the Irish people, but the machine for re-establishing in Ireland the authority of England which we had broken in pieces. The 'Provisional Parliament' may be labelled anything you like, but all the force and pretence in the world cannot make an illegitimate Government legitimate. In the profaned name of

Ireland, this alien 'Parliament' continues its ruthless violence against the men sworn to defend the principles of justice, the complete independence of our country.[47]

With even relative moderates like Plunkett angry with the actions of the Provisional Government, it was unlikely that more determined Republicans like Ruttledge, Kilroy and Maguire would respond to the amnesty offered by Cosgrave on 3 October 1922. The amnesty stated that if weapons, ammunition and explosives were handed into the National Army by 15 October then those guilty of offences against the state would be allowed to return home unmolested and fully pardoned.[48] Some Republicans availed of the amnesty, also signing a document declaring they would not take up arms again against the National Army. Most, however, ignored it. The situation was made worse by the Catholic Bishops' pastoral letter read out in all churches on 22 October, in which formal excommunication was pronounced on the Republicans.[49] For men like Joe Baker the pastoral letter was a bitter blow that caused Republicans much personal anxiety as their very souls were now in peril. After a lot of thinking, Baker concluded that 'the Bishops were not always right and on this occasion their action could have been biased'. Instead, Baker and his comrades ignored the bishops and turned instead to the mercy of the Almighty.[50]

Dr Conn Murphy, representing the Catholic Appeal Committee established by the Republicans, wrote to Archbishop Gilmartin on the matter. Their appeal was based on the argument that the Irish bishops had no right to impose 'grievous spiritual penalties' on Republicans 'solely because of their political opinions and actions'.[51] Gilmartin suggested a truce in hostilities while the appeal was heard.[52] The attempt at peace came to nothing as the Catholic Appeal Committee did not have the political authority to engage in such negotiations. The Republican leadership of Liam Lynch, Ernie O'Malley and others were digging in, preparing for an unprecedented onslaught from the Provisional Government. For Republican soldiers like Baker, the struggle had to be continued 'to the bitter end'.[53]

On 10 October 1922, the National Army issued a proclamation notifying the general public that the Army Council now had powers of arrest, internment, deportation or death.[54] This prepared the way for the executions that were to follow. Just over a week later, Commandant General Tom Maguire TD was captured. Lieutenant Nally from Ballyglass described the capture:

> On 18 October 1922 I and Comdt [David] Deasey and four others went towards Collagh Village [near Shrule]. Two of our fellows had gone with a dispatch to the General [Lawlor] and as we got into the Village we heard some shots. Capt [*sic*] Deasey told me to spread out where he had seen some men running so I went outside a hedge in a different direction. I saw two men sitting down by a ditch. I told them to put their hands up, and they did so, that was Maguire and Mr Martyn. I asked them if they had any arms and they said no.[55]

Two automatic pistols were found a few hundred yards from where the men were captured. Maguire and Martyn had dumped their guns to avoid execution if captured.[56] As the National Army began to take witness statements for Maguire's trial, it was the opinion of one of their legal officers, David C. Bergin, that 'the evidence available would be insufficient to convict the prisoner on a charge of unlawful possession of firearms or taking part in an attack on the National Forces'.[57] Major General MacEoin wrote to Bergin saying 'let this case stand for the moment. I will instruct you later on this matter.'[58] MacEoin was clearly taking instructions from a higher authority. Tom Maguire was tried by court martial in January 1923 and sentenced to death.

Maguire was replaced as O/C 2nd Western Division by Christie Macken. Macken did not last long in command as he was seriously wounded in action with the 4th Western Division in a surprise attack on Clifden, County Galway, on Sunday 28 October 1922. The battle for Clifden was launched by Petie McDonnell, one of Kilroy's senior officers, at 7 a.m. and continued all day. The National Army barracks in the town was burned and another on a nearby hill blown up by a mine. Luckily, only one combatant from each side was killed although many were wounded. The attack on Clifden caused panic throughout Mayo. William Sears expressed his concerns to General Mulcahy in a letter on 20 November:

Have just received a very grave report as to the military situation in Mayo. Kilroy fresh after his victory in Clifden is contemplating another stroke – even a more daring one than the last. The information comes from the man who warned the military about the move on Clifden.

Kilroy feels he is now strong enough to strike again. He has with him 600 men fully armed. Can command 700 if he had the arms. Has 8 machine guns; 3 armed lorries and with the window shutters taken at Clifden is making a fourth: for transport he has 7 or 8 lorries and a large number of motor cars. His little factory is turning out mines and bombs steadily.

He now proposes an attack in force in quick succession on Westport, Castlebar & Ballina. There are a hundred rifles, in each place, and he believes he can get hold of them & if he does – his scheme is to collect all rents in Mayo.

The man who brings me this will be in Dublin to-morrow (Tuesday) & would be glad of an interview with you.

He represents the people in these towns as being in a state of alarm. Again and again they have appealed for re-inforcements ... I shall be glad if you let me know if this man can have the interview he came to Dublin for. He is W. Mongey of Intelligence Staff.[59]

Up to this point, Kilroy had captured over 330 National Army soldiers. All had been released unharmed.[60] If Kilroy could take Clifden, surely he could take any of the larger towns in Mayo also? Rumours began to spread: Kilroy was marching on Claremorris, Kilroy had taken Westport and was on the outskirts of Castlebar. In fact, Kilroy was just about everywhere. Brigadier General Anthony Lawlor was now under serious pressure from MacEoin and Mulcahy to deal with this 'menace' from Newport. Putting the 4th Western Division out of action became priority number one for the National Army in the west.

While Lawlor assembled his forces in preparation for the assault on Newport, the first of seventy-seven executions to be carried out under the authority of the Irish Free State government were announced. The four young men, James Fisher, Peter Cassidy, Richard

Commandant Micheál Ó Cléirigh (second on right) with Republican Volunteers during the Civil War *c.* 1923. (Private Collection)

Twohig and John Gaffney, all from Dublin and with an average age of nineteen, were shot by firing squad at 7 a.m. at Kilmainham Jail on 17 November.[61] The executed men had been found guilty by a military court of the possession of revolvers. That evening, a deeply shocked Thomas Johnson TD, leader of the Labour Party, rose in Dáil Éireann to address those gathered:

> I prophesy a deep revulsion of feeling against the Army and against the Government. I cannot believe that that announcement states facts which would justify the execution of these men. The possession of a revolver does not justify the execution of a man, lawfully or unlawfully, and no one, I believe, despite the decision of the Dáil, and no one in this Dáil, in his heart of hearts, believes that the possession of a revolver warrants the execution of the man or the woman who possessed it.[62]

General Mulcahy and Kevin O'Higgins defended the decision to execute the men, saying the very life of Ireland as a democratic organism was at stake.[63] O'Higgins, in referring to the particular men executed, argued:

> It was better in my opinion, wiser in my opinion, more calculated to achieve the object, to achieve the deterrent object, to take simply the plain or ordinary case of the men who go out with arms to kill their fellow-countrymen, refusing to recognise the ordinary basic principle upon which civilised Government rests everywhere, refusing to recognise the sovereignty of the majority will of this Nation. And let no man think that we took action of this kind impetuously; and let no man think that we took action of this kind vindictively or in hot blood.[64]

Liam Lynch, the Chief of Staff of the Republican forces, responded to the executions with an order to shoot government TDs and senators on sight. This resulted in the murder of Sean Hales TD. The Free State government retaliated by executing Rory O'Connor, Liam Mellows, Dick Barrett and Joe McKelvey, Republican senior officers who had been held in Mountjoy since the bombing of the Four Courts.

More executions quickly followed. On the morning of 24 November 1922, as Brigadier General Lawlor, flanked by Commandant Generals Simmons and Cooney, assembled his troops on The Mall in Castlebar in preparation for an assault on Newport, Erskine Childers faced a firing squad in Dublin. The troops knelt on The Mall as Fr P. J. Joyce with outstretched hands made a sign of the cross imparting upon them general absolution before going into battle. The soldiers from Athlone, Ballina, Claremorris and Westport, supported by 'The Big Fella' armoured car, departed the town aware they were up against experienced Republican troops commanded by veterans from the Tan War. Lawlor sent Captain Joe Ruddy, one of the men implicated in the killing of John Charles Milling RM three years earlier, with a company of men on a reconnaissance-in-force to test Republican defences on the Westport to Newport road. They came under fire from Michael Kilroy and some Republican sentries as they reached Kilbride Cemetary. Ruddy knew the ground well and divided his forces. He ordered a junior officer to move around the back of the hill above them in the hope of encircling the enemy.

Ruddy, meanwhile, pursued Kilroy up the hill. It was during this pursuit that Ruddy was killed. With him died the real truth of what happened to Milling on the night of 29/30 March 1919. As Kilroy continued to withdraw towards Newport he ran into a force of National Army troops coming up the rear of the hill. As he turned to attempt an escape, Kilroy went down, wounded in the middle of the back. The bullet came out through the side of his ribs.[65] The National Army troops rushed up and took the injured Commandant General prisoner. In spite of being captured, Kilroy's war was far from over.

Operations continued around the Newport area for some days. On Saturday, after a brief artillery bombardment on the town, 4 armoured cars led some 400 National Army troops across the bridge and up into the town centre. The Republicans withdrew further west, out past Mulranny. A unit of National Army troops known as 'MacEoin's Own' advanced from Crossmolina via Keenagh and on to Shramore village. Here, six of their scouts ran into a Republican outpost under the command of Commandant P. O'Reilly. All were captured. Fighting broke out that lasted till dark, when 'MacEoin's Own', according to the Republicans, fled, leaving behind them 6 rifles, 900 rounds of ammunition, 1 lucas signal lamp, 18 Very light cartridges, 2 grenades and 4 filled pans of ammunition for a Lewis gun.[66] Newport was surrounded but the majority of the Republicans succeeded in slipping through the National Army cordon. The capture of Kilroy was Brigadier General Lawlor's only – albeit highly significant – prize. The National Army had also suffered four other casualties along with Captain Ruddy in the initial engagement. Three were Mayo men: Vice-Brigadier Joe Walsh, formerly of the West Mayo Flying Column, had been shot in the groin and died in hospital. Also killed were Volunteers Woods of Westport Quay, P. McEllin of Kiltimagh and a Murphy from Galway.[67]

One Republican correspondent – most probably the photographer J. J. Leonard – gave a graphic account of events in Newport:

> Owing to being so closely invested with large numbers of the enemy, we were in position two days and a night without rest, and knowing that the enemy hoped to be able to wear us out, and had boasted that they would capture us all at any cost, and

Jack Leonard, IRA officer, Sinn Féin organiser and professional photographer, pictured training with a Lewis gun. (Photo by Jack Leonard. Reproduced with kind permission of Anthony Leonard, The J. J. Leonard Collection of Historic Photographs)

as we were very short of ammunition, having only 50 rounds per man when the engagement started, we decided to get outside their circle. We therefore mobilised all our men on Saturday night [24 November], and although completely surrounded by the enemy, succeeded in getting completely through their lines, without they knowing it. They still had the old position surrounded on Sunday expecting we were inside. The round-up was a complete failure, and apart from the capture of the Major General [Kilroy], we made it a great success, both in the fight and in getting through their lines.[68]

On 18 December, the *Western People* published an intriguing notice: 'Owing to circumstances over which we have no control we are unable to publish a letter we have received, signed "Jack Leonard", denying the accuracy of our report of the battle of Newport.' The letter had been censored by a communications officer of the National Army in Ballina. The incident raises questions about how the National Army and the Republicans were reported in the press. The *Western People* had actually been one of the more balanced in its reports, yet as the Civil War wore on the Republican perspective was increasingly absent. Far more partisan was the *Mayo News*, which never criticised the National Army. While in public the National Army appeared a bastion of the new Irish Free State, behind the scenes the situation was radically different.

Throughout the autumn of 1922, the National Army came in for criticism on many fronts. It began with a report commissioned by Chief of Staff General Mulcahy. This stated that 'the army is very badly disciplined, frequently mutinous and very inefficient (militarily) sometimes treacherous and except in certain Barracks, dirty and slovenly'. The inefficiency of the officers was described as 'amazing'; they knew 'nothing beyond the limited tactics of ambushing, street fighting, car bombing and private assassination'. The officers were also frequently drunk, with senior officers in particular being a bad example to their men. The cleanliness of the troops themselves was described as 'exceedingly bad' with medical service 'inadequate'. Alarmingly, the report stated 'fraternisation between National Troops and Irregulars is too common and the sale of ammunition goes on'. In short, the report recommended reform on the basis of sacking 50 per cent of the junior officers and 25 per cent of the men.[69]

In the Claremorris Command Operational Area, the condition of the National Army was no different from that stated in the report. News reached William Sears TD and General Mulcahy from a number of different sources as to the behaviour of Lawlor's troops. From Tuam, Professor Whelehan TD communicated to Mulcahy that the O/C, Lohan, was 'very much addicted to drink', frequently holding himself upright against lampposts and shooting out the street lamps. The local townspeople were 'almost anxious to have the Irregulars back'.[70] Canon D'Alton of Ballinrobe wrote to Sears complaining about how a soldier who was found guilty of selling his rifle was sent to Claremorris as a prisoner where he was at once set free and given another rifle. 'How can we expect discipline or efficiency in an army where there is no drilling, no practice in arms, no marching?' Canon D'Alton also complained about the manner in which the National Army troops were treated. He described how a column of more than 100 under Commandant Finegan arrived from Ballina with the intention of attacking the enemy at Cornamona and Kilmilkin. They had received little food or sleep, only some bread and porter for breakfast. Advancing to Kilmilkin they came under fire from the Republicans and retreated without firing a shot, leaving one dead and three wounded. D'Alton said Finegan's troops arrived back in Ballinrobe 'in scattered bands, not a few without shoes or stockings'.[71]

On 6 November, Frank Shouldice wrote to GHQ complaining about the condition of Commandant McGoohan, 'who was very much under the influence of drink and absolutely incapable of carrying fire arms, not to mention effecting any discipline over his men'. His behaviour, Shouldice suggested, 'instead of inspiring a sense of security and safety in the breast of the average man or woman, as any National Army should,' was 'only bringing it into disgrace and making the name of the National Army, in the west, a byword in the mouths of their own countrymen'.[72] In early December, it was the turn of Fr Brett of Kilmaine to write to Sears complaining about the National Army's campaign in the west as being 'most unsatisfactory'. Fr Brett described how ten Republican troops and two scouts attacked the pubs in the village the previous Sunday night. He jumped on his bicycle and cycled as fast as he could to Ballinrobe for reinforcements to catch the Republicans. There was none available as Lawlor had them out on the Partry Mountains. Fr Brett finished up his letter saying he was on his way to Headford 'to reconnoitre that infested spot. We must put 100 men there. I lost the ten devils on Sunday night because there was no passion available at Ballinrobe to pursue them to Shrule'.[73]

There is no doubt General Lawlor was severely criticised by National Army supporters on the ground in Mayo, by his own GHQ and by his opponents. A Republican report 'From the West' offered yet another revealing insight:

> Lawlor, (Free State), appears to have got into disgrace over his big failure here. His extensively organised 'sweep' resulted in disaster, the Free State forces suffering numerous casualties

and having no results to show for their labour. One deserter informed me that Lawlor always does the 'Little Hun' in an attack, he forces on his men at the point of a revolver.[74]

In Lawlor's defence, he faced similar problems to other National Army senior officers throughout the country: a lack of numbers and problems in supply. Supplying Lawlor's men with even the basic essentials seems to have been a real problem. His troops had not received uniforms, underwear or even pay for four months. This lack of basic care for the troops caused disaffection and was behind a lack of fighting spirit. General Seán MacEoin, O/C Western Command, argued that such problems had resulted in the handing over of the National Army barracks to Republicans at Riverstown in County Sligo in early September. The troops at Riverstown said 'there was no point fighting for those who don't care to look after us'.[75] In order to win the campaign in the west, Lawlor required more troops. It would also be essential to take and hold ground as a guerrilla war could not be won by big sweeps. The occupying of the larger towns only left the countryside to the Republican columns who could move about quite freely.

With Kilroy captured, there were still many Republican commanders posing a serious threat to the National Army in Mayo. Frank Carty was holding north Mayo and Sligo. Ned Moane, P. J. McDonnell, Joe Baker and Dr John Madden were operating in the west and south of Mayo, while Tom Carney was active in the east. Madden and Moane's columns had between them 110 Lee-Enfield Rifles, 16,000 rounds of ammunition, 80 revolvers, 130 grenades, 15 mines, 2 Thompson sub-machine guns and 2 Lewis guns.[76] The other Republican columns were similarly well armed and supplied. There was also no shortage of recruits. Lawlor's troop numbers and equipment were completely inadequate to undertake the operations expected of him by General Mulcahy. For an operational area covering Mayo and north Galway, Lawlor had just 52 officers and 603 men.[77] Considering the strength of Republican opposition and the insufficient resources available to Lawlor, Mulcahy should have considered it lucky that Claremorris Command was able to hold on to the major towns at all. Nevertheless, Lawlor was replaced at the end of the year. On 24 January 1923, a new commanding officer for

Colonel Anthony Lawlor as President of the National Maritime Institute, formerly National Army Commander in North Galway and Mayo during the early phases of the Civil War, August–December 1922. Colonel Lawlor subsequently became O/C of the Curragh Camp. During the Second World War, Colonel Lawlor was a founding member of the National Maritime Institute and also Commander of the National Coast Watching Service. (Photograph by Pat Sweeney. Reproduced with kind permission of the Maritime Institute of Ireland)

the National Army stepped onto the platform at Claremorris railway station. His name was Hogan and, being from the west, he had a detailed knowledge of the terrain in which military operations under his command would be conducted. This knowledge coupled with additional troops and logistical support would put severe pressure on the Republican forces.

PART II – 'MAY GOD GUARD EVERY ONE OF YOU': JANUARY–APRIL 1923

Major General Michael Hogan was an officer with considerable experience. He was also the brother of Paddy Hogan, the Minister for

Agriculture in the Provisional Government. Originally from Galway, Michael Hogan had gone on the run in 1919, journeying south to join Tom Barry's flying column. During the Truce he was appointed Quartermaster of Michael Brennan's 1st Western Division. He had also served with the IRA in England, organising two raids for arms, including one in Windsor. For this, Hogan was arrested and sentenced to two years' penal servitude. However, he was released at the beginning of the Civil War. He took part in the early campaigns with his command fighting their way south from Limerick and linking up with General Daly in Tralee. At the time of his appointment to Claremorris Command he was just twenty-four years old.[78] Hogan immediately established his headquarters at Castlemacgarret, the home of Lord Oranmore, just outside Claremorris. The former workhouse was refitted as a barracks with the infantry headquarters and hospital situated there. General Hogan brought in a number of experienced officers with local knowledge. One of the first to arrive was Captain Pádraig Dunleavy, former O/C of the IRA in the town and then of the old 4th North Galway Brigade in Tuam. He was appointed communications officer. Each night, he compiled reports from the various National Army outposts in Mayo, Galway and Sligo, transmitting them via wireless to GHQ in Dublin. Dunleavy also organised and led a number of sweeps in his own district of Tuam, picking up a number of Republicans. One of them was Tom Kilgarriff, Dunleavy's former intelligence officer and IRB centre in Dunmore. Kilgarriff had been using a secret room constructed during the Tan war in a house in Washington near Dunmore called 'The White House'.[79] As well as ordering raids, Hogan ensured medical facilities were improved. The hospital in Claremorris was revamped and twenty-four hospital orderlies assigned from Tuam to assist in the treatment of a scabies epidemic that had broken out among the National Army troops.[80] At one point the outbreak practically incapacitated the entire Ballina garrison.

General Hogan set to work in the new year adopting new tactics. From now on, the National Army presence in the west would be increased. Smaller towns would be occupied and raiding for Republicans would be relentless. Existing posts included barracks at Ballina, Ballinrobe, Castlebar, Claremorris, Clifden, Newport,

Artist Frank Leah's drawing of Major General Michael Hogan, GOC Claremorris Command, featured on the front cover of the National Army journal, *An t-Óglach*, 28 July 1923. (Courtesy the Military Archives, Cathal Brugha Barracks)

THE G.O.C. CLAREMORRIS COMMAND.
Drawn by Frank Leah from a special sitting.

Westport and Tuam. New posts were established in Mayo at Ballyhaunis, Crossmolina, Foxford, Lahardane, Mulranny and Swinford. In Galway posts were set up at Athenry, Headford and Woodlawn, and at Tobercurry in Sligo. Using these posts, Hogan's forces pursued the Republicans day and night. Having served in a flying column himself, Hogan knew just how to counter their movements and close them down.

One of his most successful tactics was the use of 'cycle swoops'. Leaving their posts after dark, the National Army cycle patrols of up to thirty armed men would approach a village or townland where a Republican column was operating. The patrol would install themselves in a house for the night and at dawn begin their round-up in the locality. On other occasions, they surrounded the local church during first Mass, arresting all the men who came out. Another of Hogan's tactics was to raid a district with a motor column early in the day. The patrol would then move on. The Republicans, believing the area now safe, emerged only to discover another raid had been organised for the afternoon or evening. It was this shrewd tactical ability that confirmed General Michael Hogan as an exception in the National Army; he had a 'genuine capacity for leadership, real personal valour and a sound conception of the principles underlying warfare in the field'.[81] Notwithstanding Hogan's own abilities, his approach also demonstrates the considerable experience gained by men under Tom Barry's command during the War of Independence.

General Hogan's men rapidly captured hundreds of Republicans. Anyone who was considered an active supporter or even sympathiser of the Republican cause was arrested. The aim was to undermine Republican support throughout Claremorris Command. According to the operational reports complied by Captain Dunleavy, those arrested for the Claremorris Command area during Hogan's first three months in charge were listed as follows:[82]

Arrests for Claremorris Command Area
23/1/1923–17/4/1923

Mayo	Galway-North	Sligo	Total
212	98	12	322

Also arrested were nine women, eight deserters and one looter. The figures do not include those already arrested at the time of General Lawlor's command nor in the months that followed the end of the Civil War in April 1923. The Republicans also kept careful details on their supporters who were jailed. Some of the Cumann na mBan Mayo women who were listed as being in prison in April 1923 were: Miss N. O'Rourke, Swinford, Miss O'Hara, Knox Street, Ballina, Miss Quinn, Swinford, Miss Sweeney, Ardagh, Ballina, Miss Brennan, Main Street, Swinford, Miss Higgins, Kilkelly, Miss McMenamin, George Street, Newport and Miss O'Grady, George's Street, Newport.[83]

On 13 February, the National Army rounded up thirteen 'Irregular sympathisers' in Tuam. They marched them to the barracks in Claremorris where they had to sign a 'Form of Undertaking' promising they would not attack the National Army or give assistance to 'Irregular' forces. Upon signing they were released. If they refused to sign, they were arrested and detained. On the night of 16 February, Dunleavy reported a successful escape from Claremorris: '3 "Bolshie" prisoners named Burke and 2 brothers McCormack escaped from Union Barracks this morning. They cut away a portion of the cell door and crawled underneath. They managed to get over the Boundary wall in their feet without being noticed by the Sentry. There is no trace of their whereabouts.'[84] There was also an attempted mass breakout from Galway Jail on 5 March. Fourteen prisoners escaped, including Thomas Ruane of Ballina and Charles Gavin and Johnny Gibbons from Westport. Fifteen members of the National Army garrison in the jail were arrested on suspicion of collusion with the Republican prisoners.[85]

The majority of prisoners in Claremorris were usually transferred to Galway, Mountjoy or to the internment camps at the Curragh. On occasion the prisoners were sent to Oriel House, the headquarters of the Criminal Investigation Department. Oriel House acquired a notorious reputation for its brutal treatment of Republican prisoners during the Civil War. Tom Derrig, TD for Mayo West-North and Adjutant General of the Republican forces, lost an eye and was nearly killed. Different accounts of what happened emerged in the press. One described how Derrig made a brief dash for freedom outside Oriel House. On being caught and brought back into the hallway, Derrig went to strike one of the detectives. In raising his hand to ward off the blow, the detective accidentally discharged his revolver.[86] The Republicans claimed Derrig had been shot deliberately, as he was carrying a file detailing 'Accounts of Free State Atrocities on Republicans' when captured. One of the documents in the file referred to Lieutenant Patrick Mulchrone. The Republicans claimed Mulchrone had been murdered after his arrest on 1 November 1922:

> He [Mulchrone] was inactive for some time previous, but was attached to the Transport at Castlebar barracks while in occupation by us, using his own private car on our work. After the occupation of Castlebar by Free State troops he refused to drive for them and was instrumental in getting all the motor drivers in the town to refuse to work for them.[87]

Volunteer Jim O'Donnell claimed that Mulchrone had been shot in the head after being told to put up his hands when a raiding party led

Commandant Micheál
Ó Cléirigh, 2nd Western
Division IRA, pictured during
Civil War c. 1923. (Courtesy
Private Collection)

by Commandant Connolly from Castlebar searched Aughagowla. Mulchrone was unarmed at the time of his death.[88] Hogan's troops also became more aggressive with a 'shoot first, ask questions later' approach implemented. Dunleavy reported to GHQ on 13 February: 'Troops from Claremorris, 1 officer and 25 men and 25 from Tobbercurry saw a man on the railway line. On seeing the troops he began to run and they opened fire – he was shot dead. His name was McGuinn a native of Curry and a very active Irregular.'[89]

The National Army did not have things all their own way. The Republican response was to continue ambushes and blowing up bridges. Brigadier Tom Carney's column attacked a National Army patrol of forty-five troops at Glore near Kiltimagh on Wednesday 17 January 1923. A young girl, Mary Smyth, received terrible injuries as she was travelling in a car with National Army officers when a grenade, thrown by the Republicans, exploded near her head.[90] The Republicans received a great deal of criticism for this attack. They argued the press report of the incident was inaccurate. The girl had been sitting on the knee of Commandant McCann. The car was driven by Vice-Brigadier Byrne and contained two other girls. The Republicans also claimed they did not use grenades.[91] However, the injuries sustained by Mary Smyth were consistent with wounds sustained in an explosion. The Republican commander, Tom Carney, was also shot and wounded during the engagement.

Republican forces also sought to deny the use of strong defensive positions to the National Army in Republican areas. On 1 February, Moore Hall, the home of George Moore and his estranged brother, Colonel Maurice Moore, was burnt to the ground. Thomas Hurst of Clooneen recalled the events of that night at the claims court at Castlebar on Thursday 8 May 1924. A number of Republicans came to his home from their camp at Castlecarra. They took away 11 gallons of paraffin oil and some candles. The Republican squad then woke up James Reilly, the steward at Moore Hall, and demanded the keys to the house. Around 4 a.m. Reilly heard three or four shots. He went to the Hall and found the whole building was engulfed in flames.[92] The burning of the Hall would seem a logical move by the Republicans; the nearby area of Ballyglass was strongly Republican and they wanted to prevent the National Army using the house as a barracks in the district as had been done at Castlemacgarret in Claremorris.

In his report for 15 February, Dunleavy mentions a 'band of Irregulars' at Castlecarra:

> 5 Officers and 42 men operating with troops from Castlebar, Ballinrobe and Westport in Castlecarra district came upon a band of Irregulars. An exchange of fire followed and 3 Irregulars were captured [Joyce, Donnelly and Heneghan] along with 3 Lee-Enfield Rifles, 210 rds .303, 15 pairs of boots, 9 pairs of socks, 7 satchells, a large quantity of tobacco and cigarettes, 2 large tents, beds and bedding which the troops burned. 2 of our troops slightly wounded.[93]

This could have been the Republican column that burnt Moore Hall. Nevertheless, stories persist linking the burning of the Hall to the agrarian strife that had begun to re-emerge at this point in the Civil

War. Much of the extensive Moore Hall estate had been sold to the Congested Districts Board in 1912. As the Free State government began to release land that had been under the control of the Board it seemed to many Republicans that they were being sidelined while supporters of the government received land. This resulted in violence and intimidation by families who had failed to gain larger holdings. Moore Hall may have been destroyed to prevent government-supporting families gaining stronger influence in the district. Rumours continued alleging local cottages were furnished with the finest of curtains, tables and chairs in the decades that followed the burning.

Whatever was the real reason for the destruction of Moore Hall, it created real controversy and embarrassment in Mayo. The Moore family had marched with the French Army that landed at Killalla in 1798, with John Moore being declared 'President of Connaught' after the victory over the British forces at a battle called 'The Races of Castlebar'. During the Famine, the family had saved local tenants from starvation by buying food and improving living conditions. George Moore subsequently claimed £16,289 13s and 6d for the buildings, furniture, china, engravings and books destroyed in the fire. Judge Doyle awarded him a sum of £5,000 if the house were not rebuilt or £6,600 if there were to be a partial reconstruction with £1,700 for contents and £25 expenses. This amount was decided upon after court sittings at Castlebar, Claremorris and Westport in 1924.[94] Moore Hall was never rebuilt.

The Republican forces continued to prove impossible to defeat. On 23 February 1923, a party of National Army troops set out at 6 a.m. for Shraghmore in search of Republicans reported in the area. They discovered an arms dump with a grenade factory that the troops destroyed. They also captured eight Republican soldiers. The party were ambushed on their way back to Westport. A heavy engagement followed, which lasted until nightfall when reinforcements arrived from Newport. The National Army casualties were high, with one man killed and five others wounded, including the Westport O/C Captain Togher. One of the wounded, Lieutenant McQuaid, an assistant medical officer, died later.[95] He was the brother of John Charles McQuaid, the future Archbishop of Dublin. The National

Captain Padraig Dunleavy, National Army Communications Officer, Claremorris Command 1923. (Courtesy Dominick and Mary Dunleavy)

Army claimed he was shot deliberately in spite of wearing prominent Red Cross armbands. The Republicans denied this, saying his Red Cross markings were small badges as in the style of the old Irish Volunteers uniform and impossible to see in combat. The Republican's campaign became more sinister as they started burning out the homes of families with National Army connections. Patrick Cafferty from Charlestown, whose son was serving in the National Army, was one such victim.[96] In Belmullet, the courthouse and homes of three government supporters were burned down.[97]

The views of the Mayo population were difficult to determine, except in anonymous letters such as the following from a person in Louisburgh addressed to General Mulcahy in December 1922:

Dear Sir,

The People of Louisburgh would be grateful if you would be so kind as to send a Garrison of National troops to the village. The shopkeepers are being robbed and looted every other night.

The fact the Irregulars have a great stronghold here because they are routed from Newport Clifden & Lenane They come here to rest, while they [townspeople] have to entertain and amuse them without complaining they dare not even express their opinions. A few of us thought it would be well to call your attention I am sure there is not a village in Ireland suffering so much in silence at the present day. May the blessing of God crown yourself and your work.

I am, your's faithfully,

A Louisburgh Petitioner[98]

As the war progressed the executions quickened in pace. At first, all of the executions were carried out in Dublin. From the middle of January 1923, however, the locations varied with Dundalk, Roscrea, Carlow, Tralee, Limerick, Athlone, Waterford, Birr, Portlaoise, Cork, Wexford and Donegal all witnessing the executions of young Irishmen.[99] It was only a matter of time before the west was drawn into the bloodletting. The worst day of all was 20 January, when eleven Republicans faced a firing squad at different locations around the country. In Dundalk the soldiers who carried out the executions had to be given whiskey afterwards.[100] By April 1923, Galway and Mayo alone were absent from the horror of executions being carried out on their soil.

An attack in Headford on 9 April provided the catalyst for Claremorris Command to pass an order for execution. The attack was led by Vincent Corcoran's Republican column of fifty men. It began at 4.45 a.m. with a mine detonated against the barracks wall. This was followed up with heavy rifle and machine-gun fire on the National Army garrison. Two Republican soldiers, Dan McCormack and John Higgins, died during the attack. Sergeant Major McCarty of the National Army was severely wounded with another four also wounded. McCarty and Private Lyons died later in Galway Hospital.[101] The response from General Mulcahy was swift and severe. Six Republican prisoners in Galway Jail, charged with the possession of arms and ammunition on 21 February 1923 at Cluide, were informed on the day after the attack at Headford that they would be executed at Tuam barracks the following morning at 8 a.m.

On the night of 10 April, Frank Cunnane, Seán Newell, Michael Monaghan and Martin Moylan from the Headford district, Seamus O'Maille from Oughterard, County Galway along with John Maguire from Cross, County Mayo were put in a Crossley Tender and taken to Tuam. John Maguire wrote his last letter to his mother before leaving Galway Jail:[102]

> My Dear Mother,
>
> I am going to bid you all last farewell as this is my last day on this earth, but I hope it will not put you about in the least as I expect that God will take me to Himself. Well, dear Mother, it is sad to think that my lot was such, but I am pleased with the will of God and I hope that He will have mercy on me. Do not mourn or grieve for me dear Mother for I die in a noble cause but always pray for me. I shall pray for you and some day I hope we will all meet in heaven where we will enjoy the home our dear Redeemer has prepared for us. I am going to receive the sacraments of Penance and Holy Communion and to follow in the footsteps of the brave men who are gone before me.
>
> With all my love and blessings to dear Father, Mother, Pat, Mark, Paddy, Maryanne, Tom, Peg, Michael, Kit, Bridie, Criss, Brian and my loving little brother Joe, also to Mr. Mannion and Christie. I expect to be with my God when you receive this.
>
> From Your loving son,
>
> John

All six had been captured without resistance. O'Maille had been in his father's home in Oughterard when the National Army came looking for his brother, John. He was taken instead. The other five had been with a Republican column at Cluide in County Galway when they were captured. The six men received the last rites from three priests, Fr Donnelly, Fr King and Fr Cunningham from the cathedral nearby. For some of the prisoners their only concern was that they had nothing to leave their families as a parting memory. Moylan sent his mother his only possession, his rosary beads. Cunnane also sent his mother his beads, which he had carried throughout the Tan war. The priests gave some of them holy cards and prayers to leave to their brothers and sisters. The men spent their last night singing songs to keep their spirits strong. At dawn they attended Mass, and as 8 a.m. drew near the men were blindfolded and taken outside in two groups of three to the oratory wall. As they walked, their last thoughts were of their families, their childhood friends and their country.[103] The firing squad commander called out his orders and two volleys broke the morning silence over Tuam. The bodies of the dead were placed in coffins and buried in the workhouse yard. When the National Army pulled out of Tuam in August 1924, they dug up the coffins and took the remains of the six to Athlone where they were reinterred in Custume Barracks.

The location of Tuam as the place of execution has caused great controversy and debate ever since. Many believe Archbishop Gilmartin should have stopped the executions, or at least condemned them in the aftermath. On the day of the executions he was in Maynooth, County Kildare, at the funeral of a friend. While it was possible Gilmartin knew of the National Army's intentions, the decision to send the priests to administer confession and communion to the condemned men did not give the green light for execution. On the contrary, it supported the men and gave them great comfort in their final hours. Arriving back in Tuam on the evening of the executions, the Archbishop went to his study and wrote to Monsignor Hagan of the Irish College in Rome:

My Dear Mgr,

Mgr Luzio spent a few days here last week. I met him in Dublin yesterday. He has met all the prominent Republicans. He is to meet representatives of the Free State Government tomorrow or after. He accepts therefore to be in a position to appreciate the situation.

We had been very quiet here for the last month or so when the Irregulars made an attack on a Free State post at Headford 12 miles from Tuam killing three Free State soldiers and losing two themselves. On my return just now from Dublin I learn that six prisoners were executed here this morning as a consequence. In Dublin yesterday the opinion is that it [the Civil War] is practically over. Liam Lynch was killed in action yesterday.

> Dr Harty [Archbishop of Cashel] has very strong hopes for peace in the immediate future. Yet who can say with certainty what may happen.[104]

Gilmartin soon wrote a second letter indicating he was being blamed in some way for not halting the executions: 'I knew nothing of the executions in Tuam until they were all over and I doubt if I could have stopped them. They inspired horror all round. They were of course a sequel to the Headford attack which was insane.'[105]

Once the Free State authorities had made a decision to execute prisoners there was little that could be done to intervene. The military council's orders were made with the calculation of sending an uncompromising message to their Republican adversaries. Unquestionably, the Church did indirectly support the government's policies through its silence on the issue of executions. De Valera, in writing to Monsignor Luzio, the Pope's personal envoy to Ireland, believed the bishops' 'failure to condemn ill-treatment, the torturing and the murder of prisoners, and the inflammatory addresses of some of their members ... are scarcely worthy of Him who is Charity'.[106] Nevertheless, Tom Maguire offered a much more plausible reason for choosing the Tuam: 'It is my opinion that their [National Army] objective was to involve all of their senior officers in this policy, so that there could be no denying it afterwards.'[107] There is evidence to suggest that not all National Army generals were willing to carry out executions. Brigadier General Seán MacEoin travelled to Dublin to argue with GHQ for the reprieve of Michael Kilroy.[108] Kilroy, subsequently, was not executed. Tom Maguire had also been found guilty and sentenced to be executed in Athlone along with five others on 20 January 1923. He, too, was not executed. He never knew why and believed it was because he had a reputation for fair play.[109]

Joe Baker was captured along with fourteen of his column at Buckagh Mountain near Skerdagh on 8 March 1923. The operation had been carried out by National Army officer, Colonel Commandant P. Madden, accompanied by a platoon of thirty men who had left their barracks at 3.30 a.m. There was an initial firefight but, outflanked by a machine-gun section and with inadequate cover, Baker's column surrendered, handing over their 10 Lee-Enfield rifles and 2,000

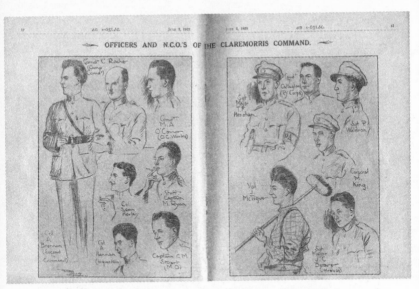

Artist Frank Leah's drawings of officers and NCOs, Claremorris Command, featured in the National Army journal *An t-Óglach*, 2 June 1923. (Courtesy the Military Archives, Cathal Brugha Barracks.)

rounds of ammunition.[110] Captain Jim Moran, a Republican officer from Callowbrack, Newport, was shot through the head and killed early in the engagement after refusing to surrender.[111] A few others escaped by hiding in the heather on the mountainside. Baker's men were taken to Claremorris where they were badly beaten by a number of Hogan's officers.[112] Commandant Seán Walsh also maintained beatings occurred at Claremorris, carried out by Hogan's officers with blackthorn sticks kept specially for the purpose.[113] Patrick Moylett was sent west by Cosgrave to investigate the ill-treatment of the prisoners. Moylett's investigation came about because Colonel Austin Brennan, Second in Command at Claremorris barracks, had taken a very strong objection to the ill-treatment of prisoners by Hogan's officers. Moylett interviewed Hogan who denied the beating of prisoners. Moylett confessed to not feeling 'very strongly against him on the matter as I knew the character of the people he had to deal with ...Whatever his faults General Hogan was a strict disciplinarian and was doing his best under extraordinary difficult circumstances

Artist Frank Leah's drawings of NCOs and men, Claremorris Command, *An t-Óglach*, 2 June 1923. (Courtesy the Military Archives, Cathal Brugha Barracks)

to restore law and order throughout his command, including his own troops'.[114] Baker and his men were transferred to Galway Jail and court-martialled. They were sentenced to death.[115] It was never carried out.

It is difficult to express the emotional trauma and sense of loss that bore down on a generation of Republicans as a result of the executions. The fact that they were carried out by fellow Irishmen intensified the sense of loss. In many families, the effects of the executions even made their mark on the following generations. Tom Kilgarriff was originally marked for execution at Tuam before being reprieved. Kilgarriff's grandson, also Tom, said 'the sacrifice of the six weighed very heavily on my Dad Kevin, and on the anniversary of this execution he always got a public anniversary Mass said for them. My uncle, Finn, a priest in California always felt that the six were in heaven.'[116]

Liam Lynch, Chief of Staff of the Republican forces, was killed on the Knockmealdown Mountains in County Tipperary on 11 April, the same day as the executions at Tuam. He had been attending a Republican Army Council meeting in the nearby Nire Valley when National Army patrols closed in. While withdrawing over the mountains, Lynch was hit by a long-range shot. Lynch urged his comrades to continue on lest they be caught. One of them was Thomas Ruane, Mayo County Councillor and senior officer of the North Mayo Brigade.[117] After his escape from Galway Jail, Ruane had made his way down to the Republican areas of south Tipperary. Ruane and his comrades tried carry Lynch with them but he was in too much pain. Lynch was captured alive with some of the National Army believing they had caught Éamon de Valera. Liam Lynch died that evening in Clonmel. Command of the Republican forces passed to Frank Aiken, who on 27 April issued an order for his troops to stand down and suspend offensive operations while taking adequate measures to defend themselves and their munitions.[118] On 24 May, after fruitless negotiations with Cosgrave's government, Aiken ordered his troops to dump their arms. De Valera applauded the Republican troops who had borne the brunt of the Civil War: 'You have saved the nation's honour, preserved the sacred national tradition, and kept open the road of independence ... may God guard every one of you and give to our country in all times of need sons who will love her as dearly and devotedly as you.'[119]

Part III – Guarding the peace: May 1923 – December 1924

In spite of the Civil War coming to an end and orders to stand down being issued, the violence on both sides continued unabated. John Melvin from Curryane near Swinford was taken out of his home in the middle of night of 21/22 April, beaten severely and shot. His body was found lying on the road nearby the following morning with a notice 'Spies and informers beware'. A number of shots were fired into the home of John McGeehin of Geesala, Ballina the same night. McGeehin, a Treaty supporter and ex-member of Belmullet District Council, was hit in the head and fatally injured.[120] The post-war period had degenerated into score-settling and mindless violence. On 21 May, the National Army shot and killed Thomas MacNicholas, 'an organiser for the IRA', while he was in their custody en route from Kilkelly to Kiltimagh. At the inquest, Private D. Murphy claimed MacNicholas had grabbed a rifle from one of the soldiers and fired a shot, wounding Volunteer Kelly in the chest. Murphy and MacNicholas had then struggled over the weapon. Incredibly, Murphy managed to fire two shots from a bolt-action rifle while in the middle of this desperate struggle, the second of which fatally wounded MacNicholas.[121] There was yet another fatal shooting on 6 June, when Republican Captain Joseph Healy from Ballina was surprised in a house at Stone Park near Claremorris. Healy was shot while attempting to escape. At the inquest, the soldiers maintained they had fired over Healy's head at a distance of 300 yards and had not intended to hit him in the abdomen.[122] Healy was unarmed and half dressed at the time of his death.

Throughout the period of the Civil War, the inquests held never really questioned the National Army's version of events. Few forensic reports, which might which might have thrown a different light on events, were forthcoming. In the aforementioned case of Joseph Healy, for example, such evidence would have ascertained whether he was in fact shot from a distance of 300 yards as the National Army maintained or killed instead from a much closer range of 25 yards as Republicans argued. One case where there was clear evidence of the murder of a prisoner was that of Captain Nicholas Corcoran, who was captured with Thomas Gill in the Messbrook district near Ballina on 13 March 1923.[123] Two days later, Captain Dunleavy reported 'Prisoner named Corcoran accidentally shot near town [Ballina] while removing mines. Died at 5.30 p.m.'[124] Dunleavy's report was very scant on detail. This was usually the case when something serious had occurred. A Sergeant Daniel Boyle faced trial for Corcoran's murder before the Lord Chief Justice and a jury of men and women at the Dublin Commission on Friday 17 November 1923. The details of the case involved four Republican prisoners who had been brought out to a railway line near Ballina to remove a suspected mined barricade. This had been standard National Army practice since 6 March that year when a Republican mine killed three officers and two soldiers attempting to uncover a suspected arms dump at Knocknagoshel, County Kerry. The following night, the Dublin Guards, one of the most notorious units of the National Army, under Brigadier General Paddy O'Daly, took nine Republican prisoners out to Ballyseedy near Tralee, tied them to a landmine and detonated it. Any survivors were mercilessly slain. One man named Stephen Fuller miraculously survived by being blown clear in the explosion.

At Ballina, Republican prisoners Corcoran, Gill, Keavney and Caulfield were ordered to remove a barricade of telegraph poles to which a notice had reportedly been attached saying 'Beware of Kerry Mines'. The prisoners refused to touch the barricade and were ordered to kneel down and say their prayers. Captain John Bannon fired a shot over their heads to frighten them and then Sergeant Boyle, saying 'I'll put the wind up them', picked up a rifle and shot Corcoran.[125] The officer, Bannon, said before the shot was fired he heard the bolt of the rifle. This means Boyle could have been under no doubt there was a round in the breech – that the rifle was loaded. With Corcoran on the ground dying, the Sergeant claimed to Captain Murtagh that he used the wrong rifle, and that his own rifle had a 'cut-off'. All Lee-Enfield rifles had a safety catch but only some had a 'cut off' that prevented the ammunition from entering the breech by sealing off the magazine. The bolt could not have been opened and closed nor the weapon fired if the safety catch had been engaged. For Boyle to say the rifle he used by mistake had no 'cut-off' was possible. But he was not challenged on this in the court. During the trial, Captain Bannon said 'Boyle was one of the best soldiers that he had ever met'. This might explain why Nicholas Corcoran was shot in the chest, three inches below the right nipple with the bullet severing the spine on its exit.

The Chief Justice addressed the jury, saying 'it might be assumed in favour of the prisoner that he did not aim and fire at the deceased with the intention of killing him or even wounding him'. This was certainly giving a great deal of latitude to Boyle's intentions as he lined up his sights on Corcoran, just 3 yards away from him. The jury took only twenty minutes to return a verdict of 'not guilty'. In times of war, justice serves those perceived to be fighting 'the good fight'.[126] The Republicans stated quite simply that Corcoran had been murdered. His name was published in a 'List of Ninety Republican Soldiers Murdered by Colonial Forces'. The list was not of Republicans killed in action but those murdered after their surrender. It gave the names, locations and dates of the deaths. It also included men murdered while in prison. In addition to Nicholas Corcoran, other Mayo men murdered were Volunteer Patrick Mulchrone based in Castlebar on 1 November 1922 and Volunteer Stenson of Charlestown on 15 March 1923.[127] Michael Kilroy also alleged Captain Patrick Mulrennan from Ballyhaunis had been shot by Brigadier General Lawlor while in Custume barracks in Athlone on 6 October 1922. Mulrennan's wound was neglected and he died shortly after. This incident was witnessed by Paddy Hegarty and Dr Francis Ferran TD.[128] The National Army stated Mulrennan had been shot during a riot by Republican prisoners. There was more tragedy to come for the Mulrennans, with Patrick's brother Seamus killed on 14 October while leading a Republican flying column in an ambush on National Army troops near Lisacul. The two brothers were buried beside each other.

On the evening of Tuesday 26 June 1923, the inaugural meeting of the Cumann na nGaedheal Party of Mayo took place in Castlebar. J. J. Collins, now a Peace Commissioner, became the first Secretary. Dr Anthony MacBride was appointed Chairman. Other prominent politicians present were Anthony Lavelle and John Hoban, both of Castlebar Urban District Council. The foundation of Cumann na nGaedheal was a natural progression for the pro-Treaty supporters of Sinn Féin. It also incorporated the broader spectrum of pro-Treaty support in the country. MacBride spoke for some time, explaining the aims of Cumann na nGaedheal as national education, the right to ownership of private property, control of public finances and a public morality based on right and wrong instead of robbery and destruction.[129]

As the evening train approached Claremorris on 30 June, men in 'The King's Carriage' began loading and checking their revolvers. Patrick Moylett looked at them and realised they were ministers of the Free State government accompanied by detectives from Oriel House. Moylett addressed them firmly: 'If you were afraid of being shot in Claremorris, you should never have left Dublin. If you show your guns, I will not leave this train and continue to Ballina.'[130] The guns remained in the pockets! W. T. Cosgrave, President of the Dáil, Kevin O'Higgins, Minister for Justice, and Paddy Hogan, Minister for Agriculture, stood on a platform in The Square, Claremorris the following morning. They were applauded by hundreds of cheering supporters. The meeting was a victory rally celebrating the end of the Civil War. It was also the official launch of the Cumann na nGaedheal Party in the west, in time for the coming election in August 1923. The rally had been preceded by a procession of Mayo women marching down Mount Street and past the platform with banners held high demanding the release of all Republican prisoners. They were wives, mothers and sisters of the Mayo men in prison. Leading them were Ann Kilroy, wife of Michael, and Margaret (Peg) Maguire, sister of Tom. It was a brave and defiant act that served as a reminder to the members of the government that the Republican ideal was still breathing, and that not all in the Free State supported their post-Civil War policies.[131]

After the dignitaries had recovered their composure, Monsignor Macken, parish priest of Claremorris, welcomed Cosgrave to the platform, referring to him as the 'saviour of the country'. Cosgrave defended his government's policies over the previous nine months and praised the National Army. Expressing hope for the future, Cosgrave confirmed his government would develop the resources of the island in the best interests of the nation. He was not, however, for softening his attitude towards the Republicans. He offered peace on his terms or 'take the consequences'. Kevin O'Higgins, who was 'most enthusiastically received', highlighted peace, order and democratic institutions as the most valuable lessons learned over the past year. Patrick Moylett sat there seething. Alongside him were eight parish priests, nine curates, three county councillors, four district councillors, members of the newly established Irish judiciary and members of the new Cumann na nGaedheal Party including J. J. Collins and Mrs Sheridan, sister of the late General Michael Collins.[132] Referring to those on the platform, Moylett wrote in his memoir:

> I found a group that one would only expect to find in such a situation ten years earlier. There were a number of former supporters of the old Irish Parliamentary Party and a sprinkling of the Unionist element. After the meeting I asked President Cosgrave what he intended to base his political party on. He replied: 'On the Unionist party and the remnant of Redmond's party. They supported me and I'll support them and without

them there would have been no Free State.' 'You are mad,' I
said to him. 'England tried to rule this country through that
bunch and she had more power behind her than you have and
she failed.'[133]

The 1923 General Election demonstrated that one third of the
population of Ireland stood behind Cosgrave. They saw his
government as a democratic alternative to Republican intimidation
where the threat to life and to the stability of the nation was very real.
Nevertheless, Cosgrave's government remained on a political knife-
edge. The Civil War had cost £7 million in compensation for killing
and destruction. Winning the conflict with the National Army had
cost a staggering £15 million.[134] The combined figure was just half the
annual budget of around £43 million available to the Irish Free State
in 1923.[135] Cosgrave was also aware of the consequential losses of the
war; lost markets, broken industries and unemployment. Cumann na
nGaedheal believed performance, not promises, was the touchstone
of the party. The election campaign had not been easy. When William
Sears TD, Charles Bewley and Fr Flatley addressed a huge crowd in
Aughagower they were heckled and booed and had to abandon the
meeting and move on Westport.[136] The Mayo constituencies were
redrawn being composed of North Mayo (4 Seats) and South Mayo
(5 Seats). Nationally the results were:[137]

Cumann na nGaedheal	62
Sinn Féin	44
Farmer's Party	15
Labour	14
Independents	17

In the Mayo constituencies revealed a county more or less equally
divided along pro- and anti-Treaty lines:[138]

COUNTY CONSTITUENCY OF NORTH MAYO – 4 SEATS
Quota (Number of votes required to secure Election) – 5,249
Total Poll – 26,241
(Candidates surplus above the quota distributed to other preference candidates)
Returning Officer: Mr M. J. Egan

Candidates	1st Pref	Total after transfers	Order of Election
Coyle, Henry (C na nG)	2,997	8,132	Coyle (3)
Crowley, Dr. John (SF)	832	5104	Dr Crowley (4)
Flynn, Charles (Farmer)	793	1138	
Heron, Archie (Labour)	647	833	
Keaveney, Michael (SF)	137	359	
Kelly, Joseph J. (C na nG)	478	1,361	
McGrath, Joseph (C na nG)	8,011	8,011	McGrath (2)
O'Connor, Oliver J. (Independent)	99	192	
O'Hara, Patrick (C na nG)	2,097	4,689	
O'Sullivan, Timothy J. (Farmer)	151	239	
Ruane, Seán T. [John]	1,002	1,704	
Ruttledge, Patrick Joseph (SF)	8,997	8,997	Ruttledge (1)

COUNTY CONSTITUENCY OF SOUTH MAYO – 5 SEATS
Quota (Number of votes required to secure Election) – 5,343
Total Poll – 32,054
(Candidate surplus above the quota distributed to other preference candidates)
Returning Officer: Mr Austin Crean

	1st Pref	Total after transfers	Order of Election
Bewley, Charles (C na nG)	2,479	3,626	
Derrig, Tom (SF)	2,148	2,551	
Kilroy, Michael (SF)	3,516	6,460	Kilroy (4)
MacBride, Joseph (C na nG)	4,758	5,417	MacBride (3)
Maguire, Tom (SF)	5.712	5,712	Maguire (2)
Nally, Martin (C na nG)	3,468	4,737	Nally (5)
O'Connor (Labour)	1,298	1,633	
O'Malley (Independent)	1,175	1,354	
Sears, William (C na nG)	6,571	6,571	Sears (1)
Tuohy, Patrick (Farmers)	929	1,046	

Victory in North Mayo was sweet for P. J. Ruttledge who, as de Valera's deputy, had a decisive result over the Minister for Industry and Commerce, Joseph McGrath, who was also a general in the National Army. In South Mayo, too, the government and the Republicans split the vote. William Sears of Cumann na nGaedheal headed the poll there. The Irish public had exercised their democratic right to renounce violence, and yet they remained strongly sympathetic to Republican ideals.[139] The Catholic Church had campaigned heavily for Cumann na nGaedheal with Archdeacon Fallon of Castlebar, Fr Brett of Ballyhaunis and Fr O'Malley of Bekan appearing with government ministers and TDs. Archdeacon Fallon found himself defending the 'Flogging Bill' on the same platform as Minister for Home Affairs, Desmond Fitzgerald, in a pre-election rally at Castlebar.[140] Flogging was just one of the measures proposed in the Public Safety Act of July 1923, which the Government had introduced to keep Republican prisoners interned. Fearful of the weapons still retained by the Republican forces, Cosgrave's government also passed an Indemnity Act on 3 August. This protected the National Army engaged in harassing Republicans.[141] For the rest of the nation, however, the oppression of the new Free State was a denial of the freedom they had suffered so much to attain. With Sinn Féin TDs refusing to enter the new Dáil, the Cumann na nGaedheal government had a possible majority of sixteen. Criticism of the government began to increase. Cosgrave was anxious to move on with the business of rebuilding the country, but with Sinn Féin still out in the cold, he was forced to keep the National Army in a state of war-readiness. A cartoon appeared in *Éire*, the Republican newssheet, with Cosgrave, cigarette in mouth, leaning into a barrel of gunpowder labelled 'Public Opinion', saying, 'I really must give up smoking.'[142] The pressure was mounting for Cosgrave and his cabinet.

The 1923 General Election marked a major turning point for the people of Mayo. With the Civil War behind them, there was a shift in the county leadership towards the prioritising of life. Enough blood had been spilled. Opposition to the government's decision to continue the detention of approximately 11,000 Republican prisoners became a unifying factor. The Catholic Church began to call for the release of the men and women who had sacrificed so much in the Tan war.

The *Mayo News*, previously the most vociferous paper in attacking the Republican cause, saw a seismic shift in its policy. At last, those in positions of influence had begun to recognise the abilities of the men and women still in jail. Conditions in the prisons were simply appalling. In spite of all the criticism Cosgrave, O'Higgins and Mulcahy received regarding the treatment of Republican prisoners, nothing was done to ease the situation. Seán Walsh was captured in February 1923. After initial stints at Swinford, Ballina and Claremorris he eventually found himself in the hell that was Galway Jail. The conditions in the prison were

> absolutely vile, so vile that nobody could possibly describe them, there were no beds of any description the prisoner had to lie on the cell floor and the only bedclothes available were pieces of coarse dirty blankets these pieces of blanket were so coarse and dirty that the place was infested with vermin. Each cell was built to accommodate one prisoner but during the Civil War period there were four prisoners in each cell, in the ordinary way there was sanitary accommodation for fifty prisoners but when the place was occupied by two hundred prisoners the sanitary accommodation was entirely insufficient result lavatories were very often choked so that prisoners were carrying excereta [*sic*] in their shoes where-ever they walked.[143]

Dr Francis Ferran, TD of the old Mayo-East constituency, had died in custody in the Curragh Camp on 10 June 1923. Originally from Magherafelt, County Derry, he had made his family home in Mayo, devoting his life to his profession and to the Irish language. Dr Ferran became involved in the national movement and trained the Fianna from 1913. He had used his medical skills to restore the severely injured P. J. Carney back to health after the attack on Bohola RIC barracks in 1920.[144] Carney left for England and was involved in an attempt to assassinate the hangman, John Ellis, who carried out most of the executions of IRA men in Ireland. As the War of Independence continued, Dr Ferran feared for the safety of his family. They went on the run together seeking shelter in a derelict house near Lough Conn. His devotion to the Republic led to his arrest and ill-treatment in Ballina. After a brief stint in Athlone he was transferred to the Curragh where in weakened health he became ill and died. His loss was yet another Ireland could ill-afford. But it did focus the minds of those who were in a position to provide the necessary leadership. In October, the Republican prisoners, led by their O/C Michael Kilroy in Mountjoy, began a hunger strike. Tom Derrig became O/C in the Curragh Camp. The issue of the hunger strike was brought a lot closer to home when sixty Republican prisoners in Castlebar Jail joined the strike. The prisoners' O/C was Paddy Horkan. He issued a stark statement to the press: 'Liberty or Death is our motto ... All men were created equal. So too all men were created Free. That our humble effort may help in speedily bringing Complete Independence to our Beloved Land we Fervently Pray. A Dia [sic] Saor Eire [God Save Ireland].'[145]

The attitude of the prison commanders was appalling. Kilroy described

> the hosing of the prisoners here, their forcible expulsion, then saturated into exercise rings, there to suffer exposure in bitter weather for thirty-seven hours, and to be hosed again and again on subsequent days, and bedding, cells, clothing etc. also hosed; the beating and kicking of men as they are dragged from their cells, and finally their confinement in overcrowded cells for three weeks, and the persistent firing on them – these things are fresh in the public mind. And in addition, as may not yet be known to the public, the torture of prisoners in the basement where men have lain, and some yet lie, handcuffed without bedding, and only partially dressed, day and night, for thirteen days is the measure of the treatment all may expect during the F.S. [Free State] effort to break the present passive resistance.[146]

It was because of treatment like this that the prisoners felt they have no alternative but to go on hunger strike. The prisoners received great support throughout the country. In Mayo, even the Cumann na nGaedheal members of the County Council temporarily united with their Republican adversaries to appeal to the government to release the prisoners.[147] But it was perhaps the older and more respected men who spoke with real wisdom. The most powerful appeal came from Charles Hughes, now Chairman of Westport Urban Council. Hughes had spent the period of the Truce rebuilding his shattered drapery business after its destruction by the Tans in 1921. His new premises offered employment and financial stability for the people of Westport during a time of real crisis in the country. Hughes addressed a packed Concert Hall in the town on 7 November 1923. He spoke with great feeling, recalling the sacrifices most of the prisoners had made in the defence of their country in the awful years before the Truce. Choosing his words carefully, Hughes stated that the people had been promised peace if they voted for a certain policy. Peace had not been delivered. There could be no peace, he argued, while thousands of their people were shut up in prison and internment camps. Hughes then introduced Miss Agnes Gallagher, who was just released from the North Dublin Union where fifty-one women were on hunger strike. Hughes then read out a statement calling on the government to release those held in jails and internment camps as it was six months since the war had ended. All present signed the statement, which was then sent on to Dublin.[148]

Cosgrave and his government, however, were not to be moved on the issue. Prisoners began to die in the most dreadful circumstances. Dr Anthony MacBride, Chairman of Castlebar Urban District Council, presided at a meeting on 5 November that passed a motion of condolence to Cosgrave on the murder of his brother Philip in Dublin. The clerk then read two resolutions seeking support for the prisoners release, one from Macroom District Council and the other from Limerick County Council. Dr MacBride told the clerk to put the resolutions in the waste paper basket, referring to the hunger strike as an 'old woman's game'. A heated discussion followed with Mrs Ryan, Mrs Carney and Mr McCormack arguing for the prisoners. MacBride was intransigent and they left.[149] The ending of the stalemate over the hunger strike required someone of greater influence to break the impasse. Cardinal Logue, Primate of Ireland, seized the initiative, issuing an appeal to the prisoners to end their hunger strike. Michael Kilroy, displaying great courage and leadership, grasped the moment and ordered his men to call off the strike: 'For the sake of Ireland and of the future we must make this sacrifice, as we consider that further deaths of Irishmen at the hands of their brother Irishmen would only perpetuate bitterness in our loved country.'[150]

Kilroy's war was finally over. Nevertheless, this resourceful commander had one last surprise to deliver. Kilroy did not permit the government to keep him locked up until they decided to release him. Instead, he chose the moment of his own liberation, escaping from the Curragh Camp on 11 May 1924. Michael Kilroy, now free, was determined not to be caught again. Like Tom Maguire, who had escaped from Custume Barracks in Athlone on 10 June 1923, he moved from house to house in the hands of those who made sure to shield them from the National Army patrols. By the end of 1924, both Kilroy and Maguire could move about freely and without the danger of arrest. Indeed they were appearing together, campaigning for Dr John Madden who won a by-election held in North Mayo. One thing both Kilroy and Maguire would have noticed immediately on their return to Mayo was the presence of a new police force, the Civic Guards.

The Civic Guards were established in 1922 as an unarmed police force for the Irish Free State. Michael Collins established a organising committee under Dáil Éireann jurisdiction and headed by Michael Staines, a Dublin TD but originally from Newport. Collins was so impressed with the organisational abilities of the RIC that thirteen members of the force sat on the committee of the Civic Guards.[151] The new force, 1,500 strong, was sent to a former artillery barracks in Kildare in the summer of 1922. The Civic Guards were offered stables as their sleeping quarters by the Free State soldiers in residence. Refusing this, most of them slept in the open with just their great-coats for warmth.[152] There was also very little to eat. When Staines, the first Commissioner, arrived with his former RIC command staff, the men refused to take orders. The presence of former RIC men in the command structure was too much for them. Leading the men was Joe Ring, who had been specially invited to join the new police force. Eventually, after a stand-off of a few weeks, the RIC staff were temporarily withdrawn. Ring, fed up with the arguing, returned to the life he knew best, as an army officer leading his own men.[153] The Civic Guards' first public appearance in Ireland was at the handing over of Dublin Castle on 17 August 1922. Major Torin of The King's

Michael Staines, originally from Newport, County Mayo, Irish Volunteer Officer North Dublin Brigade IRA, TD and First Commissioner of An Garda Síochána. (Courtesy the Garda Museum)

Shropshire Light Infantry took Staines' salute and handed over the keys. Later that evening he reported to his superiors in London:

> The new Civic Guard, 300 of whom are now quartered in Dublin Castle, are a fine body of men. They have a smart blue uniform. They are enlisted from the same class as the Royal Irish Constabulary, ie., the sons of small farmers. At present they are armed with only revolvers for guard duties and ether [*sic*] special occasions. Eventually it is intended that they shall be distributed throughout the country towns and districts as an unarmed police force. Their establishment is to be 4,000 but at the moment they are only 1,000 strong.[154]

In late August, Eoin O'Duffy replaced Michael Staines as Commissioner of the Civic Guards. The ex-RIC staff returned to assist in organising the urgently needed police force. Among them was the former District Inspector for Castlebar, Michael Horgan. In

Commandant Joe Ring (front centre with cane) and Civic Guard recruits 1922.
(Courtesy Michael Ring TD)

1924, Horgan was appointed a Superintendent in the Civic Guards at their headquarters in the old RIC Depot at the Phoenix Park. He pioneered the 'Weights and Measures' section and wrote a number of books assisting the new force in their development. Michael Horgan, after a lifetime's policing service to Ireland, retired on 1 July 1934. He died at the age of seventy-one on 29 January 1949.[155] Under Commissioner O'Duffy, the aims and purpose of the force was firmly established. The Civic Guards were to serve the people and the law regardless of the political party in power.[156] Lofty guiding principles were one thing, but the new Civic Guards first had to win the respect and confidence of the people they were to serve.

The Civic Guards arrived in Mayo at the end of February 1923. Chief Superintendent Henry O'Mara, the commander of the force, received an official welcome at Castlebar District Court on Wednesday 28 February from District Justice Philip F. Lavery.[157] On the ground, things were not as cordial. In Ballyhaunis, Sergeant O'Leary and Guards Foley, Murphy, Duggan, Piggot and McMahon settled in to the old RIC barracks. The National Army, resentful of the Civic Guards' authority, arrived and raked the police station with machine-gun fire.[158] In Carracastle, too, the Guards received a frosty reception:

> A small party of civic guards arrived to Carracastle, County Mayo, to open a station there. Believing that temporary accommodation was to be found for them in the local hall, they approached the somewhat dismal-looking structure, only to be refused admittance by the hall committee. The guards subsequently broke down the door and took occupation of the hall. The forthcoming dance for that night was postponed for one week, and a hostile, though not violent, crowd gathered round the premises, where they booed and protested at the turn of events.[159]

The Republican columns generally left the Civic Guards alone. Nevertheless, there were occasions when Civic Guard patrols were held up by armed men, stripped of their uniforms and relieved of their bicycles. Two men found guilty of an armed hold-up on two Civic Guards at Glenhest were sentenced to five years' penal servitude at the Dublin Criminal Court in July 1924.[160]

Chief Superintendant O'Mara informed the people that his men would enforce the licensing laws rigorously. The Civic Guards were particularly tenacious in tackling the illicit manufacture of poitín, which by 1923 was a thriving industry. On an island in Lough Conn they discovered the largest distillery ever uncovered in the county. The Guards, accompanied by the National Army, landed on the island after midnight. They found 500 gallons of poitín along with nine stills and a quantity of wash. There was also an amount of molasses, sugar and malt. In the subsequent court case, the man responsible for the poitín plant argued in his defence that on account of ill health he was ordered to keep a drop of spirits by the priest and the doctor. A fine of £100 mitigated to £12 was imposed.[161]

There is no doubt that policing in a county exposed to many years of violence was extremely difficult. Violent crime was common and the Guards had to deal with a number of gruesome murders involving brother against brother, husband against wife and father against son. There was also a case where a family united to murder their father. The Guards' reputation was enhanced by their ability to solve these crimes. In the case of Anne Horkan, murdered during the Truce, a Civic Guard journeyed to England to make an arrest and bring the suspect back to Mayo.[162]

In spite of all of the difficulties they faced, the Civic Guards behaved with great attention to duty. They quickly provided the presence of authority that was missing throughout the Civil War. The Guards also displayed their ability to impose their authority when necessary. Rigorous baton charges were called for during rioting in Ballyhaunis after an athletic and cycling event on 13 July 1924.[163] Impartial to the last, the Guards also began to call members of the National Army to account. Inspector Tobin successfully prosecuted a pub owner in Claremorris after Guards McCarthy, Cussin and Riordan raided the premises and discovered eight soldiers in the bar and kitchen after closing time. The soldiers claimed they had been working late at the barracks and had been allowed to go for a drink by the Provost Marshal when they were dismissed. District Justice Lavery, addressing the soldiers and the pub owner, said: 'You must understand that the Provost Marshal is not above the law and it is the duty of the Guards to enforce it. The offence has been proved.'[164]

District Justices had replaced the old Resident Magistrates. They were supported by Peace Commissioners. P. R. Hughes of Claremorris was one of the first appointed in August 1923. The new District Justices were strict and sought to implement their verdicts to the letter of the law. Many young boys were brought before them for robbery. Patrick Walsh and Michael Moffitt robbed the collection box in Ballinrobe Catholic Church. They were sentenced to four years at Galway Industrial School by District Justice William Coyne.[165] John Collins, a fourteen-year-old boy who was involved in stealing a horse at the Claremorris Fair, got three years in a reformatory from District Justice Lavery.[166] The rule of law was not always applied equally. Three former IRA officers and a civilian from Castlebar came before Acting County Court Judge M. J. Kenny in May 1924. They had gone on a drinking binge around Castlebar on 10 April 1922, robbing and terrifying people at gunpoint and molesting a married woman. They had robbed over £300, less than half of which was refunded. A number of appeals were made on behalf of the former officers, including a character references from a Castlebar Peace Commissioner who was very prominent in the new Cumann na nGaedheal Party. The ex-IRA men were given a suspended sentence of six months with a bail bond of £50. The civilian was released under the First Offenders Act.[167]

Individual Civic Guards displayed considerable bravery in the course of their duty. On Monday 13 August 1923, four women, one of them the wife of Chief Superintendent O'Mara, went swimming at Rossmalley near Westport. Teresa Durcan soon found herself in deep water and shouted for help. The other three women began to founder as they attempted to rescue their friend. On hearing the calls for help, Guard McGarry, assisted by Guard Murray and ex-Sergeant Kilroy, plunged into the water fully dressed. Aided by local man Pat McGreal, the men succeeded in pulling all of the women from the water. Mrs O'Mara and Miss Duncan were both unconscious when carried from the sea. The Guards managed to resuscitate Mrs O'Mara but were too late to save Teresa Durcan. The actions of the Guards received great praise.[168] On another occasion, Sergeant O'Driscoll and Guard Kilroy, stationed at Knock, came across salmon poachers armed with a shotgun. One of the men opened fire, wounding Guard Kilroy in the face and blowing the collar off his tunic. O'Driscoll tackled the armed poacher with such force he broke the shotgun! The men then fled into the darkness. This episode serves to emphasise how the Civic Guards, as an unarmed force, faced a population with relatively easy access to weapons.

In an era where a country had been at war with itself, the new unarmed police force gave the people an important sense of pride. Their presence among Mayo communities weary of war was a welcome one. It brought stability and marked an end to military presence. Most significant of all it heralded a return to peace. It also offered a fine example of a bright career to young Mayo men. From 1922 to 1952, Mayo, with 768 recruits, was the county to make the third highest contribution to Civic Guard rank and file. It was next only to Cork with 952 and Kerry with 861.[169] With the establishment of real peace in County Mayo, people began to at last draw breath. The years of war were at an end. The question now was what lay in store for those who had fought and survived.

* * *

On the night of 2/3 May 1916, Tom Clarke received a last visit from his wife at Kilmainham Jail in Dublin. He was to be executed at dawn with Patrick Pearse and Thomas MacDonagh. Kathleen Clarke recalled that they did not talk about themselves but instead spoke of Ireland and the future. Among Tom Clarke's last words to his wife were: 'All of us going out tonight believe we have saved the soul of Ireland. We have struck the first successful blow to freedom. Freedom is coming. But between this and freedom Ireland will go through hell. But Ireland will never lie down again.'[170]

During the years 1919–24 Mayo had gone through this hell. Many of her sons and daughters did not live to see the freedom that was coming. Throughout this period the people of the county had endured violence, political upheaval and agricultural revolution. When it was all over, many sought to rebuild lives shattered by war. For some, the Republic they had fought for had been lost so they left for America, Australia or anywhere else to dull the pain they felt. William O'Keefe, former staff officer of the South Mayo Brigade, said the youth of the country had given everything. For years they had drilled, trained and fought for Irish freedom. They were the real heroes.[171] When it was all over, they received little benefit. Many of them, their health broken by their experiences, died young. Alexander Boyd from Ballysokeery was one such case.

In 1934, de Valera's Fianna Fáil government brought in the Military Service Pensions Act. This Act established the Military Service Pensions Board, where veterans had to present statements and sometimes appear in person to give evidence to substantiate their claim for a pension and a War of Independence Medal with Cómhrac (Combat) Bar. The medal became more popularly known as 'The Black and Tan Medal' due to the colour of the ribbon attached to it. The Board decided whether or not to award pensions and/or medals to those who took part in the 1916 Rising and the War of

Independence. Alexander Boyd was turned down.[172] Boyd dispatched a long and heartfelt letter to P. J. Ruttledge, TD and former Minister for Justice, seeking assistance and additional statements to reinforce an appeal to the decision of the Pension Board. The letter, which can be read in full in the appendices, described Boyd's long years of struggle for the Irish cause. He never received an answer. Boyd's health then went into a decline from which he was not to recover. He died on 6 December 1942. His funeral at St Vincent de Paul's Church, Marino, was attended by many IRA veterans including the Minister for Defence Oscar Traynor. Boyd's medal recognising his service in the North Mayo Brigade of the IRA during the War of Independence was finally received by his widow, Ellen, on 19 February 1943.

There were many like Boyd whose lives ended prematurely. Others, however, managed to find some healing. Many years after the Civil War was over, Kevin Kilgarriff received a visit from Pádraig Dunleavy who had been his father's O/C in the IRA and then his adversary in the Civil War. Dunleavy asked for forgiveness for betraying Tom Kilgarriff by revealing his secret hiding place to the National Army in 1922. The two men became firm friends, their differences over the Treaty and the Civil War put to one side. For both men it was a mark of great courage. They understood the trials the people of the country had faced. Few veterans ever spoke about what they had experienced. For them the everlasting concern for family, faith and land took precedence over their feelings. They welcomed peace and a return to the routine of the seasons unfolding under a western sky. Occasionally, however, they would meet as old comrades and talk of the times they fought for a free and independent Ireland.

With the Civil War over and the prisoners finally released life began to return to normal. Yet the National Army still held the remains of some who had been executed during the Civil War. In 1924 W. T. Cosgrave ordered the release of the remains still held. On 6 November that year, the bodies of ten Republicans executed at Tuam and Athlone were finally returned to their families. One of them was Mayo man John Maguire. Seamus O'Maille was buried at Oughterard. The other nine were buried together at Donaghpatrick near Headford, County Galway.[173] Two of the priests from Tuam who had been with the Republicans in their last hours concelebrated

Éamon de Valera meets with IRA veterans on a visit to Castlebar 1973: (l–r) de Valera, unknown Irish Army officer, Brodie Chambers and Paddy Horkan. (Courtesy Tom Campbell Photography).

the Requiem Mass. The Maguire family followed the coffins of the dead that included their son and brother, John Maguire.

Dr Kathleen Lynn, by now a Republican TD, had travelled to south Mayo to support the Maguire family. She recorded the events in her diary.

> They had high Mass at 9 here for poor Maguire, the father & mother wonderful, by road to Headford, met 8 other funerals, terrible showers, procession to Donaghpatrick, 20,000 there, Staters round graveyard, one huge grave for all 9, all R.C. honours. McDevitt & I spoke. Put laurel wreath in grave.[174]

Dr Lynn delivered an oration honouring the memory of the young men who died. 'We all realise what the suddenness of death means

Dr Kathleen Lynn, Sinn Féin TD County Dublin. (Reference Number: SU/9/4
Reproduced by kind permission of the Royal College of Physicians of Ireland)

but we should never forget that these young boys laid down their
youthful lives that Ireland might be free.'[175] John Maguire, the last
of Mayo's war dead, was finally at peace. The graves were then closed
and the thousands assembled departed in silence to return to their
families, friends and the quiet reflection of their own thoughts.

Appendix I

United Kingdom General Election 14 December 1918

Mayo Constituencies	Population	Electorate	Elected	Votes For
Mayo East	46,729	21,635	Eamon de Valera	8,975
Mayo North	47,854	21,212	Dr John Crowley	7,429
Mayo South	48,963	21,567	William Sears	Unopposed
Mayo North	51,118	21,667	Joseph MacBride	10,195

Source: www.ark.ac.uk/elections/h1918

Appendix II

RIC County Mayo Report: Illegal Drilling by Irish Volunteers at
Westport, 4 November 1917

List of names of men identified by the Police as having taken part in Illegal Drill of Sinn
Feiners at Westport 4-11-17

No	Names	Addresses	Age	Occupation	Acts done	Witnesses to prove Acts
1	Michael J. Ring	Drummendoo	27	Farmer	In Command + gave words in drill movements	Nos 1 to 6
2	Edward Moane	Carrowbawn	28	Do [ditto – meaning 'as above']	2nd in Command	do
3	John McDonagh	High Street	47	Plasterer	marched	No 1, 2, 3, 5, + 6
4	Patrick Kettrick	do	21	Messenger Lifton's	do	do
5	John Flynn	Bridge St	23	Lime Burner	do	do
6	Bartly Cryan	High St	27	Shop Assistant	do	do
7	Martin Keane	Bridge St	23	do	do	do
8	Mick Higgins	do	25	do	do	do
9	John J. Franely	Shop St	27	do	do	do
10	John Berry	High St	20	do	do	do
11	Patrick Haran	James St	28	Solicitor's Clerk	do	do
12	John Clarke	Altamont St	20	Apprentice Fetter	do	do
13	Owen Reilly	Fair Green	24	Assistant Cattle Dealer	do	do

14	Charles Gavin	High St	20	Shop Ast	do	Nos 1,2,3, + 6
15	Patrick O'Mara	Carnalangan [?]	22	Farmer's Son	do	No 2
16	John Hestor	Westport Quay	30	Labourer	do	do
17	Stephen Burke	Doon	24	Farmer's Son	do	Nos 1, 2, 3, + 5
18	Patrick McGing	Do	32	do	do	No 2
19	James McGing	High St	27	Tailor	do	Nos 1,2,3, 5 + 6
20	Martin Geraghty	James St	24	Butcher	do	do
21	Joseph Sullivan	Octagon	22	Tailor	do	do
22	Patrick Heraty	Altamont	21	Butcher	do	1,2,3 + 5
23	Michl Massey	James St	27	Shop Ast	do	1 + 2
24	James Rush	Shop St	19	Shop Assistant	Marched	Nos 1,2,3,5+ 6
25	Michael Kearns	Mill St	21	Tailor	do	Do
26	James McKenna	Carrowbawn	21	Farmer's son	Do	Do
27	Michael J. Giblin	Churchfield	24	Do	Do	Do
28	Gus Lennon	High St	25	Tailor	Do	Do
29	Michael J. O'Malley	Ardoley	26	Farmer's son	Do	Do
30	Thomas Reidy	Bridge St	19	Shop Assistant	Do	Nos 1,2,3 + 5
31	Michael McNally	Peter St	26	Tailor	Do	Do
32	John McEvilly	Shop St	22	Shop Assistant	Do	Do
33	James Kearney	Hill St	20	Tailor	Do	Nos 1 + 3
34	John Gibbons	Quay Road	19	Teacher	Do	No 1

Note in Col 7 the Numbers shown are the Witnesses as follows:		
1	Sergt	Michael Hayes
2	Const	Patrick O'Brien
3	"	Patrick Sullivan
4	"	Francis Holland
5	"	John Tiernan
6	"	Francis J. Butler
Co Inspector		D/I Shore

Source: The British in Ireland Series. Sinn Féin Suspects. Michael Joseph Ring. National Archives of Ireland: MFA 54/134.

Appendix III

British Military Allocation for Mayo

Unit	Location	Officers	Other Ranks
2nd Border Regiment	Castlebar Barracks	12	251
Detatchment "	Castlebar Aerodrome	1	31
Detatchment "	Ballinrobe	5	114
Detatchment "	Westport	4	80
Detatchment "	Ballina	1	24
2nd Battalion Argyll & Sutherland Highlanders	Claremorris	12	389
Detachment "	Swinford	5	86
17th Lancers Detatchment	Tuam	2	46
Royal Engineers	Swinford	1	18
Detachment 5th Signal Company	Castlebar Barracks		6
Detatchment "	Claremorris		3
Detachment Royal Army Service Corps	Claremorris	2	88
Detatchment "	Swinford		1
Detatchment "	Westport		2
Detatchment "	Castlebar		3
Detatchment "	Ballinrobe		1
17th Company, Royal Army Medical Corps,	Castlebar	2	2
Detatchment "	Claremorris	1	2
Detatchment "	Swinford		1

Source: Adapted from Sheehan, William, (Collins Press, Cork, 2009), pp. 188–9.

Appendix IV

Mayo IRA Volunteers Killed in The War of Independence 1919–21

Name	Date & Location	Cause of Death
Duffy, Jim. (Volunteer)	Died Rockfield and buried secretly April 1921 Reburied Oughaval, Westport 15/01/1922.	Accidental discharge of a firearm.
Coen, Michael. (Volunteer)	01/04/1921 Lecarrow, Ballyhaunis.	Mutilated and murdered after capture by British Troops.
Corcoran, Seán. (Commandant)	1/04/1921 Crossard, Ballyhaunis.	Killed in action with RIC & British Military.
Marley, Patrick. (Adjutant)	Died 11/05/1921 Buried secretly at Rockfield. Reburied at Annagh, Glenhest 02/03/1922.	Accidental discharge of a firearm.
Tolan, Michael J. (Volunteer)	April, 1921. (exact date unknown) Leecarrow, Ballyhaunis.	Mutilated and murdered after capture by the RIC.
Feeney, Pádraig. (Volunteer)	03/05/1921 Tourmakeady.	Murdered by the RIC [Black & Tans]. RIC stated Feeney was 'shot while trying to escape'.
O'Brien, Michael. (Commandant)	03/05/1921 Partry Mountains.	Killed in action against British Troops.
O'Malley, Thomas (Volunteer)	6/05/1921 Clonkeen, Castlebar to Westport Road.	Shot dead by the RIC while trenching a road. O'Malley was unarmed.
Lally, Thomas. (Volunteer)	6/05/1921 Clonkeen, Castlebar to Westport Road.	Shot dead by the RIC while trenching a road. Lally was unarmed.

McEvilly, Seamus. (Captain)	19/05/1921 Kilmeena.	Killed in action against the RIC.
Collins, John. (Volunteer)	19/05/21 Kilmeena.	Killed in action against the RIC.
Jordan, Paddy. (Commandant)	19/05/21 Kilmeena	Fatally wounded in action against the RIC. Died in King George V Hospital [Now St Bricins Irish Military Hosptial] a specialist hospital for neurological cases.
O'Donnell, Thomas. (Volunteer)	19/05/21 Kilmeena.	Killed in action against the RIC.
Staunton, John. (Volunteer)	19/05/21 Kilmeena.	Killed in action against the RIC.
Browne, Jim. (Volunteer)	23/05/21 Lower Skerdagh.	Killed in action against the RIC.
Howley, Thomas (Volunteer)	25/05/21 Bunree.	Fatally wounded while trying to escape an RIC raid.
Paddy Boland. (Captain)	27/05/21. Derryvackna, Tooreen.	Mutilated and murdered by British Troops after capture.
Nealon, Tom (Volunteer)	25/06/21	Shot dead in an RIC raid on the North Mayo Brigade HQ Staff.
Moran, Michael. (Lieutenant)	19/01/1922 Dooagh, Achill.	Cardiac arrest at home. Death due to ill-treatment in Prison.

Source: collated from primary sources by author.

Appendix V

British Army Charge Sheet for the Court Martial of Tom Ruane, South Mayo Brigade, Claremorris Company, IRA

FORM OF CHARGE UNDER 9AA (d) RESTORATION OF ORDER IN IRELAND REGULATIONS.

The accused _Thomas Ruane_ .... civilian, of. _Claremorris Co Mayo_ ~~Galway~~ is charged with contravening the provisions of an Order made by the Competent Military Authority under Regulation 9AA. of the Defence of the Realm Regulations and in force in Ireland, as if it had been made under the Restoration of Order in Ireland Regulations, that is to say :—

~~Carrying~~
~~having~~
keeping
} {
firearms,
~~military arms,~~
~~ammunition,~~
~~explosive substances,~~
}

not under effective military control,

in that he,

at_Claremorris in the county of Mayo_ .... on _17" November_ 1920,

did, contrary to an order of the Competent Military Authority dated 28th September, 1918,

~~carry~~
~~have~~
keep
} {
Firearms,
~~military arms,~~
~~ammunition,~~
~~explosive substances,~~
}

not under effective military control,

Tom Ruane Charge Sheet Part 1. Charge Sheet for the Court Martial of Tom Ruane, South Mayo Brigade, Claremorris Company IRA. Ruane was arrested on 17 November 1920. His court martial was held at Renmore Barracks, Galway on 21 January 1921. Tom Ruane was acquitted.

Charge.
Reg. 9 AA (d),
R. O. I. R.

Contravening the provisions of an order made by the Competent Military Authority under Regulation 9 AA of the Defence of the Realm Regulations and in force in Ireland, as if it had been made under the Restoration of Order in Ireland Regulations, that is to say,

Carrying
having
keeping

firearms,
military arms,
ammunition,
explosive substances

not under effective military control,

in that he,

at *Claremorris in the County of Mayo* .... on *17ᵗʰ November 1920*

did, contrary to an order of the Competent Military Authority dated 28th September, 1918,

carry
have
keep

firearms,
military arms,
ammunition,
explosive substances,

namely :— *125 rounds of sporting ammunition*

not under effective military control.

You will be tried by Field General Court Martial on Friday 21ˢᵗ January 1921 at Renmore Barracks Galway at 10·30 a m.

Tom Ruane Charge Sheet Part 2

Summary of Evidence in the case of THOMAS BRETT, shop keeper of CLAREMORRIS and T. RUANE shop assistant in BRETT'S shop.

- - - - - - - - - - - - - - - - - - -

1st Witness for Prosecution.	Lieut. A.H.St.Clair M.C., 2nd Bn. Argyll & Sutherland Highlanders:— At CLAREMORRIS on 17th November 1920 at about 1100 hours I was ordered to take a party down to BRETT'S shop in CLAREMORRIS and search all his premises, as RUANE, one of BRETT's shop assistants was supposed to have hidden a certain amount of ammunition there. Immediately on arrival I found RUANE and placed a Guard on him I took BRETT round with me while I searched and I found in the storeroom in a sack behind some corn, 5 boxes each containing 25 sporting cartridges. These were made up in a brown paper parcel and appeared to have been put there very recently. I told BRETT to open this parcel and before doing it he shouted to RUANE who was outside the door, " I wish you fellows would label parcels when you put them away to save me the trouble of opening them " or words to that effect. I also found in the same place a .22 rook rifle. The storeroom where the above articles were found is kept locked so I asked BRETT who had the keys. He replied that only RUANE and he had them. When BRETT opened the parcel and saw that it contained cartridges he appeared to be absolutely amazed, and in my opinion it was the first time he had ever seen them. In another storeroom I found a few very mouldy and useless cartridges and also a box containing some gunpowder. I arrested both BRETT and RUANE and brought them to camp.

(Sgd) A.H.St.Clair. Lieut.

(Q) BRETT. Where did you find the rifle?

(A) In a corner in the same room as the cartridges.

The witness withdraws.

Tom Ruane Charge Sheet Part 3

1st witness.   Mr. T. BRETT states:-   I had absolutely no knowledge that any of these articles were on my premises and am prepared to make an affidavit to that effect if necessary.
With regard to the keys - I keep a master key in my possession for all my stores, but a bunch of keys is kept hanging in the shop which any of the boys in my employ and not RUANE alone have access to.   With regard to the gunpowder, I am of opinion that this was deposited in my store some 12 or 14 years ago by a Congested Districts Board Ganger and I had absolutely forgotten that it existed until Mr. St.Clair found it to-day.
                    (sgd)   Thomas Brett.

2nd Witness.   T.RUANE states:-   I had no knowledge of either the rifle or the sporting cartridges being where they were.   All the staff have access to that particular store as the keys are kept hanging in the shop.   With regard to the gunpowder - it has always been there since I entered Mr. Bretts employ.
                    (sgd)   Thomas Ruane.

        Certified that R.r. 4 c.d & e have been complied with.
        Taken down in the presence of the accused this seventeenth day of November 1920 and signed

                    C.H.A.MacMillan   Lieut.
            Adjutant, 2/Argyll & Sutherland Highlanders.

Thomas Brett will be called as a Witness for the prosecution and, in addition to giving evidence according to his statement above will prove that in his absence T. Ruane as Foreman had charge of the premises

Tom Ruane Charge Sheet Part 4

Source: courtesy of Tommy Ruane.

Appendix VI

RIC Casualties for County Mayo 1919–21

Name	RIC Number	Date	Cause of Death
Constable Doogue, Pierce.	60412	15/06/1920	Killed after being hit with a stone to the head thrown in a riot on Main Street, Belmullet, County Mayo. Doogue was in civilian clothes and on a visit to the town. He had come to the aid of beleaguered colleagues when killed.
Sergeant Armstrong, Thomas Robert.	53611	21/07/1920	Mortally wounded while on foot patrol outside The Moy Hotel, Knox Street, Ballina, County Mayo.
Sergeant Coughlan, John.	55450	22/03/1921	Mortally wounded in an ambush carried out by the West Mayo Brigade at Carrowkennedy on the Drummin Road. Sgt Coughlan was part of a four-man cycle patrol. The three other Constables were wounded.
Constable Stephens, William H.	73707	29/03/192	Mortally wounded by gun shots to the back and hip while on duty in Knox Street, Ballyhaunis, County Mayo.
Constables O'Regan, Christopher Patrick. Oakes, Herbert. Power, William. Regan, John.	67167 78855 61221 80138	3/05/1921	Killed in action in an ambush carried out by the South Mayo Brigade at Tourmakeady, County Mayo.

Constable Hopkins, Thomas.	70690	7/05/1921	Murdered by IRA while on leave to visit his father at Leface near Ballindine, County Mayo.
Sergeant Butler, Francis J.	59260	18/05/1921	Shot dead by an IRA sniper outside the RIC Barracks Newport, County Mayo.
Constable Beckett, Harry.	80290	19/05/1921	Killed in action at an ambush carried out by the West Mayo Brigade IRA at Kilmeena, County Mayo.
Constable Maguire, Joseph.	66577	23/05/1921	Killed in action at Lower Skirdagh as an eighteen-man RIC patrol surprised a resting IRA Flying Column of the West Mayo Brigade.
Constables Blythe, Sydney. Brown, James. Doherty, John. Dowling, Thomas. French, William. Stevenson, Edward James. District Inspector Creegan, Sergeant Francis.	78576 79746 57416 60016 75811 72024 59658	2/06/1921	Killed in action at an ambush carried out by the West Mayo Brigade IRA at Carrowkennedy, County Mayo.
Constables Higgins, Thomas. King, John.	62730 63068	1/07/1921	Executed after capture by members of the North Mayo IRA Flying Column in the Glenesk Mountains as the Column sought to outrun British Military patrols in pursuit.
Ex-Sergeant RIC Foody, Anthony	56773	7/07/1921	Murdered at Carralavin, County Mayo by the IRA in revenge for alleged involvement in the killing of an IRA Officer, Dwyer at The Ragg, County Tipperary.

Source: Abbott, Richard, *Police Casualties in Ireland, 1919–22* (Mercier Press, Cork, 2001).

Appendix VII

Mayo TDs For and Against the Anglo-Irish Treaty
General Election Results to the Second Dáil, 24 May 1921

Mayo North & West			
Name	Party	Re-elected/ First Elected	Position on the Treaty
Dr. John Crowley [Dr Seán Ó Cruadhlaoich]	Sinn Féin	Re-elected unopposed	Voted against
Patrick J Ruttledge [Padraic S. Ó Ruthléis]	Sinn Féin	1st elected to Dáil	Voted against
Thomas Derrig [Tomás Ó Deirg]	Sinn Féin	1st elected to Dáil	Voted against
Joseph MacBride [Seosamh Mac Giolla Bhrighde]	Sinn Féin	Re-elected unopposed	Voted for

Mayo South – Roscommon South			
Name	Party	Re-elected/ 1st Elected	Position on the Treaty
Tom Maguire [Tomás Maghuidhir]	Sinn Féin	1st elected to Dáil	Voted against
William Sears [Liam Mac Sioghuird]	Sinn Féin	Re-elected unopposed	Voted for
Daniel O'Rourke [Domhnaill Ó Ruairc]	Sinn Féin	1st elected to Dáil	Voted for
Harry Boland [Enrí Ó Beoláin]	Sinn Féin	Re-elected unopposed	Voted against

Sligo – Mayo East			
Name	**Party**	**Re-elected/ First Elected**	**Position on the Treaty**
Frank Carty [Próinsias Mac Cárthaigh]	Sinn Féin	1st elected to Dáil	Voted against
Alexander McCabe [Alasdair Mac Cába]	Sinn Féin	Re-elected unopposed	Voted against
Seamus Devins [Séumas Ó Daimhín]	Sinn Féin	1st elected to Dáil	Voted against
Dr. Francis Ferran [Dr. P Ó Fearáin]	Sinn Féin	1st elected to Dáil	Voted against
Thomas O'Donnell [Tomás Ó Domhnaill]	Sinn Féin	1st elected to Dáil	Voted for

Source: Election results, Dáil Debates, 16 August 1021. Stance on Treaty, Dáil Debates, 7 January 1922. *www/historical-debates.oireachtas.ie*

Appendix VIII

The Mayo Brigades, July 1921. A list of Mayo's various Brigades and Companies on 11 July 1921, the date the Truce was declared.

1st Western Division
South Mayo Brigade
Brigade Staff

Officer Commanding Thomas Maguire
Adjutant James Reilly
Engineering Officer Peadar McHugh
Intelligence Officer Michael Sweeney

Vice O/C Dr Tom Powell
Quartermaster Patrick Fallon
Transport Officer Thomas Mellet

1st Battalion (Cross)
Officer Commanding Michael Lynch
Vice O/C Michael Moran
Adjutant Thomas Holleran
Quartermaster Michael Shaughnessy

2nd Battalion (Ballinrobe)
Officer Commanding Thomas Lally
Vice O/C Michael Lally
Adjutant John Joyce
Quartermaster Patrick Reilly
Intelligence Officer Martin Butler

3rd Battalion (Claremorris)
No Battalion Staff on 11 July 1921
[All had been arrested and interned in Ballykinlar Camp Co. Down or Galway Jail]
Company Captains of the Claremorris Battalion Area were:
Kilcolman Patrick Fleming
Murneen Patrick Hoster
Ballyglass John Mullins
Irishtown John Callina (Callinan)
Ballindine Michael Byrne
Carrowmore Hubert Monaghan
Crossboyne James Gilmore

4th Battalion (Balla)
Officer Commanding Patrick Keville
Vice O/C John Murphy
Adjutant David R. Rochford
Quartermaster Willie Murphy
Intelligence Officer Richard Langan
Engineering Officer John Corcoran

East Mayo Brigade
Brigade Staff

Officer Commanding Patrick Mullins
Adjutant Joseph Sheehy
Engineering Officer Eugene Kelly
Communications Officer John Higgins

Vice O/C Michael Moffit
Quartermaster Liam Forde
Intelligence Officer P. J. Henry

1st Battalion [Swinford]
Officer Commanding Patrick Finn
Vice O/C James Groarke
Adjutant James Groarke
Quartermaster Andrew Muldowney

2nd Battalion [Ballaghaderreen]
Officer Commanding Patrick
Cassidy
Vice O/C Michael McDermott
Adjutant Daniel Caufield
Quartermaster Richard
Gallagher

3rd Battalion [Bohola &Kiltimagh]
Officer Commanding Sean Walsh
Vice O/C Patrick J. Grennan
Adjutant Thomas Sheehy
Quartermaster Vincent Fraine

4th Battalion [Ballyhaunis]
Officer Commanding P[addy].
Kenny
Vice O/C Dominic Byrne
Adjutant Austin Kenny
Quartermaster Patrick McNieve

Third Western Division
West Mayo Brigade
Brigade Staff

Officer Commanding Michael Kilroy
Adjutant John Gibbons
Engineering Officer T. P. Flanagan

Vice O/C Edward Moane
Quartermaster Thomas
Kitterick
Intelligence Officer Luke
Sheridan

1st Battalion [Castlebar]
Officer Commanding James Chambers
Vice O/C Patrick Cannon
Adjutant Philip Hoban
Quartermaster Mark Killelea [Killilea]

2nd Battalion [Newport]
Officer Commanding Joe
Doherty
Vice O/C J. J. Connelly
Adjutant Michael Gallagher
Quartermaster Patrick Kelly

3rd Battalion [Westport]
Officer Commanding Joseph Ring
Vice O/C James Malone
Adjutant Joseph Baker
Quartermaster Peter Lavelle

4th Battalion [Louisburgh]
Officer Commanding Patrick
J. Kelly
Vice O/C Dan Sammin
[Sammon]
Adjutant Thomas Joyce
Quartermaster James Harney

North Mayo Brigade
Brigade Staff

Officer Commanding E[amon] Gannon
Vice O/C T[om] Loftus
Adjutant T. Coen
Intelligence Officer D. Molloy
Transport Officer M. O'Connor

Communications Officer J. Doherty
Scouting Officer C. Byron
Signals Officer P. McHale
Organisation Officer J. Byron

1st Battalion (Ballina)
Officer Commanding George Delaney
Adjutant Micheál Ó Cléirigh
Quartermaster Michael Mahon
[Intelligence Officer & Engineering Officer
Phelim Callery]

2nd Battalion (Foxford)
Officer Commanding James Boyle
Vice O/C William Doherty
Adjutant James Connelly
Quartermaster John Boland

3rd Battalion (Ballycastle)
Officer Commanding Sean Langan
Vice O/C C. Munnelly
Adjutant Martin Clifford
Quartermaster Patrick Scanlon

4th Battalion (Crossmolina)
Officer Commanding William Hopkins
Officer Commanding James Flynn
Vice O/C Michael Waters
Adjutant Edward Boyle
Quartermaster Patrick Temony (Timoney)

5th Battalion (Corballa)
Officer Commanding Matthew Kilcawley
Vice O/C Thomas Finnerty
Adjutant Shemus [Seamus] Kavanagh
Quartermaster M. E. Hannon

6th Battalion (Bangor)
Officer Commanding Michael Henry

Source: Grothier, Noelle & Kinsella, Anthony (eds), 'IRA Officers and Units, 11 July 1921: the Bureau of Military History', *The Irish Sword* (Winter 2010).

Appendix IX

The Anglo-Irish Treaty, 6 December 1921

(THIS DOCUMENT IS THE PROPERTY OF HIS
BRITANNIC MAJESTY'S GOVERNMENT).

CONFIDENTIAL.

C.P. 3529 GOVERNMENT OF IRELAND
OCTOBER 11th – DECEMBER 6th 1921.

BRITISH DELEGATION.
Mr. Lloyd George.
Mr. Chamberlain.
Mr. Churchill.
Sir L. Worthington-Evans.
Sir Hamar Greenwood.
Sir Gordon Hewart.

Secretaries.
Mr. Thomas Jones.
Mr. Lionel Curtis.

IRISH DELEGATION.
Mr. Arthur Griffith.
Mr. Michael Collins.
Mr. Robert Barton.
Mr. E.J. Duggan.
Mr. Gavan Duffy.

Secretaries.
Mr. Erskine Childers.
Mr. Fionan Lynch.
Mr. John Chartres.
Mr. Diarmuid O'Hegarty.

TREATY BETWEEN GREAT BRITAIN AND IRELAND.
ARTICLES OF AGREEMENT.

1. Ireland shall have the same constitutional status in the Community of Nations known as the British Empire as the Dominion of Canada, the Commonwealth of Australia, the Dominion of New Zealand, and the Union of South Africa with a Parliament having powers to make laws for the peace, order and good government of Ireland and an Executive responsible to that Parliament, and shall be styled and known as the Irish Free State.

2. Subject to the provisions hereinafter set out the position of the Irish Free State in relation to the Imperial Parliament and Government and otherwise shall be that of the Dominion of Canada, and the law, practice and constitutional usage governing the relationship of the Crown or the representative of the Crown and of the Imperial Parliament to the Dominion of Canada shall govern their relationship to the Irish Free State.

3. The representative of the Crown in Ireland shall be appointed in like manner as the Governor-General of Canada and in accordance with the practice observed in the making of such appointments.

4. The oath to be taken by Members of the Parliament of the Irish Free State shall be in the following form:
I .... do solemnly swear true faith and allegiance to the Constitution of the Irish Free State as by law established and that I will be faithful to H.M. King George V., his heirs and successors by law, in virtue of the common citizenship of Ireland and Great Britain and her adherence to and membership of the group of nations forming the British Commonwealth of Nations.

5. The Irish Free State shall assume liability for the service of the Public Debt of the United Kingdom as existing at the date hereof and towards the payment of war pensions as existing at that date in such proportion as may be fair and equitable, having regard to any just claims on the part of Ireland by way of set off or counter-claim,

the amount of such sums being determined in default of agreement by the arbitration of one or more independent persons being citizens of the British Empire.

6. Until an arrangement has been made between the British and Irish Governments whereby the Irish Free State undertakes her own coastal defence, the defence by sea of Great Britain and Ireland shall be undertaken by His Majesty's Imperial Forces, but this shall not prevent the construction or maintenance by the Government of the Irish Free State of such vessels as are necessary for the protection of the Revenue or the Fisheries.

The foregoing provisions of this article shall be reviewed at a conference of Representatives of the British and Irish Governments to be held at the expiration of five years from the date hereof with a view to undertaking by Ireland of a share in her own coastal defence.

7. The Government of the Irish Free State shall afford to His Majesty's Imperial Forces:

(a) In time of peace such harbour and other facilities as are indicated in the Annex hereto, or such other facilities as may from time to time be agreed between the British Government and the Government of the Irish Free State; and

(b) In time of war or of strained relations with a Foreign Power such harbour and other facilities as the British Government may require for the purposes of such defence as aforesaid.

8. With a view to securing the observance of the principle of international limitation of armaments, if the Government of the Irish Free State establishes and maintains a military defence force, the establishments thereof shall not exceed in size such proportion of the military establishments maintained in Great Britain as that which the population of Ireland bears to the population of Great Britain.

9. The ports of Great Britain and the Irish Free State shall be freely open to the ships of the other country on payment of the customary port and other dues.

10. The Government of the Irish Free State agrees to pay fair compensation on terms not less favourable than those accorded by the Act of 1920 to judges, officials, members of Police Forces and other Public Servants who are discharged by it or who retire in consequence of the change of government effected in pursuance hereof.

Provided that this agreement shall not apply to members of the Auxiliary Police Force or to other persons recruited in Great Britain for the Royal Irish Constabulary during the two years next preceding the date hereof. The British Government will assume responsibility for such compensation or pensions as may be payable to any of these excepted persons.

11. Until the expiration of one month from the passing of the Act of Parliament for the ratification of this instrument, the powers of the Parliament and the Government of the Irish Free State shall not be exercisable as respects Northern Ireland, and the provisions of the Government of Ireland Act 1920, shall, so far as they relate to Northern Ireland remain of full force and effect, and no election shall be held for the return of members to serve in the Parliament of the Irish Free State for constituencies in Northern Ireland, unless a resolution is passed by both Houses of the Parliament of Northern Ireland in Favour of the holding of such elections before the end of the said month.

12. If before the expiration of the said month, an address is presented to His Majesty by both Houses of the Parliament of Northern Ireland to that effect, the powers of the Parliament and the Government of the Irish Free State shall no longer extend to Northern Ireland, and the provisions of the Government of Ireland Act, 1920 (including those relating to the Council of Ireland) shall so far as they relate to Northern Ireland, continue to be of full force and effect, and this instrument shall have effect subject to the necessary modifications. Provided that if such an address is so presented a Commission consisting of three persons, one to be appointed by the Government of the Irish Free State, one to be appointed by the Government of Northern Ireland, and one who shall be Chairman to be appointed by the British Government shall determine in accordance with the

wishes of the inhabitants, so far as may be compatible with economic and geographic conditions the boundaries between Northern Ireland and the rest of Ireland, and for the purposes of the Government of Ireland Act, 1920, and of this instrument, the boundary of Northern Ireland shall be such as may be determined by such Commission.

13. For the purpose of the last foregoing article, the powers of the Parliament of Southern Ireland under the Government of Ireland Act, 1920, to elect members of the Council of Ireland shall after the Parliament of the Irish Free State is constituted be exercised by that Parliament.

14. After the expiration of the said month, if no such address is mentioned in Article 12 hereof is presented, the Parliament and Government of Northern Ireland shall continue to exercise as respects Northern Ireland the powers conferred on them by the Government of Ireland Act, 1920, but the Parliament and Government of the Irish Free State shall in Northern Ireland have in relation to matters in respect of which the Parliament of Northern Ireland has not power to make laws under that Act (including matters which under the said Act are within the jurisdiction of the Council of Ireland) the same powers as in the rest of Ireland, subject to such other provisions as may be agreed in manner hereinafter appearing.

15. At any time after the date hereof the Government of Northern Ireland and the provisional Government of Southern Ireland hereinafter constituted may meet for the purpose of discussing the provisions subject to which the last foregoing Article is to operate in the event of no such address as is therein mentioned being presented and those provisions may include:
(a) Safeguards with regard to patronage in Northern Ireland.
(b) Safeguards with regard to the collection of revenue in Northern Ireland.
(c) Safeguards with regard to import and export duties affecting the trade or industry of Northern Ireland.
(d) Safeguards for minorities in Northern Ireland.

(e) The settlement of the financial relations between Northern Ireland and the Irish Free State.

(f) The establishment and powers of a local militia in Northern Ireland and the relation of the Defence Forces of the Irish Free State and of Northern Ireland respectively,

And if at any such meeting provisions are agreed to, the same shall have effect as if they were included amongst the provisions subject to which the powers of the Parliament and Government of the Irish Free State are to be exercisable in Northern Ireland under Article 14 hereof.

16. Neither the Parliament of the Irish Free State nor the Parliament of Northern Ireland shall make any law so as either directly or indirectly to endow any religion or prohibit or restrict the free exercise thereof or give any preference or impose any disability on account of religious belief or religious status or effect prejudicially the right of any child to attend a school receiving public money without attending the religious instruction at the school or make any discrimination as respects State aid between schools under the management of different religious denominations or divert from any religious denomination or any educational institution any of its property except for public utility purposes and on payment of compensation.

17. By way of provisional arrangement for the administration of Southern Ireland during the interval which must elapse between the date hereof and the constitution of a Parliament and Government of the Irish Free State in accordance therewith, steps shall be taken forthwith for summoning a meeting of members of Parliament elected for constituencies in Southern Ireland since the passing of the Government of Ireland Act, 1920, and for constituting a provisional Government, and the British Government shall take the steps necessary to transfer to such provisional Government the powers and machinery requisite for the discharge of its duties, provided that every member of such provisional Government shall have signified in writing his or her acceptance of this instrument. But this arrangement shall not continue in force beyond the expiration of twelve months from the date hereof.

18. This instrument shall be submitted forthwith by His Majesty's Government for the approval of Parliament and by the Irish signatories to a meeting summoned for the purpose of the members elected to sit in the House of Commons of Southern Ireland and if approved shall be ratified by the necessary legislation.

(Signed)

On behalf of the British Delegation.
D. Lloyd George.
Austen Chamberlain.
Birkenhead.
Winston S. Churchill.
L. Worthington-Evans.
Hamar Greenwood.
Gordon Hewart.

On behalf of the Irish Delegation
Art ó Griobhtha.
Michaél ó Coileain.
Riobárd Bartún.
E.S. ó Dugain.
Seórsa Ghabháin Úi Dhubhthaigh

6th December, 1921.

ANNEX.

1. The following are the specific facilities required.

DOCKYARD PORT AT BEREHAVEN
(a) Admiralty property and right to be retained as at the date hereof. Habour defences to remain in charge of British care and maintenance parties.

QUEENSTOWN
(b) Habour defences to remain in charge of British care and maintenance parties. Certain mooring buoys to be retained for the use of his Majesty's ships.

BELFAST LOUGH
(c) Harbour defences to remain in charge of British care and maintenance parties.

LOUGH SWILLY
(d) Harbour defences to remain in charge of British care and maintenance parties.

AVIATION
(e) Facilities in the neighbourhood of the above ports for coastal defence by air.

OIL FUEL STORAGE
(f) Haulbowline to be offered for sale to commercial companies under guarantee that purchasers shall maintain a certain minimum stock for Admiralty purposes.

2. A Convention shall be made between the British Government and the Government of the Irish Free State to give effect to the following conditions:
(a) That submarine cables shall not be landed or wireless stations for communication with places outside Ireland be established except by agreement with the British Government; that the existing cable landing rights and wireless concessions shall not be withdrawn except by agreement with the Irish Government; and that the British Government shall be entitled to land additional submarine cables or establish additional wireless stations for communication with places outside Ireland.
(b) That lighthouses, buoys, beacons and any navigational marks or navigational aids shall be maintained by the Government of the Irish Free State as at the date hereof and shall not be removed or added to except by agreement with the British Government.
(c) That war signal stations shall be closed down and left in the charge of care and maintenance parties, the Government of the Irish Free State being offered the option of taking them over and working them for commercial purposes subject to Admiralty inspection and guaranteeing the upkeep of existing telegraphic communication therewith.

3. A Convention shall be made between the same Governments for the regulation of Civil Communication by Air.

Source: Cabinet Papers, CAB/24/131. PRO.

Appendix X

Mayo Casualties in the RIC throughout Ireland 1919–22

Name	RIC Number	Date	Cause of Death
Constable McDonnell, James.	50616	21/01/1919	IRA ambush at Soloheadbeg, County Tipperary.
Constable Carroll, John J	62341	12/06/1920	Shot dead by the IRA in the Railway Hotel, Limerick.
Detective Sergeant Mulherin, William.	61051	26/07/1920	Shot dead by the IRA in a Chapel Porch in Bandon, County Cork.
Constable Munnelly, James.	66662	26/08/1920	Shot dead by the IRA Drumquin RIC Barracks, County Tyrone.
Constable Murphy, Edward.	69231	1/09/1920	IRA ambush on Ballaghaderreen to Frenchpark Road, at Rathmacross, County Roscommon.
Constable Gaughan, John.	64181	8/09/1920	IRA ambush near Tullow, County Carlow.
Constable McGuire, John.	69743	22/09/1920	One of six RIC policemen killed in an IRA ambush at Rineena, County Clare.

Constable Morgan, George.	70802	31/10/1920	IRA ambush at Ballyduff, County Kerry.
Sergeant Mulloy, Michael. Constable Moran, Michael.	61673 69674	20/01/1921	IRA ambush, Glenwood, County Clare.
Sergeant Bloxham, Henry J	58519	21/01/1921	Shot dead by the IRA on a two-man patrol, Waterfall, County Cork.
Constable Heffron, Thomas.	69264	26/01/1921	Shot dead by the IRA in a pub in Belfast.
Constable Moyles, Thomas.	71364	28/01/1921	Killed in an IRA ambush on an RIC patrol in Toureengarriv, County Kerry.
Constable O'Connor, Patrick James.	69676	1/02/1921	A decorated ex-British soldier who served in the First World War, O'Connor was killed in an IRA ambush at Drimoleague village near Skibbereen, County Cork.
Constable Lynch, John P.	61290	13/02/1921	IRA ambush at Ballough, County Dublin.
Sergeant Coughlan, John.	55450	22/03/1921	IRA ambush at Drummin, County Mayo.
Sergeant Higgins, John.	55504	1/04/1921	Shot dead by the IRA in Derry.
Constable Kelly, Thomas.	64253	19/04/1921	Shot dead by the IRA, RIC Barracks, Ballisodare, County Sligo.

Constable Hopkins, Thomas.	70690	7/05/1921	Shot dead by the IRA near Leface, Ballindine, County Mayo.
Constable Burke, Michael.	66998	5/06/1921	Shot dead by the IRA at Swatragh, County Derry.
Constable Clarke, Patrick.	61068	27/06/1921	Shot dead by the IRA at Cleerykeel Cross, Cliffoney, County Sligo.
Ex-Sergeant Foody, Anthony	56773	7/07/1921	Shot dead by the IRA and placard placed around his neck reading 'Revenge for Dwyer and The Ragg', at Carralavin, County Mayo.
Ex Sergeant [Disbanded] Gibbons, Tobbias.	60748	15/03/1922	Shot dead by the IRA in his hospital bed St Bride's Hospital along with another Sergeant and a civilian after the Anglo-Irish Treaty had been signed.
Sergeant Frizelle, Frederick	59994	3/05/1922	Shot dead by the IRA Ballyronan, County Derry.

Source: Abbott, Richard, *Police Casualties in Ireland*, 1919–22 (Mercier Press, Cork, 2001)

Appendix XI

Jerry Kirby, ex-RIC Sergeant Claremorris 1919–22, to Captain
William O'Keefe, Staff Officer South Mayo Brigade, Manchester
ASU and subsequently National Army, requesting a reference stating
non-involvement in Black and Tan activities during the War of
Independence.

> Lower William St
> Listowel
> Co Kerry
> January 23 1923

> Dear Willie,
> I heard you left A[bbey]feale & went to Tipperary town. I
> wrote to you to Tipperary & directed in back of letter that if
> you were not there to have the letter I sent you returned to me
> – I received back the letter again.
>   Captn English Afeale informs me he believes you are now in
> the New Barracks Limk and told me if I wanted to write you
> to direct your Letter C/O Lieut Fleming Command Transport
> so I am adopting this Course. What I want you to do is this &
> and I will forever deem it a great favour coming from you as a
> great friend viz:
>   Will you kindly by return Post send me a reference of
> Character for the 7 or 8 years you knew me in Claremorris –
> You can go on to state (1) 'I knew Sgt Jerry Kirby for 7 or 8
> years in Claremorris & was there when he resigned from the
> RIC.' (2) You know Willie I never did anything against the
> cause of Irish Freedom & You know I resigned solely from
> National Sympathy with the cause (please state the fact). You
> are aware I incurred the anger of the RIC there and not one
> of them said Good Bye to me (neither did I try for their Good

Bye). Will you kindly state this fact that you were aware I was up against the RIC & their methods & they were up against me.

(4) Will you kindly state that on my departure from Claremorris you were confined in the RIC Bks there as a Political Prisoner & and that I called in to see you. I was never in a Raid, an arrest, or a Lorry during the whole Political campaign & no man can say to me I ever stood in their way (state this). (5) I have it on reliable authority it was planned by one member of the RIC & two Black & Tans to shoot me for my persistent friendship with certain members of the IRA there (I don't know if you heard of this) but twas the case and only for I making my escape as quick as I did no doubt I would get winged possibly the crime would rest on some member of the IRA there. Well I never feared any of the IRA but I feared certain members of the RIC. (Kindly state those facts above.)

(6) I don't know were you home from London when the British military raided my House in Mt Street at 2 or 3 a.m. in the morning searched Presses & Rooms possibly for Literature or for Boys at the time who were on the run. Your family & every one there is quite aware of this fact. The same night they searched Pakie Keanes & I believe your house also at the same Hour. Please state above facts.

(7) You Know Willie I was never seen doing a turn of Duty as a Policeman with the Black & Tans & before I would do duty with them I resigned & left the old job at 19 years Service & that I left Claremorris with good wishes of every member of the Community there (which is true) and also every member of the IRA there. (Be sure & state these facts.)

(8) You were a leading member of the IRA there. Please state this fact in your letter of Character & that you never knew me to do anything whatever against the National Cause & that you are aware I resigned from National Sympathy. If you held any Commissioned Rank in the old IRA please state your Rank.

I would wish to have such a letter of Reference from you who was Resident in Claremorris & where I served as a Policeman Stating I never did anything against the National Cause & that I resigned in sympathy with that cause.

I am going to Limerick early next month & I hope to have the Pleasure of seeing you & having a long chat with you.

Connaughton is doing well. I met your Successor in Abbeyfeale (Mason) he told me you were gone to Tipperary. Connaughton told me you were home for Xmas. I hope all your family are well. Your mother was the last I said Good Bye to in Bohergorra & the poor woman imparted to me her Prayers & Blessings.

May I hope you will send me this reference by return & I shall be ever grateful & keep it as a momento. Hoping you are real well & may God Protect you now & ever.

I remain Dear Willie your sincere friend

Jerry Kirby

PS
If you can put the Army crest on the Paper you write this reference of me I should be grateful or write it on Military Paper having a Military Heading.
Sign your Name Rank etc (Officer Commanding Transport etc) now I am well known to you & I confidently leave myself in your generous hands & from all I know of you I am certain you will give me a generous reference.

Source: Celio Burke

Appendix XII

Official Proclamation issued by National Army General Headquarters, 10 October 1922. This Proclaimation announced the establishment of Military Courts and the range of punishments, which included the death penalty, for those opposing the Irish Free State. In a strange portent of what was to unfold, the *Western People* carried a number of advertisements for coffins on the same page that the Proclamation was printed. Seventy-seven Republicans were subsequently executed by the National Army between 17 November 1922 and 2 May 1923.

OGLAIGH NA h-EIREANN
PROCLAMATION
General Headquarters,
Portobello Barracks,
Dublin

To All Whom It May Concern

With a view to the speedy termination of the present state of armed rebellion and insurrection and the restoration of peace, order, and security, the Government, with the assertion of Dáil Éireann, has sanctioned the doing by, or under the authority of, the Army Council of all of the following matters or things:

1. (a) The setting up of Military Courts or committees for the inquiring into charges against persons in respect of any of the offences hereinafter mentioned, provided however, that every such Military Court or Committee shall include as a member thereof at least one person nominated by the Minister of Defence and certified by the Law Officer to be a person of legal knowledge or experience.

(b) The inquiry by such Military Courts or Committees into the cases of persons charged with any of the offences following, that is to say:

(1) Taking part in, or aiding, or abetting any attacks upon or using force against the National forces.

(2) Looting, arson, destruction, seizure, unlawful possession, or removal of, or damage to any public or private property.

(3) Having possession without proper authority of any bomb, or article in the nature of a bomb, or any dynamite, gelignite or other explosive substance, or any revolver, rifle, gun or other firearm or lethal weapon, or any ammunition for such firearm.

(4) The breach of any general order or regulation made by the Army Council, and the infliction by such Military Courts or Committees of the punishment of death or of penal servitude for any period or of imprisonment for any period or of a fine of any amount either with or without imprisonment on any person found guilty by such Court or Committee of any of the offences aforesaid, provided that no such sentence of death be executed except under the counter signature of two members of the Army Council.

(c) The removal under authority of the Army Council of any person taken prisoner, arrested, or detained by the National Forces to any place or places whether within or without the area of jurisdiction of the Government, and the detention or imprisonment of any such persons in any place or places within or without the area aforesaid.

(d) The regulation and control of the sale, possession, transfer of, and dealing in, revolvers, rifles, guns and other firearms.

2. By regulations made the 2nd day of October, 1922, the Army Council have provided for the trial by Military Courts of civilians charged with the offences specified in the preceeding paragraph and for the infliction upon any civilian convicted by a Military Court of any such offence, of any of the following punishments according to the nature and gravity of the offence:

DEATH
PENAL SERVITUDE
IMPRISONMENT
DEPORTATION
INTERNMENT
FINE

3. It is provided by the said regulations that they shall come into force upon, and shall apply as from such date as the Army Council shall determine and announce by proclamation.

4. By proclamation published the 3rd day of October, 1922, the Government announced and proclaimed as follows:

(1) Every person who is engaged in such insurrection and rebellion against the State as aforesaid, or in such armed opposition to the National Forces as aforesaid, or who has been guilty of any offence against the State, directly arising out of such aforesaid and who on or before the 15th day of October, 1922, voluntarily delivers into the possession of the National Forces all firearms, arms, weapons, bombs, ammunition and explosives, and all public and private property, now unlawfully in his possession, and quits all lands or buildings unlawfully occupied by him, and who, on or before the 15th day of October, 1922, voluntarily ceases to take part in, or aid or abet such insurrection, rebellion or armed opposition, shall be permitted to return unmolested to his house; and to every such person we hereby offer, assure and proclaim a full amnesty and pardon for all such insurrection, riot, rebellion, and opposition and offence as aforesaid.

(2) Every such person may deliver any such firearms, arms, weapons, ammunition, explosives and bombs, and any such public and private property as aforesaid, to the Officer Commanding the nearest Military position or Station, or to any such person as shall be nominated by him.

KNOW THEN, AND IT IS HEREBY ANNOUNCED AND PROCLAIMED AS FOLLOWS:

(1) After the 15th day of October, 1922, we, the Army Council, will exercise all the powers and do all the things in the first paragraph of this proclamation mentioned, or any of them, according as the same shall to us seen necessary or expedient.

(2) The said regulations as to the Trial of civilians by Military Courts made by us, the Army Council, on the 2nd day of October, 1922, shall come into force and shall apply as from the 15th day of October, 1922.

Given at General Headquarters, Portobello Barracks, Dublin, and published this 10th day of October, 1922.
Signed on behalf of the Army Council,
RISTEARD UA MAOLCATHA, General,
Commander in Chief

Source: *Western People*, 21 October 1922.

Appendix XIII

Some National Army Officers and Troops of Claremorris Command

Ballina, County Mayo. 26th Infantry Battalion, Union Barracks.	
Brigadier	Neary
Commandant	Bannon
Colonel	Bannon
Commandant	Coyle
Captain	Hanley, T.
Captain	Murtagh
Lieutenant	Merrick
Sergeant Major	Scully
Sergeant	Boyle [shot and killed Captain Nicholas Corcoran, a prisoner, at a barricade outside Ballina on 7th April, 1923.]

Ballinrobe, County Mayo. C Company, 52nd Infantry Battalion.	
Commandant	Deasey [O/C C Company, 52nd Inf Batt]
Volunteer [Private]	McCaffrey
Volunteer	Mulvehill [seriously wounded by accidental discharge of a comrade's firearm 29 April 1923]

Ballyglunin	
Commandant	Broderick
Lieutenant	Byrne
Lieutenant	Byrnes
Lieutenant	McGrath

Ballyhaunis	
Captain	Lynch, P. [O/C Ballyhaunis]

Castlebar Army Barracks	
Commandant	Galvin
Captain	O'Malley
Lieutenant	Corley, J.
Volunteer	Ansbro
Volunteer	Coyle [killed in action on 17 March 1923]
Volunteer	Dunne, Thomas.
Volunteer	Gilmartin
Volunteer	Glynn
Volunteer	McAuley

Claremorris, County Mayo. 52nd Infantry Battalion, Workhouse Barracks and Hospital. Claremorris Command HQ Staff billeted at Castlemacgarret.	
Major General	Hogan, Michael. O/C Claremorris Command
Brigadier	Brannick [appointed 5 March 1923 O/C 52nd Inf Batt]
Chaplain-General	Prendegast, Geoffrey J. [Claremorris Command]
Colonel	Brennan [Vice O/C Claremorris]
Colonel	Carroll
Colonel	Hannon, A [O/C Inspection]
Colonel	Kenna
Colonel	Morley, Seán.
Commandant	Callaghan, T. [O/C RY Corps –Railway Corps – patrolled railways to prevent Republican Forces blowing up the rails and derailing trains]
Commandant	Compton
Commandant	O'Connor, M.A. [O/C Works]
Commandant	Roche [O/C Camp]
Captain	Feeney
Captain	Flood [O/C A Company, 52nd Inf Batt]
Captain	Lennon
Captain	O'Brien
Captain	Stuart, C.M. [Command Medical Officer]

Captain	Dunleavy [Communications Officer – signs name as Padraig Dúnleibhe]
Captain	Ruane, James [Vice O/C 52nd Inf Batt]
Captain	Ryan, M. [Staff Officer]
Lieutenant	Clifford
Lieutenant	Duffy
Lieutenant	McGrath
Lieutenant	Murphy, J.
Lieutenant	Scannell, Stephen.
Lieutenant	Clifford
Sergeant Major	Beare [Wireless & Communications]
Sergeant Major	Henehan [PA – Políní Airm – Military Police]
Sergeant Major	Tierney, T.
Sergeant Major	Websey
Sergeant	Fitzgibbons
Sergeant	McGowan [Machine gun Corp]
Sergeant	Waldron
Volunteer	Healy, Joseph. [G.O.C's – General Officer Commanding – Orderly]
Volunteer	McTigue, J.
Volunteer	Sheedy [Cook]
Doctor [Rank Unknown]	Hannigan, Charles [MO Claremorris]
Assistant Paymaster	McNicholas, Peter. [Claremorris, native of Swinford]

Crossmolina, County Mayo. 26th Infantry Battalion	
Brigadier	Neary [Ballina also O/C Crossmolina]
Captain	Judge

Kiltimagh, County Mayo.	
Vice-Brigadier	Ruane, Thomas. [Recruiting Officer National Army. Mortally wounded while being arrested by Republican Forces 29 June 1922]
Captain	Ruane, Seán
Captain	McDonnell [O/C Kiltimagh]

Newport, County Mayo. 44th Infantry Battalion	
Captain	Lennon, Seán O/C Newport

Swinford, County Mayo. 61st Infantry Battalion	
Commandant	Egan
Commandant	McCann
Commandant	McTighe
Commandant	Walshe
Captain	Benson, Jack.
Captain	McHale
Quartermaster	Conlon
Volunteer	Browne
Volunteer	Clarke

Westport, County Mayo. 44th Infantry Battalion	
Brigadier	Mulloley
Colonel-Commandant	Finnegan
Colonel-Commandant	Madden
Commandant	Corcoran
Commandant	Duffy [O/C Westport – date unknown]
Commandant	Kilcoyne
Captain	Togher [O/C Westport Feb/March 1923]
Captain	Farrell [O/C Westport April 1923]
Captain	Kilroy
Captain	Lynch
Captain	Moran
Captain	Mulroy
Lieutenant	Brady
Lieutenant	Burke
Lieutenant	Hogan
Lieutenant	Loughran

Lieutenant	McQuaid [Assistant Medical Officer Westport. Mortally wounded 23 February 1923. Was the brother of the future Archbishop of Dublin John Charles. Radio Message received by Claremorris Command at 10 am. Captain Dunleavy's view was that McQuaid was shot deliberately as he had Red Cross Armbands prominently displayed. Captain Dunleavy further recommended this incident be publicised. The Republican Forces denied McQuaid was deliberately killed arguing his Red Cross markings were of the old Irish Volunteer type (small patches on the uniform) and thus impossible to see in an ambush.
Lieutenant	Munster
Lieutenant	Murphy
Lieutenant	Reid
Sergeant Major	Glynn [Recruiting Officer]
Sergeant	Brady
Corporal	Roche
Volunteer	Brady
Volunteer [Private]	Browne [KIA date unknown]
Volunteer	Collins, Michael [killed in action Shraghmore, 23 February 1923]
Volunteer	McEllin
Pte [Private]	Madden, Michael [Army Number: 14765]
Pte	Naughton, Joseph
Doctor [Rank Unknown]	Cronin [MO – Medical Officer Westport]

Aclare, County Sligo. 61st Infantry Reserve Battalion	
Commandant	Haughey, J. O/C 61ST Infantry Reserve Battalion
Captain	Flynn
Captain	McGinn

Athenry, County Galway. 34th Battalion	
Captain	Curran
Sergeant	Hargrove

Headford, County Galway. 34th Battalion	
Captain	Nugent

Moycullen, County Galway. 34th Battalion	
Lieutenant	Lenihan

Tuam, County Galway. 34th Battalion Workhouse Barracks	
Brigadier	Callinan [Previously Commandant. Promoted February 1923]
Vice-Brigadier	Broderick
Commandant	Dunleavy
Captain	Dunleavy, Pádraig [seconded periodically to Tuam from Claremorris]
Captain	Coakley
Captain	Nugent
Lieutenant	McGrath [Woodlawn Post, February 1923.]
Sergeant Major	O'Brien [Woodlawn Post]
Corporal	Looney [Woodlawn Post]

Source: Claremorris Command Operational Reports, 23 January to 17 April 1923; *An t-Óglach*, 2 June 1923. Military Archives.

Appendix XIV

Alexander Boyd to P. J. Ruttledge, Fianna Fáil Government Minister and former Officer North Mayo Brigade, regarding military pension and War of Independence Medal.

No 3. A. Philipsburg Terrace
Fairview
Dublin
25/2/42

Dear Sir,

I take the liberty of writing to you in connection with a notification I received from the Military Service Pension Board Referee, to state that Im not a person to whom the Act of 1934 applies. Enclosed you shall find that notice.

When I received it on the 20th inst, I was more than surprised that my application for pension should not bear evidences to intitle me to a pension under the act. I'm very much annoyed in mind & body over it. As I gave of my best to the Cause & my Ideals were above reproach by any one. From 1914 I have done my very best for Ireland's Cause & I had not to be asked to do it.

I did write to you before in 1939 when I was called before the Board. When before the Board I gave a satisfactory account of my services from 1916 to 1923. Mr Thomas Ruane & Mr Matt Kilcawley were up then with a crowd from Ballina & Ballysokeery areas. I was sure that the Officers in Charge would have done their best for me in their verification then, but since that time I didn't hear from the Pension Board or any of the IRA Officers in Authority.

I wrote to the Military Service Pension Board about three weeks ago and the answer I got from the Referee is the notification I have enclosed to you.

In 1913 when a young man with great ambition I left home and found myself searching for a job in England, in Liverpool I was advised by a Hotel proprietor to stand for examination for the Liverpool City Police Force, which I did, and I passed the examination and was taken into that Force which was a Corporation Force at the time.

I served in that Force for 2 yrs & 10 months and was promoted to plain Clothes Officers 6 months before I left and was also All-Round-Champion Athlete of that Force.

In the end of 1915 & beginning of 1916 I was paraded in uniform in Hatton

Garden Police Depot with 30 young Irish men out of the Force & two English men to join the English Army to fight for England. When the 32 men were about to march to a Recruiting Office to be attested for the Army.

I stepped out of the Ranks & Protested that Irishmen should not fight for England, while English men were left to take up good jobs at home. I was placed under open arrest by a Chief Superintendent of A Division the name of McGuiness, a Roscommon man, of course I didn't mind that, as Some Irishmen are liable to do anything to their fellow Irishman.

The rest were marched through the Streets to a Recruiting Office by Inspector Armstrong, an Orange man from Belfast, who had no love for an Irishman who was not his own creed. When the Recruiting Office was reached, all the Irishman objected to join as they were take by surprise by their authorities for to join the Army. So all came back again to the Parade room were I was & a Dectective from A Division the name of Griffith & a Constable the name of Jordan from Cork we were the three Spokesmen for the rest of Ring Leaders as named at our Trial for Mutiny & Riot within the Police Ranks.

When thay could not imprison us for refusing to join as we had a perfect right to protest.

While in the Police I was a member of the Irish Volunteers in Bootle England.

I came back to Ireland in 1916 and after coming back to my home in Ballysokeery Ballina I joined the Sinn Féin movement in Ballina and organised the people of the Ballysokeery. John Moylett my Brother-In-Law was also organiser. I had organised a body of Volunteers on my own in the Ballysokeery area and in March or April 1917.

The OC of No 1 Battalion in Ballina send [*sic*] down Officers of the Battalion to Elect Officers of the Company of Volunteers already organised by me.

I was elected Capt by a big vote of F Company Irish Volunteers No 1 Battalion Ballysokeery Ballina Area Co Mayo.

I drilled and trained over 100 men in that Company for over two years – during that time in Volunteers I attended meetings parades etc while on the run from RIC & Military as my house was raided by RIC on several occasions looking for me for illegal drilling & searched the house for Documents etc. When the Volunteers were reorganised and became the IRA Company in 1919 I was put on Intelligence Work for the Army in the Company and done duty in Ballysokeery & Killala Areas.

Patrick Boyd my brother was made Capt of F Company IRA then and continued on Active Service until 1923.

During the Black & Tan time in Ireland, I drilled men in the IRA as I did not want to let know to any of my Company Officers or men what I was. I continued on Active Service with the Company, I raided several houses for Firearms & Ammunition and had several engagements while doing so. I was fired at by Black

& Tans on two occasions in June 1921.

At Crosspatrick near Killala, I returned the Fire & made my escape and again at Burton St on the Killala road when the one-eyed Capt of Tans fired point-blank at me & missed as he was drunk. I made my escape & returned the fire – they were firing out of Saunders Wood at me.

I could not get home at all during that time only lying out in Stables & Barns & enduring Cold & Hunger while on the run evading Arrest & Capture.

My mothers House in Ballysokeery which was my home was raided week after week by Tans looking for me & also my brother.

And our house was going to be burned & my mother & Sisters dragged out of on the Street by the Tan soldiers wanting them to tell were we were.

My mother, God rest her soul in Peace, asked one of the Captains not to burn the house that she did not see us for years. They had Petrol & Straw to burn it. The Captain Stopped the men and took pity on my mother. They took my pictures away out of the house & also a field Glasses, and said they would get me soon and that I would be shot by them. They knew all my history from the Liverpool City Police & Military.

Even though hard pressed by Tans I continued to remain active, I watched the orange mens house in the Districts for spying & ctn to the Tans, and anything that came under my notice in the ASU or out of it. I made Private reports of same.

Some young Protestant Orangemen in 1920 were drilling in a field off the Railway Line near Killala one night and I came close up to them as I thought it was some of our own men. When I recognised who they were I fired on them & they scattered & made for Crosspatrick. One of them who carried a shotgun fired two shots at me & ran. So I put a stop to their Drilling.

I had to roam about at night and in a disguise as I was closely watched by the orange crowd too.

When the Truce came I was asked by HQ of IRA to take up Police work, I did take up that work in Company & attended the Republican Courts as OC. Made several arrests for Crime and Land Agitation.

I was brought to Ballina in the early part of 1922 to take up the position of District Officer of IRA Police. I done my best as a Police Officer to Combat Crime in phases including the troublesome Land Agitation which was rife in and around Ballina at the time. I was Brigade OC of Police before I left Ballina for the Ox Mountains with the North Mayo Flying Column of IRA.

I served with the North Mayo Flying Column and took part in nearly all the engagements in the Civil War while serving with and was in Command of men in them engagements, encluding the taking of the Free State Garrison at Ballina in September 1922.

I was put in charge of the big Lorry load of Rifles and Ammunition that we captured in the Workhouse. I took them out to Bonniconlon to the mountains.

The Lorry was Mr Davis's and the Driver was Davis's man Redmond. When at Caltra Bridge, the Bridge was broken down he refused me to drive the Lorry across – I then told him that there was only one thing for it, that he would loose his life if he would not jump the trench on the Road. I made him back the Lorry and go full speed ahead + he drove so, + we got safe to Bonniconlon and I dumped the Rifles + Ammunition in Kerrighans Barn and the next morning before the Battle when Ring was shot we divided the Rifles + Ammunition to the Column.

In March 1923 I took suddenly ill with acute Rheumatic Fever in R Culleens County Sligo while Serving with the IRA in the Column.

I was attended by Dr Connelly of Dromore West, since dead. I was very bad for about six weeks and one morning while sick in bed the Free state soldiers were raiding the village, I made my escape out of bed with the help of Mr Edward Brennan the ambulance man who was attending to me and hid in a drain until the raid was over. I remained in the drain for hours until we got word that they had gone, of course I could have waited and given myself up like more of the men in Ireland that are getting pensions for been in gaol only.

After the cease Fire order I came home but still the raids didn't stop as DO Shea of Ballina kept my movements under way all the time and our house was raided nearly every week during the Civil War and after the Civil War. Then I'm not a man that the act of 1934 applies.

In 1924 I went to Canada and would not submit to ask a Passport from the Free State to go to America.

When in Canada Eddie Brennan & I crossed the Canadian Border at Buffalo New York on a stolen ride on a Freight Train going in to the States. We succeeded to get to New York in May 1924. When in New York I was never strong owing to the severe illness I had on the mountains & I suffered with Rheumatic & stomach trouble.

I was only 1 year and 10 months in New York when I was spied on by some Free State sympathiser who heard Brennan & I crossed the Border illegally from Canada to the States.

The Federal agents came after us in New York with a warrant for our arrests. We were out of our Lodgings when they made the first raid – so we had to pack up and return to Canada again & then come home to Ireland in 1926.

When I came home again thinking I would get a rest, there was constant raids on my mother's home at Ballysokeery Ballina. DO O'Shea raided the house the 2nd day after I coming home and searched my bags for arms and ammunition, and said I had guns from America with me and in a few days after they came from Oriel House two car loads of Dectectives & Guards & made a big search including the House Stables and every bit of the Land.

My mother who was in bad health over all the Raids since the Brother & I went in the movements was beginning to feel it very much.

I decided to go back to America and get out the right way to New York – I went in 1926 again to avoid all the raids on our home.

My health never was good from all the hardship endured and I came to Ireland again for the good of my health in 1932. I suffered from Rheumatics & stomach trouble, when I came home my health improved when I got a rest.

When I was asked to join the Special Branch of the Police then forming I consented although my health was not the best.

I am suffering with duodenal ulcers of the stomach for years & I had and ulcerated stomach some years ago, and my kidneys were never good since I had the Rheumatic Fever in the mountains and I constantly on a diet, as Dr Cremen of Stephen's Green would not let me under an operation as he said it was dangerous, I have to keep myself in medicine etc and I married and has two in Family a boy & girl and its hard to keep things going in those times.

Now I will ask you not to get into a temper when You see all these sheets of fool caps explaining some of my history to You, but if You cannot do anything for me there is no other one will. I trust that You will give this Your immediate attention as You know we never failed You at any time You wanted us to do anything in Your Election.

I am not sorry for what I have done for Ireland because I believed it was a virtue in our Family to do something for the Country we saw downtrodden by misrule.

I want You Sir if You will be so kind to write a Letter to me for the Referee stating that You have known me to the IO for the ASU in Ballysokeery area & Kilalla area etc during the Black & Tan from 1919 to 1921 and also that was Capt of Volunteers – and Staff Capt in the Civil War in North Mayo Brigade of the Flying of the ASU in the Ox Mountains in Sligo where we were operating or any thing You wish to say about me during all this trouble as stated in these pages.

It is the Greatest Insult offered to me to say after all I did that I'm not a person to whom the Act applies.

I want the Letter to attach to my appeal Statement – which I am about to make out for the Referee.

I will want to have it done for about the 4th March.

I would feel very grateful to You if You would speak to the Minister for Defence for me & the Referee – because some jealous person in giving evidence in their own behalf at the Board said something about me which would not help me in my application.

Trusting this will find Your favour.
Yours Sincerely
Alexander Boyd
D/Gda [Detective Garda] 8373

Source: Private Collection

References

List of Abbreviations

BMH/WS: Bureau of Military History Witness Statements
EOMN: Ernie O'Malley Notebooks
PRO: Public Record Office/The National Archives, London
UCDA: University College Dublin Archives

Chapter 1

1 *Thoms Directory, 1923: Official Directory of Great Britain & Ireland for the Year 1923* (Alex Thom & Co., Dublin, 1923), p. 1,225.
2 Return of Royal Irish Constabulary (Sergeants, Acting-Sergeants and Constables), 1906, p. 23. Garda Museum. Numbers remained relatively static until an increase in resignations led to the introduction of the Auxiliaries and Black and Tans in July 1920.
3 Herlihy, Jim, *The Royal Irish Constabulary: A Short Genealogical Guide* (Four Courts Press, Dublin, 1997), p. 78.
4 Crown & Peace Papers: Documents relating to the cases brought forward for trial at the Quarter Sessions. The documents include details of the cases, individuals concerning the case and sentencing. On occasion, original RIC reports detailing individual cases are included or recorded.
5 Crown & Peace Papers for County Mayo, 1845–24, CSER/CP/MO, 13 April 1916. National Archives of Ireland.
6 *Ibid.*
7 *Ibid.*, 30 April 1916.
8 County Inspector's Report for Mayo, January 1919. The British in Ireland Series. National Archives of Ireland: MFA 54/66.
9 *Ibid.*
10 *Ibid.*
11 Ambrose, Joe, *Dan Breen and the IRA* (Mercier Press, Cork, 2006), p. 52.
12 County Inspector's Report for Mayo, January 1919. The British in Ireland Series. National Archives of Ireland: MFA 54/66.
13 County Inspector's Report for Mayo, February 1919. The British in Ireland Series. National Archives of Ireland: MFA 54/66.
14 *Mayoman*, 25 October 1919.
15 Gavin, Rory, 'Success for Doris Brothers ... but at a price', *Mayo News Centenary Supplement*, 2 March 1994.

16 *Ibid.*

17 *The Irish Press*, 15 January 1938. National Library of Ireland: ILB 94109.

18 *Ibid.*, 28 January 1938. National Library of Ireland: ILB 94109.

19 Horne, John (ed.), *Our War: Ireland and the Great War* (Royal Irish Academy, Dublin, 2008) p. 50.

20 O'Keefe, William T., Bureau of Military History, Witness Statements (BMH/WS) 1678, pp. 4–5. Military Archives.

21 Moore, Colonel Maurice, *An Irish Gentleman. George Henry Moore: His Travel, His Racing, His Politics* (T. Werner Laurie, London 1913); *Irish Press*, 1938. National Library of Ireland: ILB 94109.

22 Moore, Colonel Maurice. The British in Ireland Series, Sinn Féin Suspects, p. 9. National Archives of Ireland: MFA 54/130.

23 *Ibid.*, p. 15.

24 *Ibid.*, p. 11.

25 *Ibid.*, p. 9.

26 *Ibid.*, p. 8.

27 *Ibid.*, p. 6.

28 McGuire, James & Quinn, James (eds.), *Dictionary of Irish Biography*, Volume 8, (Royal Irish Academy, Cambridge University Press, 2009).

29 *Belfast Telegraph*, 2 April 1919.

30 *The Irish Times*, 2 April 1919.

31 *The Freeman's Journal*, 1 April 1919.

32 *Ibid.*

33 There are 126 books registered to Katherine Tynan-Hinkson at the National Library of Ireland.

34 Jacobite refers to support for the claim of the Catholic Stuarts as heirs to the English throne. The Catholic Irish frequently supported the attempts of the Stuarts, James II and Bonnie Prince Charlie, to regain the Crown.

35 Tynan, Katherine, *The Wandering Years* (Constable and Co., London, 1922), p. 52.

36 *Ibid.*, p. 51.

37 *Mayo News*, 6 May 1916.

38 'Seachtar na Casca' [Easter Week], TG4, November 2010.

39 *Mayoman*, 19 June 1920.

40 Ring, Michael Joseph. The British in Ireland Series. Sinn Féin Suspects. National Archives of Ireland: MFA 54/134.

41 *Ibid.*

42 *Connaught Telegraph*, 26 January 1918.

43 EOMN, Brodie Malone, P17b/109, p. 66A. University College Dublin Archives (UCDA).

44 Hevey, Thomas, BMH/WS 1668, pp. 15–16. Military Archives.

45 Bonsall, Penny, *The Irish RMs: The Resident Magistrates in the British Administration of Ireland* (Four Courts Press, Dublin, 1997), p. 146.

46 *Connaught Telegraph*, 23 March 1918.

47 Donnelly, Stephen, BMH/WS 1548, pp. 5–9. Military Archives.
48 Bonsall, *The Irish RMs*, p. 147.
49 Tynan, *Wandering Years*, p. 52.
50 *The Irish Times*, 2 April 1919.
51 Milling, John Charles. British in Ireland Series. Sinn Féin Suspects. National Archives of Ireland: MFA 54/130.
52 *Ibid.*
53 National Registry for Births, Deaths and Marriages. Birth Certificate of Joseph Ruddy, Westport, Mayo, Volume 4, p. 427, 1892, 3rd Quarter. Joseph was born on 5 July 1892 to Thomas Ruddy and Mary Ruddy née O'Neal.
54 Hevey, Thomas, BMH/WS 1668, p. 16. Military Archives.
55 *Connaught Telegraph*, 13 October 1917.
56 Records of the Parish of Aughaval (Tuam) [Westport], County Mayo, P.158.08, Preacher's Book 8, 1916–20. Representative Church Body Library.
57 Dwyer, T. Ryle, *The Squad* (Mercier Press, Cork, 2005), pp. 47–8.

CHAPTER 2

1 *Mayoman*, 29 November 1919.
2 Officially known as the Prisoners Temporary Release for Ill-Health Act 1913.
3 *Mayoman*, 3 January 1920.
4 *Ibid.*
5 Sheehan, William, *Hearts and Mines: The British 5th Division, Ireland, 1920–1922* (The Collins Press, Cork, 2009).
6 Lloyd George Papers, LG/F/32/5/50, Intelligence Report, District Inspector RIC, Castlebar, County Mayo dated 7/06/1918 relayed to Lloyd George, Prime Minister 10/06/1918. Parliamentary Archives.
7 Bennett, Richard, *The Black and Tans* (Edward Hulton, London, 1959), p. 211.
8 February 1922, War Diary, 2nd Battalion Border Regiment, 1919–21. Kings Own Border Regiment Museum.
9 *Mayoman*, 6 March 1920.
10 *Ibid.*, 14 June 1919.
11 *Ibid.*
12 *Ibid.*, 24 January 1920.
13 County Inspector's Report for Mayo, January 1920. The British in Ireland Series. National Archives of Ireland: MFA 54/69.
14 Waldron, Kieran, *The Archbishops of Tuam, 1700–2000* (Nordlaw Books, Galway, 2008), pp. 100–3.
15 www.tuamarchdiocese.org/category/archdiocese/history/
16 O Rioghbhardain [O'Riordan], Liam S., BMH/WS 888, pp. 6–7. Military Archives.
17 County Inspector's Report for Mayo, December 1919. The British in Ireland Series. National Archives of Ireland: MFA 54/65.

18 *Mayoman*, 24 July 1920.
19 Walsh, Richard [Dick], BMH/WS 400, pp. 31–2. Military Archives.
20 Karsten, Peter, 'In Civil Military Relations: The Military and Society. A Collection of Essays', *Irish Historical Studies* (November 1983).
21 White, G. & O'Shea, B., *Irish Volunteer Soldier, 1913–23*, (Osprey Publishing, Oxford, 2003), pp. 16–20.
22 Walsh, Richard [Dick], BMH/WS 400, p. 86. Military Archives.
23 'Frongoch: Ollscoil na Réabhlóide' [Frongoch: University of Revolution], TG4, April 2007.
24 Inspector General RIC, Monthly Report, February 1920. The British in Ireland Series. National Archives of Ireland: MFA 54/69.
25 *Ibid.*
26 Walsh, Richard [Dick], BMH/WS 400, p. 85. Military Archives.
27 Lyons, Patrick, BMH/WS 1645, p. 4. Military Archives.
28 Mulcahy Papers, P7/0/3, Conversation with Lt General Peadar McMahon, 15 May 1963, pp. 4–5. UCDA.
29 White & O'Shea, *Irish Volunteer Soldier*, pp. 12–14.
30 Donnelly, Stephen, BMH/WS 1548, pp. 4–5. Military Archives.
31 *Ibid.*, p. 10.
32 Patrick Joseph Ruttledge became TD for Mayo North and was an organiser of the Republican courts system that began to replace the British court system in Ireland in 1920.
33 Walsh, Richard [Dick], BMH/WS 400, p. 66. Military Archives.
34 Tom Barry in *Guerrilla Days in Ireland* offers an interesting insight to the different personalities of the IRA GHQ staff. See chapter 21, pp. 175–86.
35 Dunleavy, Pádraig, BMH/WS 1489, p. 9. Military Archives.
36 EOMN, Tom Maguire, 17b/100 and 120, p. 146A. UCDA.
37 Walsh, Richard [Dick], BMH/WS 400, p. 89–90. Military Archives.
38 *Western People*, 8 October 1955.
39 Walsh, Richard [Dick], BMH/WS 400, pp. 40, 89. Military Archives.
40 Maguire, Tom, British Military Intelligence File, WO 35/207/123. PRO.
41 *Ibid.*
42 EOMN, Tom Kitterick, 17b/96, p. 35B. UCDA.
43 Walsh, Richard [Dick], BMH/WS 400, p. 121. Military Archives.
44 EOMN, Dr John Madden, 17b/113, p. 61A and p. 61B. UCDA.
45 Hevey, Thomas, BMH/WS 1668, p. 24. Military Archives.
46 Gibbons, Seán, BMH/WS 927, p. 6. Military Archives.
47 Walsh, Richard [Dick], BMH/WS 400, pp. 130–2. Military Archives.
48 *Ibid.*, p. 135.
49 *Ibid.*, p. 118.
50 EOMN, Tom Kitterick, p. 93A. UCDA.
51 EOMN, Brodie Malone, P17b/109, p. 69A. UCDA.
52 Gibbons, Seán, BMH/WS 927, p. 63. Military Archives.
53 EOMN, Tommy Heavey, P17b/120, p. 46A. UCDA.

54 *Ibid.* For Patrick Marley see the *Mayo News*, 4 March 1922. For Jim Duffy see the *Mayo News*, 18 March 1922.

55 Baker, Joe, *My Stand for Freedom: Autobiography of an Irish Republican Soldier* (Westport Historical Society, Mayo, 1988), p. 24.

CHAPTER 3

1 Records of the Parish of Kilcolman (Tuam), County Mayo, Period 1832–69, 1, 1916–29, P.180.5.2, Vestry Book, 28 March 1920. Church Representative Body Library.

2 Barry, Tom, *Guerrilla Days in Ireland* (Anvil Books, Dublin, 1989), pp. 3–4.

3 Dáil Debates, 21 January 1919. www.historical-debates.oireachtas.ie

4 Dáil Debates, 18 June 1919. www.historical-debates.oireachtas.ie

5 *Ibid.*

6 County Inspector's Report for Mayo, July 1920. The British in Ireland Series. National Archives of Ireland: MFA 54/69.

7 County Inspector's Report for Mayo, January 1920. The British in Ireland Series. National Archives of Ireland: MFA 54/69.

8 *Ibid.*

9 *Mayoman*, 10 April 1920.

10 *Ibid.*

11 *Ibid.*, 24 April 1920.

12 *Ibid.*, 10 April 1920.

13 *Ibid.*

14 Bennett, *The Black and Tans*, p. 40.

15 *Mayoman*, 8 May 1920.

16 *Ibid.*, 15 May 1920.

17 *Ibid.*

18 Campbell, Fergus, *Land and Revolution: Nationalist Politics in the West of Ireland, 1892–1921* (Oxford University Press, Oxford, 2005), pp. 240–1.

19 *Mayoman*, 22 May 1920.

20 *Ibid.*

21 Campbell, *Land and Revolution*, p. 255

22 *Ibid.*, p. 254.

23 Maguire, Conor Alexander, BMH/WS 708, p. 3. Military Archives.

24 Tomlinson, Mike, Varley, Tony & McCullagh, Ciaran (eds.), *Whose Law & Order? Aspects of Crime and Social Control in Irish Society* (Sociological Association of Ireland, Belfast, 1988) p. 62.

25 *Mayoman*, 5, 26 June 1920.

26 *Ibid.*, 12 June 1920.

27 Sligo Prison, General Register of Prisoners, June–October 1920, MFGS/51/098. National Archives of Ireland.

28 *Mayoman*, 21 August 1920.

29 Sligo Prison, General Register of Prisoners, June–October 1920, MFGS/51/098. National Archives of Ireland.

30 *Mayoman*, 13 November 1920.

31 Walsh, Seán, BMH/WS 1733, pp. 20–2. Military Archives.

32 While undertaking research for this publication the following information regarding the case was related to me by historians at the Public Record Office: The files on this case are likely to be at the Public Record Office at Kew, London. However, to date the files for the RIC for this period are vast and have not been catalogued. It is highly likely the files will be uncovered as a search for other materials is being conducted.

33 *Mayoman*, 19 June 1920.

34 *Mayoman*, *Mayo News*, *Western People* and *Connaught Telegraph*, June 1920.

35 *Mayoman*, 19 June 1920.

36 County Inspector's Report for Mayo, June 1920. The British in Ireland Series. National Archives of Ireland: MFA 54/69.

37 *Ibid.*

38 *Ibid.*

CHAPTER 4

1 Cabinet Papers, CAB/24/109, British Cabinet Conference on the Situation in Ireland, 23 July 1920. PRO.

2 *Ibid.*, p. 2.

3 *Ibid.*, pp. 3–4.

4 Dwyer, *The Squad*, pp. 107–19.

5 Cabinet Papers CAB/24/109, British Cabinet Conference on the Situation in Ireland, 23 July 1920, p. 6. PRO.

6 *Ibid.*, p. 12.

7 *Ibid.*, p. 18.

8 *Ibid.*, pp. 19–20.

9 Herlihy, Jim, *The Royal Irish Constabulary. A Complete Alphabetical List of Officers and Men, 1816–1922* (Four Courts Press, Dublin, 1999); Cruise, Richard Francis Raleigh, Serial Number 60,575, General Register for the RIC. National Archives of Ireland: MFA 54/16.

10 Coleman, Patrick, BMH/WS 1683, p. 23. Military Archives.

11 *Ibid.*, p. 13. See also Tom Kenny, 'Joe Togher, A Galway Volunteer', *Galway Advertiser*, 9 April 2009.

12 War Diary, 2nd Battalion, Argyll and Sutherland Highlanders, 1920–22. Argyll and Sutherland Highlander Museum.

13 *New York Times*, 21 July 1920.

14 Waldron, *Archbishops of Tuam*, pp. 106–7; *Mayoman*, 24 July 1920.

15 B4/8–ii/6, Eyewitness accounts of Black and Tan activity. Tuam Diocesan Archive.

16 Abbott, Richard, *Police Casualties in Ireland 1919–1922*, p. 119; *Mayoman*, 11 September 1920; O'Callaghan, Micheál, *Fight for Freedom. Roscommon's Contribution to the Fight for Independence*. Boyle, County Roscommon. 1991.

17 *Western People*, 16 October 1920.

18 Coleman, Patrick, BMH/WS 1683, p. 9. Military Archives.

19 Rev. Br Ward Collection, CD 77/11. Military Archives. Br Ward was Acting Principal of Westport CBS August 1913 to September 1926. He was present when a number of intelligence documents were handed over for destruction to Mr Jack Finnerty, Shop St, Westport, by John Gibbons Quay Rd., Westport in the presence of Edward Moane, Carrowbawn, Westport. On his suggestion the documents should be kept for historical purposes they were handed over to him and buried in an airtight container for two years. On leaving Westport he took them with him to Drogheda and kept them safely until the 1950s when he deposited the documents with the Bureau of Military History.

20 *Mayoman*, 25 September 1920.

21 B4/8-ii/8, Correspondence between General Macready and Dr Gilmartin, 3 July 1920. Tuam Diocese Archive.

22 *Ibid.*, 21 July 1920.

23 *Western People*, 6 November 1920.

24 County Inspector's Report for Mayo, October 1920. The British in Ireland Series. National Archives of Ireland: MFA 54/70.

25 *Western People*, 18 January 1920.

26 Robinson, Sir Henry, *Memories: Wise and Otherwise* (Cassell and Co., London, New York and Melbourne, 1923), pp. 164–70.

27 Walter Hume Long to Rev. Fr John Flatley, 947/224, June–September 1918. Wiltshire and Swindon History Centre.

28 Rev. Fr John Flatley to Walter Hume Long, 947/225, November 1920–January 1921. Wiltshire and Swindon History Centre.

29 Rev. Fr John Flatley to Captain Frank Siltzer, 947/225, November 1920–January 1921. Wiltshire and Swindon History Centre; *Hansard*, House of Commons, 29 November 1920.

30 B4/8-ii/36, Rev. Fr John Flatley to General Sir Neville Macready. Tuam Diocese Archive.

31 B4/08-ii/04. Tuam Diocese Archive.

32 *Western People*, 27 November 1920.

33 Hegarty-Thorne, Kathleen, *They Put The Flag A Flyin'. The Roscommon Volunteers, 1916–23*, 2nd Edition, (Generation Organisation, Oregon, 2007), p. 465.

34 Hegarty, Patrick, BMH/WS 1606, p. 22–3. Military Archives.

35 *Mayoman*, 26 March 1921.

36 O'Keefe, William T., BMH/WS 1678, p. 5–15. Military Archives. O'Keefe lists the following men from Claremorris in the Manchester ASU: James

Ryan, Mount Street; Joe Dillon, Rockfield; Matt Cribbon, Bekan; Tom Dolan and Pat Duffy, Belisker; and Stephen Clancy, Cloonbrook. O'Keefe also lists the following Claremorris men who took part in the Connaught Rangers Mutiny in India 1921 and were sentenced to life imprisonment: Val Delaney, The Square Claremorris; and J. J. Buckley and Eugene Egan, Convent Road, Claremorris.

37 Mayo County Council Minute Book, Volume 8, p. 315. Mayo County Council.

38 *Ibid.*, Volume 9, p. 17.

39 *Ibid.*, pp. 8, 473.

40 *Ibid.*, pp. 410, 473.

41 *Ibid.*, p. 31.

42 Sir Winston Churchill Archive Trust, CHAR 2/111/95, Archbishop Gilmartin to Winston Churchill, 9 December 1920. Churchill Archives Centre.

43 Sir Winston Churchill Archive Trust, CHAR 2/111/117–18, Winston Churchill to Archbishop Gilmartin, 14 December 1920. Churchill Archives Centre.

44 Sir Winston Churchill Archive Trust, CHAR 2/111/92. Archbishop Gilmartin to Winston Churchill, 17 December 1920. Churchill Archives Centre.

45 Relatio Status 1920, B4/01-1/05, Report on the condition of Tuam Diocese in 1920 by Archbishop Gilmartin to Pope Benedict XV. Tuam Diocese Archive. (Translation courtesy of Peter Molloy, St Paul's Secondary School, Oughterard, County Galway.)

46 *Mayo News*, 22 January 1921 listed the names of the Claremorris men in Ballykinlar Camp as: Michael Joseph Heaney, Aloysius Heaney, W. Macken, T. Donoghue, T. Rooney, Jim Gallagher and Patrick Tulier. Claremorris men awaiting court martial in Galway Town Hall were listed as: John Tulier, Will Kenney, Harry Burke, John Griffin, T. Ruane and Joe Brennan.

47 RIC officers, DI Owen Spellman. National Archives of Ireland: MFA 24/10 and MFA 24/117. DI Owen Spellman remained in the RIC until the force was disbanded in 1922. He retired to his wife's home place of Stoneyford, County Kilkenny. Together they ran the village post office. Spellman became a bee-keeper in his spare time and won many prizes at the County Fairs. He died on 4 September 1948 and was buried in Stoneyford RC Church graveyard.

48 County Inspector's Report for Mayo, January 1921. The British in Ireland Series. National Archives of Ireland: MFA 54/71.

49 County Inspector's Report for Mayo, December 1920. The British in Ireland Series. National Archives of Ireland: MFA 54/70.

50 Coleman, Patrick, BMH/WS 1683, pp. 11–16. Military Archives.

51 *Western People*, 15 January 1921.

52 B4/08-ii/06. Tuam Diocese Archive.

53 Cabinet Papers, CAB/23/23, pp. 341–2, Cabinet Meeting 29 December 1920. PRO.

Chapter 5

1 County Inspector's Report for Mayo, February 1920. British in Ireland Series. National Archives of Ireland: MFA 54/69.
2 *Mayoman*, *Mayo News*, 5 February 1921.
3 Sheehan, *Hearts and Mines*, pp. 95–6.
4 Lally, *The Tan War*, p. 72. See also The Border Regiment, War Diary, 1919–21. King's Own Border Regiment Museum.
5 Ryder, Kathleen (ed.), 'South Mayo's Fight for Freedom', *The Bridge: Ballinrobe Parish Magazine*, 1968–9, p. 29.
6 MacEoin, Uinseann, *Survivors* (Argenta Publications, Dublin, 1980) p. 284.
7 *Mayo News*, 12 March 1921.
8 *Mayoman*, 12 March 1921.
9 B4/08-ii/04, Fr O'Malley to Archbishop Gilmartin, 11 March 1921. Tuam Diocese Archive.
10 Lally, *The Tan War*, pp. 92–7.
11 B4/08-ii/04, Fr O'Malley to Archbishop Gilmartin, 11 March 1921. Tuam Diocesan Archives.
12 Kilroy, Michael, BMH/WS 1162, p. 5. Military Archives.
13 *Mayo News*, 26 March 1921.
14 Kilroy, Michael, BMH/WS 1162, p. 5. Military Archives.
15 *Ibid.*, pp. 4–7.
16 *Ibid.*, p. 10.
17 Hughes, Harry & Ryan, Áine, *Charles Hughes: Lankill to Westport, 1876–1949* (Portwest Ltd., Mayo, 2007), pp. 137–8.
18 *Mayoman*, 9 April 1921.
19 *Ibid.*, 2 April 1921; Abbott, *Police Casualties in Ireland*, p. 216.
20 *Mayo News*, 5 November 1921.
21 *Western People*, 21 May 1921.
22 Cassidy, Patrick, BMH/WS 1017, pp. 12–13. Military Archives.
23 Wilkins, Charles H., District Inspector RIC, Service Number: 72, 157. The British in Ireland Series. National Archives of Ireland: MFA 24/17.
24 Sobolewski, Peter & Solan, Betty (eds.), *Kiltimagh: Our Life & Times*. Historical Journals and Periodicals, Mayo County Library.
25 Mayo County Council Minute Book, Volume 8, p. 70. Mayo County Council.
26 *Mayoman*, 9 April 1921. See also RIC Officers and Constables, White, William Eugene, District Inspector RIC, Service Number: 71, 611. The British in Ireland Series. National Archives of Ireland: MFA 24/17.
27 Collins Papers, Mayo Brigade Group IX, A/0749, GHQ to North Mayo Brigade. Military Archives.

28 *Western People*, 23 April 1921.

29 *Ibid.*, 4 February 1922.

30 Collins Papers, Mayo Brigade Group IX, A/0749 III, GHQ to Comdt Tom Maguire, 15 April 1921. Military Archives.

31 *Ibid.*

32 *Ibid.*

33 *Ibid.*

34 Ryder, 'South Mayo's Fight for Freedom', p. 33.

35 Lally, *The Tan War*, p. 115.

36 *Ibid.*, pp. 114–15.

37 Buckley, Donal, *The Battle for Tourmakeady: Fact or Fiction* (Nonsuch Press, Dublin, 2008), p. 68.

38 Ryder, 'South Mayo's Fight for Freedom', p. 34; Buckley, *The Battle for Tourmakeady*, p. 68.

39 Ryder, 'South Mayo's Fight for Freedom', pp. 35–6.

40 Ibberson, Major Geoffrey, BMH/WS 1307, p. 2. Military Archives.

41 Lally, *The Tan War*, p. 127.

42 *Mayo News*, 5 November 1921.

43 *Ibid.*, 26 November 1921.

44 Lally, *The Tan War*, p. 140–1.

45 MacEoin, *Survivors*, p. 286.

46 *Mayoman*, 14 May 1921.

47 Lally, *The Tan War*, p. 144.

48 *Mayoman*, 14 May 1921.

49 Walsh, Richard [Dick], BMH/WS 400, p. 67. Military Archives.

50 WO 35/207/123, C419380, British Intelligence Document on Commandant Thomas Maguire. PRO.

51 Cabinet Papers, CAB/24/123, Survey of the State of Ireland for the week ended 9 May 1921. PRO.

52 *Mayoman*, 30 April 1921.

53 *Ibid.*, 21 May 1921.

54 Feehan, John, BMH/WS 1692, pp. 71–2. Military Archives.

55 Abbott, *Police Casualties in Ireland*, p. 244.

56 Kilroy, Michael, BMH/WS 1162, pp. 20–2.

57 *Ibid.*, p. 22.

58 EOMN, Paddy Cannon, P17b/136, p. 51A. UCDA.

59 For further notes on the Anti-Guerilla Warfare course run by the British 5th Division consult Sheehan, *Hearts and Mines*, pp. 280–6.

60 Kilroy, Michael, BMH/WS 1162, p. 24. Military Archives.

61 Kitterick, Thomas, BMH/WS 872, pp. 31–2. Military Archives. [Some accounts appear to imply there were two machine guns, one at each RIC position. Other accounts mention only one machine gun. As Kitterick was in Cummins' farmyard – in the middle of the two RIC positions and underneath the IRA column when the action began – it is thought by the

author that he was best placed to judge the number of machine guns in action.]

62 Kilroy, Michael, BMH/WS 1162, p. 29. Military Archives.

63 *Ibid.*, p. 30.

64 *Ibid.*, p. 29.

65 Kitterick, Thomas, BMH/WS 872, p. 31. Military Archives.

66 Gibbons, Seán, BMH/WS 927, p. 28. Military Archives.

67 Donnellan, Peter, District Inspector RIC, Service Number: 60,047. National Archives of Ireland: MFA 24/16.

68 B4/08-ii/04 1920–21, Statement of John Pierce to RIC Divisional Commissioner R. F. Cruise. Tuam Diocese Archive.

69 Hevey, Tommy, BMH/WS 1668, p. 26. Military Archives.

70 Abbott, *Police Casualties in Ireland*, p. 246.

71 EOMN, Michael Kilroy, P17b/138, p. 11B–12A. UCDA.

72 *Ibid.*, p. 36B.

73 *Mayoman*, 21 May 1921.

74 *Ibid.*

75 EOMN, Tommy Heavey, P17b/120, pp. 48B–49A. UCDA.

76 EOMN, Paddy Cannon, P17b/136, p. 55A. UCDA.

77 EOMN, Brodie Malone, P17b/109, p. 71A. UCDA.

78 Hevey, Tommy, BMH/WS 1668, pp. 46–7. Military Archives. [Ernie O'Malley attempted to get to the bottom of this incident in a series of interviews with Mayo men who were at Carrowkennedy. O'Malley managed to discover that a court martial of the Louisburgh section was held following Carrowkennedy. However, he was unable to find out further details of exactly who was involved or what the outcome was.

79 Kilroy, Michael, BMH/WS 1162, pp. 62–3. Military Archives.

80 *Ibid.*, p. 62.

81 Hevey, Tommy, BMH/WS 1668 pp. 47–8. Military Archives.

82 Kitterick, Thomas, BMH/WS 872, p. 41. Military Archives.

83 EOMN, Thomas Kitterick, p. 38A. UCDA.

84 *Mayoman*, 11 June 1921.

85 EOMN, Brodie Malone, P17b/109, p. 72A. UCDA.

86 Kitterick, Thomas, BMH/WS 872, p. 42. Military Archives.

87 EOMN, Tom Kitterick, p. 39A. UCDA.

88 Hevey, Tommy, BMH/WS 1668, p. 49. Military Archives.

89 EOMN, Paddy Duffy, P17b/113, 138, p. 5B. UCDA.

90 Keane, Vincent, 'The Irish Volunteers in Westport, Part IV', *Cathair na Mart: Journal of the Westport Historical Society*, 2010.

91 *Mayoman*, 28 May 1921.

92 *Western People*, 25 June 1921.

93 *Ibid.*

94 Hegarty-Thorne, *They Put the Flag A-Flyin*, p. 482.

95 Collins Papers, Mayo Brigade Group IX, A/0749VI. Military Archives.

96 Abbott, *Police Casualties in Ireland*, p. 261.

97 EOMN, Matt Kilcawley, 136, 137, p. 62B. UCDA.

98 *Western People*, 16 July 1921.

99 Kitterick, Thomas, BMH/WS 872, p. 52. Military Archives.

100 *Western People*, 16 July 1921.

101 *Ibid.*

Chapter 6

1 Moylett, Patrick, Memoir, P78, pp. 37–9. UCDA.

2 *Ibid.*, pp. 265–7.

3 *Ibid.*, pp. 269–71.

4 Lloyd George Papers, LG/F/91/7/7-24, 19 November 1920. Parliamentary Archives.

5 Lloyd George Papers, LG/F/91/7/7-24, 23 November 1920. Parliamentary Archives.

6 Dwyer, *The Squad*, pp. 172–202.

7 Moylett, Patrick, Memoir. P78, p. 333. UCDA. Erskine Childers served in the Boer War and with British Naval Intelligence in the First World War, Robert Barton served as an officer in the Royal Dublin Fusiliers, John Chartres was a suspected British intelligence officer.

8 Mulcahy Papers, P7a/15, IRA Mayo Brigade Strength Report. UCDA.

9 MacEoin, *Survivors*, p. 288.

10 County Inspector's Monthly Report for Mayo, August 1921. The British in Ireland Series. National Archives of Ireland: MFA 54/73.

11 War Diary, 2nd Battalion, Argyll and Sutherland Highlanders, 1920–22. Argyll and Sutherland Highlander Museum.

12 Dunleavy, Pádraig, Commandant No 4 Brigade, Tuam, 2nd Western Division 1921–2. Pádraig Dunleavy Papers. Private Collection.

13 Mulcahy Papers, P7a/15, South Mayo Brigade Intelligence Report July 1921. UCDA.

14 Collins Papers, Mayo Brigade, Group IX, A/0749, South Mayo Brigade Intelligence Reports and GHQ responses. Military Archives.

15 Mulcahy Papers, Division Munitions Reports, September 1921 [Including the Mayo Brigades], P7a/15. UCDA.

16 Collins Papers, Mayo Brigade, Group IX, A/0749, Report on East Mayo Brigade by McNeill and Chadwick. Military Archives.

17 Ruane, Senator Seán T., BMH/WS 1588, p. 21. Military Archives.

18 Collins Papers, Mayo Brigade, Group IX, A/0479, Report on East Mayo Brigade by McNeill and Chadwick. Military Archives.

19 EOMN, Johnny Griely, P17b/113, p. 3A. UCDA.

20 Collins Papers, Mayo Brigade, Group IX, A/0479, Report on East Mayo Brigade by McNeill and Chadwick. Military Archives.

21 *Ibid.*

22 Collins Papers, 1st Western Division, Group IX, A/0674, Correspondence
    concerning a search by members of the East Mayo Brigade for E. Corbett,
    Transport Officer, 1st Western Division, and a shooting incident at
    Kiltimagh on 14 October 1921 in which O/C 2nd Brigade, 1st Western
    Division was involved. Military Archives.

23 Collins Papers, Mayo Brigade, Group IX, A/0749, Reports on training
    camps in East Mayo Brigade Area, 22 September 1921. Military Archives.

24 Collins Papers, Mayo Brigade, Group IX, A/0749, Correspondence involving
    AG Department of Finance, D/I, Prisoners' Dependents' Fund and ADJ
    East Mayo Brigade regarding compensation for dependents of Comdt Sean
    Corcoran. Military Archives.

25 Collins Papers, Mayo Brigade, Group IX, A/0749, North Mayo Brigade
    to Adjutant General IRA concerning murder of Volunteer Michael Tolan.
    Military Archives.

26 *Ibid.*

27 *Western People*, 4 February 1922.

28 *Ibid.*

29 Conor Alexander Maguire continued to serve as a member of the County
    Council, attending only periodically due to other duties.

30 *Mayo News*, 28 November 1921.

31 *Ibid.*

32 EOMN, Johnny Griely, P17/b/113, p. 3A. UCDA.

33 Coogan, Tim Pat, *Michael Collins: A Biography* (Hutchinson, London, 1990),
    p. 295.

34 Lynn, Kathleen, The Lynn Diaries, 7 December 1921. Royal College of
    Physicians of Ireland Heritage Centre.

35 Mayo County Council Minute Book, Volume 9, p. 126. Mayo County Council.

36 *Mayo News*, 10 December 1921.

37 *Ibid.*

38 MacEoin, *Survivors*, pp. 289–90.

39 EOMN, Tom Maguire, P17b/100, p. 148B. UCDA.

40 *Mayo News*, 7 January 1922.

41 *Ibid.*

42 *Ibid.*

43 Mayo County Council Minute Book, Volume 9, p. 151. Mayo County
    Council.

44 *Mayo News*, 7 January 1922.

45 Dáil Debates, 4 January 1922. www.historical-debates.oireachtas.ie

46 Dáil Debates, 21 December 1921. www.historical-debates.oireachtas.ie

47 Cabinet Papers, CAB/24/131, Articles of the Anglo-Irish Treaty, 6 December
    1922, Article 4, p. 1. PRO.

48 Dáil Debates, 21 December 1921. www.historical-debates.oireachtas.ie

49 Professor Alfred O'Rahilly MA PhD of UCD had an article published by
    the *Irish Independent* and subsequently by the *Mayo News*, 7 January 1922,

in which he offered a profound analysis of the Anglo-Irish Treaty of 1921. It convinced many to vote for the Treaty. The one elephant in the room, however, was partition, which was perhaps the only aspect on which the Professor's projections did not work out.

50 Dáil Debates, 6 January 1922. www.historical-debates.oireachtas.ie

51 *Mayo News*, 24 September 1921.

52 *Ibid.*, 24 December 1921.

53 *Western People*, 21 January 1922.

54 War Diary, 2nd Battalion, Argyll and Sutherland Highlanders, 1920–22. Argyll and Sutherland Highlander Museum.

55 Ferguson, K., *King's Inns Barristers, 1868–2004* (The Honourable Society of King's Inns, Dublin, 2005), p. 178.

56 *Mayo News*, 29 October 1921.

57 Dáil Debates, 13 September 1922. www.historical-debates.oireachtas.ie

58 Compensation Claims for County Mayo, FIN 1/649, British Proposal from Mr Waterfield to Howell Thomas of Provisional Government and Compensation Ireland Commission, 7 September 1922. National Archives of Ireland.

59 Cabinet Papers, CAB/24/138, p. 2, Letter from the British Cabinet to the Provisional Government regarding Compensation for Malicious Injuries to Property. PRO.

60 Compensation Claims for County Mayo, FIN 1/1556, Mr A. V. G. Thornton, County Solicitor, to Provisional Government Ministry of Finance, 16 December 1922. National Archives of Ireland.

61 Compensation Claims for County Mayo, FIN 1/649, Alfred Cope Scheme of Payment, October 1921. National Archives of Ireland.

62 Cabinet Papers, CAB/24/138, p. 2–3, Letter from the British Cabinet to the Provisional Government regarding Compensation for Malicious Injuries to Property. PRO.

63 Dáil Debates, 6 March 1923. www.historical-debates.oireachtas.ie

64 Collins Papers, Mayo Brigade, Group IX, A/0749, Chief of Staff Richard Mulcahy to Commandant General Michael Kilroy, O/C 2nd Western Division, 12 October 1921; A/0749, Correspondence re expenses incurred by the West Mayo Brigade, 16 September to 22 October 1921. Military Archives.

65 Liaison and Evacuation Papers, 4/4, Captain Seán Walshe to Chief Liaison Officer, 30 January 1922. Military Archives.

66 Liaison and Evacuation Papers, 4/4, Captain Seán Walshe to Chief Liaison Officer, 18 January 1922. Military Archives.

67 Collins Papers, Mayo Brigade, Group IX, A/0749, Commandant Joe Ring to GHQ, 20 October 1921. Military Archives.

68 Collins Papers, A/0971, Seán Cawley to Michael Collins, undated [spring 1922]. Military Archives.

69 Dáil Debates, 2 March 1922. www.historical-debates.oireachtas.ie

70 Collins Papers, A/0971. Military Archives.
71 Cabinet Papers, CAB/24/134, p. 2, Weekly Survey of the State of Ireland. PRO.
72 *Ibid.*
73 Abbott, *Police Casualties in Ireland*, p. 281. Inquest Report, *The Irish Times*, 17 March 1922
74 *The Irish Times*, 17 March 1922.
75 Patrick Moylett, BMH/WS 767, p. 17. Military Archives.
76 Liaison and Evacuation Papers, 4/10, Letters concerning the shooting of ex-Sergeants Gibbons and Gilmartin and a civilian Patrick Cassidy. Military Archives. All that remains are the cover notes for these files. There is still a possibility the files may turn up but it is unlikely.
77 Ruane, Senator Seán T, BMH/WS, pp. 26–7. Military Archives.
78 *Connaught Telegraph*, 1 April 1922.
79 Liaison and Evacuation Papers, 4/10, 19 March 1922. Military Archives.
80 Long Papers, Correspondance of R. F. Cruise to Walter Hume Long, 'Memorandum On Terms of Disbandment of the Royal Irish Constabulary', 947/194. Wiltshire and Swindon Archives.
81 *Connaught Telegraph*, 8 April 1922.
82 *Ibid.*
83 *Ibid.*
84 EOMN, Tommy Heavey, P17b/120, p. 52B. UCDA; *Connaught Telegraph*, 8 April 1922.
85 *Mayo News*, 22 April 1922.
86 Cabinet Papers, CAB/23/30, p. 17, British Cabinet Conference, 16 May 1922. PRO.
87 *Ibid.*
88 Mayo County Council Minute Book, Volume 9, p. 217. Mayo County Council.
89 *Ibid.*, p. 218.
90 *Ibid.*, p. 219.
91 *Western People*, 29 April 1922.
92 Mayo County Council Minute Book, Volume 9, p. 223. Mayo County Council.
93 *Ibid.*
94 *Mayo News*, 6 May 1922.
95 *Connaught Telegraph*, 8 April 1922.
96 *Mayo News*, 6 May 1922.
97 *Ibid.*
98 *Ibid.*
99 *Western People*, 13 May 1922.
100 *Mayo News*, 20 May 1922.
101 *Ibid.*, 3 June 1922.
102 *Ibid.*, 27 May 1922.

103 *Western People*, 3 June 1922.
104 Coogan, *Michael Collins*, p. 329.
105 *Mayo News*, 24 June 1922.
106 *Western People*, 24 June 1922.
107 Coogan, *Michael Collins*, pp. 372–7.

CHAPTER 7

1   Seán MacEoin Papers, P151/155, Commandant General E. J. Cooney to General MacEoin, 24 July 1922. UCDA.
2   Lawlor, Anthony Teasdale, Personnel Records, AIR/76/290. PRO.
3   'The Four Court Guns', *An Cosantóir* (November 1979).
4   Cabinet Papers, CAB/24/138, Report on the Situation in Ireland for the Week Ending 22 July 1922. PRO.
5   *Mayo News*, 8 October 1921.
6   *Western People*, 22 July 1922.
7   British Military Intelligence File, Michael Kilroy, WO 35/207/110. PRO.
8   Baker, *My Stand for Freedom*, p. 72.
9   *Mayo News*, 21 March 1925.
10 National Army Operational Reports, Claremorris Command, 23 January to 17 April 1923. Military Archives.
11 Neeson, Eoin, *The Civil War 1922–23* (Poolbeg, Dublin, 1989), p. 249.
12 Seán Walsh Papers. Private Collection.
13 *Mayo News*, 16 August 1924.
14 *Ibid.*, 5 August 1922.
15 EOMN, Tommy Heavey, P17b/120, p. 53A. UCDA.
16 *Mayo News*, 5 August 1922.
17 *Ibid.*
18 Erskine Childers Collection, 6/40/1, 'From the West, January 23rd, 1923', Reports between Director of Publicity of IRA and President, Ministers of Dáil Éireann, Chiefs of IRA. Military Archives.
19 MacEoin, *Survivors*, pp. 292–3.
20 *Western People*, 19 August 1922.
21 *Ibid.*
22 Coogan, *Michael Collins*, p. 403 and footnote 78 p. 448. [Coogan states he was shown an unpublished account of Collins' death by one of the Mayo men present at Béal na mBláth.]
23 *Western People*, 26 August 1922.
24 *Ibid.*, 2 September 1922.
25 Mayo County Council Minute Book, Volume 9, pp. 306–7. Mayo County Council.
26 *Ibid.*
27 O'Dwyer, Martin, *Death Before Dishonour* (Tipperary, 2010), pp. 14–17.
28 EOMN, Tommy Heavey, P17b/120, p. 54B. UCDA.

29   *Western People*, 2 September 1922.

30   *Mayo News*, 20 September 1924.

31   *Ibid.*, 5 August 1922.

32   Baker, *My Stand for Freedom*, p. 58.

33   *Ibid.*, p. 60.

34   *Western People*, 16 September 1922.

35   *Ibid.*, 23 September 1922.

36   *Ibid.*

37   Baker, *My Stand for Freedom*, p. 60.

38   Mayo County Council Minute Book, Volume 9, p. 325. Mayo County Council.

39   Baker, *My Stand for Freedom*, p. 62.

40   *Western People*, 23 September 1922.

41   Ó Flanagáin, Peadar, 'Brigadier-General Joe Ring: "A brave soldier whose courage was never in doubt"', *Cathair na Mart: Journal of the Westport Historical Society*, 1987.

42   *Western People*, 23 September 1922.

43   Dáil Debates, 9 September 1922. www.historical-debates.oireachtas.ie

44   Dáil Debates, 11 September, 1922. www.historical-debates.oireachtas.ie

45   Dáil Debates, 12 September 1922. www.historical-debates.oireachtas.ie

46   *Mayo News*, 7 October 1922.

47   Box 39, Number 206, Count George Plunkett to Archbishop Gilmartin, 5 October 1922. Galway Diocesan Archive.

48   *Western People*, 14 October 1922.

49   Neeson, *The Civil War*, p. 173.

50   Baker, *My Stand for Freedom*, pp. 79–80.

51   De Valera Papers, P150/1654, Dr Murphy, Catholic Appeal Committee, to Archbishop Gilmartin, 2 November 1922. UCDA.

52   De Valera Papers, P150/1654/7, Archbishop Gilmartin to Dr Conn Murphy, 31 October 1922. UCDA.

53   Baker, *My Stand for Freedom*, p. 80.

54   *Western People*, 21 October 1922.

55   MacEoin Papers, P151/167(5), Lieutenant Nally, National Army, Witness Statement at the Trial of Commandant General Thomas Maguire, 27 November 1922. UCDA.

56   MacEoin Papers, P151/167(4), Commandant David Deasey, National Army, 27 November 1922. UCDA.

57   MacEoin Papers, P151/167(2), Assistant Legal Staff Officer David C. Bergin, GHQ Western Command, Custume Barracks, Athlone. UCDA.

58   MacEoin Papers, P151/167(1), Major General Seán MacEoin, National Army, GHQ Western Command. UCDA.

59   Mulcahy Papers, P7/B/75, William Sears TD to General Richard Mulcahy. UCDA.

60   Childers Papers, Adjutant General IRA GHQ to Director of Publicity, 17 February 1923. Military Archives.

61 O'Dwyer, Martin, *Seventy-Seven of Mine Said Ireland* (Tipperary, 2006), pp. 18–26.

62 Dáil Debates, 17 November 1922. www.historical-debates.oireachtas.ie

63 *Ibid.*

64 *Ibid.*

65 EOMN, Michael Kilroy, P17b/101, p 58A. UCDA.

66 Childers Papers, Director of Publicity IRA, 'Description of the Battle for Newport'. Military Archives.

67 *Connaught Telegraph*, 2 December 1922.

68 Childers Papers, Director of Publicity IRA, 'Description of the Battle for Newport'. Military Archives.

69 Mulcahy Papers, P7/a/141, Army Indiscipline Report (Civil War). UCDA.

70 Mulcahy Papers, P7/b/74, Richard Mulcahy to the Chief of the General Staff, 30 September 1922. UCDA.

71 Mulcahy Papers, P7/b/75, Canon D'Alton to William Sears TD. UCDA.

72 MacEoin Papers, P151/164(10), Frank Shouldice to General Seán MacEoin, 6 November 1922. UCDA.

73 Mulcahy Papers, P7/b/75, Rev. Fr T. Brett to William Sears TD, 7 December 1922. UCDA.

74 Childers Papers, Group 40 Publicity, 60/40/1, Republican Report 'From the West', 23 January 1923. Military Archives.

75 Mulcahy Papers, P7/b/74, General Seán MacEoin to Commander in Chief Richard Mulcahy, 19 October 1922. UCDA.

76 General Weekly Reports and Statistics, Claremorris Command, 24 February 1923. Military Archives.

77 Mulcahy Papers, P7/b/74, Report detailing numbers and locations of National Army troops under General Lawlor's command on 18 December 1921. UCDA.

78 *An t-Óglach*, 28 July 1923. Military Archives.

79 Clair Kilgarriff, granddaughter of Tom Kilgarriff. Interview with author.

80 National Army Operational Reports, Claremorris Command, 17 February 1923 and 30 January 1923. Military Archives.

81 Mulcahy Papers, P7/a/141, Army Indiscipline Report. UCDA.

82 National Army Operational Reports, Claremorris Command. Military Archives.

83 *Éire, The Irish Nation*, 21 April 1923.

84 National Army Operational Reports, Claremorris Command, 16 February 1923. Military Archives.

85 National Army Operational Reports, Claremorris Command, 6 March 1923. Military Archives.

86 *Mayo News*, 14 April 1923.

87 T. O'Derrig Papers, Accounts of Free State Atrocities on Republicans, A/0990 Lot 2 4(A), Captured Documents, IRA letter to AAG from P Much[?], Divisional O/C Field HQ 4th Western Division, 7 February 1923. Military Archives.

88 O'Donnell, Jim, 'Recollections based on the diary of an Irish Volunteer, 1898–1924', *Cathair na Mart: Journal of the Westport Historical Society*, 1992.

89 National Army Operational Reports, Claremorris Command, 13 February 1923. Military Archives; Sobolewski & Solan, *Kiltimagh: Life & Times*.

90 *Mayo News*, 27 January 1923.

91 Box 40 Number 222, *Poblacht na h-Éireann*, 2 March 1923. Galway Diocesan Archives.

92 *Mayo News*, 17 May 1924.

93 National Army Operational Reports, Claremorris Command, 15 February 1923. Military Archives.

94 *Mayo News*, 24 May 1924.

95 National Army Operational Reports, Claremorris Command, 23 February 1923. Military Archives.

96 National Army Operational Reports, Claremorris Command, 26 March 1923. Military Archives.

97 National Army Operational Reports, Claremorris Command, 31 March 1923. Military Archives.

98 Mulcahy Papers, P7/b/74, Louisburgh civilian to General Mulcahy, 8 December 1922. UCDA.

99 O'Dwyer, *Seventy-Seven of Mine Said Ireland*, pp. 14–16.

100 Pádraig Dunleavy Papers, Captain O'Connor to Colonel O'Higgins, National Army QM, 1 February 1923. Private Collection.

101 National Army Operational Reports, Claremorris Command, 10 April 1924. Military Archives.

102 O'Dwyer, *Seventy-Seven of Mine Said Ireland*, p. 350.

103 *Ibid.*, pp. 335–52.

104 Rector John Hagan Papers, HAG 1/1923/197, Archbishop Gilmartin to Monsignor John Hagan, Rector of the Pontifical Irish College, Rome, 11 April 1923. Irish College, Rome.

105 Rector John Hagan Papers, HAG 1/1923/215, Archbishop Gilmartin to Monsignor John Hagan, Rector of the Pontifical Irish College, Rome, 23 April 1923. Irish College, Rome.

106 Coogan, Tim Pat, *De Valera* (Hutchinson, London, 1993), p. 353.

107 MacEoin, *Survivors*, p. 294.

108 EOMN, Michael Kilroy, p. 58A. UCDA.

109 Mac Eoin, *Survivors*, p. 294.

110 National Army Operational Reports, Claremorris Command, 8 March 1923. Military Archives; Baker, *My Stand for Freedom*, pp. 94–6.

111 O'Donnell, 'Recollections based on the diary of an Irish Volunteer, 1898–1924, Part II', *Cathair na Mart: Journal of the Westport Historical Society*, 1992.

112 Baker, *My Stand for Freedom*, p. 96.

113 Seán Walsh Papers, Document II, pp. 25–6. Private Collection.

114 Patrick Moylett, Memoir, P78, pp. 425–6. UCDA.

115 Baker, *My Stand for Freedom*, p. 96.

116 Letter to the author on Tom Kilgarriff and the North Galway Brigade, 2nd Western Division, IRA, 9 September 2009.

117 Thomas Ruane obituary in the *Western People*, 14 June 1969. Miscellaneous Newspaper Article Collection. Mayo County Library.

118 *Mayo News*, 5 May 1923.

119 Coogan, *De Valera*, p. 355.

120 *Mayo News*, 28 April 1923.

121 *Ibid.*, 26 May 1923.

122 O'Dwyer, *Death before Dishonour*, pp. 287–8; *Mayo News*, 9 June 1923.

123 National Army Operational Reports, Claremorris Command, 13 March 1923. Military Archives.

124 National Army Operational Reports, Claremorris Command, 16 March 1923. Military Archives.

125 *Western People*, 15 September 1923.

126 *Mayo News*, 17 November 1923.

127 *Éire, The Irish Nation*, 21 April 1923.

128 EOMN, Michael Kilroy, p. 58A; EOMN, Tommy Heavey, p. 55B. UCDA. Reference to Dr Francis Ferran see *Éire, The Irish Nation*, 23 June 1923.

129 *Éire, The Irish Nation*, 30 June 1923.

130 Patrick Moylett, Memoir, p. 427. UCDA.

131 *Éire, The Irish Nation*, 21 July 1923.

132 *Mayo News*, 7 July 1923.

133 Moylett, Memoir, pp. 427–8. UCDA.

134 Cosgrave, President William T., *Policy of the Cumann na nGaedheal Party* (Cahill & Co., Dublin, 1927), p. 3.

135 *Mayo News*, 31 March 1923.

136 *Ibid.*, 25 August 1923.

137 Coogan, *De Valera*, p. 361.

138 *Western People*, 8 September 1923.

139 *Ibid.*

140 *Mayo News*, 11 August 1923. See also Dáil Debates, 2 July 1923. www.historical-debates.oireachtas.ie

141 Coogan, *De Valera*, p. 356.

142 *Éire, The Irish Nation*, 30 August 1924.

143 Sean Walsh Papers, p. 28. Private Collection.

144 *Ibid.*

145 *Mayo News*, 3 November 1923.

146 Childers Papers, Michael Kilroy, Hunger Strike Statement by O/C Prisoners' Mountjoy, 13 October 1923. Military Archives.

147 *Mayo News*, 27 October 1923.

148 *Ibid.*, 10 November 1923.

149 *Ibid.*

150 Childers Papers, Michael Kilroy, O/C Prisoners, Kilmainham Jail, 23 November 1923. Military Archives.

151 Brady, Conor, *Guardians of the Peace* (Gill & Macmillan, Dublin, 1974), pp. 44–5.

152 *Ibid.*, p. 53.

153 Allen, Gregory, *The Garda Síochána* (Gill & Macmillan, Dublin, 1999), p. 15.

154 Cabinet Papers, CAB 24/138, Report on the Situation in Ireland for the Week Ending 19 August, 1922. PRO.

155 Biographical detail of Michael Horgan, former Superintendent Civic Guards and District Inspector Royal Irish Constabulary. Garda Museum.

156 Brady, *Guardians of the Peace*, p. 76.

157 *Mayo News*, 3 March 1923.

158 Brady, *Guardians of the Peace*, p. 79.

159 McNiffe, Liam, *A History of the Garda Síochána* (Wolfhound Press, Dublin, 1999), p. 29.

160 *Mayo News*, 26 July 1924.

161 *Ibid.*, 5 May 1923.

162 *Ibid.*, 1 December 1923.

163 *Ibid.*, 19 July 1924.

164 *Ibid.*, 5 May 1923.

165 *Ibid.*, 2 June 1923.

166 *Ibid.*, 21 July 1923.

167 *Ibid.*, 31 May 1923.

168 *Ibid.*, 18 August 1923.

169 McNiffe, *History of the Garda Síochána*, p. 48.

170 'Seachtar na Casca', TG4, November 2010.

171 William O'Keefe Jnr in conversation with the author (2009).

172 Military Service Pensions Board to Alexander Boyd, 14 February 1942. Private Collection

173 As Seamus O'Maille was from the Connemara Brigade, he was buried separately at Oughterard. The other nine were: Micheal Walsh, Derrymore; Herbert Collins, Headford; Stephen Joyce, Caherlistrane; and Martin Burke, Caherlistrane; Martin Moylan, Annaghdown; Mickey Monaghan, Headford; Frank Cunnane, Kilcoona; John Newell, Headford; and John Maguire, Cross. Walsh, Collins, Joyce and Burke were executed in Custume Barracks, Athlone, 20 January 1923. Moylan, Monaghan, Cunnane, Newell, O'Maille and Maguire were executed in Tuam, 11 April 1923.

174 The Lynn Diaries, October 1924. Royal College of Physicians of Ireland Heritage Centre.

175 *Mayo News*, 8 November 1924.

Bibliography

Primary Sources

Belfast
Police Museum
Photographic Collection
Medal Collection

Public Record Office Northern Ireland
Correspondence relating to the court martial of prisoners at Ballykinlar Internment
    Camp, County Down

Cambridge
Churchill Archive Centre, Churchill College
Correspondence between Sir Winston Churchill, Secretary for War, and
    Archbishop of Tuam, Dr Thomas Gilmartin, regarding the 'Truce of God'
    December 1920

Carlisle
King's Own Royal Border Regiment Museum
The Border Regiment, 2nd Battalion, War Diary, 1919–22

Chippenham
Wiltshire and Swindon Archives
Viscount Walter Hume Long Papers

Dublin
Dáil Éireann and Oireachtas Library
William Sears TD biographical details

Garda Museum
Photographic Collection
RIC Constabulary Lists, Officers and Men [Microfilm]
Biographies

National Archives of Ireland
Crown and Peace Papers for County Mayo, 1775–1931
RIC County Inspector's Reports for County Mayo [Microfilm]

RIC Personnel Records for Officers and Constables [Microfilm]
Sinn Féin Suspects: John Charles Milling, Michael Joseph Ring [Microfilm]
Sligo Jail Register 1920 [Microfilm]
Department of Finance Compensation Claims Papers 1921–3

National Library of Ireland
Photographic Collections [Digital]

Military Archives
Captured Documents Collection [Second, Third and Fourth Western Divisions]
Rev Br Ward Collection
Childers Papers
Collins Papers – Mayo Brigade Group IX
Liaison and Evacuation Papers
The Military Archives Photographic Collection
An t-Oglach, 1919–24
Claremorris Command, National Army Operational Reports, January–April
    1923
Claremorris Command, Reports and Statistics, January–October 1923
Claremorris Command, Intelligence Reports, Christie Macken O/C Second
    Western Division, September 1923
Claremorris Command, Republican Military Activity Reports, 1923
Bureau of Military History: Brennan, John P. WS 1278. Cannon, Patrick Joseph
    WS 830. Cassidy, Patrick WS 1017. Coleman Patrick [Pappy] WS 1683.
    Donnelly, Stephen WS 1548. Dunleavy, Pádraig WS 1489. Feehan, John
    WS 1692. Gibbons, Sean WS 927. Hegarty, Patrick [Paddy] WS 1606.
    Henry, Michael WS 1732. Heavey, Thomas WS 1668. Hewson, George WS
    1569. Howley, Thomas WS 1122. Ibberson, Geoffrey WS 1307. Kelly, P. J.
    (Paddy) WS 1735. Ketterick, Thomas WS 872. Kilroy, Michael WS 1162.
    Lyons, Patrick WS 1645. McHugh, Michael WS 1632. McMahon, Peadar
    WS 1730. Maguire, Conor Alexander WS 708. Moane, Edward [Ned] WS
    896. Molloy, Dominick WS 1570. Mooney, Martin WS 1602. Moylett,
    Patrick WS 767. O'Hora, William J. WS 1554. O'Keefe, William T. WS
    1678. O'Riordan [Rioghbhardain], Liam S. WS 888. O'Sheil, Kevin WS
    1770. Ruane, Seán T. WS 1588. Timony, John WS 1620. Walsh, Richard
    WS 400. Walsh, Sean WS 1733.

Representative Church Body Library
Parish Records [Vestry Books and Preacher's Books] for Christ Church Castlebar,
    Kilcolman, Claremorris and Crossboyne, Aughaval, Westport

Royal College of Physicians Heritage Centre
Dr Kathleen Lynn Diaries

University College Dublin Archives
Mulcahy Papers
MacEoin Papers
De Valera Papers
Ernie O'Malley Notebooks: Interviews with Paddy Cannon, Tom Carney, Paddy
    Duffy, Grady, Johnny Griely, Tommy Heavey, Peter Hegarty, Matt Kilcawley,
    Tom Kitterick, Christie Macken, Dr John Madden, Tom Maguire, Brodie
    [also Broddie] Malone, Taylor O'Flynn, Paddy O'Malley, James Slattery. [All
    extracts in the text were transcribed and typed by Cormac K. H. O'Malley
    and Dominic Price]

Galway
Galway Diocesan Archives
Box 39:
No. 190 Letter from Dr O'Shea to Chief Secretary regarding abuse suffered at
    the hands of the British Military in Galway Diocese
No. 200 Appeal by Cumann na mBan to the Irish Bishops in 1922
No 201 Bishop's Pastoral containing prisoner's letter to Archbishop of Dublin
No 206 Letter from Count Plunkett to Archbishop Gilmartin

Box 40:
No 38 Letter from Archbishop Gilmartin to Bishop O'Doherty, 5 April 1922
No 40 *An t-Óglach*, 12 April 1922
No 59 Mary McSweeney's letter to Cardinal Logue and Bishops of Ireland
No 66 Letter from Cardinal Logue, Armagh to Bishop O'Doherty referring to
    rumours about Monsignor Luzio's visit
No 216 Brown envelope containing documents inserted by Bishop Michael
    Browne with appropriate reference to 1916–23
No 222 Blue File containing historical political documents

Box 47:
No 14 Green File: Cutting from the *Leader* 1923 leading article referring to Irish
    Bishops and Soldiers of the Republic

Tuam Diocese Archives
Black and Tan Reports
Relatio Status 1921
Parish Priest Reports 1920–1

London
Parliamentary Archives
David Lloyd George Papers

Public Record Office/The National Archives
Cabinet Papers, 1918–24
Sinn Féin Suspects: Michael Kilroy, Anthony Teasdale Lawlor, Tom Maguire,
    Patrick Moylett

Mayo
Mayo County Council
County Council Minute Books for 1920–3

Mayo County Library
Miscellaneous Newspaper Article Collection
Historical Mayo Maps Collection
Bureau of Military History Witness Statements

Rome
Irish College Archives
Monsignor John Hagan Papers 1903–30.

Stirling
Argyll and Sutherland Highlander Museum
Argyll and Sutherland Highlanders, 2nd Battalion, War Diary, 1920–2

NEWSPAPERS

Belfast Telegraph
Connaught Telegraph
Eire, The Irish Nation
Irish Independent
Mayoman
Mayo News
The Freeman's Journal
The Irish Times
Western People

INTERNET

www.historical-debates.oireachtas.ie

DOCUMENTARIES

'Frongoch: Ollscoil na Réabhlóide' [Frongoch: University of Revolution], TG4,
    April 2007
'Seachtar na Casca' [Easter Week], TG4, November 2010

Articles

Ryder, Kathleen (ed.), 'South Mayo's Fight for Freedom', *The Bridge*: Ballinrobe Parish Magazine 1968–69.

All the following from *Cathair na Mart: Journal of the Westport Historical Society*
Boran, Marie. 'Politics and Revolution: Local Government in Ireland', 1998
Conway, P. J. 'Ambush at Castlehill during the Civil War', 1991
Curry, John. 'The Murder of John Charles Milling – Resident Magistrate', 2002
Duffy, Jarlath. 'The Islandeady Ambush', 1990
Garvey, Rosemary. 'Senior Citizens: Letters from George Augustus Moore (1852–1933) to John Frederick Garvey (1856–1940)', 1993
Glavey, Michael. 'County Mayo Prisoners of War Relief Fund', 1994
hÓgáin, Seán. 'The Tourmakeady Ambush, May 1921 – Part 1', 2002
Hughes, Michael (Contributed by Carmel Hughes). 'Statement of Micheal Hughes. Castlebar Battalion IRA', 1999
Joyce, John. 'The National Movement, 1916–21 period as it relates to areas south of Westport – Drummin, Carrowkennedy, Liscarney, Lankill, Cordarragh', 1990
Keane, Vincent. 'Westport and the Irish Volunteers – Part 1', 2002
Keane, Vincent. 'Westport Sluagh. Na Fianna Éireann (Irish National Boy Scouts)', 2006–7.
Lane, Padraig J. 'The Lambert-Brookhill Estate. A Record of Mayo Property 1694–1946', 1996
May, Patrick E. 'A Short History of the IRA in Islandeady 1919–21', 1995
Moran, Anthony. 'The Night the Tans Came', 1998
Murphy, Clare C. 'Conflict in the West: The Ranch Wars Continue Part 1 1911–1912', 1995
Murphy, Clare C. 'Conflicts in the West: The Ranch Wars Continue Part 2 1911–1912', 1996
Ó Flanagáin, Peadar. 'Brigadier-General Joe Ring: "A brave soldier whose courage was never in doubt"', 1987
O'Donnell, Jim. 'Recollections based on the Diary of an Irish Volunteer 1898–1924, Part 1', 1990
O'Donnell, Jim. 'Recollections based on the Diary of an Irish Volunteer 1898–1924, Part 2', 1991
Tunney, Peter. 'From Derrykillew to Frongoch, under the Defence of the Realm Act', 1985

Books

Abbot, Richard. *Police Casualties in Ireland 1919–1924* (Mercier Press, Cork, 2000)

Allen, Gregory. *The Garda Síochána* (Gill & Macmillan, Dublin, 1999)

Barry, Tom. *Guerilla Days in Ireland* (Anvil Books, Dublin, 1981)

Baker, Joe. *My Stand for Freedom: Autobiography of an Irish Republican Soldier* (Westport Historical Society, Mayo, 1988)

Bennett, Richard. *The Black and Tans* (Edward Hulton & Co., London, 1959)

Bonsall, Penny, *The Irish RMs: The Resident Magistrates in the British Administration of Ireland* (Four Courts Press, Dublin, 1997)

Brady, Conor. Guardians of the Peace (Gill & Macmillan, Dublin, 1974)

Breen, Daniel, *My Fight for Irish Freedom* (Anvil Books, Tralee, 1964)

Buckley, Captain Donal. *The Battle of Tourmakeady: Fact or Fiction. A Study of the IRA Ambush and its Aftermath* (Nonsuch Publishing, Dublin, 2008)

Campbell, Fergus. *Land and Revolution: Nationalist Politics in the West of Ireland, 1892–1921* (Oxford University Press, 2005)

Chappell, Mike. *The British Army in World War I (1). The Western Front 1914–16. Men-at-Arms* (Osprey Publishing, Oxford, 2003)

Chappell, Mike. *The British Army in World War I (2). The Western Front 1916–18. Men-at-Arms* (Osprey Publishing, Oxford, 2005)

Coleman, Marie. *Longford and the Irish Revolution, 1910–1923* (Irish Academic Press, Dublin, 2003)

Coogan, Tim Pat. *Michael Collins* (Hutchinson, London, 1990)

Coogan, Tim Pat. *De Valera. Long Fellow, Long Shadow* (Hutchinson, London, 1993)

Cottrell, Peter. *The Anglo-Irish War. The Troubles of 1913–1922* (Osprey Publishing, Oxford, 2006)

Cottrell, Peter. *The Irish Civil War, 1922–23* (Osprey Publishing, Oxford, 2008)

Crozier, Brigadier-General F. P. *Ireland Forever* (Cedric Chivers Ltd., Bath, 1971)

Doyle, J., Clarke, F., Connaughton, E. & Somerville, O. *An Introduction to the Bureau of Military History, 1913–1921* (Military Archives, Dublin, 2002)

Dwyer, T. Ryle. *The Squad* (Mercier Press, Cork, 2005)

Ferriter, Diarmaid. *Judging Dev* (Royal Irish Academy, Dublin, 2007)

Herlihy, Jim. *The Royal Irish Constabulary. A Complete Alphabetical List of Officers and Men, 1816–1922* (Four Courts Press, Dublin, 1999)

Horne, John (ed.). *Our War: Ireland and the Great War* (Royal Irish Academy, Dublin, 2008)

Hughes, Harry & Ryan, Áine. *Charles Hughes: Lankill to Westport, 1876–1949* (Portwest Ltd., Mayo, 2007)

Lally, Micheál. *The Tan War* (Mayo, 2009)

Mac Eoin, Uinseann. *Survivors* (Argenta Publications, Dublin 1980)

McNiffe, Liam. *A History of the Garda Síochána* (Wolfhound Press, Dublin, 1999)

Moore, Colonel Maurice Henry. *An Irish Country Gentleman. George Henry Moore: His Travels, His Racing, His Politics* (T. Werner Laurie, London, 1913)

Murphy, David. *Irish Regiments in the World Wars* (Osprey Publishing, Oxford, 2007)

Ó Mórdha, An Chornail Muiris. Ó Rinn, Liam. D'aistrigh. *Túa agus Fás Óglach na hÉireann 1913–1917*, (Oifig Díolta Foillseacháin Rialtais, Baile Átha Cliath, 1936). [English language versions of this series of newspaper articles written by Colonel Maurice Moore appeared in the *Irish Press* throughout 1938. The articles are bound in two volumes and available for consultation at the National Library of Ireland: ILB 94109

O'Callaghan, Micheál. *Fight for Freedom. Roscommon's Contribution to the Fight for Independence* (Boyle, County Roscommon, 1991)

O'Dwyer, Martin. *Seventy-Seven of Mine Said Ireland* (Tipperary, 2006)

O'Dwyer, Martin. *Death before Dishonour* (Tipperary, 2010)

O'Malley, Edward. *Memories of a Mayoman* (Foilseacháin Náisiúnta Teoranta, Dublin, 1981)

Reddiough, James (ed.). *But They Are Forever Young. A History of the East Mayo Brigade 1913–1921* (Mayo, 2005)

Robinson KCB, Sir Henry. *Memories: Wise and Otherwise* (Cassell and Co., London, New York and Melbourne, 1923)

Sheehan, William. *British Voices from the Irish War of Independence, 1918–21* (The Collins Press, Cork, 2007)

Sheehan, William. *Hearts and Mines: The British 5th Division, Ireland, 1920–22* (The Collins Press, Cork, 2009)

Thom, Alex. *Thoms Directory 1923: Official Directory of Great Britain and Ireland for the Year 1923* (Alex Thom & Co., Dublin, 1923)

Waldron, Kieran. *The Archbishops of Tuam, 1700–2000* (Nordlaw Books, Galway, 2008)

Walker, B. M. *Parliamentary Election Results in Ireland, 1801–1922* (Royal Irish Academy, Dublin, 1978)

Walker, B. M. *Parliamentary Election Results in Ireland, 1918–1992* (Royal Irish Academy, Dublin, 1992)

Walsh, Oonagh. *Ireland's Independence, 1880–1923* (Routledge, London and New York, 2002)

White, G. & O'Shea, B. *Irish Volunteer Soldier, 1913–23* (Osprey Publishing, Oxford, 2003)

Index

*Page numbers in **bold** indicate photos*